Young Children's Cognitive Development

*Interrelationships Among Executive Functioning,
Working Memory, Verbal Ability,
and Theory of Mind*

International Workshop
Young Children's Cognitive Development:
Interrelationships Among Executive Functioning, Working Memory, Verbal Ability And Theory Of Mind

From left to right: Philip Zelazo, Klaus Oberauer, Helen Tager-Flusberg, Claire Hughes, Claudia Mähler, Susan Gathercole, Claudia Roebers, David Bjorklund, Marcus Hasselhorn, Winfried Kain, Josef Perner, Lou Moses, Selin Öndül, Ulrike Metz, Sylvia Bach, Beate Sodian, John Towse, Barbara Schöppner, Wolfgang Schneider, Christof Zoelch, Nora Gaupp, Mößle Thomas, Dietmar Grube, Daniela Kloo, Nelson Cowan. *Not in the picture:* Susanne Koerber, Kathrin Lockl.

Young Children's Cognitive Development

*Interrelationships Among Executive Functioning,
Working Memory, Verbal Ability,
and Theory of Mind*

Edited by

Wolfgang Schneider
University of Würzburg

Ruth Schumann-Hengsteler
Catholic University of Eichstätt–Ingolstadt

Beate Sodian
University of München

LEA

LAWRENCE ERLBAUM ASSOCIATES, PUBLISHERS
2005   Mahwah, New Jersey   London

Lawrence Erlbaum Associates, Inc., Publishers
10 Industrial Avenue
Mahwah, New Jersey 07430

Cover design by Kathryn Houghtaling Lacey

Library of Congress Cataloging-in-Publication Data

Young children's cognitive development : interrelationships among executive functioning, working memory, verbal ability, and theory of mind / edited by Wolfgang Schneider, Ruth Schumann-Hengsteler, Beate Sodian.
    p.   cm.
  Includes bibliographical references and index.
  ISBN 0–8058–4906–8 (alk. paper)
  1. Cognition in children—Congresses. I. Schneider, Wolfgang, 1950 June 19– II. Schumann-Hengsteler, Ruth, 1957–   III. Sodian, Beate, 1956–
BF723.C5Y67 2004
155.4'13—dc22   2004047104

Printed in the United States of America
10 9 8 7 6 5 4 3 2 1

Contents

Contributors

David F. Bjorklund, *Department of Psychology, Florida Atlantic University, Boca Raton, FL 33431, USA*

Stephanie M. Carlson, *Department of Psychology, University of Washington, Box 351525, Seattle, WA 98195–1525, USA*

Christopher A. Cormier, *Department of Psychology, Florida Atlantic University, Boca Raton, FL 33431, USA*

Nelson Cowan, *Department of Psychology, University of Missouri, 210 McAlester Hall, Columbia, MO 65211, USA*

Olivia Fernandez, *Department of Psychology, University of Würzburg, Röntgenring 10, 97070 Würzburg, Germany*

Dietmar Grube, *Department of Psychology, Georg-August-Universität Göttingen, Goßlerstr. 14, 37073 Göttingen, Germany*

Marcus Hasselhorn, *Department of Psychology, Georg-August-Universität Göttingen, Goßlerstr. 14, 37073 Göttingen, Germany*

Christian Hülsken, *Department of Psychology, University of München, Leopoldstr. 13, 80802 München, Germany*

Robert M. Joseph, *Department of Anatomy and Neurobiology, Boston University School of Medicine, 715 Albany Street L-814, Boston MA 02118-2526, USA*

Winfried Kain, *Department of Psychology, University of Salzburg, Hellbrunnerstr. 34, 5020 Salzburg, Austria*

Kathrin Lockl, *Department of Psychology, University of Würzburg, Röntgenring 10, 97070 Würzburg, Germany*

Claudia Mähler, *Department of Psychology, Georg-August-Universität Göttingen, Goßlerstr. 14, 37073 Göttingen, Germany*

Louis J. Moses, *Department of Psychology, 1227 University of Oregon, Eugene, OR 97403 USA*

Ulrich Müller, *Department of Psychology, University of Victoria, 3800 Finnerty Road, Victoria BC V8P 5C2, Canada*

Klaus Oberauer, *Department of Psychology, University of Potsdam, Karl-Liebknecht Str. 24–25, 14476 Golm, Germany*

Josef Perner, *Department of Psychology, University of Salzburg, Hellbrunnerstr. 34, 5020 Salzburg, Austria*

Li Qu, *Department of Psychology, University of Toronto, Toronto, Ontario, M5S 3G3, Canada*

Justin S. Rosenberg, *Department of Psychology, Florida Atlantic University, Boca Raton, FL 33431, USA*

Mark A. Sabbagh, *Department of Psychology, Queens University, Kingston, Ontario, K7L 3C3 Canada*

Wolfgang Schneider, *Department of Psychology, University of Würzburg, Röntgenring 10, 97070 Würzburg, Germany*

Ruth Schumann-Hengsteler, *Department of Psychology, Catholic University of Eichstätt-Ingolstadt, Ostenstraße 26, 85071 Eichstätt, Germany*

Katja Seitz, *Department of Psychology, Catholic University of Eichstätt-Ingolstadt, Ostenstraße 26, 85071 Eichstätt, Germany*

Beate Sodian, *Department of Psychology, University of München, Leopoldstr. 13, 80802 München, Germany*

Helen Tager-Flusberg, *Department of Anatomy and Neurobiology, Boston University School of Medicine, 715 Albany Street L-814, Boston MA 02118-2526, USA*

John Towse, *Department of Psychology, Fylde College, University of Lancaster, Bailrigg, Lancaster, LA1 4YF, UK*

Philip D. Zelazo, *Department of Psychology, University of Toronto, Toronto, Ontario, M5S 3G3, Canada*

Christof Zoelch, *Department of Psychology, Catholic University of Eichstätt-Ingolstadt, Ostenstraße 26, 85071 Eichstätt, Germany*

Chapter 1

Introduction and Overview

Wolfgang Schneider
University of Würzburg

Ruth Schumann-Hengsteler
Catholic University of Eichstätt-Ingolstadt

Beate Sodian
University of München

The study of cognitive development has undergone considerable changes during the last three decades. In the 1970s, the field was dominated by information processing views that assumed parallel and closely interrelated developmental changes in different cognitive domains, thus emphasizing a domain-general perspective of cognitive development. This perspective changed during the course of the 1980s and 1990s as the importance of domain-specific processes was confirmed in numerous studies, reflected in different developmental patterns in foundational domains (Wellman & Gelman, 1998). Research on children's developing understanding of the mental domain has become paradigmatic for the domain-specific approach to cognitive development. Although initially the primary focus of theory of mind research was on children's acquisition of core conceptual distinctions (e.g., between belief and reality), the developmental relations between conceptual development and other cognitive functions have attracted considerable research interest in recent years. Interrelations among theory of mind or metacognitive knowledge, working memory, language acquisition, and executive functions have been studied empirically. Several theoretical proposals have been made to account for the observed associations. However, there is still little exchange between researchers working in the memory and information processing traditions and researchers working in conceptual development.

Thus, the main purpose of this book is to discuss and integrate findings from prominent research areas in developmental psychology that are typically studied in isolation but are clearly related. For instance, young children's ability to regulate their actions (executive functions) is related to the ability to perform theory of mind (ToM) tasks that require the inhibition of prepotent responses (e.g., ignore one's own knowledge of the situation and take the perspective of another person). An interesting question is whether executive functions represent a precursor of ToM or whether ToM understanding predicts the development of executive functions. Another interesting and understudied issue is to what extent children's level of verbal ability (e.g., their understanding of sentences) and their working memory are important predictors of performance on both executive functioning and theory of mind tasks. For example, it is reasonable to assume that individual differences in vocabulary and verbal understanding are particularly important for predicting performance on executive functioning and ToM tasks in samples of young children (i.e., 3–4-year-olds), whereas among older children individual differences in working memory and executive functioning, rather than verbal abilities, may be better predictors of ToM performance.

During the last two decades, numerous studies have been conducted to investigate developmental trends in the areas addressed in the title of this book. More recently, several cross-sectional and longitudinal studies were carried out to test the specific predictions outlined previously. The chapters in this book give a detailed account of the major outcomes of this research. First, the state of the art concerning current understanding of the relevant constructs (working memory, ToM, executive functioning) and their developmental changes is presented, followed by chapters that deal with interactions among the core concepts. Thus, one outstanding feature of this volume is its focus on theoretically important relationships among determinants of young children's cognitive development—topics considered to be hot issues in contemporary developmental psychology. Most of the contributions to the book are based on presentations made at an international workshop at Castle Hirschberg, Bavaria, in May of 2002.

In the first part of the volume, five teams of researchers present theoretical analyses and overviews of empirical evidence regarding the core constructs: working memory, executive functions, and theory of mind. Chapter 2, by Towse and Cowan, describes recent developments in the area of working memory. In its first section, it focuses on two different approaches to working memory, namely, the models of Baddeley and Hitch and of Cowan. This section ends with a comparison of these two approaches, which is stimulating because the two authors each stand behind one of the two models. Hence, the similarities are outlined without neglecting the distinct differences. The second section consists of an empirical approach comparing different working memory span procedures on the basis of their assumed processing demands. Here, the authors conclude that different span measures may reflect—depending on the age of the children—quite different processing demands (for similar arguments, see also chap. 3 by Zoelch and colleagues). The last section again takes a theoretical focus, when the authors emphasize that working memory development may not be adequately described by taking into account only the amount of information that has to be processed but that it is also important to consider variables that might be age dependent, such as processing speed, storage time, strategic variations, or variations in representational format. Finally, Towse and Cowan relate the concept of working memory to that of executive functions by referring to the core system of Baddeley's (1996) model, that is, the central executive.

It is exactly here where the chapter 3 by Zoelch, Seitz, and Schumann-Hengsteler takes up: They discuss, on a theoretical as well as an empirical basis, how central executive processing within the Baddeley and Hitch working memory framework could be measured. A primary attempt is made at an empirical evaluation of Baddeley's (1996) theoretical conceptualization of central executive processes within a developmental context. Therefore, the authors adjust seven different measures of central executive processes to children between 5 and 10 years of age. Each of these different operationalizations of central executive processing is discussed with respect to its processing demands—in particular, when different age groups will be faced with them. Empirically, Zoelch et al. demonstrate different developmental trends for the four different central executive subfunctions and report a correlational pattern that is in accordance with Baddeley's theoretical assumptions. Furthermore, they discuss on the basis of their findings the criteria that should be taken into account when creating and evaluating working memory measurement tools within a developmental context.

In the following chapter by Zelazo, Qu, and Müller, the focus is switched from working memory to the role of executive functions (EF). The main part of the chapter is dedicated to reviewing the state of the art with respect to the definition of EF. Here the authors start with a functional approach, describing EF as mainly a planning procedure and—this is emphasized— as a domain-general construct. A crucial distinction is then made between hot and cool EF, depending on whether an action or thought occurs in a motivationally significant context or not. In particular, hot EF are relevant for social, emotional, and moral development. At that point, the authors point out a relation to ToM: Zelazo et al. argue on the basis of the CCC theory (Cognitive Complexity and Control) on complexity, that, basically, ToM is EF as expressed in the content domain of self and social understanding. They close the chapter by reporting a first study that documents the relative difficulty that children have with tasks that reflect both ToM and EF. In their conclusions, they clearly state that ToM doesn't cause EF and EF doesn't cause ToM; rather, both reflect the development of similar cognitive mechanisms and neural systems.

The chapters on working memory and EF are followed by an overview of the theory of mind literature. In the past 20 years, theory of mind has been one of the most active fields of cognitive development. Based on a conceptual analysis of what it means to be able to impute mental states to oneself and to others, Wimmer and Perner (1983) conducted the first systematic investigation of belief understanding in children. Since then, several hundred studies have addressed the issue of whether or not age-related changes in children's solutions of the false belief task reflect a genuine developmental phenomenon. In chapter 5, Sodian reviews the developmental evidence for both first- and second-order belief understanding and the mastery of related concepts as well as the theoretical accounts that have been proposed for these phenomena. If belief understanding is a genuine developmental phenomenon (and there is good reason to believe that it is), what is it the development of? Whereas earlier accounts (simulation as well as conceptual change accounts) have focused on the mental domain, more recent theories have linked theory of mind development to broader cognitive changes, such as perspective-representation, the acquisition of syntax, and EF. Because the developmental relation of ToM and EF has been demonstrated in a large body of empirical studies, and because of its implications for neurocognitive development, the ToM-EF link has become an area of both theoretical and empirical innovation in recent years and is at the core of this book.

The second part of this volume deals with the interplay among the core concepts previously outlined and with developmental trends in the interaction. There is broad agreement that EF is a heterogeneous construct including inhibition, working memory, cognitive flexibility, and planning, as well as monitoring skills. Moses, Carlson, and Sabbagh (chap. 6) ask which aspects of executive function underlie the EF-ToM relation. The empirical findings strongly suggest that working memory, in combination with inhibitory control, is important for ToM development. There is ample evidence against a simple working memory account because ToM tasks with parallel working memory demands are solved at different ages, and only tasks with high inhibitory demands have been found to correlate closely with executive function measures. With respect to theories about the causal relation between executive control and ToM development, Moses et al. argue that the view that a certain level of executive functioning is a prerequisite for ToM development is best supported by the empirical data (especially by longitudinal data). The authors also argue that EF is probably important for conceptual development, that is, for ToM to emerge in the first place, rather than merely for overcoming performance problems, as expression accounts suggest.

In chapter 7, Bjorklund, Cormier, and Rosenberg take an evolutionary perspective on the ToM-EF relation. While evolutionary psychology generally favors domain-specific accounts, Bjorklund et al. argue that, in human evolutionary history, a domain-general process—the evolution of increased inhibitory ability resulting from brain expansion—led to better intentional control over individuals' behavior and that this ability proved to be most highly adaptive in the social domain, where it was applied to dealing with everyday challenges in social groups. Enhanced social-cognitive abilities resulting from increased inhibitory control altered the hominids' ecology and thereby produced new selective pressures that eventually resulted in the emergence of new, more sophisticated domain-specific social-reasoning abilities, supported by a theory of mind.

Whereas most studies of the EF-ToM relationship focused on first-order ToM, Sodian and Hülsken (chap. 8) studied advanced ToM abilities in children with deficient inhibitory control (children with attention deficit hyperactivity disorder [ADHD]). Consistent with the few studies previously conducted on ToM in children with ADHD, there was no difference between children with ADHD and normally developing controls in second-order belief understanding, as well as in a test of advanced social understanding. However, children with ADHD were shown to be delayed as indicated by a test of advanced understanding of epistemic states (knowing, guessing correctly, knowing by inference), requiring online representation of a person's informational access, independently of behavioral outcome. These findings indicate that the development of EF may be important for certain aspects of advanced ToM development in elementary school age. The findings certainly support an expression account, but they may also be consistent with an emergence account, based on theoretical assumptions about an interaction of the conceptual content of mindreading tasks with their inhibitory demands.

Several contributions to this book emphasize that developmental changes in the prefrontal cortex relate to developmental changes observed for EF and ToM functioning. In chapter 9, Kain and Perner report on the current evidence from neuroimaging studies for the neural basis of ToM and EF. Although neuroimaging studies with children are still scarce, the empirical data summarized in this chapter show that both ToM and EF recruit spatially proximal brain regions. Regarding developmental differences, the overview given in this chapter indicates that, when working on EF tasks, children's prefrontal regions are more broadly activated than those of adults. Overall, the authors emphasize that the relationship between ToM and EF performance depends considerably on the particular kinds of executive functioning and ToM tasks one is dealing with. Accordingly, generalizations about the relationship between the two constructs are difficult to justify based on findings from neuroimaging studies and thus should be avoided.

In chapter 10, Hasselhorn, Mähler, and Grube relate ToM to phonological working memory and verbal abilities. In particular, the authors look for so-called developmental dependencies between these three aspects of cognitive development in preschool children. The chapter starts with two empirical studies: In both of the studies, verbal ability aspects such as understanding, comparison, and word fluency as well as two measures of phonological working memory (i.e., digit span and nonword repetition) are incorporated and related to ToM. With respect to the latter, the focus is laid on first- and second-order false beliefs. On the basis of correlational and covariational data analyses, the authors discuss various potential developmental trajectories. Finally, they propose a hypothetical model, the relay race model, based on the assumption that, in the beginning, phonological working memory, and, later in development, verbal abilities are major pacemakers for the development of ToM.

Developmental disorders are especially important for understanding the EF-ToM relationship. Tager-Flusberg and Joseph (chap. 11) longitudinally studied the relationship between impairments in ToM and EF in autistic children. Their findings indicate that working memory, combined with inhibitory control and planning, contributed to ToM performance in autistic children and adolescents, independently of nonverbal mental age and language ability. Again, a simple working memory account was not supported because working memory by itself was not significantly correlated with ToM independently of general cognitive ability and language. Working memory combined with inhibitory control was a significant concurrent predictor of ToM, whereas planning ability predicted progress in ToM development in autistic persons. The authors discuss the implications of these findings for emergence versus expression accounts of the EF-ToM relationship, arguing that the combination of working memory and inhibitory control appears to be most closely related to performance aspects (expression) of ToM, whereas planning seems to be more deeply and conceptually related to ToM development—a conclusion that is also supported by independent research on the relation of ToM and planning abilities in normally developing children (Bischof-Köhler, 2000).

Although a few longitudinal studies tap developmental changes in some of the constructs discussed in this volume, only one recent study deals with the development of all of these concepts. Schneider, Lockl, and Fernandez (chap. 12) report on the first results of the Würzburg Longitudinal Study that was initiated in 2001 with 3-year-old children and is supposed to last until 2005. This longitudinal study was stimulated by a similar investigation conducted by Astington and Jenkins (1999), which emphasized the role of language development for the development of ToM and EF. Overall, the findings of the Würzburg study confirm and extend the findings by Astington and Jenkins, again highlighting the importance of language development (in particular, sentence comprehension) for children's performance on both ToM and EF tasks when this relationship is investigated with comparably young children (i.e., 3-year-olds). Although the study is not complete (at the time of this writing), findings from subsequent measurement points seem to indicate that the importance of individual differences in language proficiency for ToM and EF performance is reduced with increasing age.

In the final chapter, Oberauer discusses the findings presented in the various chapters of this volume and their implications for our understanding of the interplay among ToM, EF, and working memory functions. The author already served as a discussant at the workshop at Castle Hirschberg and extends the comments he made at that occasion to the revised evidence presented in this volume. One of the major conclusions he draws from the available evidence is that a narrow definition of EF should be used in empirical studies, because (limited) construct validity can be demonstrated only for such a conception that focuses on supervisory and control processes, in particular, the inhibition of prepotent responses. Another conclusion is that working memory capacity seems to contribute to the emergence of ToM understanding, even though the existing evidence is not particularly strong. Finally, the author generates interesting speculations regarding the developmental function of the constructs under investigation in this volume, discussing the issue of whether they all come together and develop at about the same pace. The readers of this book are invited to take on these hypotheses and speculations and develop them further. We hope that they can share our discussant's view and find the chapters valuable and helpful.

ACKNOWLEDGMENTS

The workshop at Castle Hirschberg, Bavaria, in May 2002, from which the contributions to the present volume originated, was funded by a grant from the German Research Foundation (Deutsche Forschungsgemeinschaft) to the German Research Group on Cognitive Development.

REFERENCES

Astington, J. W., & Jenkins, J. M. (1999). A longitudinal study of the relation between language and theory-of-mind development. *Developmental Psychology, 35*, 1311–1320.

Baddeley. A. (1996). *Working memory.* New York: Oxford University Press.

Bischof-Köhler, D. (2000). *Theory of mind, Zeitverständnis und Handlungsorganisation* [Theory of mind, understanding of time, and organization of actions]. Bern, Switzerland: Huber.

Wellman, H. M., & Gelman, S. A. (1998). Knowledge acquisition in foundational domains. In W. Damon (Ed. in Chief), D. Kuhn, & R. S. Siegler (Vol. Eds.), *Handbook of child psychology, Vol. 2: Cognition, perception, and language* (pp. 523–574). New York: Wiley.

Wimmer, H., & Perner, J. (1983). Beliefs about beliefs: Representation and constraining function of wrong beliefs in young children's understanding of deception. *Cognition, 13*, 103–128.

Chapter 2

Working Memory and Its Relevance for Cognitive Development

John Towse

University of Lancaster

Nelson Cowan

University of Missouri

I suppose it is tempting, if the only tool you have is a hammer, to treat everything as if it were a nail.
—Maslow (1966, pp. 15–16)

In the present chapter, we attempt to cover three principal issues. First, we introduce and discuss some of the key findings relevant to understanding models of working memory in children, including ideas of executive functioning. Second, we attempt to provide evidence for our contention that relying on a single index of working memory—as often happens—may restrict the appreciation of important cognitive and developmental processes. This may be especially pertinent when considering how working memory relates to other developmental processes. Accordingly, we suggest new measures of working memory to complement those already in use. Third, we argue that it is important to be careful in thinking about the questions to be asked of working memory processes, and we offer questions that may enrich understanding in the area.

These three issues serve as an illustration of the potential relevance of Maslow's remark at the opening of this chapter. There exists the threat that researchers have a single index (or a small number of indices) for working memory and as a consequence are left to interpret psychological processes according to the particular perspective offered by that performance index. However, we also recognize that this situation is not immutable, and new perspectives on working memory are emerging. There are also other reasons for concluding that we could benefit from the opportunity to reflect on where we have reached: On the one hand, there is widespread recognition of the importance and relevance of working memory within cognitive and developmental psychology (see Miyake & Shah, 1999). And of course the adoption of the terminology and attention on the discipline is undoubtedly flattering. And yet, on the other hand, communications with an ever-wider audience bring the risk that conceptual ideas become simplified to the point where they no longer represent our level of understanding in a valid way. In reaching a wider audience (in essence, as research findings become corporatized), messages can lose their important nuances, subtleties, and controversies. Nonetheless, here, too, there are reasons to be upbeat and positive about the outlook and to hope that there can be successful application of theoretical ideas while retaining a measure of vibrancy in the debate about the interpretation of knowledge.

SECTION 1: MODELS OF WORKING MEMORY

Background to Baddeley's Model of Working Memory

The model of working memory evolved considerably over time, gradually becoming more specific and elaborated. Initially at least, data served the role of characterizing working memory, not testing the model against some sharply defined alternative. In other words, several ideas about working memory developed in the absence of a formally specified model. Nonetheless, Baddeley and Hitch (1974) laid important foundations for subsequent research. Their work successfully welded together a number of important concepts connected with immediate memory. Among these were, first, the realization that immediate memory is fragile and limited to a small number of independent items (Miller, 1956). The definition of items is necessarily elusive, insofar as they can vary according to the availability of conceptual or semantic representations that lead to coherence (maybe individual letters, maybe words with many more letters). Second was the notion that rehearsal of items can serve an important function in warding off the effects of forgetting, which can be pernicious and rapid (Brown, 1958; Peterson & Peterson, 1959). Such forgetting was originally thought of as reflecting time–based decay (but see, e.g., Crowder, 1993). Third, it is apparent that verbal memory is influenced by the physical properties of verbal information, such as the confusions among the sounds of letters (Conrad, 1964). Fourth, a structural model of processes was envisaged, with a flow of information among the components of the system, most likely a concept influenced by Broadbent (1958, 1971).

Baddeley and Hitch (1974) were responsible for setting the stage for research that followed and, to a lesser extent, for interpreting existing findings. Moreover, their work was primarily influential in proposing a general framework, according to which memory was thought of as allied to and integrated with cognitive processing. They certainly distinguished between a central workspace and a dedicated verbal memory system, but beyond this many details were left open. It was only with subsequent research that the specification of a multicomponent system emerged, later to be masterfully integrated into a coherent framework by Baddeley (1986). Thus, data from Baddeley, Thomson, and Buchanan (1975) revealed that immediate serial recall of verbal information is closely tied to the real-time articulation of the memory stimuli. In particular, memory for words is inversely proportional to their length so that sequences of short words are better remembered than equivalent sequences of long words. The phonological properties of verbal items have also been shown to be relevant, allowing the appreciation of the early finding that overlapping phonological codes (e.g., for the letters *b, c, e, p*) disrupt memory performance (Baddeley, 1966). Baddeley, Lewis, and Vallar (1984) confirmed the importance of verbal labeling in the translation of visual-based memory codes into verbal ones. They showed that articulatory suppression—the repeated utterance of a simple phrase—could eliminate the word length effect and the phonemic similarity effect for visually presented material. This was assumed to occur because suppression occupied and therefore blocked the rehearsal process that would otherwise be available for the recoding of information into a verbal form.

Figure 2.1 provides a simplified schematic account of Baddeley's (2000) model of working memory. It proposes a multicomponent architecture, in

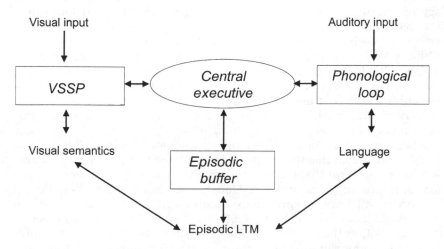

FIG. 2.1. Adaptation of Baddeley's model of working memory. From "The Episodic Buffer: A New Component of Working Memory," by A. D. Baddeley, 2000, *Trends in Cognitive Science*.

which there are two major slave systems, the phonological loop and the visuospatial sketch pad, together with a recently proposed third system, the integrative episodic buffer. All of these systems are thought to be under the control of the so-called central executive. The central executive is the hub of the system, although the other components are important and largely independent of each other. The phonological loop is a verbal-based system, which, it is proposed, comprises a relatively passive phonological store together with an articulatory control process. This phonological loop system is used to encode printed items as well as to refresh phonological representations in working memory to prevent them from becoming inactive. The visuospatial sketch pad holds, as one would expect, visual and spatial representations. At least, according to some accounts, these are thought to be separable (see Logie, 1995; Pearson, 2001), although, because stimuli will often contain elements of both visual and spatial information, a division between them is sometimes just a convenient research device concerning emphasis, rather than a phenomenological reality.

Although working memory was proposed as a theoretical account of adult memory performance, it has been fruitfully applied to a range of developmental issues. In several cases, research showed that changes in memory among primary school children can be attributed to the strategies that children use. Verbal recoding of visually presented material (whether images or words) is not ubiquitous (see Halliday & Hitch, 1988). At around the age of 8 years, children exhibit, with consistency, phenomena such as word length effects and phonological similarity effects even when material is presented in a nonverbal form. Convergent with these results, children younger than about 7 years of age are susceptible to visual similarity effects in attempting to remember pictorial stimuli (Hitch, Woodin, & Baker, 1989). They show confusion between items with visually overlapping features. This has been taken to suggest that their memory may be based on relatively untransformed visual representations of the initial stimuli. Exploring this last idea in more detail, Walker, Hitch, Dewhurst, Whiteley, and Brandimonte (1997) compared memory for recently exposed images with longer term memories for the same stimuli, investigating how attributes of the original material may be either duplicated in internal representations or may be transformed and abstracted.

Working memory has not simply been used to expose some of the processes involved in qualitative shifts in memory. Quantitative changes have also been analyzed. For example, just as the word length effect demonstrated that verbal memory performance relates to pronunciation duration, developmental changes in articulation speed may form one component of improved memory (Hitch, Halliday, & Littler, 1989). As discussed in more detail later, research also documented a relationship between memory ability and concurrent cognitive tasks (Case, Kurland, & Goldberg, 1982) so that, as these concurrent tasks become executed more efficiently through development, memory improves to a corresponding degree.

Furthermore, it is apparent that memory performance is an intricate amalgam of both immediate and longer term memory processes. Hulme,

Maughan, and Brown (1991) noted that recall performance for words is superior to that of (otherwise-matched) nonwords, with both types of memoranda sensitive to the syllabic length of the stimuli. They argued that words benefit from the availability of a redintegration process. This potentially allows the recovery of the target from a partially degraded representation (a target item may be uniquely identified even with only some of the original information) and involves the application of semantic knowledge to the memory representation. Because pronunciation time affected all items equally, the data imply that rehearsal speed is a factor independent from redintegration. The study also illustrates how some processes (redintegration) can make a detectable, qualitative difference to recall, whereas others (word length) affect memory in a proportional way.

In work that shows some parallels with Hulme et al. (1991), Gathercole, Willis, Baddeley, and Emslie (1994) showed that children's memory for nonwords is sensitive to the wordlikeness of the material, the overlap between the stimuli and familiar phonotactic representations in words (see also Thorn & Gathercole, 1999). Gathercole et al. showed that memory for nonwords varies across children and relates to vocabulary acquisition. The ability to retain unfamiliar phonological items (nonwords that are distinct from items in the lexicon) may be important for the acquisition of novel vocabulary and may be one important function of the phonological loop of working memory.

Having provided some general background to some of the important research cornerstones in working memory, we now turn to some issues of executive control. Baddeley's (1986, 2000) model of working memory is interesting in the context of cognitive development because it explicitly acknowledges the role of executive skills. Moreover, executive skills encompass a range of mechanisms for regulating thought and behavior, and these are potentially relevant to other themes in the book. For example, the central executive has been argued to take on functions of mental control, including inhibitory action. Thus, among adults, the executive has been argued to play an important role in shaping responses on a random generation task, where individuals try to inhibit prepotent or overlearned stereotypical responses (Baddeley, 1986; Baddeley, Emslie, Kolodny, & Duncan, 1998). Also, the central executive is thought to have controlling powers that influence the flow of information (so that the slave systems are directed appropriately). Aspects of this control function resonate with some features within Zelazo's Cognitive Complexity and Control (CCC) model (see Zelazo, this volume; Zelazo & Jacques, 1996) and in particular the developmental growth of reflexivity and informational access at different levels of consciousness. Furthermore, the central executive may be involved in the retention of information during a complex task as well as possessing a control function (Baddeley & Hitch, 1974, though see also Baddeley & Logie, 1999, for a shift in position; see also Daneman & Carpenter, 1980; Just & Carpenter, 1992).

Characterizing the interrelationship between memory and ongoing mentation is important in and of itself. It is also relevant in the context of the present volume because there have been arguments, for example, that theory of mind (ToM) tasks may impose nontrivial demands on children's ability to manipulate and remember critical aspects of an experimental situation (Gordon & Olson, 1998). Consider a false belief task, whereby a child is witness to a state of the world (a marble placed in a box) but is also exposed to another, different view of the world (witnessing that a puppet had only seen an earlier scenario, in which a marble was in a basket, and thus a different location). False belief questions probe the child's understanding of the puppet's knowledge. Therefore, the task requires that children acknowledge not only the real state of the world but also alternative beliefs based on different perspectives, where these alternate beliefs are tenable because of particular circumstances (such as whether another individual is able to witness a critical event).

As one considers the complexity of the situation, and the number of different pieces of information that are potentially relevant to the false belief task, it begins to look plausible that working memory constraints might affect false belief computations. Children's ability to respond correctly to false belief questions may depend on their ability to hold in mind multiple, contradictory representations, as well as their ability to access these representations appropriately (inhibiting their knowledge of reality to uncover others' beliefs). As Gordon and Olson (1998) note, working memory may be an important support structure for ToM abilities and not just for the expression of these abilities. While short-term memory (STM) performance has not been a useful unique predictor of false belief (Jenkins & Astington, 1996), paradigms such as backward span (Davis & Pratt, 1995) and counting span (Keenan, Olson, & Marini, 1998) are more strongly associated with false belief tasks. Gordon and Olson (1998) added to this view, reporting that false belief performance was related to a dual-task paradigm in which children needed to integrate two tasks and keep track of the point they had reached on each one. While it is not our intention to analyze these data in particular, we see these studies as offering a motivation for understanding what working memory involves, as a potential means for appreciating the constraints on other cognitive domains.

However, although the central executive is potentially relevant in different ways to cognitive development as we just described, unfortunately the research field lacks unequivocal evidence that the central executive does all (or indeed any) of these functions in the way that has been proposed. That is, these functions have the status of candidate executive operations. In addition, the promiscuous way in which central executive has acquired functions is potentially a substantial problem. It may generate the illusion that different aspects of research refer to some common mental mechanism, whereas they may just share a verbal label (however, see Miyake et al., 2000, for a body of evidence pointing to how executive functions may have both common and disparate elements). In the domain of working memory span (to be discussed in more detail later) one function ascribed to the executive is that it can act as a general-purpose system that shares resources between different requirements of the task. Counting span requires the participant to find the number of target objects in an array and remember this number during additional counts. The difficulty of the counting component of the task has been argued to determine the ability to remember the answers (Case et al., 1982). In this paradigm, the executive has a free-floating role in which two functions trade off against each other; that is, they compete for and share the limited capacity system resources. A task such as random generation provides a substantial contrast (Baddeley, 1966; for performance among primary school children, see Towse and Mclachlan, 1999). Here, the executive is invoked as a mechanism by which unwanted responses (such as those that form stereotyped sequences, as in the string 1 ... 2 ... 3 ... 4 when generating random numbers) are inhibited or suppressed and a mechanism by which new strategies for less predictable responses can be generated.

The number of executive roles is problematic, and this is compounded by their heterogeneity. It should be apparent that these mental processes, of resource sharing in one situation and response inhibition in another, are very different. Other executive functions have been proposed, and these are different again. Carrying out all the suggested functions is a substantial burden on this abstract system (for further discussion, see Towse & Houston-Price, 2001; Zoelch, Seitz, & Schumann-Hengsteler, this volume).

In summary, we outlined some key aspects of Baddeley's (1986, 2000) model of working memory. What has been proposed is a multicomponent architecture based on storage systems that are tied to particular domains and controlled by an executive system. Working memory components interact, yet they also have considerable independence. Verbal memory is heavily linked to articulation and rehearsal activities, although it is also clear that this is not the complete story. The development of working memory involves qualitative changes in the way that information is remembered as well as quantitative changes arising from the efficiency of rehearsal and speed-related processes. The executive system is a complex controlling device, which has been given responsibility for a variety of cognitive tasks. Given the degree to which memory representations are used in mental activities, working memory is an important contributor to many cognitive phenomena.

Background to Cowan's Model: Implications for Development and Executive Skills

Cowan's model (e.g. Cowan, 1999) is inherently hierarchical in its structure. Whereas Baddeley's (1986) model outlined a two-layer system (with slave systems at one level and the central executive at another), Cowan's model has three levels, and the distinctions between them are even more marked. Long-term representations form one level of memory. Activated Long-Term Memory (LTM) representations form a second level of memory, and these are a subset of the first level. These representations are in a more accessible state than the full set of memory representations. The focus of

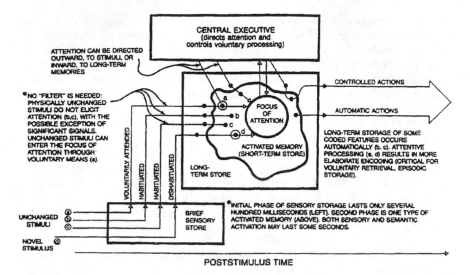

FIG. 2.2. Illustration of Cowan embedded process model of attention. © 1998 by the American Psychological Corporation. Reprinted with permission.

attention, a subset of activated representations, forms a further, third level of mental process. The model developed from ideas presented by Cowan (1988) and is shown in Fig. 2.2.

Baddeley (2000) proposed an episodic buffer as a fourth component of his Working Memory model. This brings the two models somewhat closer together, in that this episodic buffer sits between the two slave systems—being the place where modality-based representations are extracted and become integrated—and the central executive (which controls its operations). However, it is worth noting that the nature of the hierarchies is different: Cowan outlines a group of mechanisms that have a different grain size so that they are subsets or supersets of each other. They therefore form embedded processes. Hierarchies in Baddeley's model reflect instead a chain of command for quite separate processing systems, where the emphasis is on the cognitive architecture and its structural characteristics. So even though both models might be thought to have three levels, the way in which these levels are envisaged to relate to each other is quite different.

Cowan's (1999) vision of working memory is that it is a collective term referring to the set of mental processes that result in representations being available in an unusually accessible state. The level of accessibility is important because the representations can influence how any task with a mental component is carried out. Memories per se are not effective in shaping mental contents. It is only when these memories are accessible (through increased activation) that they can achieve this.

Furthermore, Cowan, Elliott, and Saults (2002) noted that working memory is not just the activated portion of long-term memory (the second embedded level referred to previously). This is because the set of activated representations are not just free-floating, independent, and unconnected. Features need to be bound together, and there needs to be some way to recover the temporal sequence in which events take place and to mark other episodic information; for example, determining which elements were activated after others. This additional (in one sense, contextual) information also forms part of working memory. Such bindings are thought to occur only when representations are in the focus of attention, and once established the links rapidly become incorporated within long-term memory. Hence, the emphasis here on the collective nature of the term *working memory* as a set of processes that, in concert, produce representations that are memorable and that can be used in other circumstances.

An important aspect of Cowan's (1999) model is that the focus of attention is quite limited. Cowan (2001) argued that the average capacity of the focus of attention for normal adults is about four unconnected chunks. Although this is in one sense a revision of Miller's (1956) magic number 7 or minor adjustment of Broadbent's (1975) capacity estimate of three chunks, Cowan's (2001) analysis represents an attempt to consider the appropriate methods for evaluating capacity limits in immediate memory, and the legitimate interpretations from memory performance from a range of paradigms. Fundamentally, Cowan (2001) offers a critical analysis of whether previous claims of limited capacity are warranted and concludes by endorsing this stance. This limited capacity may be rooted in the nature of memory representations. If the items in memory are represented by a set of features (Cowan, 2001, considered pulsing feature detectors), then the degree of featural overlap increases as the number of chunks increases. Features rapidly become confusable with each other as the number of independent items increases.

In summary, Cowan (1999) offers a model of memory that, like Baddeley's (2000), emphasizes the links between memory and attentional functioning. Cowan's model is hierarchical, comprising a set of embedded systems so that the focus of attention is a subset of active memory representations, itself a subset of long-term memory. The model postulates different constraints on different faculties, not just in size but also in type; the focus of attention being capacity limited and activation being time limited and susceptible to interference. The model emphasizes the multiple routes to developmental change because the various constraints can be relaxed through biological and cognitive change.

Comparing Models of Working Memory

It is important to recognize some of the obstacles in comparing the Baddeley (2000) and Cowan (1999) models of working memory, particularly from a developmental perspective. First, the two approaches have not received the same degree of empirical scrutiny. A far greater body of research has been built on Baddeley's framework, investigating the structural characteristics of the system components. Second, both models converge or concur in several important respects; thus, they do not dispute the validity of several memory phenomena or suppositions. Unsurprisingly, perhaps, they are not entirely different, and as a consequence it is not possible to identify points of divergence in every situation. Third, it could be argued that the models are moving closer to each other, for example, in the postulation of an episodic buffer for working memory (Baddeley, 2000, although see previous comments). Fourth, where these theoretical differences are sharpest (in describing the distinction between immediate and long-term memory representations) the models are more abstract, which decreases the scope for a simple experimental test to discriminate between them. Fifth, in neither case do these models stand or fall by developmental data alone. Sixth, as one turns to younger children, both approaches become increasingly coy about making straightforward predictions because the memory strategies that children have at their disposal are fewer and more primitive.

All these caveats notwithstanding, the two approaches can be separate in some respects. As already referred to, Baddeley's model is more modular in outlook. Each of the working memory slave systems operates largely independently of others. Thus verbal and visuospatial tasks can be combined much more easily than two tasks from the same domain (e.g., Baddeley, Grant, Wight, & Thomson, 1975). Each component is thought to be neurologically distinct, and thus there is considerable autonomy amid interacting systems. Cowan's (1999) approach is more cautious in considering the division of labor according to the type of memory involved. In part, this reflects a concern about representations that incorporate multiple sources of information (e.g., tactile sensory memories or acoustically derived spatial codes). It also follows from the emphasis on memory processes rather than memory domain codes. This makes Baddeley's model particularly suited to explaining data from experiments where stimuli are created to have domain-specific properties.

From the perspective of cognitive development, Baddeley's (2000) model emphasizes that working memory systems per se may not undergo major developmental changes, arguing instead that it is the way the systems are used (e.g., through increases in articulation rate or translation between modalities of representation allowing a more appropriate memory code to be formed) that leads to older children performing better on memory tasks (see Hitch & Towse, 1995). In contrast, Cowan suggested that acoustic information may be lost more rapidly in younger children (e.g., Cowan, Nugent, Elliott, & Saults, 2000) and that the capacity of the focus of attention and the rate of transfer of information into that focus of attention also change with age (Cowan et al., 2002). Thus the rate of forgetting, and not just the rate at which memories are encoded, may differ across ages. The models therefore differ in that Cowan makes more specific predictions about the nature of developmental change in memory per se.

Another point of divergence is that Cowan's (1999) model is more explicit in identifying multiple sources of change in processing efficiency. Thus, in Baddeley's (2000) model there has been an emphasis on articulation speed, as already discussed. Although it has not been claimed that this is sufficient (and potentially the model could be elaborated to reflect the different ways in which developmental change takes place), Cowan has been more forthright in questioning the idea that a central, global processing rate is sufficient. For example, there may be separate processing rate parameters involved in memory search activities and in phonological processing operations, explaining why these predict independent sources of variance in children's memory performance (Cowan et al., 1998). We also noted that adopting a position whereby memory is affected by a variety of processing factors helps to account for findings that are sometimes argued to pose problems for Baddeley's model of working memory. Thus, Kemps, De Rammelaere, and Desmet (2000) noted that increases in visual memory ability could not be accounted for in terms of rehearsal speed or the phonological loop. Yet, as already indicated, this is troublesome only to the extent that these variables are the only relevant constraints on working memory. Of course, one needs a principled way of expanding the number of degrees of freedom through which memory can vary, lest there be an unmanageable proliferation of parameters. However, because the empirical data already offer evidence of two different speed-limited processes and phenomena associated with each, this modification could hardly be regarded as being reckless.

It has already been noted that the models differ in terms of the extent to which they are hierarchical and modular. It has also been pointed out that Cowan's (1999) model is more process oriented, emphasizing how activation of features of stimuli is important—indeed fundamental—for the memorability of stimuli. Placing activation at the forefront of the model provides a contrast to Baddeley's (2000) model, wherein the core issues revolve around the appropriate laying down, refreshing, and decay of domain-specific memory traces.

To conclude, even though there are strong points of similarity, it is possible to distinguish the Baddeley and Cowan models of working memory in a number of ways. In general, we view the presence of alternative approaches to working memory as being very healthy (as do others, too; see Miyake & Shah, 1999) because it is through the contrasts that research can be focused in a productive way. It facilitates the appreciation of the benefits and drawbacks of looking at memory phenomena from particular vantage points and draws out different aspects of memory phenomena. These include a consideration of the number and the nature of developmental changes in working memory, the characteristics of memory systems themselves, and the strategies adopted by children to preserve information for future recall.

A Focus on Working Memory Span Tasks

The notion that working memory is limited in the number of things that can be remembered simultaneously, during ongoing processing, leads to the emphasis on tests of working memory that assess how many items can be remembered. The situation is akin to that of the juggler, whose reputation is built solely on the number of balls, or sticks, or knives, or other items that can be juggled simultaneously. In our fascination with the juggling, we seem to ignore whether there are other issues to be considered. Does our juggler have the ability to interact with an audience, to make them feel involved in what he or she is accomplishing, as they laugh or gasp or cheer at the performance? Does our juggler have the ability to develop a story as part of the juggling act, to change the tempo and potentially break up the monotony of just juggling? Indeed, does our juggler have any other tricks (up his or her sleeve or anywhere else)? As we begin to generate, or reflect on, these and other questions, it becomes apparent that judging the quality of a juggler is more complex than it initially seems—and so it would seem with working memory. There are some fundamental attributes to working memory, and complex span tests clearly generate a reasonably stable, efficient, and predictive score. Notwithstanding, there is more to working memory than just remembering in sequence a large set of unrelated words.

Our own work, in collaboration with others, illustrates this issue. We recently studied a group of children who were given several widely used tests of working memory. Among these tests was one of reading span, and we dwell on this task for a while to illuminate several empirical findings and theoretical conclusions. In the implementation of reading span that we used, children read aloud a series of incomplete sentences from a computer screen. They generated an appropriate word to complete the sentence before it was removed from view and the next sentence appeared. Thus, they might see "The rocket went into outer _____" and they would be expected to say "space." After all sentences in a series were complete, children were cued to recall the completion words they had produced, recapitulating the order of production. The provision by children of the expected completion word shows that they have, at least in broad terms, engaged in appropriate comprehension processes. Children began with sets of two sentences to read and therefore two words to remember. In those cases where children could remember all the target words on at least one of three attempts, the number of sentences in the series was increased (from two to three, from three to four, etc.) and the procedure continued. When children were unable to recall the words at a given length, testing stopped. Figure 2.3 provides a prototypical test scenario, in which a child remembers the target words from two of the three two-sentence lists but fails to remember the target words from the three-sentence trials. The child makes a variety of recall errors, including failing to remember an item altogether and making serial order and item errors.

With such a procedure, one can estimate the reading span for a particular child, the highest sequence length for which the child can correctly remember the target words. Indeed, one can take different measures of memory performance. One can identify the point at which recall errors first appeared in the children's memory responses. Alternatively, one can note the point where the majority of the three recall attempts were unsuc-

<u>**Sentence and response**</u>	<u>**Recall attempt**</u>	<u>**Outcome**</u>
There are twelve months in a ___ year I wear socks on my ___ feet	Year... feet	✓
Every day I wash and comb my ___ hair Ben ran fast and won the ___ race	Hair ... fast	✗
The opposite of cold is ___ hot Cows eat the long green ___ grass	Hot ... grass	✓
Food and water makes plants ___ grow Mary got home and unlocked the ___ door We see things with our ___ eyes	grow... ?...?	✗
The dog was happy and wagged his ___ tail Mum and I read a story from a ___ book If I hear a joke it makes me ___ laugh	Book... laugh... tail	✗
At night I go to bed and fall ___ asleep The next number after four is ___ five Jane skips with a skipping ___ rope	Asleep... five... book	✗

FIG. 2.3. An example testing protocol showing success and failure at reading span.

cessful. Alternatively still, it is possible to determine the point where none of the three recall efforts were successful. In each case, one can derive an estimate of memory ability but according to different criteria. For the purposes of obtaining stable measurements, and simplifying the process of analysis, these three separate points along the forgetting function can be combined into an overall measure of memory recall.

It is worth noting at this point that a variety of research studies have confirmed that measures of reading span are good predictors of children's cognitive abilities, for example correlating with assessments of scholastic attainment (e.g., Hitch, Towse, & Hutton, 2001) and measures of early reading development (e.g., Leather & Henry, 1994). Tests of working memory are superior to tests of short-term memory as predictors of a range of cognitive tasks (see Daneman & Carpenter, 1980). Because the working memory span task requires both language-processing ability (in reading aloud, understanding the sentence, and generating a suitable completion) and memory (retaining the final word for later recall), it is not surprising that there is a popular argument that the task reflects the capacity to combine these two different mental functions of processing and retention. According to some influential views (Daneman & Carpenter, 1980; Daneman & Hannon, 2001), these mental functions are separate and play off or trade off each other, and span reflects the residual ability to remember once processing has been accomplished. That is, working memory span represents a dual-task paradigm.

On the basis of several important studies over a number of years, Randy Engle and colleagues (e.g., Engle, Tuholski, Laughlin, & Conway, 1999; Kane & Engle, 2003) concluded that working memory span is a critical window on the capacity to engage in controlled attention and as an index of a domain-general skill that involves the maintenance of information in the face of interference. According to this position, WM = STM + controlled attention. Therefore, working memory and short-term memory partially overlap. At the same time, short-term memory tasks involve just the retention of information, whereas working memory tasks are constructed in such a way as to "present a secondary task to interfere with the primary retention task" (Kane & Engle, 2003, p. 639).

Several aspects of their model are germane to the present discussion. They emphasise the domain-general nature of working memory capacity. So, although they acknowledge the impurity of particular tasks, and therefore recognize that performance must also be made up of domain-specific processes, they hold that the core, underlying construct of working memory involves a general ability. They also suggest that working memory capacity may be substantially linked to general fluid intelligence. The working memory construct is quite closely allied to the idea of central executive in Baddeley's model. "Thus, when we use the term 'WM [working memory] capacity' . . . we are really referring to the capability of the executive-attention component of the working memory system" (Kane & Engle, 2003, p. 638). It should be recognized that the authors argue that controlled attention is not wholly a function of the number of items being remembered; therefore, working memory capacity may be strained by the maintenance of just a single item (e.g., when interference is especially pernicious). However, the authors' empirical work often involves a comparison of individuals who have been prescreened into the upper and lower quartiles on an operation span test. Therefore, the groups differ in terms of their ability to remember items at the same time as they complete a sequence of arithmetic problem verifications. The notion of capacity as the ability to remember more or fewer items on working memory problems is woven into the fabric of their theoretical garments. Finally, it is clear that their approach to understanding working memory lies in an individual-difference approach. It is through the relationship between working memory span on the one hand and complex cognitive skills on the other that the functioning of working memory is to be understood. This is something we return to later.

SECTION 2: THE MULTIFACETED NATURE
OF WORKING MEMORY IN CHILDREN

In this section, we analyze further the idea of the working memory span paradigm as a dual-task situation, in which performance is determined by the ability to share mental resources between the memory and processing requirements. According to this view, attentional processes serve to preserve memory traces in an accessible state. However, at least in the case of primary-school children, it is clear to us that there is more to the story. In particular, we wish to point to some of the additional phenomena that can influence how children perform working memory tasks. Paradoxically, it may be that because the memory and the processing activities take place at separate points in time, memory is at the mercy of the processing events. Therefore, in a reading span task, engaging in reading comprehension for a presented sentence leaves memory activity on hold. When reading processing is slow, either because of some developmentally immature apparatus, weak strategies, or experimentally imposed delays, then memory representations are left to wither for longer. This results in lower estimates of working memory, whether for younger children, for poorer readers, or for participants completing more time-consuming experimental conditions.

Towse, Hitch, and Hutton (1998) have reported strong correlations between estimates of children's working memory span and the duration required to complete the processing phase of the task, a finding that is consistent with this emphasis on the temporal dynamics of working memory tasks. We have also reported that this relationship is not true in the same way for adults, specifially that processing rate for this population is not a reliable determinant of span (Towse, Hitch, & Hutton, 2000; see also Engle, Cantor, & Carullo, 1992). Therefore, restricting the scope to children between 8 and 11 years of age, where data have been collected, we can note that statistically controlling for individual differences in children's processing (in reading times) attenuates the relationship between working memory span and external ability measures. It is certainly worth adding the further caveat that partialling out processing time does not account for all of the variance between working memory and cognitive abilities, such as reading and number skills (Hitch et al., 2001). However, controlling for processing time may attenuate this relationship to the point where working memory span is no more predictive of ability than short-term memory span (Hutton & Towse, 2001). That is, it may go some way to explaining the special status of working memory span tasks in children, so that WM = STM + controlled attention can be simplified to WM = STM + variation in skill at processing. Although other studies appear to show that working memory tasks are better predictors than short-term memory tasks of children's scholastic abilities (e.g., Leather & Henry, 1994), few studies we are aware of have fully take into account the modulating effect that the processing task has on working memory. Therefore, this remains an important issue for further investigation, particularly in light of differences we have referred to between children and adults.

We argue that it is feasible to conclude, therefore, that working memory capacity is driven by more than just the ability to combine mental resources for some cognitive task alongside memory operations. In other words, working memory capacity in children is not singly determined by resource-sharing ability. (Similarly, it is not necessarily the case that WM = STM + controlled attention, unless the latter parameter is defined so broadly as to risk being overinclusive.) Indeed, the notion that working memory is the umbrella term for a series of embedded processes (Cowan, 1999) serves to illustrate how one might ask whether there should be such a sharp divide between the two aspects of the working memory span task, the processing and the memory, because memories, as a set of highly activated representations, are memories because of the processing operations that have taken place. Thus, the processing may become part of the memory trace itself and not simply play the role of a secondary task.

To return to the study at hand, we investigated whether there might be yet further attributes relevant to working memory performance. To do so, we examined not only the quality of memory recall responses but also the timing of the successful response sequences. For every correctly recalled response sequence, we measured the preparatory interval (the initial pause before the child began to respond), word durations (the time taken to articulate the words in recall) and the interword intervals (the temporal gaps between each response). Thus, rather than respond to the multifaceted nature of working memory by collecting data from multiple tasks, we sought to collect multiple measures of processing from a particular task of interest, giving prominence to different measures of response timing.

A body of research established some important phenomena associated with response timing in short-term memory tasks when individuals were asked to remember sequences of digits and words. It is clear that recall response times are coherent measures in that they are sensitive to appropriate experimental manipulation. Moreover, they are interpretable within a theoretical framework and possess certain stable characteristics. First, response durations change significantly over development; children become quicker to say the response words and the preparatory interval declines, and they pause for shorter amounts of time between each word (Cowan et al., 1998). Second, however, what differentiates children with higher spans from their peers with lower spans are the pauses and the word durations, not the preparatory intervals. Third, when children are given more stimuli to remember, the interword pauses increase but the preparatory intervals do not (Cowan et al., 1998). Fourth, when the articulation duration of the stimuli are increased (e.g. using multisyllabic rather than monosyllabic words) the interword pauses do not increase (Cowan et al. 1998), which contrasts with the robust and widely cited phenomenon that memory performance itself declines as a function of word length (Baddeley et al., 1975; see also Cowan, Nugent, Elliott, & Geer, 2000). Fifth, individual differences in pauses during recall offer a significant predictor of memory performance that is distinguishable from overall speed of processing functions. Cowan et al. (1998) found that both interword pauses and estimates of speeded articulation correlated with span, but did not correlate with each other. Sixth, although it is the case that children with superior memory span recall items more quickly for equivalent sequences, overall recall length at the maximal span level is longer for children who have higher spans (Tehan & Lalor, 2000).

Therefore, it is apparent that for studies of short-term memory, analysis of recall timing delivers a variety of potentially important phenomena, permitting quite detailed inferences about memory processes. Cowan et al. (1998) argued that interword pauses provide an index of memory search and recovery operations during recall. These operations incorporate representations from all list items. Yet, given that pauses do not increase as word length increases, the search process does not rely on verbal rehearsal in any straightforward way. Furthermore, a variety of analyses indicate that pauses reflect processes that are separate from the preparatory interval because these two variables often show different patterns of sensitivity. Although it has been argued that forgetting of memory items can occur during recall (Cowan et al., 1992), in the context of response timing there does not seem to be a fixed temporal window of opportunity within which responses must occur and beyond which errors are inevitable. This conclusion is based on the finding that participants differ in the length of overall response durations at their maximal level. Evidently, the strategy for accessing internal representations is relevant. Further, insofar as pause measures are correlated with span and independent of other speed measures, we can deduce that pause measures do not simply reflect some global speed of processing variable (Kail & Salthouse, 1994). Finally, the developmental changes in (different) response timing processes emphasize the multifaceted nature of cognitive development.

There are two important gaps in our knowledge of response timing that we sought to address through empirical study. First, we examined the relevance of response timing for working memory paradigms, as opposed to short-term memory paradigms. It is apparent from the arguments articulated earlier that working memory and short-term memory are distinguishable (in methodology and in predictive prowess), and it is possible that, as a consequence, response timing exhibits quite a different profile in working span tasks. Second, we evaluated the extent to which phases of the response were related to external cognitive abilities, in particular scholastic skills. An important driving force behind the interest in working memory measures, as we have already seen, is the powerful and reliable correlations between working memory and cognitive ability. Is it the case that the patterns of recall contribute to the predictive power of working memory tests?

To this end, across two experiments, children and adults were given a reading span test, a counting span test (in which an array was counted with its cardinal value being remembered) and a listening span test (participants listened to a sentence and decided whether it was true or not and remembered the last word in the sentence). Various measures of ability were collected. These included reading and numerical skills attainment and high school grade percentiles (for counting span and listening span). It is also relevant to note that counting span and listening span were assessed alongside digit span. This provided a control task so that working memory

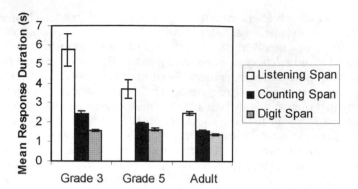

FIG. 2.4. Mean duration (in seconds) of recall within correct responses at each group to two-item lists in Experiment 2 of Cowan et al., 2003. © 2003 by the American Psychological Corporation. Reprinted with permission.

performance could be compared directly with short-term memory performance and performance could be verified against findings in the existing literature.

One of the most striking aspects of the results was the length of the response pauses in the case of reading span and listening span. Whereas the response durations of words were comparable to measures obtained from previous studies involving STM tasks—important in showing that children were not globally slower—the preparatory intervals and, even more so, the interword pauses were much slower. Although previous research might suggest (for children around the age of 8 years of age) preparatory intervals lasting about 0.6 s and pause durations of approximately 0.2 s (values corroborated by digit span data in Cowan et al., 2003), the preparatory intervals in reading span were more than 3 s and the pause durations more than 2 s. This can also be observed from the overall response durations shown in Fig. 2.4. Children were clearly doing something very different with reading span and listening span compared with digit span tasks or counting span tasks (where pauses were more like digit span, though still longer).

Despite differences in the absolute lengths of the response duration segments, in general the pattern of performance matched previous findings. This can be illustrated by the differences in response duration according to recall abilities. Children with better memories recalled items more quickly, though they took longer to recall their answers at the terminal level. Children did not all operate within a constant window of recall opportunity. Sensitivity to list length was also examined, and the first and second interword pauses were equivalent, showing no sharp gain in moving toward the end of the list.

In several different ways, the data reinforce our view that there is great value in multiple measures of working memory. Response timing measures help us to reach a number of conclusions. We would argue, on the basis of the results just described, that there can be important differences between working memory tasks, with the data helping to throw new light on how working memory tasks function. The differences challenge some claims that working memory measures are fundamentally alike (e.g., Turner & Engle, 1989) because they all involve a combination of concurrent mental operations and memory. In the present data, the overall response times in reading span and listening span were substantially different from those of counting span (and digit span). Basically, participants were taking far longer to recall the memory items when the processing element involved the comprehension of linguistic material rather than numerical calculations. Our interpretation of these data is that in tasks like reading span and listening span, participants have representations that are not just about the target word itself but also about the processing event that generated it. This rich memory means that participants have other words (from the sentence) to think about and reject and also have the potential to use these words as cues to the target item itself. This makes the memory search process more protracted. In the counting span test, the processing operations have considerable overlap, involving in each case the enumeration of target objects always beginning with the same sequence (counting up from 1). There is little in the way of distinctive information in the processing that can contribute to the identification of the memory items, making memory recall much quicker. Likewise, in digit span, there is no accompanying contextual information to the presentation of the numerical memory items.

We also note that other empirical data are consistent with the view that working memory tests may be distinguishable. For example, Hitch et al. (2001) noted that, for the children they studied, although both reading span and operation span correlated with the rate of completion of the processing requirements, the form of that relationship was different. Operation span changed with numerical processing speed more than reading span changed with reading speed. One explanation for this finding is that representations of the sentences provided support for the memory items, making the rate of forgetting slower than that of operation span, where arithmetic formed the processing event. This of course fits very well with the interpretation just outlined.

Further evidence to distinguish working memory span tests in the way outlined was reported by Copeland and Radvansky (2001). They reported that, among adults, a reading span task was accompanied by a reverse phonemic similarity effect (so that lists of rhyming items were remembered better than lists of nonrhyming items), whereas an operation span test followed by equivalent memory words (because a word followed each sum) produced the conventional similarity effect in which rhyming or overlapping phonological content hampered recall performance. Copeland and Radvansky suggested that their reading span task was influenced by semantic representations of the sentences. The processing events for reading span provided a scaffold on which recall can be attempted, and in such cases a phonological rhyme provides a helpful cue.

Moving on from a consideration of experimental analysis of response segments to individual differences in recall, it was a stated aim of the study to assess the commonality between response timing measures and cognitive abilities. For reading span, response timing measures correlated with standardized tests of reading and number skills, and this was separable from the relationship between memory performance per se and cognitive ability. Furthermore, among older children, response timing measures across span tasks (listening span, counting span, and digit span) correlated with cognitive ability after controlling for span scores themselves. This offers further evidence that response time measures afford a different and distinctive insight into memory processes.

We would argue that working memory span tests are complex multifaceted paradigms, and the predictive power of working memory span tests in children arises from the interplay between a series of cognitive processes. There is no single answer to the question, "What makes working memory special?" We have advocated the conclusion that there are differences between working memory span tests. Our second conclusion is that there are different processes contributing to any particular working memory task. Different and distinctive measures of working memory performance are available. The data do not challenge the view that the family of working memory tests share some important attributes or the view from some findings that they may be comparable. Clearly, it remains the case that working memory tests generally predict complex cognitive skills. Instead, what the data challenge is the conclusion that because there are some points of comparability they can be regarded as the same tests or that they can always be measured by a global parameter. Some measures may be highly effective in capturing particular phenomena. Yet other measures may provide additional and complementary sources of evidence about the composition of working memory. We regard it as important to acknowledge both sides of this coin.

A further potential implication following from these conclusions is that different theoretical models of working memory span performance may be applicable to particular instantiations of the task. Thus, accounts that focus on the importance of inhibiting irrelevant information when accessing target memoranda may be most suited to tasks like reading span. This is because here we have evidence that memory for processing events is used at the point of recall and therefore may interfere. Models that propose that controlled attention contributes to the task may have most to say about tasks in which the processing and memory events are more distinct. In operation span tasks in which an arithmetic operation is followed by a memory word, there is a greater element of dual tasking (at one point encoding and transforming a sum, at another point encoding a word), and processes that facilitate the execution of independent operations may be germane. It is possible that task–switching models, emphasizing the loss of memories during processing, captures a phenomenon that cuts across span tasks (e.g., see Towse et al., 1998). Nonetheless, it is quite conceivable that it has a greater impact in some situations than others, such that slow processing is more damaging for operation span than reading span (Hitch et al., 2001). The exciting—and at the same time challenging—perspective is that different models of span may be explaining different aspects of a family of tasks.

We believe that the data warrant a third, more specific, conclusion, too. We feel that the data reaffirm how different aspects of response timing can usefully be differentiated. Preparatory intervals, the gap between the response cue and the start of the participants' recall sequence are not the same as the intervals that occur between each word, and neither of these are simply reflections of the word recall responses. Unsurprisingly, it remains an important challenge to fully articulate the set of processes involved at each phase of the response. Nonetheless, these data, along with others, fully warrant the attempt to specify what the various phases represent.

The empirical data, then, make a case for the value of gathering different measures of working memory. This better allows for the capture of a range of working memory skills and mechanisms. There is a methodological advantage in the use of different tests, also. Different tests provide a useful source of converging evidence for conclusions that are appropriate with a particular data set. Because a working memory test, by design, is quite complex in structure it can sometimes be difficult to identify precisely which aspect of any task is crucial in shaping the results. Different tests can help to isolate the relevant variables. In addition, if the processing event in working memory tests is manipulated, there are various ways in which this might be accomplished (e.g. Towse et al., 1998). Establishing the same pattern of results across different working memory tests allows stronger conclusions to be drawn, in that idiosyncratic effects of particular manipulations or particular characteristics of certain measures can be ruled out. For example, we can be fairly confident that the long preparatory intervals in reading span are not the result of children generating this memory item for themselves since slow responses were also found in listening span, where children instead verified the semantic legitimacy of the presented material. As a second example, where Towse et al. (1998) manipulated the processing duration of the working memory trials, they inevitably resorted to different ways of lengthening the processing phase of counting arrays, arithmetic sums, and incomplete sentences. It becomes harder to argue that findings represent artifacts of how the processing material was altered. In sum, with a complex task, there are advantages in collecting convergent evidence from different paradigms to make the conclusions more robust.

In this section, we relied on empirical data from working memory span tests, to advance our view that there are several important attributes that contribute to recall performance. Working memory span is not just a function of a global memory ability. Rather, there are multiple processes, skills, traits, and possibly strategies that give rise to the characteristics of working memory span. Indeed, we argued that it is oversimplified to regard all working memory span tasks as comparable; there are reasons to distinguish span tasks and to consider how differences between them might affect the way children handle the task requirements. As part of our belief that multiple measures of working memory help to understand the task, we also argued that the analysis of the duration of the various phases of recall offers an important set of evidence about working memory processes.

SECTION 3: ASKING THE RIGHT QUESTIONS ABOUT WORKING MEMORY

Drawing on Working Memory Theory for Cognitive Development

Research into memory development has been captivated by the attempt to explain a few salient research questions. In particular, the dominant agenda item has been "How much?"; therefore, empirical research is directed at the attempt to identify memory capacity in children and chart its changes. Associated with this question is the issue of whether changes in memory performance—an increase in digit span or reading span, for example—occur because there is a growth in memory capacity or because of the way a relatively fixed and invariant capacity is used (see Case, 1985; Dempster, 1981; Kail, 1991; Pascual-Leone, 1970). This is a difficult question to address, and Cowan (2001) argued that a variety of converging evidence is probably required for its resolution. There are different ways in which stimuli can be delivered so that participants have little opportunity to recode items or chunk them into higher order units, which would of course give rise to the impression of capacity changes.

We fully recognize that measurement of memory capacity has played an important part in the collective understanding of memory and that capacity constraints may be a fundamental memory characteristic. Much of the chapter thus far has framed questions about working memory in terms of how many items an individual can successfully retain in mind and produce at a relevant time. However, it need not follow from this stance that capacity constraints are the only characteristic of memory, that there is a single, catch-all variable that can explain memory phenomena. Indeed, we have already noted that estimates of response timing processes shows the multiple and partially independent components of memory performance. The model of working memory outlined by Cowan (1999) explicitly recognizes the point that some aspects of the system may be capacity limited (in particular, the focus of attention), and other aspects may be limited by different parameters (e.g. the level of activation).

Thus, we argue that researchers who wish to incorporate aspects of working memory into their particular studies of cognitive development should be aware that the question "How much?" is not the only one that can or should be asked of memory. There is a need to be sensitive to parallel questions. Other questions that may be pertinent include the following:

"How long?" It is important to consider the extent to which memories need to be kept in an active state for different durations. One would expect children to forget more information when they have to remember it for longer intervals (in the case of working memory span tasks, see Towse & Hitch, 1995; Towse et al., 1998). Potentially, one could look to various causal explanations for this phenomenon (in particular, degradation in the quality of representations in the absence of any sustaining process—so called time-based decay—or the influence of interference from competing memory traces). Yet the phenomenon exists and is worthy of consideration regardless of how the details of it should be best explained. Data from Cowan et al. (2000) on the rate of forgetting of acoustic information could also be interpreted in this context.

"What tricks?" Cowan (2001) has shown that estimates of capacity (the "how much" question) vary according to the degree to which ancillary mnemonic processes are allowed to combine (i.e., chunk) memory items into meaningful clusters. The example of SF (Ericsson, Chase, & Faloon, 1980) is a good case study of an exceptional ability to recode a sequence into higher order units or chunks and therefore bypass the conventional limits on memory capacity. Yet the phenomenon usually illustrates how one can circumvent memory limits rather than substantially change them.

"What form?" This issue arises out of the premise that not all memories are created equal, and the modality of the memory representation can have an important influence on its characteristics. In fact, it is probably an oversimplification to see all memories as exclusively belonging to one modality because in many cases there will be multiple codes, including forms of semantic coding. Nonetheless, the modality of presentation can be important as it forms the initial source of a representation. Similarity or overlap in the features that code for a memory are particularly important, such that phonological similarity is important (Baddeley, 1966), as is visual similarity (Hitch, Halliday, Schaafstal, & Schraagen, 1988) and semantic similarity (Poirier & Saint-Aubin, 1995). In some cases, the direction of similarity effect can be reversed so that similar items become well remembered (Copeland & Radvansky, 2001), which may arise because the rhyme can be used as a recall cue.

"From what?" Rather than ignoring the mental processes that give rise to the memoranda, it might well be fruitful to consider the source of the information being retained. These may be derived from processes that the participant engages in, or the items may be self-generated, which is known to affect the quality or durability of the memory representations (Slamecka & Graf, 1978). A further illustration of the issue at hand comes from the research described in detail earlier. Cowan et al. (2003) showed that response timing patterns are quite different for reading span and counting span tasks. Although these both represent working memory span tasks, the processing in the former case (sentence comprehension) produces a much richer and distinctive memory than the processing in the latter case (enumeration of object arrays). We already referred to the argument that this can explain why responses are much slower for reading span than, say, counting span, with children having more elaborated memories and therefore more cues for recall when sentence comprehension forms a context.

"What cause?" Killeen (2001) provides an overview of Aristotle's four "becauses," noting the complementary nature of different causal accounts of psychological phenomena. Formal causes are abstract models or logical maps that explain behavior, and much of this chapter, in considering different models of working memory, evaluate how satisfactory these are with respect to phenomena of interest. In considering the material causes of developmental change and individual differences—that is, the agent(s) responsible for an event—we argue that there does not seem to be a logical reason why they must be the same. Moreover, the causal explanation could involve both biology and learning. And because there are multiple parameters that change with development, it may well be important to understand the dynamics and interactions among them. Some changes may be little more than epiphenomenal, some may be efficient causes (the triggers for change) and others may represent the developmental change itself.

Thus, it is possible that differences in the speed of cognitive processing produce working memory differences. Yet is it also possible that working memory differences produce speed differences (just as a computer with more memory may run a program faster)? Moreover, a basic difference in working memory at a young age could allow more able children to learn processing strategies and acquire knowledge more efficiently than less able children by a later age point. One reason to think of this as at least plausible is that a person might have to attend to several aspects of a stimulus array at the same time to bind them together in memory to form a new concept (see also Andrews & Halford, 2002, for a wider discussion). Clearly, understanding the direction of causality adds to the complexity of the task of discriminating between potential sources of developmental change in theory of mind, executive function, and working memory.

Killeen (2001) also refers to the final cause of behavior (i.e., its functional significance) and this is an issue taken up by Cowan (2001) in referring to the reasons why limited capacity may be important. Restrictions in working memory may help younger children to focus on the most germane aspects of the environment and to remember the immediate precursors of an event. As children accumulate experiences and their mental world becomes enriched, their growing working memory allows them to interpret events in a more sophisticated and complex way.

Working Memory and Executive Skills

The issue of executive skills is important, indeed fundamental, to the current volume. Yet despite this importance its nature has remained elusive and controversial. In the case of working memory, it also takes on a promiscuous role, acquiring functions from a variety of paradigms, with seemingly little regard for how well or how coherently these functions sit alongside each other (for more details, see Towse & Houston-Price, 2001). Thus, in the domain of working memory span, which has formed a core component of the present chapter, one influential idea is that the executive can act as a general-purpose system that shares resources between different task requirements of processing and storage. Counting span requires the participant to find the number of target words in an array and remember this number during additional counts. The difficulty of the counting requirement has been argued to shape the ability to remember the answers (Case et al., 1982). In this paradigm, the executive has a free-floating role in which two functions trade off against each other; that is, they compete for the limited capacity of the executive system. Engle et al. (1999) set out a somewhat different view, according to which the executive is responsible for controlled attention, which means the maintenance of representations in an accessible state in the presence of interference. The processing requirements provide interference for memory items, and in this sense the account preserves the notion of competition for mental resources between the two subtasks that make up working memory span.

Random generation has also been hailed as an executive task (e.g., Baddeley, 1966; for random generation data among primary-school children, see Towse & Mclachlan, 1999; Zoelch et al., this volume). In this instance, the executive is invoked as a mechanism by which unwanted responses (e.g., those that form stereotyped sequences) are inhibited or suppressed or a mechanism by which new strategies for less predictable responses can be generated (Baddeley et al., 1998). The control function in random generation is the selection of unconnected responses, which is made difficult by the very natural process of having associations between responses. In general, little mention is made of a direct role of memory representations, and instead the emphasis is on the management of internal associations between response alternatives and the selection of appropriate strategies for generating responses.

Leaving to one side a specification of how something like the central executive could carry out the range of tasks assigned to it, there are a number of indications that links exist at some level between working memory functioning, executive control processes, and atypical development, such as autism. We have already noted the logical and empirical relationship between ToM and working memory (Gordon & Olson, 1998). It is also becoming apparent that working memory span tasks, though not synonymous with executive function tasks, do correlate with them, both in adults and in children (e.g., Lehto, 1996; Lehto, Juujarvi, Kooistra, & Pulkkinen, 2003; Miyake et al., 2000). There is some preliminary evidence that autistic individuals generate random sequences differently from controls (Williams, Moss, Bradshaw, & Rinehart, 2002) and, more generally, a body of evidence that is consistent with autism being connected to aberrant executive functioning (Russell, 1997; but see also Perner & Lang, 1999).

Nonetheless, a substantial research program is required to specify the links between these different research domains in a more sophisticated and satisfactory way. Our collective understanding of a topic such a working memory per se has developed enormously over the past 30 years. Yet it is apparent that we have much more to learn. Furthermore, attempts to examine the connections between working memory and other concepts have not always reflected the range of issues that could be argued to be important in understanding what working memory represents. Just as there is a need to ask a range of questions about working memory, we need to consider a variety of questions about executive functioning.

CONCLUSION

Working memory is a dynamic and evolving area of psychological research. It combines fundamental research into adults' performance, with developmental perspectives as well as applied studies. It is an area of intense study, and, not surprisingly, there are several controversies and uncertainties. Although working memory research has not tackled issues of preschool children in any particular detail, nonetheless it is clear that developmental processes incorporate both qualitative and quantitative changes. Tasks involving working memory come in different shapes and guises. Some of these clearly incorporate elements of temporary retention of information, where the focus is very much on the number of independent memories that an individual can cope with. Other tasks focus more on the executive or control aspects of performance. This family of tasks reveals the complexity of working memory and the use of incorporating different measures into an assessment of performance because working memory cannot be meaningfully rendered down to a single dimension. To take up Maslow's (1966) challenge, we need to ensure that we can resort to more than just a research hammer when we consider how to deal with the range of psychological issues that we would like to confront.

REFERENCES

Andrews, G., & Halford, G. S. (2002). A cognitive complexity metric applied to cognitive development. *Cognitive Psychology, 45,* 153–219.
Baddeley, A. D. (1966). Short-term memory for word sequences as a function of acoustic, semantic and formal similarity. *Quarterly Journal of Experimental Psychology, 18,* 362–365.
Baddeley, A. D. (1986). *Working memory.* Oxford, UK: Clarendon Press.
Baddeley, A. D. (2000). The episodic buffer: A new component of working memory. *Trends in Cognitive Sciences, 4*(11), 417–423.
Baddeley, A. D., Emslie, H., Kolodny, J., & Duncan, J. (1998). Random generation and the executive control of working memory. *Quarterly Journal of Experimental Psychology, 51*(4), 819–852.
Baddeley, A. D., Grant, S., Wight, E., & Thomson, N. (1975). Imagery and visual working memory. In P. M. A. Rabbitt & S. Dornic (Eds.), *Attention and performance V* (pp. 205–217). London: Academic Press.
Baddeley, A. D., & Hitch, G. J. (1974). Working memory. In G. Bower (Ed.), *The psychology of learning and motivation: Advances in research and theory* (pp. 47–89). New York: Academic Press.

Baddeley, A. D., Lewis, V. J., & Vallar, G. (1984). Exploring the articulatory loop. *Quarterly Journal of Experimental Psychology, 36*, 233–252.

Baddeley, A. D., & Logie, R. H. (1999). Working memory: The multiple component model. In A. Miyake & P. Shah (Eds.), *Models of working memory* (pp. 28–61). New York: Cambridge University Press.

Baddeley, A. D., Thomson, N., & Buchanan, M. (1975). Word length and the structure of short-term memory. *Journal of Verbal Learning and Verbal Behavior, 9*, 176–189.

Broadbent, D. E. (1958). *Perception and communication.* London: Pergamon.

Broadbent, D. E. (1971). *Decision and stress.* London: Academic Press.

Broadbent, D. E. (1975). The magic number seven after fifteen years. In A. Kennedy & A. Wilkes (Eds.), *Studies in long-term memory* (pp. 3–18). London: Wiley.

Brown, J. (1958). Some tests of the decay theory of immediate memory. *Quarterly Journal of Experimental Psychology, 10*, 12–21.

Case, R. (1985). *Intellectual development: Birth to adulthood.* New York: Academic Press.

Case, R., Kurland, M., & Goldberg, J. (1982). Operational efficiency and the growth of short-term memory span. *Journal of Experimental Child Psychology, 33*, 386–404.

Conrad, R. (1964). Acoustic confusion in immediate memory. *British Journal of Psychology, 55*, 75–84.

Copeland, D. E., & Radvansky, G. A. (2001). Phonological similarity in working memory. *Memory and Cognition, 29*(5), 774–776.

Cowan, N. (1988). Evolving conceptions of memory storage, selective attention, and their mutual constraints within the human information processing system. *Psychological Bulletin, 104*, 163–191.

Cowan, N. (1999). An embedded-process model of working memory. In A. Miyake & P. Shah (Eds.), *Models of working memory* (pp. 62–101). New York: Cambridge University Press.

Cowan, N. (2001). The magical number 4 in short-term memory: A reconsideration of mental storage capacity. *Behavioral and Brain Sciences, 24*(1), 87–185.

Cowan, N., Day, L., Saults, J. S., Keller, T. A., Johnson, T., & Flores, L. (1992). The role of verbal output time in the effects of word length on immediate memory. *Journal of Memory and Language, 31*, 1–17.

Cowan, N., Elliott, E. M., & Saults, J. S. (2002). The search for what is fundamental in the development of working memory. In R. Kail & H. Reese (Eds.), *Advances in child development and behavior, 29*, 1–49.

Cowan, N., Nugent, L. D., Elliott, E. M., & Geer, T. (2000). Is there a temporal basis of the word length effect? A response to Service (1998). *Quarterly Journal of Experimental Psychology, 53*(3), 647–660.

Cowan, N., Nugent, L. D., Elliott, E. M., & Saults, J. S. (2000). Persistence of memory for ignored lists of digits: Areas of developmental constancy and change. *Journal of Experimental Child Psychology, 76*, 151–172.

Cowan, N., Towse, J. N., Hamilton, Z., Saults, J. S., Elliott, E. M., Lacey, J. F., Moreno, M. V., & Hitch, G. J. (2003). Children's working memory processes: A response-timing analysis. *Journal of Experimental Psychology: General, 132*(1), 113–132.

Cowan, N., Wood, N. L., Wood, P. K., Keller, T. A., Nugent, L. D., & Keller, C. V. (1998). Two separate verbal processing rates contributing to short-term memory span. *Journal of Experimental Psychology: General, 127*(2), 141–160.

Crowder, R. G. (1993). Short-term memory: Where do we stand? *Memory and Cognition, 21*, 142–145.

Daneman, M., & Carpenter, P. A. (1980). Individual differences in working memory and reading. *Journal of Verbal Learning and Verbal Behavior, 19*, 450–466.

Daneman, M., & Hannon, B. (2001). Using working memory theory to investigate the construct validity of multiple-choice reading comprehension tests such as the SAT. *Journal of Experimental Psychology: General, 130*(2), 208–223.

Davis, H. L., & Pratt, C. (1995). The development of children's theory of mind: The working memory explanation. *Australian Journal of Psychology, 47*, 25–31.

Dempster, F. N. (1981). Memory span: Sources of individual and developmental differences. *Psychological Bulletin, 89*, 63–100.

Engle, R. W., Cantor, J., & Carullo, J. J. (1992). Individual differences in working memory and comprehension: A test of four hypotheses. *Journal of Experimental Psychology: Learning, Memory and Cognition, 18*, 972–992.

Engle, R. W., Tuholski, S. W., Laughlin, J. E., & Conway, A. R. A. (1999). Working memory, short-term memory and general fluid intelligence: A latent variable approach. *Journal of Experimental Psychology: General, 128*(3), 309–331.

Ericsson, K. A., Chase, W. G., & Faloon, S. (1980). Acquisition of a memory skill. *Science, 208*, 1181–1182.

Gathercole, S. E., Willis, C. S., Baddeley, A. D., & Emslie, H. (1994). The children's test of non-word repetition: A test of phonological working memory. *Memory, 2*, 103–127.

Gordon, A. C. L., & Olson, D. R. (1998). The relation between acquisition of a theory of mind and the capacity to hold in mind. *Journal of Experimental Child Psychology, 68*, 70–83.

Halliday, M. S., & Hitch, G. J. (1988). Developmental applications of working memory. In G. Claxton (Ed.), *New directions in cognition* (pp. 193–222). London: Routledge and Keegan Paul.

Hitch, G. J., Halliday, M. S., & Littler, J. E. (1989). Item identification time and rehearsal rate as predictors of memory span in children. *Quarterly Journal of Experimental Psychology, 41*(2), 321–337.

Hitch, G. J., Halliday, S., Schaafstal, A. M., & Schraagen, J. M. C. (1988). Visual working memory in young children. *Memory and Cognition, 16*(2), 120–132.

Hitch, G. J., & Towse, J. N. (1995). Working memory: What develops? In F. E. Weinert & W. Schneider (Eds.), *Memory performance and competencies: Issues in growth and development* (pp. 3–21). Hillsdale, NJ: Lawrence Erlbaum Associates.

Hitch, G. J., Towse, J. N., & Hutton, U. M. Z. (2001). What limits working memory span? Theoretical accounts and applications for scholastic development. *Journal of Experimental Psychology: General, 130*(2), 184–198.

Hitch, G. J., Woodin, M. E., & Baker, S. (1989). Visual and phonological components of working memory in children. *Memory and Cognition, 17*(2), 175–185.

Hulme, C., Maughan, S., & Brown, G. D. A. (1991). Memory for familiar and unfamiliar words: Evidence for a long-term memory contribution to short-term memory span. *Journal of Memory and Language, 30*, 685–701.

Hutton, U. M. Z., & Towse, J. N. (2001). Short-term memory and working memory as indices of children's cognitive skills. *Memory, 9*, 383–394.

Jenkins, J. M., & Astington, J. W. (1996). Cognitive factors and family structure associated with theory of mind development in young children. *Developmental Psychology, 32*, 70–78.

Just, M. A., & Carpenter, P. A. (1992). A capacity theory of comprehension: Individual differences in working memory. *Psychological Review, 99*(1), 122–149.

Kail, R. (1991). Developmental change in speed of processing during childhood and adolescence. *Psychological Bulletin, 109*, 490–501.

Kail, R., & Salthouse, T. A. (1994). Processing speed as a mental capacity. *Acta Psychologica, 86*, 199–255.

Kane, M. J., & Engle, R. W. (2003). The role of prefrontal cortex in working memory capacity, executive attention, and general fluid intelligence: An individual difference perspective. *Psychonomic Bulletin and Review, 9*(4), 637–671.

Keenan, T., Olson, D. R., & Marini, Z. (1998). Working memory and children's developing understanding of mind. *Australian Journal of Psychology, 50*, 76–82.

Kemps, E., De Rammelaere, S., & Desmet, T. (2000). The development of working memory: Exploring the complementarity of two models. *Journal of Experimental Child Psychology, 77*(2), 89–109.

Killeen, P. R. (2001). The four causes of behaviour. *Current Directions in Psychological Science, 10*(4), 136–140.

Leather, C. V., & Henry, L. A. (1994). Working memory span and phonological awareness tasks as predictors of early reading ability. *Journal of Experimental Child Psychology, 58*, 88–111.

Lehto, J. (1996). Are executive function tests dependent on working memory capacity? *Quarterly Journal of Experimental Psychology, 49*(1), 29–50.

Lehto, J. E., Juujarvi, P., Kooistra, L., & Pulkkinen, L. (2003). Dimensions of executive functioning: Evidence from children. *British Journal of Developmental Psychology, 21*, 59–80.

Logie, R. H. (1995). *Visuo-spatial working memory.* Hillsdale, NJ: Lawrence Erlbaum Associates.

Maslow, A. (1966). *The psychology of science.* New York: Harper & Row.

Miller, G. A. (1956). The magic number seven, plus or minus two: Some limits on our capacity for processing information. *Psychological Review, 63*, 81–97.

Miyake, A., Friedman, N. P., Emerson, M. J., Witzki, A. H., Howerter, A., & Wager, T. D. (2000). The unity and diversity of executive functions and their contributions to complex "frontal lobe" tasks: A latent variable analysis. *Cognitive Psychology, 41*, 49–100.

Miyake, A., & Shah, P. (1999). *Models of working memory.* New York: Cambridge University Press.

Pascual-Leone. J. (1970). A maturational model for the transition rule in Piaget's developmental stages. *Acta Psychologica, 32*, 301–345.

Pearson, D. G. (2001). Imagery and the visuo-spatial sketchpad. In J. Andrade (Ed.), *Working memory in perspective* (pp. 33–59). Hove, UK: Psychology Press.

Perner, J., & Lang, B. (1999). Development of theory of mind and executive control. *Trends in Cognitive Sciences, 3*(9), 337–344.

Peterson, L. R., & Peterson, M. J. (1959). Short term retention of individual verbal items. *Journal of Experimental Psychology, 58*, 193–198.

Poirier, M., & Saint-Aubin, J. (1995). Memory for related and unrelated words: Further evidence on the influence of semantic factors in immediate serial recall. *Quarterly Journal of Experimental Psychology, 48*(2), 384–404.

Russell, J. (Ed.). (1997). *Autism as an executive disorder.* Oxford, UK: Oxford University Press.

Slamecka, N. J., & Graf, P. (1978). The generation effect: Delineation of a phenomenon. *Journal of Experimental Psychology: Human Learning and Memory, 4*, 592–604.

Tehan, G., & Lalor, D. M. (2000). Individual differences in memory span: The contribution of rehearsal, access to lexical memory, and output speed. *Quarterly Journal of Experimental Psychology, 53*(4), 1012–1038.

Thorn, A. S. C., & Gathercole, S. E. (1999). Language-specific knowledge and short-term memory in bilingual and non-bilingual children. *Quarterly Journal of Experimental Psychology, 52*, 303–324.

Towse, J. N., & Hitch, G. J. (1995). Is there a relationship between task demand and storage space in tests of working memory capacity? *Quarterly Journal of Experimental Psychology, 48*(1), 108–124.

Towse, J. N., Hitch, G. J., & Hutton, U. (1998). A reevaluation of working memory capacity in children. *Journal of Memory and Language, 39*(2), 195–217.

Towse, J. N., Hitch, G. J., & Hutton, U. (2000). On the interpretation of working memory span in adults. *Memory and Cognition, 28*(3), 341–348.

Towse, J. N., & Houston-Price, C. M. T. (2001). Reflections on the concept of the central executive. In J. Andrade (Ed.), *Working memory in perspective* (pp. 240–260). Hove, UK: Psychology Press.

Towse, J. N., & Mclachlan, A. (1999). An exploration of random generation among children. *British Journal of Developmental Psychology, 17*(3), 363–380.

Turner, M. L., & Engle, R. W. (1989). Is working memory capacity task dependent? *Journal of Memory and Language, 28*, 127–154.

Walker, P., Hitch, G. J., Dewhurst, S. A., Whiteley, H. E., & Brandimonte, M. A. (1997). The representation of nonstructural information in visual memory: Evidence from image combination. *Memory and Cognition, 25*(4), 484–491.

Williams, M. A., Moss, S. A., Bradshaw, J. L., & Rinehart, N. J. (2002). Random number generation in autism. *Journal of Autism and Developmental Disorders, 32*(1), 43–47.

Zelazo, P. D., & Jacques, S. (1996). Children's rule use: Representation, reflection and cognitive control. In R. Vasta (Ed.), *Annals of child development* (pp. 119–176). London: Jessica Kingsley Press.

Chapter 3

From Rag(Bag)s to Riches: Measuring the Developing Central Executive

Christof Zoelch
Katja Seitz
Ruth Schumann-Hengsteler
Catholic University of Eichstätt-Ingolstadt

What is the central executive and how does it develop during childhood? After its first description as the ragbag of working memory (Baddeley, 1986; Baddeley & Hitch, 1974), the central executive recently turned out to be a complex system of various processes (Baddeley, 1996; Towse & Houston-Price, 2001). Although the role of the central executive in working memory is currently being specified in more detail, little is as yet known about the development of central executive processes.

In this chapter we discuss, on a theoretical as well as an empirical basis, how central executive processing within the Baddeley and Hitch (1974) working memory framework can be measured. In particular, we focus on the extent to which developmental aspects have been considered so far and to what extent they have to be taken into account when measurement tools for children are created. First, we briefly compare different working memory traditions with one another and show their implications on operationalizations that were designed up to the present. However, the focus of this chapter will be on the attempt to empirically evaluate Baddeley's (1996) conceptualization of the central executive functions within a developmental context. For this purpose, we adjusted seven different measures of central executive processes to children between 5 and 10 years of age.

For each of these measures, we discuss the adjustability to younger children and show developmental trends, and finally we look for relational patterns among the seven measures. In the last paragraph, we summarize our three main points:

1. Different central executive subfunctions show various obvious developmental trends.
2. In the developmental approach of our study, we find a correlational pattern that is in accordance with the theoretical assumptions about those central executive functions, which should be tapped by the measures respectively employed.
3. Coming back to the theoretical concept of a nonunitary working memory, we argue, on the basis of our data, which criteria should be taken into account when working memory measurement tools are created within a developmental context.

MODELS OF WORKING MEMORY AND THE CENTRAL EXECUTIVE

Working memory is responsible for the temporal storage and manipulation of information; therefore, it has been proven to have great significance for human cognition, such as language comprehension (Gathercole & Baddeley, 1993), mental arithmetic (Ashcraft, 1992; Seitz & Schumann-Hengsteler, 2002), and syllogistic reasoning (Gilhooly, 1998). Whereas current models of working memory mainly deal with adult cognition (for an overview, see Miyake & Shah, 1999), some traditional theories of working memory (Case, Kurland, & Goldberg, 1982; Pascual-Leone & Baillargeon, 1994) mainly focus on developmental aspects. Two rather contrary neo-Piagetian models of working memory are Pascual-Leone's model of growing working memory capacity, and Case's model of growing processing efficiency.

Pascual-Leone's (1994) mathematical model of the development of attentional capacity contains schemes and hardware operators that determine cognitive performance. Essential to his model of the working memory (or originally, the field of mental attention; Pascual-Leone & Baillargeon, 1994) is its capability to explain cognitive development. This is basically done using the concept of the M–capacity, which is the maximum number of information units that can be activated simultaneously within a mental operation. M-capacity or M-space is supposed to increase simply with age or (biological) maturation until it reaches a level of seven information units in adults. By contrast, Case and colleagues (Case et al., 1982) propose in their model of the working memory a general capacity that is shared by both storage and processing functions and that remains more or less unchanged all of one's life. Case et al. found that the working memory span (assessed with the counting span task) increases with development. They described development not as a change in resources but as a more efficient use of (constant) capacities. As development goes on, mental processing becomes faster and more automatized and thus sets capacities free for the storage of information.

The use of measurement tools based on neo-Piagetian models of working memory as a storage and processing device is still widespread in cognitive developmental psychology (Gathercole & Pickering, 2000a). Well-established span procedures of this kind are the counting span (Case et al., 1982), the reading span (Daneman & Carpenter, 1983), or the Mr. Peanut task (de Ribaupierre & Bailleux, 1994, 1995; Kemps, De Rammelaere, & Desmet, 2000). Although traditional span measures like the reading span are considered to measure an overall working memory capacity, they are also used in context of working memory models that assume modality specific processing and storage resources, for example, the Baddeley and Hitch model (Baddeley, 1986, 1990; Baddeley & Hitch, 1974; Gathercole & Pickering, 2000a; Towse, Hitch, & Hutton, 1998). Certainly, this kind of complex span task measures processing capacities of a working memory, but the exact processes that are supposed to be responsible for the performance in such a span task often remain ill-defined.

Baddeley and Hitch (Baddeley & Hitch, 1974, 1994, 2000) developed their working memory model in a clearly experimental tradition. Its capability to account for a wide range of data with only a few, albeit broad, concepts led to widespread use in several fields of cognitive psychology. The model originally consisted of three components, a superordinate controlling system, the so-called central executive, and two subsidiary slave systems dealing with modality-specific information, the phonological loop and the visual-spatial sketch pad (VSSP). Recently, an extension of the concept was made: A fourth component, the episodic buffer, was introduced (Baddeley, 2000, 2002). Baddeley proposed the episodic buffer to unravel inconsistencies concerning the integration of information from the slave systems and from long-term memory. The episodic buffer has not yet been empirically established, and so far no assumptions on its developmental aspects have been made.

In contrast to other approaches of working memory—for instance, Pascual-Leone's model—the architecture of Baddeley and Hitch's model is relatively simple (for an actual debate on the two models see Baddeley & Hitch, 2000; Kemps et al., 2000; Pascual-Leone, 2000). What has changed over the past 30 years is the specification of the different systems, mainly the two subsystems. The phonological subsystem was soon fractionated into a passive storage component and an active rehearsal mechanism, which aided understanding of the various empirical effects and the nature of this slave system (Baddeley & Hitch, 1994; Baddeley, Thomson, & Buchanan, 1975; see Gathercole & Baddeley, 1993, for an overview). Subsequently, the division into a passive storage component and an active rehearsal mechanism was also introduced for the VSSP (Logie, 1995) and is at the moment being discussed on the basis of two further dimensions: the static-dynamic and the visual-spatial dichotomy (Pickering, Gathercole, Hall, & Lloyd, 2001; Schumann-Hengsteler, 1995; Schumann-Hengsteler,

Strobl, & Zoelch, 2004). Strong efforts in research on the phonological loop and the visual–spatial sketch pad not only led to an extension and differentiation of these concepts but also yielded a fundamental understanding of their development (Gathercole & Baddeley, 1993; Gathercole & Hitch, 1993; Hitch & Halliday, 1983; Logie & Pearson, 1997; Schumann-Hengsteler, 1995).

In contrast, the central executive, formally known as the area of residual ignorance (Baddeley & Hitch, 1977) or the ragbag of working memory, lived in the shadows until Baddeley (1996), among others, started to disentangle this component. At first, Baddeley and Hitch (1974) supposed the central executive to have both storage and processing functions, and the executive of working memory was also proposed to show similarities to Norman's and Shallice's (1986) concept of the SAS (the supervisory attentional system). This led to the view of the central executive as a controller for the allocation of attentional resources (Baddeley, 1993; Baddeley & Hitch, 1994). For this reason, its role as coordinator for the storage and retrieval of information in the subsystems and in the long-term memory was emphasized. In later proposals, the aspect of attentional control was still dominant, when the fractionation of central executive processes into the capacity to focus attention, to switch this focus, and to divide attentional focus between two concurrent tasks occurred. Baddeley (1996) assumed four main functions of the central executive:

1. The coordination of simultaneous tasks and task switching.
2. The control of encoding and retrieval strategies of temporarily stored information (also when retrieved from the long-term store).
3. The selection of attention and inhibitory processes.
4. The retrieval and manipulation of long-term stored information.

As a result, the central executive changed into a pure processing system without any storage function but with a responsibility for almost every high-level cognitive process (see also Andrade, 2001).

More recently, American working memory concepts had a notable influence on the British tradition (Cowan, 2001; Towse & Cowan, this volume). These concepts (see Miyake & Shah, 1999, for a detailed overview) all consider working memory as a system that actively manipulates temporarily held information. Information that is only held passively (without any regard to the modality) does not require working memory capacity but is held only in a (not always clearly defined) short-term store. Attentional processes play a more significant and explicit role, and working memory is mostly a unitary system, meaning that it is not fractionated into subsystems (Just & Carpenter, 1992).

The influence of unitary working memory concepts on the Baddeley and Hitch (1994) model can be seen in recent considerations on the central executive. A general purpose processor, a multifunctional unit for higher order processing demands, is discussed (Towse & Houston-Price, 2001).

Essential to this view is the aspect of a general processing capacity and how it is used in complex span tasks. Similarities between different working memory concepts were also noted earlier by Just and Carpenter (1992), who claimed a correspondence of Baddeley's central executive with their concept of working memory (see also Towse & Houston-Price, 2001, for a critical discussion of this notion). The view of working memory as a structure with modality–specific storage systems and a central processing unit resulted in different operationalizations for storage and processing capacities. However, Baddeley's initial idea of fractionating the processing capacities by using different empirical tools is still to be realized, especially in a developmental context.

What do we know about developmental aspects of working memory in general and the central executive in particular? There is considerable amount of data on the development of the phonological subsystem and a growing number of findings on the development of the visuospatial scratch pad. However, up to now only little effort has gone into the exploration of the developing central executive. The latter is remarkable insofar as it is supposedly responsible for many aspects that are crucial to cognitive development (Thorn & Gathercole, 2000).

In general, a developmental increase in capacity for both subsystems can be observed, but different courses of development for the VSSP and the phonological loop are discussed (see Hitch, 1990, who proposed the method of developmental fractionation). The word/digit span as a measure of phonological loop capacity increases from two or three items at the age of 4 years to six or seven items in early adulthood (Hulme, Thomson, Muir, & Lawrence, 1984; Isaacs & Vargha-Khadem, 1989). The loop is used more pervasively with ongoing development, which is accompanied by the increasing tendency to recode nonverbal stimuli verbally. A spontaneous use of the subvocal rehearsal process takes place from age 7 years on (Gathercole, Adams, & Hitch, 1994). The subsequent development of the loop is supposed to be due to qualitative and quantitative changes in the subvocal rehearsal process (i.e., the usage of cumulative rehearsal strategies and the improvement in the efficiency and speed of the rehearsal mechanism; Gathercole & Baddeley, 1993). An increasing use of the knowledge base additionally supports the phonological loop. This is demonstrated by a superior recall of familiar words in contrast to unfamiliar words (Gathercole, Willis, Baddeley, & Emslie, 1994; Gathercole, Adams, & Hitch, 1994).

There is evidence for an increase in the capacity of the visuospatial subsystem as well (Isaacs & Vargha-Khadem, 1989), but, unlike the case of the phonological loop, it still remains unclear to what extent strategic processes and their enhanced use, as well as their growing efficiency, are responsible for these changes. The temporal memory for spatial-dynamic information is commonly measured by means of the Corsi block test and increases from a span of about 2.5 blocks in 5-year-olds up to about 6 blocks in 15-year-olds (Isaacs & Vargha-Khadem, 1989; Schumann-Hengsteler & Pohl, 1996). The static-visual component of visual-spatial working memory is frequently examined with the matrix task. Here, the developmental increase ranges from 4.5 squares in 4-year-olds to 7.5 squares in 10-year-olds to about 10 squares in adults (Strobl, Strametz, & Schumann-Hengsteler, 2002). Different courses of development for the visual and the spatial system were shown by means of developmental fractionation (Logie & Pearson, 1997). Recent developmental investigations strengthen the idea of two dichotomous systems of the VSSP but consider them to be rather static versus dynamic than visual versus spatial (Pickering et al., 2001; Schumann-Hengsteler et al., 2004).

Research on the development of the central executive is still in its infancy. The influence of the neo-Piagetian tradition both on theoretical concepts and on operationalizations of the developing executive is strong. Therefore, a preference for complex working memory tasks, like the listening span or digit span backwards, can be observed (Gathercole & Pickering, 2000a). Only rarely are attempts undertaken to measure the central executive's development by means of more specific measures, like random generation (Towse & Mclachlan, 1999) or the trail-making task (McLean & Hitch, 1999), which are discussed by Baddeley in his 1996 proposal. With the complex span tasks, like reading span (Daneman & Carpenter, 1980), operation span (Turner & Engle, 1989), counting span (Case et al., 1982), listening span or digit span backwards (Gathercole & Pickering, 2000a), a dramatic increase of performance from kindergarten children to adolescents is found. These measurement tools definitely require resources for the coordination of simultaneous storage and operational processes and additionally ask for other central executive processes as defined by Baddeley (1996). Yet it remains unclear as to what extent each of these central executive processes (coordination of simultaneous tasks, control of strategies, selective attention and inhibition, retrieval and manipulation of long-term stored information) are involved in the respective tasks.

According to Thorn and Gathercole (2000), developmental changes in complex span tasks can be explained as a result of growing processing efficiency (but constant capacities) on the one hand (Case et al., 1982) and changed attentional resources, as suggested by Swanson (1999), on the other. The latter approach claims that, with ongoing development, the availability of attentional resources changes, which results in more efficient processing. So both approaches explain the developmental increase in complex span tasks with changes in functional capacity rather than storage capacity (Thorn & Gathercole, 2000, pp. 425–426). The proposal of a general factor (Gathercole, 1999; Swanson, 1999) to explain central executive functioning is tempting and certainly helps to describe developmental changes, too, but cannot provide evidence to prove the assumption of a nonunitary central executive. It can be concluded that empirical as well as theoretical approaches toward the development of the central executive are one-dimensional rather than nonunitary. As it seems, however, a transposition of Baddeley's (1996) concept of a nonunitary central executive into a developmental context must inevitably start with operation-alizations of the four different executive processes proposed by Baddeley: coordination of simultaneous tasks, control of strategies, selective atten-tion and inhibition, and retrieval and manipulation of information from the long-term store.

What could a methodological approach to the fragmentation of the central executive in general, and particularly in a developmental context, look like? Examining patients with executive control deficits after severe frontal lobe damage may provide one possible way to tackle executive processes. Baddeley and Wilson (1988) proposed this neuropsychological approach and called the functional lack in executive control dysexecutive syndrome. Although the association of cognitive functions with anatom-ical structures may bear certain risks, it provides further methodologi-cal inspiration: Related fields, like the research on executive functions or attentional research, also correlate (frontal) brain structures with cogni-tive functions. It is useful not only to take a closer look at the measure-ment tools used within these fields but also to relate to the underlying theoretical concepts. For instance, research on executive functions deals, among other things, with the role of attentional resources and with the coordination and the monitoring of ongoing processes. For this reason, it can provide a useful link to a methodological approach and the theoretical concept of central executive processes. D'Esposito and Grossmann (1998) regard working memory processes, like temporal activation or manipula-tion of information, as basic operations that are significant for executive functions (but see also Stratta et al., 1997, who did not find a correlation between impaired executive functions and disturbed working memory processes). Furthermore, theories on the development of executive func-tions may be an inspiration for the work on concepts of the developing central executive (for a developmental concept of executive functions see Zelazo & Mueller, 2003; Zelazo, Mueller, Frye, & Marcovitch, 2003, and in this volume).

The developmental aspect itself represents another potential pathway to the dissociation of executive processes. Given specific assumptions as to which processes constitute the central executive and how they have to be measured, developmental fractionation, as proposed by Hitch (1990) or Logie (Logie & Pearson, 1997), may provide further evidence for the non-unitary nature of the executive. The idea of different factors of working memory or the central executive, respectively, was also taken up by Ober-auer and colleagues (Oberauer, Süß, Schulze, Wilhelm, & Wittmann, 2000; Oberauer, Süß, Wilhelm, & Wittman, 2003): A combined analysis of per-formance in different working memory tasks resulted in factors that reflect different facets of working memory. The next paragraph provides an empirical approach to the measurement of developing executive pro-cesses, which is done by giving seven central executive tasks, with differ-ent demands on the four central executive processes proposed by Baddeley (1996), to children of different age groups and to adults.

DEVELOPMENTAL OPERATIONALIZATIONS
OF THE CENTRAL EXECUTIVE

In our attempt to explore the four different central executive functions as defined by Baddeley (1996) within a developmental context, we adapted seven different measures so that they could be used with kindergarten children. In the following paragraphs, we introduce each measurement tool, discuss the central executive processes that are predominantly tapped, and give a summary of the most important results. The recently discussed general purpose processor (Towse & Houston-Price, 2001) is not covered in the following section, as its capacity must be involved in all tasks. A further quantification of general purpose processor capacity seems difficult at the moment, so the concept does not seem to be helpful for the investigation of a nonunitary central executive. Our aim was to relate each measurement tool to the respective central executive process. This was not exactly easy in every case, as the established central executive tasks are rather complex: Breaking them down to the predominantly demanded processes required some simplification. Still, we propose an assignment of each task to one or two of the four central executive processes.

Altogether 112 subjects of five age groups participated in the study. There were two different age groups of kindergarteners: 25 younger (mean age 5;3) and 21 older children (mean age 6;6). Twenty-four second graders (mean age 8;3), 18 fourth graders (mean age 10;4) and 24 adults (mean age 22;9 years) completed the sample. All subjects were tested individually in two sessions. Each session lasted about 30 min. The seven tasks were given in random order.

Random Generation

Random generation represents a genuine central executive task that was originally proposed by Baddeley (Baddeley, 1966, 1996; Baddeley, Emslie, Kolodny, & Duncan, 1998). The main effort in the task is generating a random series out of a given set of ordered items, like the numbers from 1 to 10. Other response sets, such as letters, spatial positions, or different hand movements (Zoelch, Jung, & Schumann-Hengsteler, 2000), were also explored (see also Brugger, 1997, for an overview). Vandierendonck and colleagues (Vandierendonck, 2000; Vandierendonck, De Vooght, & Van der Goten, 1998a) introduced the so-called random interval tapping task, where subjects have to tap random time intervals. The authors claim that this method is relatively independent of modality, meaning that no subsystem is involved.

In addition to the widespread use of random generation with several clinical populations (Brugger, Monsch, Salmon, & Butters, 1996; Kramer, Larish, Weber, & Bardell, 1999; Robertson, Hazlewood, & Rawson, 1996) and in dual-task studies (Logie, Gilhooly, & Wynn, 1994; Seitz & Schumann-Hengsteler, 2000; Vandierendonck, De Vooght, & Van der Groten, 1998b), first promising attempts to apply random generation tasks to kindergarten and elementary school children exist: Towse and Mclachlan (1999) investigated random number generation in 5- to 11-year-old children and concluded that this type of task is adjustable to children as young as 5 years old. From that age on, children were able to understand instructions for the random production. However, the results showed age effects for randomness in several measures.

Some task-immanent aspects of random generation have proven to be crucial for performance (for a critical overview on human random concepts and their cognitive demands, see Treisman & Faulkner, 1987). One is the number of items to be randomized: The larger a response set is, the more stereotyped and nonrandom the generated random series (Towse, 1998; Towse & Valentine, 1997). A second important factor is the response frequency of random generation: The faster random series of numbers have to be created, the less random they are (Baddeley et al., 1998; Towse, 1998). From a central executive point of view, random generation tasks claim a continuous change of retrieval strategies (i.e., the control of encoding and retrieval strategy component of the central executive is involved). The second major central executive resource demanded in this task is selective attention and inhibition (inhibition of stereotyped or recurring responses, such as "1, 2, 3 ..." or a familiar telephone number).

Taking into account the memory load constraints in younger children, we decided to use a random number generation task with a response set of only four numbers (1, 2, 3, 4). Subjects were told to imagine that they had a bag with four balls in it, each of the balls with a different number on it. Then they were to imagine that one ball was taken out, its number stated, and the ball then thrown back into the bag. This procedure was to be continued until the experimenter stopped it. The subjects were told to orally generate the random series (of the four balls) in a given production interval of 2 s. The timing of the production was trained before the experiment started. Every subject produced a series of 60 numbers within 2 minutes.

For the resulting random number series different measures (redundancy, Evan's random generation [RNG] index, Guttmann's null-score, turning point index, and adjacency, see Towse & Neil, 1998) were computed. Overall, a strong general age effect was found indicating more random production with increasing age. Marked differences between the younger kindergarten sample and the other age groups (particularly in redundancy, Evan's RNG index, adjacency, see Fig. 3.1) emphasize the high level of stereotyped responses within this youngest age group. This shows that the younger children have clear limitations with respect to the inhibition of stereotyped responses like "2, 3, 4" or "3, 2, 1." As Fig. 3.1 shows, there is no strong developmental trend from the age of 8 years onwards.

Stroop Task

In the original Stroop task (Stroop, 1935), color words written in congruent and incongruent colors are presented. Subjects have to name the color

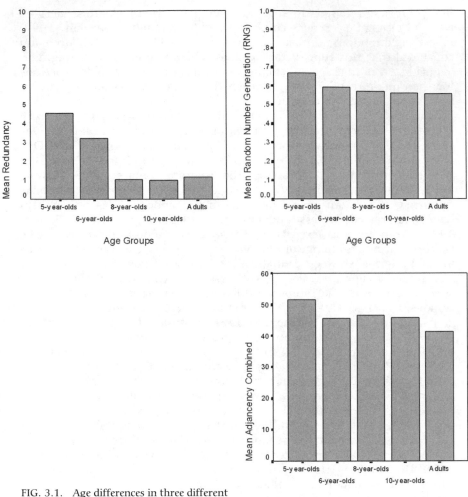

FIG. 3.1.   Age differences in three different
random generation indices.

each word is written in and avoid reading the color name. Solution times
show a dramatic increase when congruently colored words are contrasted
with incongruently colored words (for an overview, see MacLeod, 1991).
The task was originally developed as a measure of inhibition capacity, but
it also serves perfectly for the measurement of the selective attention component of the central executive. It predominantly requires a focused attention on naming the color of the words and an inhibition on reading the
color names. To a lesser extent, retrieval of long-term stored information
is necessary to name the seen color. In addition to extensive literature on

the Stroop effect in adults, fortunately, developmental adaptations do exist (Bull & Scerif, 2001; Demetriou, Spanoudis, Christou, & Platsidou, 2001; Jansen, Mannhaupt, Marx, & Skowronek, 1999; Patnaik, 2002; Wright, Waterman, Prescott, & Murdoch-Eaton, 2003) that show the practicability of the task for elementary school and kindergarten children as well.

In our study, a version by Jansen et al. (1999) was used. Pictures of four different types of vegetables were presented to the subjects. Vegetables and fruits and their colors had to be named separately. Then, congruent colors of vegetables that were presented in black and white had to be named. After this, the actual test was carried out: A series of vegetables and fruits was presented, but this time in incongruent colors. The child was asked to name the original color of each vegetable or fruit as quickly and correctly as possible (e.g., a red lemon is presented—correct answer is "yellow"). Figure 3.2 shows the solution times for naming the color of 32 color-incongruent objects.

Because the solution times and the accuracy of the solution showed a comparable result pattern, we only report the solution times here. The results showed a clear age effect over the five age groups. The large differences between the three youngest age groups point toward major developmental changes in the selective attention and inhibition processes between the ages of 5 and 8 years.

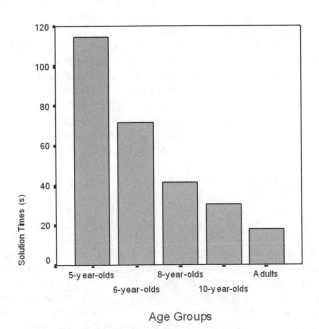

FIG. 3.2. The Stroop task: Age differences in solution times for naming color-incongruent objects.

Color Span Backwards and Visual Decision Span

Due to their theoretical background in the neo-Piagetian tradition, span tasks make two demands of working memory in general: first, a constantly increasing memory load and, second, an executive processing requirement. One of the first complex span tasks was proposed by Daneman, Carpenter, and Just (1982). In this reading span task, two (disconnected) sentences are initially presented. The subject has to read and verify each sentence and keep the last word in mind. The task demand is to recall these words in the order of their presentation. The number of sentences is constantly increased until the subject produces incorrect word sequences. Turner's (Turner & Engle, 1989) operation span task and Case's (Case et al., 1982) counting span task follow the same principle: Both require the processing of information (i.e., solving of mental arithmetic sums or counting dots) as well as the maintenance of information (i.e., the temporal storage of either arithmetic results or different numbers of dots). Gathercole and Pickering (2000a) adapted this type of task for kindergarten and elementary school children: In this listening span task, sentences are presented acoustically, and the children are asked to verify each sentence ("chairs have legs" — "yes"; "bananas have teeth" — "no") followed by the immediate serial recall of each sentence's last word ("legs, teeth") (Gathercole & Pickering, 2000a, p. 381). The average listening span is defined as the maximum number of words correctly recalled in serial order. Another widely used span task is the backward digit span. This task requires the storage of orally presented digits and their recall in reverse order ("4, 7, 3" → "3, 7, 4").

According to Baddeley's process specification, a backward digit span task predominantly demands capacity to control the encoding and retrieval strategies for following the reversed serial order during recall. Resources of selective attention and inhibition may also be involved but to a lesser extent. In contrast, complex span tasks require the coordination of simultaneous tasks (switching between storage and processing) and the control of retrieval strategies (keeping the correct serial order). Additionally, complex span tasks, like the one used by Daneman and Carpenter (1983), necessitate the retrieval of long-term stored information (i.e., arithmetic facts).

In our study, we used two span tasks: a color span backwards and a complex span task like that proposed by Gathercole and Pickering (2000a) called visual decision span. Because the ability to use digits verbally is very heterogeneous in kindergarten children, we modified the commonly used digit span backwards into a color span backwards. Buttons of different colors were presented one after another, and the subjects had to recall the sequence in reversed order. Prior to the experiment, every child was asked to name the colors to control that the span procedure was not affected by a different knowledge of color names. To make sure that possible phonological recoding strategies were not affected by a different length of the color names, only colors with monosyllabic (German) names were selected. Within an extensive instruction period, the backward demand of the task was explained. The span procedure provided two color sequences

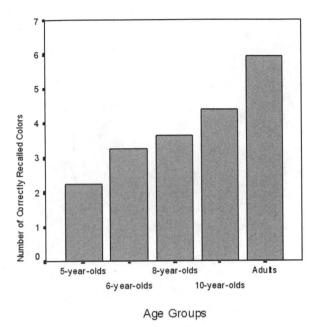

FIG. 3.3.   Age differences for color span backwards.

of the same length on each level and was stopped as soon as both color sequences of one level were incorrectly recalled. Color span backwards was defined as the length of the last color sequence correctly recalled. Figure 3.3 displays color span backwards for the five age groups.

In addition to a general developmental increase in performance, two substantial gaps are striking: a difference of about 1 item between the 5-year-olds and the 6-year-olds on the one hand and a difference of 1.5 items between the 10-year-olds and the adults on the other. Additionally, an analysis of the colors correctly recalled, which did not take serial order into account, showed a similar age effect. For this span, an advantage of 0.3 to 0.5 items for each age group was observed, and no interaction of either of the span measures with age was found. Therefore, we can conclude that the age-dependent effect caused by the backward serial order aspect was rather small. In addition, the gap between the 10-year-olds' and adults' performance strongly suggests that the development of processes used in color span backwards is not completed at the age of 10 years. Adults' superior performance may be due to an efficient control of encoding and retrieval strategies for mastering the reverse recall. Further investigations with children aged 11 to 15 years should clarify the developmental gains up to adulthood.

As a second, more complex span task, we employed a modified version of the listening span task used by Gathercole and Pickering (2000a), that

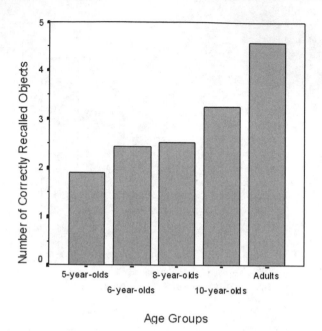

FIG. 3.4.   Age differences in visual decision span.

is, the visual decision span. In contrast to the original version, pictures of objects were presented one at a time. The subjects were asked to decide whether the object they saw was eatable or not. The application of visual stimuli together with the concept of edibility was carried out to make the verification task easier to understand for our younger age groups. After the presentation, the subjects had to recall the objects in the order of their presentation. The visual decision span was defined as the number of objects recalled correctly.

As displayed in Fig. 3.4, again a strong age effect was found with striking differences between 10-year-olds and adults. As in color span backwards, a moderate age-related increase up to the age of 10 years was observed. In addition, the very low span of less than two items for the 5-year-olds is remarkable. One possible explanation may be that younger children have severe difficulties in switching between storage and processing. This is in line with Towse et al.'s (1998) explanation of children's performance in complex span tasks: given that no refreshment of the information that is to be stored is possible, forgetting occurs to a more dramatic degree because of longer switching procedures. All in all, there are striking similarities between the developmental trends of the two span tasks in our study, as well as clear differences to the Stroop task. We discuss this in a later section in more detail.

Trail Making Test B

In the trail making test B (Reitan, 1958), subjects have to connect in alternating order (1-A-2-B-3-C) digits and letters that are placed randomly on a sheet of paper. The dependent variables are the time taken to solve the task and the number of errors. Beyond its general purpose of measuring the control of retrieval strategies and the task switching capacity, the test certainly requires access to long-term memory for using sequences of numbers and letters. McLean and Hitch (1999; see also D'Elia & Satz, 1989) adapted the task for elementary-school children by replacing the letter series with a recurring two-color sequence: children had to connect digits that were placed in circles of two different colors (1 pink - 1 yellow - 2 pink - 2 yellow).

In our adaptation of the trail making test, we wanted to avoid numbers because counting skills are rather heterogeneous in kindergarten-age children. For this purpose, a series of eight yellow circles with ascending size and a series of eight green circles with ascending size were presented. The subjects had to connect the circles according to the following directions:

> Start with the smallest circle in color green, then go on to the circle of the same size in color yellow, then look out for the next larger circle of color green . . . and so forth . . . until you reach the biggest circle of color yellow; try to do this as fast as you can without making any mistakes!

After a training period, the test version was administered and the solution times were taken (see Fig. 3.5).

With the change from the letter and number series to a green and yellow series of circles increasing in size, the demands of the task changed considerably. Access to long-term memory is not involved anymore, and the control of retrieval strategies is minimized. The predominant central executive process necessary to solve our trail making task is task switching. However, no switching between storage and processing, but an alternation between circle color and circle size, is required. There was a strong age effect in the sense of a decrease in solution times. The prominent difference between the two youngest age groups supports the hypothesis of an inefficient task switching process in 5-year-olds, as already discussed in the section on span measures.

Mental Fusion Task

The mental fusion task was proposed by Brandimonte and colleagues (Brandimonte, Hitch, & Bishop, 1992). At first, a card with a seemingly abstract image (e.g., a semicircle whose flat side is pointing upwards; see Fig. 3.6) is shown for 2 s. After this, the card is removed and another card with another image is presented for the same duration (e.g., a triangle whose tip is pointing upwards). Then, the first image is shown again, and

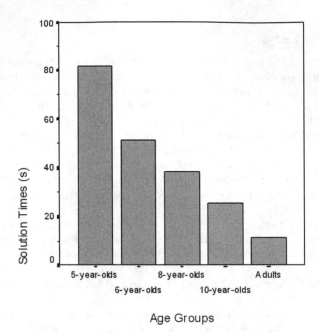

FIG. 3.5. Age differences in the trail making task.

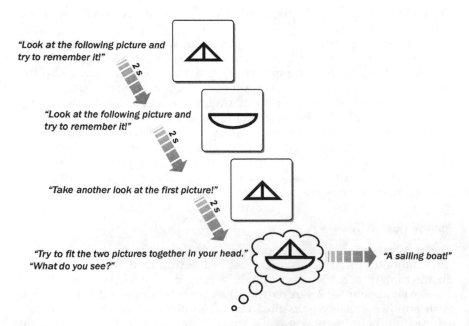

FIG. 3.6. Example for a mental fusion trial.

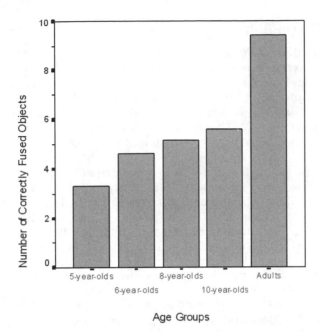

FIG. 3.7.   Age differences in the mental fusion task.

the subject is asked to mentally fuse the two images and tell which object results from the mental fusion (e.g., a sailing boat).

Manipulation of and access to long-term memory is the core central executive process that is required for task solution. The temporal storage and mental manipulation of the two pictures is carried out by the visuo-spatial slave system. Apart from this, the access to long-term memory resources by aligning the fused images with long-term stored informa-tion and naming the obtained objects is attributed to the central executive. We implemented 10 trials and calculated a sum score of correctly fused objects. To ensure that potential age differences are not caused by diffi-culties in identifying and naming the fused objects, each test person was shown the fused pictures and asked to name them subsequent to the exper-iment. Figure 3.7 shows the distribution of means across age groups.

The big age effect is to a large extent due to differences between adults and children. Additionally, a marked difference between 5-year-olds and 6-year-olds is observable. On average, the older age group of the kinder-garten children solved one item more than the younger group. The gaps between the 5- and the 6-year-olds and between the 10-year-olds and the adults may arise from a more efficient access to long-term memory in the older age groups. In particular, higher efficiency here may reflect a faster access. Studies within other modalities (i.e., the mental fusion of orally presented syllables) will provide further evidence.

Decision-Making Task

Finally, a decision making task was conducted. Here, selective attention to a given criterion is required, while concurrent inhibition of other reaction tendencies is needed. So far, the ability to selectively attend and react to a given stimulus and to suppress the concurrent tendency to react to another stimulus is measured by several attentional tasks of the GO/NOGO type (Dowsett & Livesey, 2000; Foeldnyi, Giovanoli, Tagwerker-Neuenschwander, Schallberger, & Steinhausen, 2000; Mähler & Hasselhorn, 2001).

In our task, a search criterion was presented at the beginning of each trial. The subjects were instructed to react with "yes" if the search criterion (e.g., a yellow ball) appeared with the stimulus (e.g., a child with a yellow ball) and to react with "no" if the search criterion was absent (e.g., child without a ball) or showed different characteristics (e.g., child with a red ball). Each trial contained 10 search pictures, half of them with and half of them without the criterion. Six trials were given. The difficulty of the task was varied by increasing the number of search criteria and by using criteria with and without color information. At the beginning, a search criterion without color information was presented (the criterion was presented in black and white)—the glasses ("look out for the glasses, no matter what color they have")—then a criterion with color information was presented ("look out for the yellow ball, but be aware that the ball needs to be colored yellow"; see Fig. 3.8 for an example). The number of criteria increased up to three. Correct responses and solution times were taken as dependent variables. Because both reveal a comparable age effect, we report only the solution times here.

"Look out for the yellow ball!"

FIG. 3.8.   Example of a decision-making task.

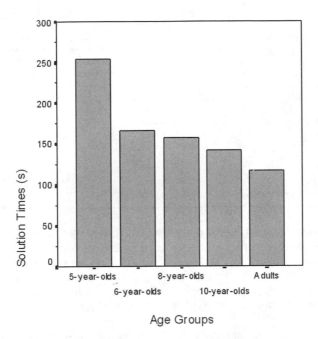

FIG. 3.9.   Age differences in the decision-making task.

Figure 3.9 indicates the age differences in the decision-making task. The performance of the 5-year-olds differed greatly from that of the older children. Particularly with regard to this severe gap, we have to wonder whether qualitative changes in central executive processing may occur in addition to quantitative increases of resources: It could be postulated that selective attention and inhibition processes emerge between the ages of 5 and 6 years.

ARE THERE DIFFERENT COURSES OF DEVELOPMENT FOR DIFFERENT CENTRAL EXECUTIVE PROCESSES?

One of the leading intentions behind the use of the seven different measurement tools was to look for different developmental trends. To compare developmental trends in the different dependent variables, we calculated an effect size measure for the factor age within each measurement tool. To prove the hypothesis of different developmental trends in different variables, we looked at large gaps between two age groups. This was done by using the effect size measure of the factor age effect and comparing the effect size of the whole sample with the effect size measures of the sample without the 5-year-olds or without the adults, respectively. Two obvious

TABLE 3.1
Effect Size Measures for Central Executive Measurement Tools

Measurement Tools	Effect Size Measure ε for Different Conditions		
	ε for Whole Sample	ε Without 5-Year-Olds	ε Without Adults
Color span backwards	1.22	1.04	0.49
Mental fusion task	1.42	1.36	0.49
Decision-making task	0.73	0.53	0.61
Visual decision span	1.14	1.06	0.60
Stroop task	1.41	1.61	1.17
Trail making task	1.26	1.07	0.96
Random generation—adjacency	0.29	0.26	0.17

tendencies could be found for our data. There are two major gaps: between the kindergarten samples and the other age groups on the one hand and between the 10-year-olds and our adult subjects on the other hand. Table 3.1 provides three different effect size measures for the age effect in every central executive task: the effect size for the overall sample, the effect size of the sample excluding the 5-year-olds, and the effect size of the sample excluding the adults.

From a comparison of the effect size measures, it becomes apparent that the developmental trend is a different one for different tasks: a relatively large gap between adults and 10-year-olds can be found for color span backwards, the mental fusion task, and visual decision span. Excluding the adults from the analysis leads to dramatically diminished effect size measures for the age effect of these variables (see column 4 in Table 3.1). This indicates that the development of the required processes is not finished at the end of elementary-school age. To define the developmental trends between 10-year-olds and adults more specifically, age groups older than 10 years and younger than adults need to be examined.

Other measures, such as the Stroop task, the trail making test, and the decision-making task show a quite moderate and more linear developmental trend. Excluding 5-year-olds or adults from the sample leads to similar changes in the age effect (see column 3 and column 4 in Table 3.1). In addition, remarkable gaps between 5- and 6-year-olds, as found for the Stroop task, the trail making task, and the decision-making task (see Fig. 3.2, Fig. 3.5, Fig. 3.9, and Table 3.1), suggest different interpretations. On the one hand, some of the central executive processes that are basically required in these tasks may not have been developed yet or may still be underdeveloped. Contrarily, it could also be assumed that young children are able to cope with the tasks but that the complexity of the task is not linear across age groups. Furthermore, the interplay between different processes, particularly in complex tasks, may not yet work properly in younger children.

Finally, the measure for randomness shows only a weak developmental trend altogether. In accordance with Towse (1998), we think that the analysis of randomness in a random generation task requires a multivariate approach and cannot be demonstrated so easily by one measure only. So, for further studies, a multivariate approach may be more appropriate.

To underpin the hypothesis of different developmental trends, post hoc analyses with Student-Newman-Keul tests for differences between the age groups were applied. Different homogeneous subgroups were identified by these analyses: Five distinct groups for the trail making task, four groups for the Stroop task and color span backwards, three groups for the mental fusion task and the visual decision task, and only two groups for the decision-making task and the random generation measure were identified.

In summary, the analyses of the age effects showed different developmental trends for our seven tasks, and this is taken as preliminary evidence for the assumption of different developmental trends for the four central executive processes (Baddeley, 1996). Particularly for the complex, multiprocess tasks, such as visual decision span and color span backwards, older age groups (between 10 years and adulthood) need to be examined in further studies because the development is not yet completed in these groups. Furthermore, aspects of complexity within the different tasks should be taken into account for future task modifications. This is also important for controlling potential floor and ceiling effects within the different tasks. Also, the involvement of the modality-specific working memory subsystems calls for additional examination because it still remains a partially open question as to what extent the subsystems are involved in the central executive task performance. Finally, the construction of tasks with comparable measures, such as complex span tasks, provides the opportunity to compare different executive processes via developmental fractionation. The idea of a multitrait-multimethod matrix seems plausible only for clearly defined executive processes and distinct measures of central executive functioning.

SHOULD DIFFERENT MEASUREMENT TOOLS BE USED FOR DIFFERENT EXECUTIVE PROCESSES?

Finally, we have to ask about the relation between the seven measurement tools applied in our study and the four different central executive processes proposed by Baddeley (1996). Figure 3.10 shows a proposal of these relations. It seems apparent that no measurement tool requires just one central executive process alone. It also has to be noted that the modality-specific requirements of the tasks (i.e., their phonological and visual-spatial demands) undoubtedly exist but are not involved in this figure.

For an empirical demonstration of the diversity of the different processes in our tasks, a correlational analysis was applied. The resulting correlational pattern is provided in Table 3.2. Partial correlational coefficients that are adjusted for chronological age in months were used.

Three measures that are assumed to tap selective attention or inhibition capacity show significant correlations: color span backwards, decision

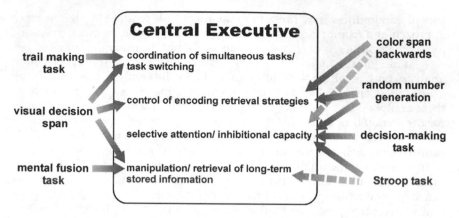

FIG. 3.10. The relational pattern between different measurement tools and central executive processes.

making, and Stroop task. Within the selective attention/inhibition measures, the highest degree of association was obtained between the Stroop task and the decision-making task (partial $r = .39$, $p < .01$). The requirement to inhibit prepotent responses (i.e., the obvious color of an object instead of its original color or the given serial order instead of the reverse serial order) is one of the fundamental similarities in these tasks. The capacity to inhibit prepotent or stereotyped response alternatives is also a relevant aspect in the random generation task, but the correlations between random generation and other attentional measures are rather weak, except

TABLE 3.2
Correlational Matrix for Central Executive Measurement Tools

Variable	1	2	3	4	5	6	7	8
1. Age	—	—	—	—	—	—	—	—
2. Color span backwards	.74**	—	.02	−.21*	.21*	−.34**	−.33**	−.15
3. Mental fusion task	.83**	.61**	—	−.21*	.23*	−.17	.14	−.05
4. Decision making task	−.42**	−.44**	−.46**	—	−.10	.39**	.34**	.17
5. Visual decision span	.69**	.61**	.67**	−.36**	—	−.23*	−.14	−.06
6. Stroop task	−.65**	−.65**	−.61**	.54**	−.57**	—	−.67**	.26**
7. Trail making task	−.63**	−.64**	−.58**	.50**	−.52**	.81**	—	.28**
8. Random generation adjacency	−.27**	−.30**	−.25*	.27**	−.23*	.37**	.38**	—

Note. Simple correlations are shown in the lower triangle; partial correlation coefficients adjusted for chronological age in month are shown in the upper triangle.
*$p < .05$. **$p < .01$.

for the Stroop task (partial $r = .26$, $p < .01$). Although the processes of selective attention and inhibition capacity are rather connected, they may play different roles in our tasks.

The control of retrieval and encoding strategies is an aspect immanent to tasks that require temporal storage of information as well as subsequent recall of information. The correlation between color span backwards and visual decision span (partial $r = .21$, $p < .05$) supports the hypothesis that both tasks share at least one process. In addition, the visual nature and the demand to keep serial order (which is an aspect of retrieval and encoding strategies) may also contribute to the correlation.

Visual decision span taps the integration of long-term memory information, a characteristic that is also covered by the mental fusion task. The latter task requires information from the knowledge base to combine visual objects and name the fused object correctly, whereas visual decision span necessitates long-term stored facts for its verification demand. The two tasks correlate moderately but significantly (partial $r = .23$, $p < .05$).

A correlation between the mental fusion task and the decision-making task was not expected, although both tasks are based on visual processes. The involvement of visual processes, however, is true for almost all of our tasks. The correlations between the trail making and the decision-making task (partial $r = .34$, $p < .01$) and between the trail making task and the color span backwards (partial $r = .33$, $p < .01$) may also reflect that both tasks require visual processes.

The correlations between the trail making test and the Stroop task (partial $r = .67$, $p < .01$), between random generation and the Stroop task (partial $r = .26$, $p < .01$), between the decision-making task and the trail making task (partial $r = .34$, $p < .01$) and between the trail making test and random generation (partial $r = .28$, $p < .01$) may be explained in terms of timing aspects: All tasks require solution processes with timing constraints ("solve it as fast as you can"; "try to keep a 2 s response frequency").

In general, the specific measurement of different central executive processes is possible in children and provides one pathway to the fractionation of the central executive into different subprocesses. The correlational analyses revealed evidence for this. However, it has to be noted that phonological or visual-spatial processes have not been taken into account so far and may have a modifying function on the subjects' performance. This is particularly important because we know that there are different developmental trends in these working memory subsystems, too.

MEASURING THE DEVELOPING CENTRAL EXECUTIVE OF A NONUNITARY WORKING MEMORY MODEL

Finally, some comments on the operationalizations used in our study should be made. Our empirical findings clearly support the notion of different central executive processes. Because every task we used is based on different executive processes and was furthermore adapted to developmental needs, some aspects have to be considered for the future use of these measurement tools.

As mentioned previously, the mental fusion task requires retrieval of long-term information as well as the mental fusion of visual objects. Undoubtedly, mental imagery is required, and the question remains whether such a complex process is spontaneously available in kindergarten children. For that reason, we propose to control for the complexity of the objects that are to be fused. Potential criteria for an analysis of complexity may be the familiarity and the degree of abstraction. Because younger children's nonverbal abilities seem better developed than their verbal skills, the mental imagery pathway to the long-term retrieval function of the central executive seems an interesting approach. Nevertheless, it has to be taken into account that the task may be solved differently by younger children than by older children and adults. To test this hypothesis, the role of visual-spatial imagery processes could be dissociated by applying a verbal analogue of the task (i.e., demanding to mentally fuse syllables into a new word). Although this version of the mental fusion task certainly requires a large amount of phonological processing, it may help to specify the amount of executive processes that are relevant to such a task.

The notion of disentangling the role of the subsystems in central executive tasks by varying the modality of these tasks seems plausible for other tasks as well, for example for random generation. Attempts to vary the modality of the response alternatives (Baddeley et al., 1998; Towse, 1998; Towse & Valentine, 1997) have demonstrated that different aspects of the subsystems are relevant for different randomization tasks. These findings led to experimental studies on the dissociation of central executive interference from phonological or visual-spatial interference. For instance, motor- and spatially based random generation tasks were used (Zoelch et al., 2000; see also Vandierendonck, De Vooght, & Van der Goten, 1998a, for a modality-free randomization task). The use of nonverbal random generation tasks may reduce other problems as well: Stereotyped behavior in random number generation tasks may be an effect of overloaded attentional capacities caused by the constant maintenance of response alternatives. As spatially based random generation tasks such as key pressing do not require the temporal storage of all response alternatives, storage capacities are freed up for monitoring the output regarding its randomness as well as its response frequency.

Although the Stroop task has a strong experimental tradition, different working memory processes that are required for this task have still not been well defined (see also Demetriou et al., 2001). Certainly, inhibition of irrelevant information is crucial to almost every working memory task that requires the selection of information to be remembered. The dissociation of attentional focusing and inhibitory capacity within the Stroop task is one step. However, when the task is applied to young children, additional aspects, such as the complexity of the task (i.e., the number of different objects to be named) and the duration of the task (i.e., the length of the overall series), should be examined.

Considerable efforts have gone into the development of complex span tasks over the last few years (Hitch, Towse, & Hutton, 2001; Miyake, Friedman, Emerson, Witzki, & Howerter, 2000; Towse et al., 1998) resulting in appropriate adaptations of these tasks even for primary-school children (Gathercole & Pickering, 2000a). However, it is still desirable to minimize verbal demands in this type of span task. Our visual decision span and the color span backwards may provide a first step in that direction: Both tasks are applicable to younger children or subgroups with language difficulties.

In general, reducing task complexity and keeping verbal task demands to a minimum are some of the basic factors that should be taken into consideration when central executive tasks are applied to younger children. Our version of the trail making task was constructed according to this argument: Complexity can be varied via the number of the different colors, via the spatial arrangement of the items that have to be connected as well as via the variation of distinct object forms. The same holds true for the decision-making task: The decision criteria can be varied in number and type.

Using complex tasks with several demands leads to the question of which additional processes may be attributed to the central executive. Towse and Houston-Price (2001) proposed the role of a general-purpose processor to be one of central executive's major functions. Because many high-level functions are attributed to the central executive, the idea of a general-purpose processor seems tempting. Apart from its major role in central executive functioning, however, the general-purpose processor bears a certain risk: To some extent, it resembles the beginning of Baddeley and Hitch's (1977) central executive conception. Because diverse processing demands are required in almost every (complex) working memory task, the processing unit may become the new ragbag of working memory. Here, an exact specification of storage and processing aspects is a difficult but possible way to disentangle single aspects of the overall processing unit. The same is true for selective attention processes within the central executive: They seem to be more or less relevant to almost every working memory task. Additionally, up to now it has not been empirically proven whether the selective attention component plays a more significant role in younger age groups than in older ones. Therefore, a measure solely for the ability to focus attention within the working memory framework seems to be necessary. Because the attentional focus on a subject of interest is limited in capacity and, therefore, always requires the suppression of irrelevant information, inhibition should also be one of the central executive's basic purposes (see also Hasher & Zacks, 1989).

The notion of attentional capacities proves to be particularly relevant also from a developmental point of view: Many processes that are automatized in older children and adults require resources in younger children's processing. Hasher and Zacks (1979) claimed that effortful processes change developmentally into automatized processes so they demand less capacity. Together with Case et al.'s (1982) notion of a changing the use of operation and storage space, this idea seems plausible for the development of the central executive as well: Basic processes, such as encoding and retrieval strategies, may require less capacity in older children and adults than in younger children. Because complex working memory tasks rely on several processes simultaneously, this may soon lead to a functional overload in younger children. A potential fallback strategy to cope with such an overload may be to process different task components successively instead of simultaneously. For this reason, solution times will increase. The notion of temporal aspects for the explanation of central processing capabilities is not new to the working memory model of Baddeley and Hitch, although it does not explicitly "offer a temporal framework within which to explain 'central' working memory capacity phenomena" (Towse et al., 1998, p. 215).

One potential way to control the processing demands within working memory tasks is to vary the complexity in these tasks: If complex versions of a task cannot be solved, whereas simple versions of the same task can be coped with, this may be taken as evidence that the bad task performance is not caused by a general lack of executive processes but by a functional overload. As long as the structural differences within central executive functioning in adults and children are not clear, this explanation seems plausible. Furthermore, the idea of different developmental courses of the diverse central executive processes can be strengthened if the processes are defined clearly and operationalizations are adapted to developmental aspects. This means that the control of complexity in working memory tasks seems indispensable and should be taken into account to control for potential functional overloads. Only then can the idea of developmental fractionation (Hitch, 1990) be realized for the central executive. Fractionating the executive may not only put a new complexion on developmental concepts like the good strategy user or good information processing (Pressley, 1995), but it might also provide further progress toward diagnosis and intervention within the field of learning disabilities (Gathercole & Pickering, 2000a, 2000b; McLean & Hitch, 1999).

ACKNOWLEDGMENTS

The study described in this chapter is part of a research project that is supported by a grant from the German Research Foundation to the third author (Schu840/5-3). We are grateful to Nora Gaupp, Martina Seybel, and Carina Barthle for their help and contribution on the experiments. Correspondence concerning this article should be addressed to Christof Zoelch, Department of Developmental and Educational Psychology, Catholic University of Eichstätt-Ingolstadt, Ostenstr. 26-28, D-85071 Eichstätt, Germany. Electronic mail may be sent to christof.zoelch@ku-eichstaett.de.

REFERENCES

Andrade, J. (2001). The working memory model: Consensus, controversy, and future directions. In J. Andrade (Ed.), *Working memory in perspective* (pp. 281–310). Philadelphia: Psychology Press.

Ashcraft, M. H. (1992). Cognitive arithmetic: A review of data and theory. *Cognition, 44,* 75–106.

Baddeley, A. D. (1966). The capacity for generating information by randomization. *Quarterly Journal of Experimental Psychology, 18,* 119–129.

Baddeley, A. D. (1986). *Working memory.* Oxford, UK: Oxford University Press.

Baddeley, A. D. (1990). *Human memory: Theory and practice.* Boston: Allyn and Bacon.

Baddeley, A. D. (1993). Working memory or working attention? In A. D. Baddeley & L. Weiskrantz (Eds.), *Attention: Selection, awareness, and control: A tribute to Donald Broadbent* (pp. 152–170). Oxford, UK: Oxford University Press.

Baddeley, A. D. (1996). Exploring the central executive. *Quarterly Journal of Experimental Psychology, 49,* 5–28.

Baddeley, A. D. (2000). The episodic buffer: A new component of working memory. *Trends in Cognitive Science, 4*(11), 417–423.

Baddeley, A. D. (2002). Is working memory still working? *European Psychologist, 7,* 85–97.

Baddeley, A., Emslie, H., Kolodny, J., & Duncan, J. (1998). Random generation and the executive control of working memory. *Quarterly Journal of Experimental Psychology, 51,* 819–852.

Baddeley, A. D., & Hitch, G. J. (1974). Working memory. In G. Bower (Ed.), *The psychology of learning and motivation* (pp. 47–89). New York: Academic Press.

Baddeley, A. D., & Hitch, G. J. (1977). Working memory. In G. Bower (Ed.), *Human memory* (pp. 191–241). New York: Academic Press.

Baddeley, A. D., & Hitch, G. J. (1994). Developments in the concept of working memory. *Neuropsychology, 8,* 485–493.

Baddeley, A. D., & Hitch, G. J. (2000). Development of working memory: Should the Pascual-Leone and the Baddeley and Hitch models be merged? *Journal of Experimental Child Psychology, 77,* 128–137.

Baddeley, A. D., Thomson, N., & Buchanan, M. (1975). Word length and the structure of working memory. *Journal of Verbal Learning and Verbal Behaviour, 14,* 575–589.

Baddeley, A. D., & Wilson, B. (1988). Frontal amnesia and the dysexecutive syndrome. *Brain and Cognition, 7,* 212–230.

Brandimonte, M. A., Hitch, G. J., & Bishop, D. V. (1992). Manipulation of visual mental images in children and adults. *Journal of Experimental Child Psychology, 53,* 300–312.

Brugger, P. (1997). Variables that influence the generation of random sequences: An update. *Perceptual and Motor Skills, 84,* 627–661.

Brugger, P., Monsch, A. U., Salmon, D. P., & Butters, N. (1996). Random number generation in dementia of the Alzheimer type: A test of frontal executive functions. *Neuropsychologia, 34,* 97–103.

Bull, R., & Scerif, G. (2001). Executive functioning as a predictor of children's mathematics ability: Inhibition, switching, and working memory. *Developmental Neuropsychology, 19,* 273–293.

Case, R., Kurland, D. M., & Goldberg, J. (1982). Operational efficiency and the growth of short-term memory span. *Journal of Experimental Child Psychology, 33,* 386–404.

Cowan, N. (2001). The magical number 4 in short-term memory: A reconsideration of mental storage capacity. *Behavioral and Brain Sciences, 24,* 87–185.

Daneman, M., & Carpenter, P. A. (1980). Individual differences in working memory and reading. *Journal of Verbal Learning and Verbal Behavior, 19,* 450–466.

Daneman, M., & Carpenter, P. A. (1983). Individual differences in integrating information between and within sentences. *Journal of Experimental Psychology: Learning, Memory, and Cognition, 9,* 561–584.

Daneman, M., Carpenter, P. A., & Just, M. A. (1982). Cognitive processes and reading skills. *Advances in Reading/Language Research, 1,* 83–124.

D'Elia, L., & Satz, P. (1989). *Colour trails 1 and 2*. Odessa, FL: Psychological Assessment.

Demetriou, A., Spanoudis, G., Christou, C., & Platsidou, M. (2001). Modeling the Stroop phenomenon: Processes, processing flow, and development. *Cognitive Development, 16*, 987–1005.

De Ribaupierre, A., & Bailleux, C. (1994). Developmental changes in a spatial task of attentional capacity: An essay toward an integration of two working memory models. *International Journal of Behavioral Development, 17*, 5–35.

De Ribaupierre, A., & Bailleux, C. (1995). Development of attentional capacity in childhood: A longitudinal study. In F. Weinert, & W. Schneider (Eds.), *Memory performance and competencies: Issues in growth and development* (pp. 45–70). Hillsdale, NJ: Lawrence Erlbaum Associates.

D'Esposito, M., & Grossmann, M. (1998). The physiological basis of executive function and working memory. *Neuroscientist, 2*, 345–352.

Dowsett, S. M., & Livesey, D. J. (2000). The development of inhibitory control in preschool children: Effects of "executive skills" training. *Developmental Psychobiology, 36*, 161–174.

Foeldnyi, M., Giovanoli, A., Tagwerker-Neuenschwander, F., Schallberger, U., & Steinhausen, H.-C. (2000). Reliabilitaet und Reteststabilitaet der Testleistungen von 7–10jaehrigen Kindern in der computerunterstuetzten TAP [Reliability and stability of the computerized attention test battery (TAP) for children aged 7–10]. *Zeitschrift für Neuropsychologie, 11*, 1–11.

Gathercole, S. E. (1999). Cognitive approaches to the development of short-term memory. *Trends in Cognitive Science, 3*, 410–419.

Gathercole, S. E., Adams, A.-M., & Hitch, G. J. (1994). Do young children rehearse? An individual-differences analysis. *Memory and Cognition, 22*, 201–207.

Gathercole, S. E., & Baddeley, A. D. (1993). *Working memory and language*. Hove: Erlbaum.

Gathercole, S. E., & Hitch, G. J. (1993). Developmental changes in short-term memory: A revised working memory perspective. In A. F. Collins, S. E. Gathercole, & M.A. Conway (Eds.), *Theories of memory* (pp. 189–209). Hillsdale, NJ: Lawrence Erlbaum Associates.

Gathercole, S. E., & Pickering, S. J. (2000a). Assessment of working memory in six- and seven-year-old children. *Journal of Educational Psychology, 92*, 377–390.

Gathercole, S. E., & Pickering, S. J. (2000b). Working memory deficits in children with low achievements in the national curriculum at 7 years of age. *British Journal of Educational Psychology, 70*, 177–194.

Gathercole, S. E., Willis, C. S., Baddeley, A. D., & Emslie, H. (1994). The Children's Test of Nonword Repetition: A test of phonological working memory. *Memory, 2*, 103–127.

Gilhooly, K. J. (1998). Working memory, strategies, and reasoning tasks. In R. H. Logie & K. J. Gilhooly (Eds.), *Working memory and thinking. Current issues in thinking and reasoning* (pp. 7–22). Hove, UK: Psychology Press.

Hasher, L., & Zacks, R. T. (1979). Automatic and effortful processes in memory. *Journal of Experimental Psychology: General, 108*, 356–388.

Hasher, L., & Zacks, R. T. (1989). Working memory, comprehension, and aging: A review and a new view. In G. H. Bower (Ed.), *The psychology of learning and motivation* (pp. 193–225). Orlando, FL: Academic Press.

Hitch, G. J. (1990). Developmental fractionation of working memory. In G. Vallar & T. Shallice (Eds), *Neuropsychological impairments of short-term memory* (pp. 221–246). New York: Cambridge University Press.

Hitch, G. J., & Halliday, M. S. (1983). Working memory in children. *Philosophical Transaction of the Royal Society of London, B302*, 325–340.

Hitch, G. J., Towse, J. N., & Hutton, U. (2001). What limits children's working memory span? Theoretical accounts and applications for scholastic development. *Journal of Experimental Psychology: General, 130*, 184–198.

Hulme, C., Thomson, N., Muir, C., & Lawrence, A. (1984). Speech rate and the development of short-term memory span. *Journal of Experimental Child Psychology, 38*, 241–253.

Isaacs, E. B., & Vargha-Khadem, F. (1989). Differential course of development of spatial and verbal memory span: A normative study. *British Journal of Developmental Psychology, 7*, 377–380.

Jansen, H., Mannhaupt, G., Marx, H., & Skowronek, H. (1999). *BISC Bielefelder Screening zur Frueherkennung von Lese-Rechtschreibschwierigkeiten* [Bielefeld Screening Battery for Early Diagnosis of Problems in Reading and Writing]. Göttingen: Hogrefe.

Just, M. A., & Carpenter, P. A. (1992). A capacity theory of comprehension: Individual differences in working memory. *Psychological Review, 99*, 122–149.

Kemps, E., De Rammelaere, S., & Desmet, T. (2000). The development of working memory: Exploring the complementarity of two models. *Journal of Experimental Child Psychology, 77*, 89–109.

Kramer, A. F., Larish, J. L., Weber, T. A., & Bardell, L. (1999). Training for executive control: Task coordination strategies and aging. In D. Gopher & A. Koriat (Eds.), *Attention and Performance XVII* (pp. 617–652). Cambridge, MA: MIT Press.

Logie, R. H. (1995). *Visuo-spatial working memory.* Hove, UK: Erlbaum.

Logie, R. H., Gilhooly, K. J., & Wynn, V. (1994). Counting on working memory in arithmetic problem solving. *Memory and Cognition, 22*, 395–410.

Logie, R. H., & Pearson, D. G. (1997). The inner eye and the inner scribe of visuospatial working memory: Evidence from developmental fractionation. *European Journal of Cognitive Psychology, 9*, 241–257.

MacLeod, C. M. (1991). Half a century of research on the Stroop effect: An integrative review. *Psychological Bulletin, 109*, 163–203.

Mähler, C., & Hasselhorn, M. (2001, 1 September). *"Achte auf den Fuchs und nur auf den Fuchs!" Zur Entwicklung einer Arbeitsgedächtnisfunktion im Grundschulalter* ["Pay attention to the fox and only to the fox!" On the development of a working memory function in elementary school children]. Poster presented at the 15. Tagung der Fachgruppe Entwicklungspsychologie der Deutschen Gesellschaft für Psychologie, Potsdam, Germany.

McLean, J. F., & Hitch, G. J. (1999). Working memory impairments in children with specific arithmetic learning difficulties. *Journal of Experimental Child Psychology, 74*, 240–260.

Miyake, A., Friedman, N. P., Emerson, M. J., Witzki, A. H., & Howerter, A. (2000). The unity and diversity of executive functions and their contributions to complex "frontal lobe" tasks: A latent variable analysis. *Cognitive Psychology, 41*, 49–100.

Miyake, A., & Shah, P. (1999). *Models of working memory: Mechanisms of active maintenance and executive control.* Cambridge, UK: Cambridge University Press.

Norman, D. A., & Shallice, T. (1986). Attention to action: Willed and automatic control of behaviour. In R. J. Davidson, G. E. Schwartz, & D. Shapiro (Eds.), *Consciousness and self regulation: Advances in research and theory* (pp. 1–18). New York: Plenum Press.

Oberauer, K., Süß, H.-M., Schulze, R., Wilhelm, O., & Wittmann, W. W. (2000). Working memory capacity-facets of a cognitive ability construct. *Personality and Individual Differences, 29*, 1017–1045.

Oberauer, K., Süß, H.-M., Wilhelm, O., & Wittman, W. W. (2003). The multiple faces of working memory: Storage, processing, supervision, and coordination. *Intelligence, 31*, 167–193.

Pascual-Leone, J. (2000). Reflections on working memory: Are the two models complementary? *Journal of Experimental Child Psychology, 77*, 138–154.

Pascual-Leone, J., & Baillargeon, R. (1994). Developmental measurement of mental attention. *International Journal of Behavioral Development, 17*, 161–200.

Patnaik, N. (2002). Selective attention in normal and learning disabled children. *Psychological Studies, 47*, 113–120.

Pickering, S. J., Gathercole, S. E., Hall, M., & Lloyd, S. A. (2001). Development of memory for pattern and path: Further evidence for the fractionation of visuo-spatial memory. *Quarterly Journal of Experimental Psychology: Human Experimental Psychology, 54*, 397–420.

Pressley, M. (1995). What is intellectual development about in the 1990s? Good information processing. In F. E. Weinert & W. Schneider (Eds.), *Memory performance and competencies: Issues in growth and development* (pp. 375–404). Hillsdale, NJ: Lawrence Erlbaum Associates.

Reitan, R. M. (1958). Validity of the Trail Making Test as an indicator of organic brain damage. *Perceptual and Motor Skills, 8*, 271–276.

Robertson, C., Hazlewood, R., & Rawson, M. D. (1996). The effects of Parkinson's disease on the capacity to generate information randomly. *Neuropsychologia, 34,* 1069–1078.

Schumann-Hengsteler, R. (1995). *Die Entwicklung des visuell-räumlichen Gedächtnisses* [On the development of visual spatial memory]. Göttingen, Germany: Hogrefe-Verlag für Psychologie.

Schumann-Hengsteler, R., & Pohl, S. (1996, July). *Children's temporary memory for spatial sequences in the Corsi blocks.* Paper presented at the International Conference on Memory, Padua, Italy.

Schumann-Hengsteler, R., Strobl, M., & Zoelch, C. (2004). Temporal memory for locations: On the encoding of spatio-temporal information in children and adults. In G. L. Allen (Ed.), *Human spatial memory: Remembering where* (pp. 101–124). New York: Erlbaum.

Seitz, K., & Schumann-Hengsteler, R. (2000). Mental multiplication and working memory. *European Journal of Cognitive Psychology, 12,* 552–570.

Seitz, K., & Schumann-Hengsteler, R. (2002). Phonological loop and central executive processes in mental addition and multiplication. *Psychologische Beitrage, 44,* 275–302.

Stratta, P., Daneluzzo, E., Prosperini, P., Bustini, M., Mattei, P., & Rossi, A. (1997). Is Wisconsin Card Sorting Test performance related to working memory capacity? *Schizophrenia Research, 27,* 11–19.

Strobl, M., Strametz, D., & Schumann-Hengsteler, R. (2002). *Effekte der Aufgabenkomplexität und Matrixgröße auf die Matrix-Muster-Aufgabe* [The effects of task complexity and size on the matrix task]. Eichstätt, Germany: Catholic University of Eichstätt-Ingolstadt.

Stroop, J. R. (1935). Studies of interference in serial verbal reactions. *Journal of Experimental Psychology, 18,* 643–662.

Swanson, H. L. (1999). What develops in working memory? A life span perspective. *Developmental Psychology, 35,* 986–1000.

Thorn, A. S. C., & Gathercole, S. E. (2000). The development and impairment of working memory. *Revue de Neuropsychologie, 10,* 417–439.

Towse, J. N. (1998). On random generation and the central executive of working memory. *British Journal of Psychology, 89,* 77–101.

Towse, J. N., Hitch, G. J., & Hutton, U. (1998). A reevaluation of working memory capacity in children. *Journal of Memory and Language, 39,* 195–217.

Towse, J. N., & Houston-Price, C. M. T. (2001). Reflections on the concept of the central executive. In J. Andrade (Ed.), *Working memory in perspective* (pp. 240–260). Philadelphia: Psychology Press.

Towse, J. N., & Mclachlan, A. (1999). An exploration of random generation among children. *British Journal of Developmental Psychology, 17,* 363–380.

Towse, J. N., & Neil, D. (1998). Analyzing human random generation behavior: A review of methods used and a computer program for describing performance. *Behavior Research Methods, Instruments and Computers, 30,* 583–591.

Towse, J. N., & Valentine, J. D. (1997). Random generation of numbers: A search for underlying processes. *European Journal of Cognitive Psychology, 9,* 381–400.

Treisman, M., & Faulkner, A. (1987). Generation of random sequences by human subjects: Cognitive operations or psychological process? *Journal of Experimental Psychology: General, 116,* 337–355.

Turner, M. L., & Engle, R. W. (1989). Is working memory capacity task dependent? *Journal of Memory and Language, 28,* 127–154.

Vandierendonck, A. (2000). Analyzing human random time generation behavior: A methodology and a computer program. *Behavior Research Methods, 32,* 555–565.

Vandierendonck, A., De Vooght, G., & Van der Goten, K. (1998a). Does random time interval generation interfere with working memory executive functions? *European Journal of Cognitive Psychology, 10,* 413–442.

Vandierendonck, A., De Vooght, G., & Van der Goten, K. (1998b). Interfering with the Central Executive by Means of a Random Interval Repetition Task. *Quarterly Journal of Experimental Psychology, 51,* 197–218.

Wright, I., Waterman, M., Prescott, H., & Murdoch-Eaton, D. (2003). A new Stroop-like measure of inhibitory function development: Typical developmental trends. *Journal of Child Psychology and Psychiatry and Allied Disciplines, 44*, 561–575.

Zelazo, P. D., & Mueller, U. (2003). Executive function in typical and atypical development. In U. Goswami (Ed.), *Blackwell handbook of childhood cognitive development* (pp. 445–469). Malden, MA: Blackwell Publishers.

Zelazo, P. D., Mueller, U., Frye, D., & Marcovitch, S. (2003). The development of executive function. *Monographs of the Society for Research in Child Development, 68*(3), 11–27.

Zoelch, C., Jung, S., & Schumann-Hengsteler, R. (2000, December). *Central executive interference in a spatial working memory task.* Poster presented at the International Conference on Spatial Cognition Scientific Research and Applications, Rome, Italy.

Chapter 4

Hot and Cool Aspects
of Executive Function:
Relations in Early Development

Philip D. Zelazo
Li Qu
University of Toronto

Ulrich Müller
University of Victoria

Although executive function (EF) can be understood as a domain-general functional construct, a distinction may be made between the relatively hot affective aspects of EF associated with ventral and medial regions of prefrontal cortex (VM-PFC), including the anterior cingulate cortex (ACC) and the more purely cognitive, cool aspects associated with dorsolateral prefrontal cortex (DL-PFC; Zelazo & Müller, 2002; cf. Metcalfe & Mischel, 1999; Miller & Cohen, 2001). Whereas cool EF is more likely to be elicited by relatively abstract, decontextualized problems, hot EF is required for problems that involve the regulation of affect and motivation (i.e., regulation of basic limbic system functions), including problems in the content domain of self and social understanding. In this chapter, we address the relation between hot and cool EF in the context of research on theory of mind (ToM) and EF. The relation between ToM and EF is now well established, although the nature of the relation remains a matter of debate. We argue that ToM is one manifestation of EF, mainly hot EF, as expressed in a particular content domain.

When adequately defined, the conceptual relation between ToM and hot EF becomes clearer. We first examine the definitions of these constructs and then review research establishing a functional relation between ToM and cool EF. Finally, we briefly consider empirical evidence that hot and cool EF are closely related in typical development.

DEFINITIONS OF EXECUTIVE FUNCTION AND THEORY OF MIND

Executive Function

Although EF is not synonymous with prefrontal cortical function, the construct of EF was originally derived from analysis of the consequences of damage to prefrontal cortex. Early studies of patients with prefrontal damage revealed a peculiar pattern of impairments despite preservation of basic cognitive functions, including many aspects of language, memory, and intelligence (e.g., Luria, 1973). The impairments, which have a kind of family resemblance, include (but are not limited to) failures to make wise judgments, poor planning of future actions, and difficulty inhibiting inappropriate responses (e.g., Stuss & Benson, 1986; Tranel, Anderson, & Benton, 1994; Wise, Murray, & Gerfen, 1996). The construct of EF is intended to capture the psychological abilities whose impairment is presumed to underlie these manifest deficits: the ability to make wise judgments, the ability to plan, the ability to inhibit inappropriate responses, and so on.

Different researchers have emphasized different aspects of EF, such as working memory (e.g., Baddeley, 1996), inhibition (e.g., Diamond, 1996), and aspects of attention (Posner & Rothbart, 1998; Stuss, Floden, Alexander, Levine, & Katz, 2001; Stuss et al., 1999), among others. These proposals single out important components of EF but generally fail to capture the full range of phenomena relevant to EF. In contrast, Luria's (e.g., 1973) approach to neurological systems suggests a way to capture the diversity of the processes associated with EF without simply listing them and without hypostasizing homuncular abilities. For Luria, prefrontal cortex and other neurological systems consist of interactive functional systems that involve the integration of subsystems. Subsystems have specific roles to play but cannot be considered outside of the larger systems of which they are a part. Zelazo, Carter, Reznick, and Frye (1997) took seriously Luria's suggestion that EF is a function and not a mechanism or cognitive structure, and they attempted to characterize that function. Functions are essentially behavioral constructs defined in terms of their outcome—what they accomplish. To a large extent, the task of characterizing a complex function such as EF is a matter of describing its hierarchical structure, characterizing its subfunctions, and organizing these subfunctions around their constant common outcome. In the case of EF, the outcome is deliberate problem solving, and functionally distinct phases of problem solving can be organized around the constant outcome of solving a problem. Figure 4.1 presents a familiar looking flow chart and illustrates how different aspects of EF contribute to the eventual outcome.

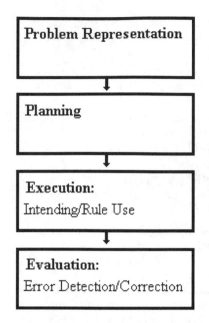

FIG. 4.1. A problem-solving framework for understanding temporally and functionally distinct phases of executive function, considered as a functional construct. From "Early Development of Executive Function: A Problem Solving Approach," by P. D. Zelazo, A. S. Carter, J. S. Reznick, & D. Frye, 1997. *Review of General Psychology, 1*. Copyright 1997 by American Psychological Association. Reprinted with permission.

For example, consider the Wisconsin Card Sorting Test (WCST; Grant & Berg, 1948), which is widely regarded as "the prototypical EF task in neuropsychology" (Pennington & Ozonoff, 1996, p. 55). The WCST taps numerous aspects of EF, and, as a result, the origin of errors on this task is difficult to determine (e.g., see Delis, Squire, Bihrle, & Massman, 1992). To perform correctly on the WCST, one must first construct a representation of the problem space, which includes identifying the relevant dimensions. Then, one must choose a promising plan—for example, sorting according to shape. After selecting a plan, one must keep the plan in mind long enough for it to guide one's thought or action and actually carry out the prescribed behavior. Keeping a plan in mind to control behavior is referred to as intending; translating a plan into action is rule use. Finally, after acting, one must evaluate one's behavior, which includes both error detection and error correction.

Inflexibility can occur at each problem-solving phase, so there are several possible explanations of poor performance on the WCST—and on global EF tasks more generally. For example, perseveration could occur after a rule change in the WCST either because a new plan was not formed or because the plan was formed but not carried out. As a descriptive framework, the delineation of problem-solving phases does not explain EF, but it does allow us to ask more precisely when in the process of problem solving performance breaks down. In addition, the framework accomplishes the following:

1. It clarifies the way in which diverse aspects of EF work together to fulfill the higher order function of problem solving.

2. It avoids conceptualizing EF as a homuncular ability (e.g., as a central executive [Baddeley, 1996] or a supervisory attentional system [Shallice, 1988]).
3. It suggests relatively well-defined measures of EF (e.g., measures of rule use for which problem representation, planning, and evaluation are not required).
4. It allows us to capture key aspects of EF, including goal selection, conceptual fluency, and planning in novel situations (e.g., Tranel et al., 1994), that occur even in situations that do not demand resistance to interference.
5. It permits the formulation of specific hypotheses regarding the role of more basic cognitive processes (e.g., procedural memory, priming, suppression of attention) in different aspects of EF.

Although EF can be understood as a domain-general functional construct, a distinction may be made between the relatively hot affective aspects of EF associated with VM-PFC, including ACC, and the more purely cognitive, cool aspects associated with DL-PFC (Zelazo & Müller, 2002; cf. Metcalfe & Mischel, 1999; Miller & Cohen, 2001). Whereas cool EF is more likely to be elicited by relatively abstract, decontextualized problems (e.g., sorting by color, number, or shape on the WCST; Grant & Berg, 1948), hot EF is required for problems that involve the regulation of affect and motivation (i.e., the regulation of basic limbic system functions). Hot EF, as opposed to cool EF, is invoked when people care about the problems they are attempting to solve.

This characterization of hot EF in contradistinction to cool EF is consistent with several recent proposals regarding the function of VM-PFC. For example, based on single-cell recordings of neurons in orbitofrontal cortex (OFC) together with neuroimaging data and evidence that VM-PFC damage impairs performance on simple tests of object reversal and extinction, Rolls (e.g., 1999, 2000, 2004) suggests that VM-PFC, and OFC in particular, is required for the flexible representation of the reinforcement value of stimuli. A rather different theory has been proposed by Damasio (e.g., 1994; see also Bechara, 2004). According to this theory, the somatic marker theory, VM-PFC is required for processing learned associations between affective reactions and specific scenarios, and this processing plays a crucial but often overlooked role in decision making. Despite their differences, however, both approaches capture the important fact that the control of thought and action depends on different cortical systems, depending on whether or not it occurs in motivationally significant contexts.

Traditionally, research on EF in human beings has focused almost exclusively on cool EF, using measures such as the WCST and the Tower of London (Shallice, 1988). Recently, however, there has been growing interest in hot EF as well—in particular in what might be called affective decision making or decision making about events that have emotionally significant consequences (i.e., meaningful rewards, losses). To study affective decision making, researchers have developed a number of useful measures, including measures of gambling (e.g., Bechara, 2004), risky decision making (e.g., Rogers, Everitt, et al., 1999; Rogers, Owen, et al., 1999), and guessing with feedback (e.g., Elliot, Frith, & Dolan, 1997; for comparisons among measures, see Manes et al., 2002; Monterosso, Ehrman, Napier, O'Brien, & Childress, 2001).

One widely used measure of hot EF is the Iowa Gambling Task. Like many measures of EF, this task requires cognitive flexibility, reversal of responding, and responding on the basis of relatively abstract, future-oriented information despite the presence of a more immediate, salient alternative. However, what makes this task a measure of hot EF, as opposed to cool EF, is that these functions are assessed in the context of meaningful rewards and losses.

In an initial study using the Iowa Gambling Task (Bechara, Tranel, Damasio, & Anderson, 1994), VM–PFC patients and healthy control participants were presented with four decks of cards that, when turned, revealed a combination of gains and losses (measured in play money). Participants were given a stake of $2,000 and asked to win as much money as possible by choosing cards from any of the four decks (one card per trial). They were not told how many trials there would be (100), but they were told that some of the decks were better than the others. In fact, the task was designed so that choosing consistently from two of the decks (the advantageous decks) would result in a net gain, whereas choosing consistently from the other two (the disadvantageous decks) would result in a net loss. Each card from the disadvantageous decks provided a higher reward than each card from the advantageous decks ($100 vs. $50), but the variable (and unpredictable) losses associated with cards from disadvantageous decks were much larger on average than the losses associated with the advantageous decks. Notice that the task is structured so that information about the gains associated with each deck is presented before information about losses, both across trials and within trials. Therefore, participants will initially represent the disadvantageous decks as more reinforcing than the advantageous decks, but eventually they must reverse these representations and use them to control their behavior despite the allure of the disadvantageous decks.

Bechara et al. (1994) found that both patients and controls indeed preferred the disadvantageous cards at the outset. Over trials, however, controls were increasingly likely to select from the advantageous decks, whereas patients were not. Subsequent studies (e.g., Bechara, Damasio, Tranel, & Damasio, 1997) confirmed and extended these findings, and similar impairments on the Iowa Gambling Task have been documented in pathological gamblers (Cavedini, Riboldi, Keller, D'Annucci, & Bellodi, 2002) and individuals abusing cocaine (Monterosso et al., 2001), heroin (Petry, Bickel, & Arnett, 1998), alcohol (Mazas, Finn, & Steinmetz, 2000), and a combination of drugs (Bechara et al., 2001; Grant, Contoreggi, & London, 2000).

Bechara and colleagues noted that their patients appeared to lack concern for future consequences, even though their intellectual abilities were largely preserved (Bechara et al., 1994). Concern for future consequences is a general feature of EF (i.e., qua goal-directed problem solving), but in the Iowa Gambling Task, these consequences are concrete and meaningful—healthy participants care about what they are doing. One general class of problems that is likely to invoke hot EF as opposed to cool EF is the class of social problems, including predicting other people's emotions and behavior and deciding how best to respond. For example, patients with VM-PFC damage exhibit impairments in recognizing facial expressions, and they often fail to attribute fear, anger, and embarrassment to story protagonists (e.g., Blair & Cipoloth, 2000; Damasio, Tranel, & Damasio, 1990; Keane, Calder, Hodges, & Young, 2002; Russell, Bachorowski, & Fernadandez-Dols, 2003).

Social situations are almost always motivationally significant because other people's behavior often has emotional consequences for us, if not direct consequences for our physical well-being. For this reason, it is not surprising that many case studies of VM-PFC damage are marked by disturbances of interpersonal behavior. Phineas Gage, for example, was a responsible and affable fellow before an iron tamping rod was blown through the ventromedial regions of his PFC in a work-related accident (Harlow, 1848, 1868; see Damasio, Grabowski, Frank, Galaburda, & Damasio, 1994). After the accident, however, he became irresponsible and abrasive, despite preserved general cognitive and motor skill. Contemporary VM-PFC patients, such as EVR, resemble Gage in manifesting a behavioral profile that has been referred to as acquired sociopathy (e.g., Saver & Damasio, 1991). Although not necessarily violent, these patients are often grossly insensitive to the consequences of their behavior—both for themselves and for others. For example, they may make disastrous financial decisions and have severe difficulty maintaining personal relationships (e.g., Dimitrov, Phipps, Zahn, & Grafman, 1999; Rolls, Hornak, Wade, & McGrath, 1994).

Unlike adults with VM-PFC damage, who may be able to rely on rules of conduct worked out prior to their injuries, children with VM-PFC damage often display significant impairments in moral reasoning and simple perspective taking, and they often have histories of violence and criminal activity. This suggests that VM-PFC may play an especially crucial role in social, emotional, and moral development (Anderson, Bechara, Damasio, Tranel, & Damasio, 1999). For example, Price, Daffner, Stowe, and Mesulam (1990) described patient G. K., who sustained bilateral damage to VM-PFC during his first 7 days of life and was identified by age 8 years as having serious behavioral problems. In addition to chronic impulsive and reckless behavior, G. K. displayed a stunning lack of regard for other people's perspectives. For example, Price et al. (1990) write, "When restricted for inappropriate behavior by a ward attendant, he escaped from the locked psychiatric unit, scratched the attendant's card with broken glass, signed his own name, and reentered the ward. When confronted, he denied his involvement" (p. 1384).

Examples of affective problems include many social situations, but the social versus nonsocial distinction fails to capture the difference between hot and cool EF. For one, even abstract problems such as the WCST are often administered by another person, whereas canonical measures of hot EF, such as object reversal (Rolls et al., 1994) or gambling (Bechara et al., 1994), need not be. Indeed, the inadequacy of the social versus nonsocial distinction can be seen even in Damasio's (1994) attempt to defend it:

> Thus the bioregulatory and social domain seem to have an affinity for the systems in the ventromedial sector, while systems in the dorsolateral region appear to align themselves with domains which subsume knowledge of the external world (entities such as objects and people, their actions in space-time; language; mathematics, music). (p. 183)

But of course, people and their actions in space-time are clearly social.

In contrast, the distinction between two types of problem solving that put differential demands on the regulation of affect and motivation makes considerable sense from a neuroanatomical point of view, and it is supported by task analyses. First, VM-PFC has close connections with the limbic system, whereas these connections are less direct in the case of DL-PFC (indeed, they are partly mediated by VM-PFC). Second, measures of VM-PFC, such as extinction, object reversal, and gambling, are not (necessarily) social, but they do require revising one's appraisal of the affective significance of stimuli. In all cases, one must learn to avoid or ignore something that previously elicited (appetitive) approach.

When thinking about the development of hot and cool EF, it is important to keep in mind that measures of these functions need to be arranged according to developmental level. An important determinant of developmental level is task complexity, or, more appropriately, the complexity of the cognitive processes that a task requires. The importance of complexity has long been recognized in the developmental literature (e.g., Inhelder & Piaget, 1964), and it is also starting to be appreciated in the neuroscience literature (Dias, Robbins, & Roberts, 1996; Stuss et al., 1999; Waltz et al., 1999; Wise et al., 1996). One influential complexity theory has been proposed by Halford and colleagues. Halford, Wilson, and Phillips (1998) suggest that as children develop they are able to understand increasingly complex relations among objects. Halford et al. define complexity in terms of the number of relations that can be processed in parallel. According to these authors, each argument of a relation, such as "X" in the relation "X is greater than Y," represents a source of variation, or a dimension. Processing a single relation (i.e., a unary relation) is less complex than a binary relation, which is less complex than processing a ternary relation, and so on.

The cognitive complexity and control theory (CCC) theory (e.g., Frye, Zelazo, & Burack, 1998; Zelazo & Frye, 1998) also emphasizes the importance of complexity, and this theory is specifically intended to be a theory of EF and its development. This approach defines complexity in terms

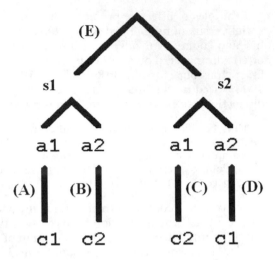

FIG. 4.2. Hierarchical tree structure depicting formal relations among rules. s_1 and s_2 = setting conditions; a_1 and a_2 = antecedent conditions; c_1 and c_2 = consequences. From "Theory of Mind and Rule-Based Reasoning," by D. Frye, P. D. Zelazo, and T. Palfai, 1995. *Cognitive Development, 10,* p. 486. Copyright 1995 by Elsevier. Reprinted with permission.

of the hierarchical structure of children's rule systems, rather than the number of relations that can be processed in parallel. According to this theory, age-related changes in EF—considered as a functional construct— are due to age-related changes in the maximum complexity of the rules that children can formulate and use when solving problems. These age-related changes in maximum rule complexity are, in turn, made possible by age-related increases in the degree to which children can reflect on the rules they represent.

On this account, rules are formulated in an ad hoc fashion in potentially silent self-directed speech. These rules link antecedent conditions to consequences, as when we tell ourselves, "If I see a mailbox, then I need to mail this letter." When children reflect on the rules they represent, they are able to consider them in contradistinction to other rules and embed them under higher order rules, in the same way that we might say, "If it's before 5 p.m., then if I see a mailbox, then I need to mail this letter, otherwise, I'll have to go directly to the post office." In this example, a simple conditional statement regarding the mailbox is made dependent on the satisfaction of yet another condition (namely, the time).

The tree diagram in Fig. 4.2 illustrates the way in which hierarchies of rules can be formed—the way in which one rule can be embedded under another higher order rule and controlled by it. Rule A, which indicates that Consequent 1 (c_1) should follow Antecedent 1 (a_1), is incompatible with rule C, which connects a_1 to c_2. Rule A is embedded under, and controlled by, a higher order rule (rule E) that can be used to select rules A and B, as opposed to rules C and D. This higher order rule makes reference to setting conditions (s_1 and s_2) that condition the selection of lower order rules. Notice that to formulate higher order rules and deliberate between rules C and D, on the one hand, and rules A and B on the other, children need to be aware that they know both pairs of lower order rules. Thus, increases in reflection on lower order rules are logically required for increases in embedding to occur. However, it is the increases in embedding that provide the metric for measuring the degree of complexity of the entire rule system that needs to be kept in mind (i.e., in working memory) to perform particular tasks. That is, complexity is measured as the number of degrees of embedding in the rule systems that children formulate when solving a particular problem. More complex rule systems permit the more flexible selection of certain rules for acting when multiple conflicting rules are possible. This allows for flexible responding, as opposed to perseveration; it allows for cognitive control, as opposed to stimulus control.

According to CCC theory, there are several age-related changes in EF that occur during childhood, and for each developmental transition a general process is recapitulated. Specifically, a rule system at a particular level of complexity is acquired, and this rule system permits children to exercise a new degree of control over their reasoning and their behavior. However, the use of this rule system is subject to limitations that cannot be overcome until yet another level of complexity is achieved. In particular, the rule system cannot be selected when there is a salient, conflicting rule system. Consequently, according to the CCC theory, abulic dissociations—dissociations between having knowledge and actually using that knowledge—occur until incompatible pieces of knowledge are integrated into a single, more complex rule system via their subordination to a new higher order rule.

On this account, reflection and higher order rule use are the primary psychological functions accomplished by systems involving prefrontal cortex, but different regions of prefrontal cortex are associated with reflection on different kinds of rules or rules in different contexts (i.e., abstract vs. motivationally significant). That is, the CCC theory applies both to cool EF and to hot EF and suggests that complexity is an important dimension of the development of EF in both cool, cognitive contexts and hot, emotional contexts. For example, from this perspective, a task such as object reversal is a relatively simple measure of hot EF, whereas the Iowa Gambling Task is relatively complex. Similarly, delayed response is a relatively simple measure of cool EF, whereas the WCST is relatively complex. This account predicts that performance on measures of hot and cool EF at the same level of complexity should be related because complexity is an important determinant of difficulty in both cases and because hot and cool EF both rely on common underlying mechanisms of reflection and the formulation and use of verbal rules.

The importance of considering complexity when attempting to understand EF is reflected in the measures that elicit characteristic failures of EF (e.g., perseveration, knowledge–action dissociations) in children at different ages (as shown in Table 4.1). Developmental research indicates not only that failures of EF occur in different contexts at different ages but also that these contexts can be ordered in terms of complexity. For example, one of the most widely studied examples of infant perseveration is the

TABLE 4.1
Tasks Revealing Characteristic Failures of EF (e.g., Perseveration)
at Different Ages

Age	Tasks
~9 months	A-not-B, delayed response, object retrieval
~2 years	Invisible displacement, mazes, multistep/multilocation search
~2.5 years	Scale models, forced-choice deductive card sort, object naming
~3 years	DCCS, Luria's hand game and tapping, Children's Gambling Task, moral reasoning, delayed self-recognition
~4 years	Flexible Item Selection Task (FIST)
~6–12 years	WCST, Stroop Color-Word

A-not-B error. As originally described by Piaget (1954), the A-not-B error occurs when infants (typically between the ages of about 8 and 10 months of age) successfully retrieve an object at one location (location A) and are then allowed to search for it when it is conspicuously hidden at another location (location B). Remarkably, infants at this age often search at the first location despite having last seen the object at location B. The basic finding has proven to be robust (for a recent meta-analysis, see Marcovitch & Zelazo, 1999). Whereas Piaget attributed the error to an immature understanding of the object concept, contemporary researchers are more likely to argue that infants have difficulty using a representation of an object's location to override a prepotent response (e.g., Diamond, 1996)—that is, that infants exhibit a failure of EF.

Older children are unlikely to err on a simple A-not-B task, but they do exhibit failures of EF on more complex measures. For example, DeLoache (1987) observed changes between 2.5 and 3 years of age in children's ability to use a three-dimensional model of a room to guide the search for an object hidden in the room. In particular, DeLoache (see DeLoache, Pierroutsakos, & Troseth, 1996, for review; see also O'Sullivan, Mitchell, & Daehler, 2001) observed that 2.5-year-olds often committed perseverative errors, searching for the object at the location where it had been found on a previous trial. Three-year-olds, in contrast, searched successfully. DeLoache suggested that the age-related changes observed in this task reflect an increase in representational flexibility: 2.5-year-olds persist in thinking of the model as a three-dimensional object (e.g., a toy room) rather than thinking of it in terms of the thing it represents (viz., the room).

There is also a large body of research indicating that 3-year-olds have difficulty switching between incompatible perspectives on a single object—they perseverate in representing objects in a particular way even when it is no longer appropriate to do so. In tasks assessing understanding of appearance and reality, for example, children are shown a misleading object such as a sponge painted to look like a rock and asked about its appearance ("What does it look like?") and its true nature or function ("What is it really?"). Three-year-olds are much more likely than 5-year-olds to give the same answer to both questions (Flavell, Green, & Flavell, 1986).

Further evidence of representational inflexibility in 3-year-olds has been obtained in research on numerous topics, including reasoning about physical causality (e.g., Frye, Zelazo, Brooks, & Samuels, 1996), moral reasoning (e.g., Zelazo, Helwig, & Lau, 1996), reasoning about delayed representations (e.g., Povinelli, Landau, & Perilloux, 1996; Zelazo, Sommerville, & Nichols, 1999), generation of multiple labels for a single object (e.g., Doherty & Perner, 1998; Markman, 1989; but see Deák & Maratsos, 1998), and affective decision making as measured by a child analogue of the Iowa Gambling Task called the Children's Gambling Task (Kerr & Zelazo, 2004). In each case, younger preschoolers seem to have difficulty switching between conflicting representations; they tend to perseverate on a salient representation, and there are age-related increases in EF between about 3 and 5 years of age.

Whereas most of these measures would be considered measures of cool EF, some, such as moral reasoning and the Children's Gambling Task, would be considered measures of hot EF. As can perhaps be seen from the table, measures of hot and cool EF of comparable complexity are generally passed by children at the same age. It should be kept in mind, however, that like VM-PFC and DL-PFC, hot and cool EF are parts of a single coordinated system, and in the normal case they work together—even in a single situation. Thus, as Damasio (e.g., 1994) suggests, decision making is normally biased in an adaptive fashion by physiological reactions that predict rewards and punishments; hot EF is working in the service of cool EF. Conversely, it seems likely that a successful approach to solving some affective problems is to reconceptualize the problem in relatively neutral, decontextualized terms and try to solve it using cool EF. For these reasons, it is probably impossible to design a task that is a pure measure of hot or cool EF (although it is clearly possible to design tasks that emphasize one or the other). For example, the Iowa Gambling Task may be a relatively good measure of hot EF, but research indicates a role for working memory functions usually associated with DL-PFC (Hinson, Jameson, & Whitney, 2002; Manes et al., 2002).

Theory of Mind

Theory of mind is often used as an umbrella term to refer to understanding human action in terms of mental states, such as intentions, desires, beliefs, and so on (see Wellman, Cross, & Waston, 2001, for a meta-analysis). Many or most studies of ToM have focused on 3- to 5-year-olds, given that there are important changes in performance on classic measures of ToM such as the false belief task (Wimmer & Perner, 1983). In this task, children are told a story in which a person hides a desired object at location A. Without the person's knowledge, the object is transferred to location B, and children are asked to predict where the person will search for the object. To understand that the person will falsely believe that the object is still in location A, children must understand that the situation can be seen from two separate perspectives—the child's and the person's—and that those perspectives produce incompatible judgments. Three-year-olds typically fail to consider the difference in perspective, whereas older children switch judgments flexibly in line with whichever perspective is being asked about.

Although many studies of ToM have focused on 3- to 5-year-olds, the development of ToM is continuous, beginning in late infancy (Moore, 1996) and extending into adulthood. Indeed, although most healthy adults may routinely assume that other people have some mental states, it is a common experience for adults to fail to appreciate that others may have mental states that differ from their own. For example, authoritarian parents may assume their children's plans for the future resemble their own. Thus, like EF, it is necessary to consider ToM as a developmental phenomenon unfolding on a spectrum of complexity, rather than as an all-or-none phenomenon.

Indeed, rather than something that one does or does not have, the formulation and use of inferences regarding mental states is a dynamic and integrative process that involves not only the formulation of rules for making inferences but also the maintenance of inferences in working memory, the strategic activation or inhibition of attention, and, ultimately, the motivation to consider perspectives other than one's own. At least four steps are involved in successfully inferring another person's mental states and using that inference to predict their behavior (cf. Flavell, Miller, & Miller, 2002). First, one must appreciate that one may have a different perspective from someone else in a particular situation. Second, one needs to formulate a hierarchy of inferences for determining the other person's mental states vis-à-vis one's own. Third, one has to keep track of changes in the environment and in the other person's behavior so as to make appropriate adjustments to one's ideas about the person's mental states. Fourth, one has to deduce likely behavior based on inferred mental states. In everyday situations, this dynamic process must occur rapidly, and it is likely to be very resource demanding. In contrast, many laboratory tests of ToM are well-defined and relatively easy, which may be in part why people with Asperger's syndrome sometimes appear to function normally when tested in the laboratory and exhibit deficits in social problem solving outside of the lab (Clark, Prior, & Kinsella, 2002). People may also approach simple laboratory measures of ToM using alternative strategies—for example, without focusing on the others' emotional states or feelings. A person can predict others' strategies and activities on the first- and second-order false-belief tasks, for example, through logical reasoning and game theory (Colman, 2003; Zhang & Hedden, 2003), even if these approaches are unlikely to be adopted in everyday situations. Indeed, Bowler (1992) found that people with Asperger's syndrome can pass second-order ToM tasks, but they typically did not use mental state terms to explain their answers. Bowler hypothesized that people with Asperger's syndrome can solve problems through cognitive reasoning, which is relatively slow compared to normal people's fast affective responses. Because the social environment and interpersonal communication require rapid information exchange and response, the slow strategy used by people with Asperger's syndrome may cause them to appear odd and cumbersome.

THE RELATION BETWEEN THEORY OF MIND AND EXECUTIVE FUNCTION

The link between ToM and EF was perhaps first noted in the context of research on individuals with autism. For example, Russell, Mauthner, Sharpe, and Tidswell (1991) tested healthy 3- to 4-year-olds and children with autism on a measure of strategic deception called the windows task. In this task, the child is presented with two boxes that have transparent windows on them. The windows face the child and reveal the contents of the boxes. On each trial, one of the boxes is baited, and the child is instructed to tell the experimenter (who cannot see the content of the boxes) where to look. The experimenter searches where instructed, and the child receives the contents of the other box. Thus, this was a zero-sum competitive game in which the successful strategy was to deceive the experimenter by pointing to the incorrect, unbaited box. Despite repeated failures to receive the rewards, 3-year-olds and children with autism (unlike 4-year-olds) continued to point to the baited box. In a striking display of extensive perseveration, many of these children perseverated for the full 20 trials (but see also Samuels, Brooks, & Frye, 1996).

Later studies (e.g., Russell, Jarrold, & Potel, 1994) demonstrated that difficulties in this task are EF difficulties rather than difficulties in deception per se. The social aspect of deception can be separated from the EF requirements by removing the opponent from the task. Children were merely required to point to a visibly empty box rather than a baited one, whereupon they were given the concealed prize. Russell et al. (1994) found that 3-year-olds still perseverated extensively even in this version (see also Hughes & Russell, 1993; Russell, Hala, & Hill, 2003).

At around the same time, Ozonoff, Pennington, and Rogers (1991) examined high-functioning children with autism, believing that, although ToM and EF are not related functionally, both are dependent on prefrontal cortex, which develops abnormally in people with autism. These authors found that these children were impaired both on measures of ToM (e.g., a mental-physical distinction task, a false belief task, and a second-order belief attribution task) and on tasks assessing EF (e.g., Tower of Hanoi and WCST).

EF has also been studied in relation to ToM in typically developing children. For example, Frye, Zelazo, and Palfai (1995) found that children's performance on ToM tasks was correlated with their ability to make inferences using embedded if-if-then rules, as assessed by the Dimensional Change Card Sorting (DCCS) task. In the DCCS, children are presented with colored shapes that would be sorted differently if one were sorting by color or by shape. Children are first required to sort the cards by one dimension (e.g., color), and then the other (e.g., shape). Subsequent research using a wide variety of measures of EF, such as the day/night Stroop and the bear/dragon task (e.g., Carlson & Moses, 2001; Carlson, Moses, & Breton, 2002; Carlson, Moses, & Hix, 1998; Cole & Mitchell, 2000; Davis & Pratt, 1995; Gordon & Olson, 1998; Hala, Hug, & Henderson, 2003; Hala & Russell, 2001; Hughes, 1998a, 1998b; Keenan, Olson, & Marini, 1998; Lang & Perner, 2002; Perner, Lang, & Kloo, 2002) has confirmed that EF is related to performance on measures of ToM, and a meta-analysis has found the relation to be strong ($d = 1.06$; Perner & Lang, 1999).

In an extensive series of studies, Carlson and Moses (2001) found that performance on some measures of EF—those that involve conflict between two perspectives on a situation, such as the DCCS—were better predictors of ToM than performance on delay tasks, such as the gift delay task, in which children are required not to peek while the experimenter noisily wraps a gift. The relation between EF and ToM remained substantial even when age, sex, IQ, and other variables were controlled. In a subsequent study, these authors examined the relative contributions of working memory and performance on conflict EF tasks to the prediction of ToM performance. Although significantly correlated with performance on ToM tasks, working memory was no longer related when age, IQ, and gender were controlled. By contrast, performance on the conflict EF tasks remained significant. These authors also showed that conflict tasks were just as strongly related to measures of ToM that lacked a salient prepotent response alternative but still required embedded hierarchical reasoning (e.g., understanding sources of knowledge, judging mental state uncertainty; see Moore, Pure, & Furrow, 1990).

In addition to behavioral evidence about the close developmental relation between ToM and EF, there is neurophysiological evidence from imaging and lesion studies that ToM tasks rely on the same regions of the prefrontal cortex (PFC) as EF—particularly hot EF (Frith & Frith, 2000; Siegal & Varley, 2002, for reviews). For example, imaging studies have shown that ToM reasoning involves activation of medial PFC, especially the paracingulate gyrus and the ACC (Brodmann areas 8 and 9, and the ACC; Calder et al., 2002; Castelli, Frith, Happé, & Frith, 2002; Fletcher et al., 1995; Gallagher et al., 2000; Goel, Grafman, Sadato, & Hallett, 1995; Vogeley et al., 2001)—regions that are also activated in EF tasks that require conditional responding (Petrides, 1995). Interestingly, adults with Asperger's syndrome show activation not in Brodmann area 8 but in Brodmann areas 9 and 10 when comprehending stories that involve mental states, suggesting that patients with Asperger's syndrome reason about mental states in a different manner than controls (Happé & Frith, 1996). A study using high-density ERP found that left PFC is involved in ToM tasks but not in understanding false photos (Sabbagh & Taylor, 2000). Imaging studies have also highlighted the importance of right VM-PFC in understanding mental state terms (Baron-Cohen et al., 1994; Brownell, Griffin, Winner, Friedman, & Happé, 2000). Finally, a study that compared patients with either damage to VM-PFC or DL-PFC with controls, found that both types of patient were similarly unimpaired on less complex theory of mind tasks (first- and second-order) but that VM-PFC patients but not DL-PFC failed more complex ToM tasks that required understanding of more complex social situations (the faux pas task; Stone, Baron-Cohen, & Knight, 1998).

At present, the nature of the relation between EF and ToM remains a matter of debate. One approach, by Perner and his colleagues (Perner, Stummer, & Lang, 1999), focuses on changes occurring around 4 years of age. According to Perner et al. (1999), ToM is an integral part of EF, required for the inhibition of incorrect action schemas, as assessed by measures of EF. On this analysis, an important change in children's ToM occurs with the emergence of metarepresentation (Perner, 1991). Metarep- resentation refers to the explicit understanding that a representation rep- resents a situation (referent) as being in a certain way (sense). Four-year- olds' metarepresentational understanding that "mental states are based on representations . . . that have causal force and make people do things" (Perner & Lang, 2000, p. 153) makes possible the inhibition of incorrect action tendencies that are activated by salient stimuli: "Inhibitory control is not achieved until the causal/representational nature of mental states is understood" (Perner et al., 1999, p. 145). In other words, the main problem faced by children younger than 4 years of age is the failure to understand representational relations.

Perner et al.'s (1999) proposal regarding the relation between ToM and EF contrasts with the suggestion that ToM is simply one class of prob- lems for which EF is required. In keeping with CCC theory (Frye et al., 1998; Zelazo & Frye, 1998), the approach presented here sees both ToM and EF as life span developmental phenomena (e.g., Phillips, MacLean, & Allen, 2002; Saltzman, Strauss, Hunter, & Archibald, 2000; Zelazo, Craik, & Booth, 2004). According to CCC theory, the critical requirement for 4- year-olds' ToM is taken to be the emergence of the ability to formulate and use a higher order rule that allows them to reason as follows: "If you're asking me, then the answer is that the candy is in location B, but if you're asking about Maxi, then the answer is that the candy is in loca- tion A." Similarly, as discussed by Zelazo and Sommerville (2001), chil- dren must consider temporal perspectives as such (i.e., as distinct from objective time: before vs. later) when they are asked to reason about their own past false beliefs. For example, 3-year-olds typically fail Gopnik and Astington's (1988) representational change task, where they must appre- ciate that they have changed from thinking Smarties candy to thinking sticks, even when the contents of the box did not change. According to CCC theory, they fail this task because the task requires them to differ- entiate between the history of the self (one category of variation) and the history of the world (another category of variation). Instead, children assimilate the subjective series to the objective series and reason within a single dimension. Notice that when similar tasks only require reason- ing within a single dimension, 3-year-olds perform well. For example, in a control task used by Gopnik and Astington (1988, Exp. 1), most 3-year-olds were able to judge that *now* there is a doll in a closed toy house but *before* there was an apple.

Although ToM reasoning at any age requires the maintainance and manipulation of specific concepts pertaining to mental states and their implications for human behavior, the acquisition of certain mental concepts (e.g., belief) may well require a certain level of EF development (e.g., see Moses, Carlson, & Sabbagh, this volume). For example, to appreciate the concept of false belief, children must be able to adopt multiple perspectives. From this perspective, then, ToM is simply EF as manifested in a particular content domain, and it follows that levels of ToM development may be determined by levels of EF development in general. More specifically, however, the current proposal is that ToM is hot EF as expressed in the content domain of self and social understanding. Hot EF develops in parallel with cool EF, and both are parts of an interactive functional system.

There is relatively little research comparing the development of both cool and hot EF. However, in a preliminary study, Hongwanishkul, Happaney, Lee, and Zelazo (in press) administered two cool EF tasks, the DCCS and Self-Ordered Pointing (SOP; a measure of spatial working memory; Petrides & Milner, 1982), as well as two hot EF tasks, the Children's Gambling Task and a delay of gratification task based on Thompson, Barresi, and Moore (1997). The SOP and DCCS are considered measures of cool EF because they involve problem solving on the basis of relatively abstract information. The Children's Gambling Task, on the other hand, taps hot EF insofar as it requires flexible reappraisals of the emotional valence of particular stimuli. Delay of gratification also measures hot EF because it requires acting on the basis of future-oriented information despite initial tendencies to approach the immediate rewards.

Results indicated that all four tasks showed significant age-related improvements between the ages of 3 and 5 years. Moreover, performance on the SOP was related to performance on both the DCCS and the Children's Gambling Task. At the same time, however, only the cool EF tasks were strongly related to verbal mental age, performance mental age, and parent ratings of children's effortful control (based on the Children's Behavior Questionnaire [CBQ]; Rothbart, Ahadi, Hershey, & Fisher, 2001). These results therefore suggest both similarities and differences between hot and cool EF (or both unity and diversity; cf. Miyake, Friedman, Emerson, Witzki, & Howerter, 2000), as might be expected based on the functional characterization of EF presented here.

Another recent experiment in our laboratory was designed more specifically to compare performance on two measures of EF that were closely matched for complexity and differed only in that one type of task (the mentalistic tasks) required sorting according to a character's belief and the other (the nonmentalistic tasks) required sorting the same stimuli according to behavioral regularities. The nonmentalistic tasks were considered measures of cool EF, requiring cognitive flexibility and reversal of responding in the context of relatively arbitrary information. In contrast, the mentalistic tasks were considered measures of hot EF, and specifically measures of ToM, because they required cognitive flexibility and reversal of responding in the context of concrete, social information.

In the mentalistic tasks, 3- to 5-year-old children were introduced to a story character, such as a little red bear, and were told, "Little bears like to eat from little bowls because if they ate from big bowls they'd be too full. They don't like to eat from big bowls. No way!" Then another puppet was introduced and children were told, "This is Mother, and today it's Mother's turn to feed the bears. Mother knows that little bears like to eat from little bowls, not big bowls." Two bowls, a little blue bowl and a big red bowl, were displayed in front of the child throughout, and on each of five preswitch trials children were told "Look, here comes the little red bear. Mother knows that little bears like to eat from little bowls, not big bowls. Which bowl will Mother give to the little red bear?" Children were asked to point to the bowl that Mother would give to the little red bear.

After the five preswitch trials, a new puppet, Grandmother, was introduced along with the postswitch rules. Children were told, "Now it's Grandmother's turn to feed the bears. Grandmother lives far away, and she doesn't know that little bears like little bowls. She thinks that bears like bowls that match their color. So, she thinks that red bears eat from red bowls, not blue bowls." Five postswitch trials were administered exactly like the preswitch trials. The postswitch rules were repeated after every trial, and children were asked to point to the bowl that Mother would give to the little red bear.

The nonmentalistic condition differed from the mentalistic condition only in that the rules were presented as behavioral regularities rather than justified by reference to the puppet's knowledge or belief. Thus, for example, children were told, "In Mother's game, little bears get little bowls, not big bowls," during the preswitch trials. On the postswitch trials, children were told, "This is Grandmother, and now Grandmother is going to feed the bears. Grandmother's game is a little bit different than Mother's game. In Grandmother's game, bears get bowls that match their color. So, red bears get red bowls, not blue bowls."

Results showed that children performed similarly on mentalistic and nonmentalistic tasks, and that older children performed significantly better on both types of tasks than younger children. As far as we know, this experiment is the first to explore the relative difficulty of ToM and EF (or hot EF and cool EF) using tasks that are closely matched in task format.

CONCLUSION

Although it is clear that much more work is needed to elucidate the nature of the relation between ToM and EF, it seems reasonable to propose that ToM just is EF as manifested in the content domain of self and social understanding. On this account, it is not that ToM causes EF or that EF causes ToM. Rather, both ToM and EF are viewed as things one does, and they depend on common underlying cognitive mechanisms and neural systems. The development of these mechanisms, which include the formulation and use of increasingly complex rules, and these neural structures, which include interacting regions of prefrontal cortex, unfolds across a wide range of ages.

ACKNOWLEDGMENTS

The preparation of this chapter was supported in part by grants from NSERC of Canada and the Canada Research Chairs Program to Phil Zelazo. We thank Dr. Helena Hong Gao for providing helpful comments on an earlier draft of this manuscript. Please address correspondence to Philip David Zelazo, Department of Psychology, University of Toronto, Toronto, Ontario, Canada, M5S 3G3 (electronic mail: zelazo@psych.utoronto.ca).

REFERENCES

Anderson, S. W., Bechara, A., Damasio, H., Tranel, D., & Damasio, A. R. (1999). Impairment of social and moral behavior related to early damage in human prefrontal cortex. *Nature Neuroscience, 2*(11), 1032–1038.

Baddeley, A. (1996). Exploring the central executive [special issue]. *Quarterly Journal of Experimental Psychology: Human Experimental Psychology, 49,* 5–28.

Baron-Cohen, S., Ring, H., Moriarty, J., Schmitz, B., Costa, D., & Ell, P. (1994). Recognition of mental state terms: Clinical findings in children with autism and a functional neuroimaging study of normal adults. *British Journal of Psychiatry, 165,* 640–649.

Bechara, A. (2004). The role of emotion in decision-making: Evidence from neurological patients with orbitofrontal damage [special issue]. *Brain and Cognition, 55,* 30–40.

Bechara, A., Damasio, H., Tranel, D., & Damasio, A. (1997). Deciding advantageously before knowing the advantageous strategy. *Science, 275,* 1293–1295.

Bechara, A., Dolan, S., Denburg, N., Hindes, A., Anderson, S. W., & Nathan, P. E. (2001). Decision-making deficits, linked to a dysfunctional ventromedial prefrontal cortex, revealed in alcohol and stimulant abusers. *Neuropsychologia, 39,* 376–389.

Bechara, A., Tranel, D., Damasio, H., & Anderson, S. W. (1994). Insensitivity to future consequences following damage to human prefrontal cortex. *Cognition, 50,* 7–12.

Blair, R. J. R., & Cipoloth, L. (2000). Impaired social response reversal: A case of "acquired sociopathy." *Brain, 123,* 1122–1141.

Bowler, D. (1992). Theory of mind in Asperger's syndrome. *Journal of Child Psychology and Psychiatry, 33,* 877–893.

Brownell, H., Griffin, R., Winner, E., Friedman, O., & Happe, F. (2000). Cerebral lateralization and theory of mind. In S. Baron-Cohen, H. Tager-Flusberg, & D. J. Cohen (Eds.), *Understanding other minds: Perspectives from developmental cognitive neuroscience* (2nd ed., pp. 306–333). Oxford, UK: Oxford University Press.

Calder, A. J., Lawrence, A. D., Keane, J., Scott, S. K., Owen, A. M., Christoffels, I., & Young, A. W. (2002). Reading the mind from eye gaze. *Neuopsychologia, 40,* 1129–1138.

Carlson, S. M., & Moses, L. J. (2001). Individual differences in inhibitory control and theory of mind. *Child Development, 72,* 1032–1053.

Carlson, S. M., Moses, L. J., & Breton, C. (2002). How specific is the relation between executive function and theory of mind? Contributions of inhibitory control and working memory. *Infant and Child Development, 11,* 73–92.

Carlson, S. M., Moses, L. J., & Hix, H. R. (1998). The role of inhibitory processes in young children's difficulties with deception and false belief. *Child Development, 69,* 672–691.

Castelli, F., Frith, U., Happé, F., & Frith, C. (2002). Autism, Asperger syndrome and brain mechanisms for the attribution of mental states to animated shape. *Brain, 125,* 1839–1849.

Cavedini, P., Riboldi, G., Keller, R., D'Annucci, A., & Bellodi, L. (2002). Frontal lobe dysfunction in pathological gambling patients. *Biological Psychiatry, 51,* 334–341.

Clark, C., Prior, M., & Kinsella, G. (2002). The relationship between executive function abilities, adaptive behaviour, and academic achievement in children with externalising behaviour problems. *Journal of Child Psychology and Psychiatry and Allied Disciplines, 43,* 785–796.

Cole, K., & Mitchell, P. (2000). Siblings in the development of executive control and a theory of mind. *British Journal of Developmental Psychology, 18,* 279–295.

Colman, A. M. (2003). Depth of strategic reasoning in games. *Trends in Cognitive Sciences, 7,* 2–4.

Damasio, A. R. (1994). *Descartes' error.* New York: Putnam.

Damasio, H., Grabowski, T., Frank, R., Galaburda, A. M., & Damasio, A. R. (1994). The return of Phineas Gage: Clues about the brain from the skull of a famous patient. *Science, 264,* 1102–1105.

Damasio, A. R., Tranel, D., & Damasio, H. (1990). Individuals with sociopathic behaviour caused by frontal damage fail to respond autonomically to social stimuli. *Behavioural Brain Research, 41,* 81–94.

Davis, H. L., & Pratt, C. (1995). The development of children's theory of mind: The working memory explanation. *Australian Journal of Psychology, 47,* 25–31.

Deák, G. O., & Maratsos, M. (1998). On having complex representations of things: Preschoolers use multiple words for objects and people. *Developmental Psychology, 34,* 224–240.

Delis, D. C., Squire, L. R., Bihrle, A., & Massman, P. J. (1992). Componential analysis of problem-solving ability: Performance of patients with frontal lobe damage and amnesic patients on a new sorting test. *Neuropsychologia, 30,* 683–697.

DeLoache, J. S. (1987). Rapid change in the symbolic functioning of very young children. *Science, 238,* 1556–1557.

DeLoache, J. S., Pierroutsakos, S. L., & Troseth, G. L. (1996). The three R's of pictorial competence. *Annals of Child Development, 12,* 1–48.

Diamond, A. (1996). Evidence for the importance of dopamine for prefrontal cortex functions early in life. *Philosophical Transcripts of the Royal Society of London, 351*(1346), 1483–1493.

Dias, R., Robbins, T. W., & Roberts, A. C. (1996). Dissociation in prefrontal cortex of affective and attentional shifts. *Nature, 380,* 69–72.

Dimitrov, M., Phipps, M., Zahn, T. P., & Grafman, J. (1999). A thoroughly modern Gage. *Neurocase, 5,* 345–354.

Doherty, M., & Perner, J. (1998). Metalinguistic awareness and theory of mind: Just two words for the same thing? *Cognitive Development, 13,* 279–305.

Elliott, R., Frith, C. D., & Dolan, R. J. (1997). Differential neural response to positive and negative feedback in planning and guessing tasks. *Neuropsychologia, 35,* 1395–1404.

Flavell, J. H., Green, F. L., & Flavell, E. R. (1986). Development of knowledge about the appearance-reality distinction. *Monographs of the Society for Research in Child Development, 51*(1, Serial No. 212).

Flavell, J. H., Miller, P. H., & Miller, S. A. (2002). *Cognitive development* (4th ed.). Upper Saddle River, NJ: Prentice-Hall.

Fletcher, P. C., Happé, F., Frith, U., Baker, S. C., Dolan, R. J., Frackowiak, R. S. J., & Frith, C. D. (1995). Other minds in the brain: A functional imaging study of "theory of mind" in story comprehension. *Cognition, 57,* 109–128.

Frith, C., & Frith, U. (2000). The physiological basis of theory of mind: Functional imaging studies. In S. Baron-Cohen, H. Tager-Flusberg, & D. J. Cohen (Eds.), *Understanding other minds: Perspectives from developmental cognitive neuroscience* (2nd ed., pp. 334–356). Oxford, UK: Oxford University Press.

Frye, D., Zelazo, P. D., Brooks, P. J., & Samuels, M. C. (1996). Inference and action in early causal reasoning. *Developmental Psychology, 32*, 120–131.

Frye, D., Zelazo, P. D., & Burack, J. A. (1998). I. Cognitive complexity and control: Implications for theory of mind in typical and atypical development. *Current Directions in Psychological Science, 7*, 116–121.

Frye, D., Zelazo, P. D., & Palfai, T. (1995). Theory of mind and rule-based reasoning. *Cognitive Development, 10*, 483–527.

Gallagher, H. L., Happé, F., Brunswick, N., Fletcher, P. C., Frith, U., & Frith, C. D. (2000). Reading the mind in cartoons and stories: An fMRI study of "theory of mind" in verbal and nonverbal tasks. *Neuropsychologia, 38*, 11–21.

Goel, V., Grafman J., Sadato, N., & Hallett, M. (1995). Modeling other minds. *Neuroreport, 6*, 1741–1746.

Gopnik, A., & Astington, J. W. (1988). Children's understanding of representational change and its relation to the understanding of false belief and the appearance reality distinction. *Child Development, 59*, 26–37.

Gordon, A. C. L., & Olson, D. R. (1998). The relation between acquisition of a theory of mind and the capacity to hold in mind. *Journal of Experimental Child Psychology, 68*, 70–83.

Grant, D. A., & Berg, E. A. (1948). A behavioral analysis of degree of reinforcement and ease of shifting to new responses in a Weigl-type card-sorting problem. *Journal of Experimental Psychology, 38*, 404–411.

Grant, S., Contoreggi, C., & London, E. D. (2000). Drug abusers show impaired performance in a laboratory test of decision making. *Neuropsychologia, 38*, 1180–1187.

Hala, S., Hug, S., & Henderson, A. (2003). Executive function and false belief understanding: Two tasks are harder than one. *Journal of Cognition and Development, 4*, 275–298.

Hala, S., & Russell, J. (2001). Executive control within strategic deception: A window on early cognitive development? *Journal of Experimental Child Psychology, 80*, 112–141.

Halford, G., Wilson, W. H., & Phillips, S. (1998). Processing capacity defined by relational complexity: Implications for comparative, developmental, and cognitive psychology. *Behavioral and Brain Sciences, 21*, 803–864.

Happé, F., & Frith, U. (1996). Theory of mind and social impairment in children with conduct disorder. *British Journal of Developmental Psychology, 14*, 385–398.

Harlow, J. M. (1848). Passage of an iron rod through the head. *Boston Medical Surgery Journal, 39*, 389–393.

Harlow, J. M. (1868). Recovery from passage of an iron through the head. *Massachusetts Medical Society Publish, 2*, 327–346.

Hinson, J. M., Jameson, T. L., & Whitney, P. (2002). Somatic markers, working memory, and decision making. *Cognitive, Affective and Behavioral Neuroscience, 2*, 341–353.

Hongwanishkul, D., Happaney, K., Lee, W. S. C., & Zelazo, P. D. (in press). Assessment of hot and cool executive function in young children: Age-related changes and individual differences. *Developmental Neuropsychology.*

Hughes, C. (1998a). Finding your marbles: Does preschoolers' strategic behavior predict later understanding of mind? *Developmental Psychology, 34*, 1326–1339.

Hughes, C. (1998b). Executive function in preschoolers: Links with theory of mind and verbal ability. *British Journal of Developmental Psychology, 16*, 233–253.

Hughes, C., & Russell, J. (1993). Autistic children's difficulty with mental disengagement from an object: Its implications for theories of autism. *Developmental Psychology, 29*, 498–510.

Inhelder, B., & Piaget, J. (1964). *The early growth of logic in the child: Classification and seriation* (E. A. Lunzer & D. Papert, Trans.). New York: Harper & Row.

Keane, J., Calder, A. J., Hodges, J. R., & Young, A. W. (2002). Face and emotion processing in frontal variant frontotemporal dementia. *Neuropsychologia, 40*, 655–665.

Keenan, T., Olson, D. R., & Marini, Z. (1998). Working memory and children's developing understanding of mind. *Australian Journal of Psychology, 50*, 76–82.

Kerr, A., & Zelazo, P. D. (2004). Development of "hot" executive function: The Children's Gambling Task [special issue]. *Brain and Cognition, 55*, 148–157.

Lang, B., & Perner, J. (2002). Understanding of intention and false belief and the development of self-control. *British Journal of Developmental Psychology, 20,* 67–76.

Luria, A. R. (1973). *The working brain: An introduction to neuropsychology* (B. Haigh, Trans.). New York: Basic Books.

Manes, F., Sahakian, B., Clark, L., Rogers, R., Antoun, N., Aitken, M., & Robbins, T. (2002). Decision-making processes following damage to the prefrontal cortex. *Brain, 125,* 624–639.

Marcovitch, S., & Zelazo, P. D. (1999). The A-not-B error: Results from a logistic meta-analysis. *Child Development, 70,* 1297–1313.

Markman, E. (1989). *Categorization and naming in children: Problems of induction.* Cambridge, MA: MIT Press.

Mazas, C. A., Finn, P. R., & Steinmetz, J. E. (2000). Decision-making biases, antisocial personality, and early-onset alcoholism. *Alcoholism: Clinical and Experimental Research, 24,* 1036–1040.

Metcalfe, J., & Mischel, W. (1999). A Hot/Cool-System analysis of delay of gratification: Dynamics of willpower. *Psychological Review, 106,* 3–19.

Miller, E. K., & Cohen, J. D. (2001). An integrative theory of prefrontal cortex function. *Annual Review of Neuroscience, 24,* 167–202.

Miyake, A., Friedman, N. P., Emerson, M. J., Witzki, A. H., & Howerter, A. (2000). The unity and diversity of executive functions and their contributions to complex "frontal lobe" tasks: A latent variable analysis. *Cognitive Psychology, 41,* 49–100.

Monterosso, J., Ehrman, R., Napier, K. L., O'Brien, C. P., & Childress, A. R. (2001). Three decision-making tasks in cocaine-dependent patients: Do they measure the same construct? *Addiction, 96,* 1825–1837.

Moore, C. (1996). Theories of mind in infancy. *British Journal of Developmental Psychology, 14,* 19–40.

Moore, C., Pure, K., & Furrow, D. (1990). Children's understanding of the model expression of certainty and uncertainty and its relation to the development of a representational theory of mind. *Child Development, 61,* 722–730.

O'Sullivan, L. P., Mitchell, L. L., & Daehler, M. W. (2001). Representation and perseveration: Influences on young children's representational insight. *Journal of Cognition and Development, 2,* 339–365.

Ozonoff, S., Pennington, B. F., & Rogers, S. J. (1991). Executive function deficits in high-functioning autistic individuals: Relationship to theory of mind. *Journal of Child Psychology and Psychiatry, 32,* 1081–1105.

Pennington, B. F., & Ozonoff, S. (1996). Executive functions and developmental psychopathology. *Journal of Child Psychology and Psychiatry, 37,* 51–87.

Perner, J. (1991). *Understanding the representational mind.* Cambridge, MA: MIT Press.

Perner, J., & Lang, B. (1999). Development of theory of mind and cognitive control. *Trends in Cognitive Science, 3,* 337–344.

Perner, J., & Lang, B. (2000). Theory of mind and executive function: Is there a developmental relationship? In S. Baron-Cohen, H. Tager-Flusberg, & D. J. Cohen (Eds.), *Understanding other minds: Perspectives from developmental cognitive neuroscience* (2nd ed., pp. 150–181). Oxford, UK: Oxford University Press.

Perner, J., Lang, B., & Kloo, D. (2002). Theory of mind and self-control: More than a common problem of inhibition. *Child Development, 73,* 752–767.

Perner, J., Stummer, S., & Lang, B. (1999). Executive functions and theory of mind: Continue complexity or functional dependence? In P. D. Zelazo, J. W. Astington, & D. R. Olson (Eds.), *Developing theories of intention: Social understanding and self-control* (pp. 133–152). Mahwah, NJ: Lawrence Erlbaum Associates.

Petrides, M. (1995). Functional organization of the human frontal cortex for mnemonic processing: Evidence from neuroimaging studies. In J. Grafman, K. J. Holyoak, & F. Boller (Eds.), *Annals of the New York Academy of Sciences* (Vol. 769, pp. 85–96). New York: New York Academy of Sciences.

Petrides, M., & Milner, B. (1982). Deficits on subject-ordered tasks after frontal- and temporal-lobe lesions in man. *Neuropsychologia, 12,* 323–330.

Petry, N. M., Bickel, W. K., & Arnett, M. (1998). Shortened time horizons and insensitivity to future consequences in heroin addicts. *Addiction, 93,* 729–738.

Phillips, L. H., MacLean, R. D. J., & Allen, R. (2002). Age and the understanding of emotions: Neuropsychological and sociocognitive perspectives. *Journals of Gerontology: Series B: Psychological Sciences and Social Sciences, 57,* 526–530.

Piaget, J. (1954). *The construction of reality in the child.* New York: Basic Books.

Posner, M. I., & Rothbart, M. K. (1998). Summary and commentary: Developing attentional skills. In J. E. Richards (Ed), *Cognitive neuroscience of attention: A developmental perspective* (pp. 317–323). Mahwah, NJ: Lawrence Erlbaum Associates.

Povinelli, D. J., Landau, K. R., & Perilloux, H. K. (1996). Self-recognition in young children using delayed versus live feedback: Evidence of a developmental asynchrony. *Child Development, 67,* 1540–1554.

Price, B. H., Daffner, K. R., Stowe, R. M., & Mesulam, M. M. (1990). The comportmental learning disabilities of early frontal lobe damage. *Brain, 113,* 1383–1393.

Rogers, R. D., Everitt, B. J., Baldacchino, A., Blackshaw, A. J., Swainson, R., Wynne, K., Baker, N. B., Hunter, J., Carthy, T., Booker, E., London, M., Deakin, J. F. W., Sahakian, B. J., & Robbins, T. W. (1999). Dissociable deficits in the decision-making cognition of chronic amphetamine abusers, opiate abusers, patients with focal damage to prefrontal cortex, and Tryptophan-depleted normal volunteers: Evidence for monoaminergic mechanisms. *Neuropsychopharmacology, 20,* 322–339.

Rogers, R. D., Owen, A. M., Middleton, H. C., Williams, E. J., Pickard, J. D., Sahakian, B. J., & Robbins, T. W. (1999). Choosing between small, likely rewards and large, unlikely rewards activates inferior and orbital prefrontal cortex. *Journal of Neuroscience, 20,* 9029–9038.

Rolls, E. T. (1999). *The brain and emotion.* Oxford, UK: Oxford University Press.

Rolls, E. T. (2000). The orbitofrontal cortex and reward. *Cerebral Cortex, 10,* 284–294.

Rolls, E. T. (2004). The functions of the orbitofrontal cortex [special issue]. *Brain and Cognition, 55,* 11–29.

Rolls, E. T., Hornak, J., Wade, D., & McGrath, J. (1994). Emotion-related learning in patients with social and emotional changes associated with frontal lobe damage. *Journal of Neurological and Neurosurgery Psychiatry, 57,* 1518–1524.

Rothbart, M. K., Ahadi, S. A., Hershey, K. L., & Fisher, P. (2001). Investigations of temperament at three to seven years: The Children's Behavior Questionnaire. *Child Development, 72,* 1394–1408.

Russell, J., Hala, S. M., & Hill, E. (2003). The automated windows task: The performance of preschool children, children with autism, and children with moderate learning difficulties. *Cognitive Development, 18,* 111–137.

Russell, J., Jarrold, C., & Potel, D. (1994). What makes strategic deception difficult for children-the deception or the strategy? *British Journal of Developmental Psychology, 12,* 301–314.

Russell, J., Mauthner, N., Sharpe, S., & Tidswell, T. (1991). The "window task" as a measure of strategic deception in preschoolers and autistic subjects. *British Journal of Developmental Psychology, 9,* 331–349.

Russell, J. A., Bachorowski, J., & Fernadandez-Dols, J. (2003). Facial and vocal expressions of emotions. *Annual Review of Psychology, 54,* 329–349.

Sabbagh. M. A., & Taylor, M. (2000). Neural correlates of theory-of-mind reasoning: An event-related potential study. *Psychological Science, 11,* 46–50.

Saltzman, J., Strauss, E., Hunter, M., & Archibald, S. (2000). Theory of mind and executive functions in normal human aging and Parkinson's disease. *Journal of the International Neuropsychological Society, 6,* 781–788.

Samuels, M. C., Brooks, P. J., & Frye, D. (1996). Strategic game playing in children through the windows task. *British Journal of Developmental Psychology, 14,* 159–172.

Saver, J. L., & Damasio, A. R. (1991). Preserved access and processing of social knowledge in a patient with acquired sociopathy due to ventromedial frontal damage. *Neuopsychologia, 29,* 1241–1249.

Shallice, T. (1988). *From neuropsychology to mental structure.* New York: Cambridge University Press.

Siegal, M., & Varley, R. (2002). Neural systems involved in "theory of mind." *Nature Reviews Neuroscience, 3*, 463–471.

Stone, V. E., Baron-Cohen, S., & Knight, R. T. (1998). Frontal lobe contributions to theory of mind. *Journal of Cognitive Neuroscience, 10*, 640–656.

Stuss, D. T., & Benson, D. F. (1986). *The frontal lobes.* New York: Raven Press.

Stuss, D. T., Floden, D., Alexander, M. P., Levine, B., & Katz, D. (2001). Stroop performance in focal lesion patients: Dissociation of processes and frontal lobe lesion location. *Neuropsychologia, 39*, 771–786.

Stuss, D. T., Toth, J. P., Franchi, D., Alexander, M. P., Tipper, S., & Craik, F. I. M. (1999). Dissociation of attentional processes in patients with focal frontal and posterior lesions. *Neuropsychologia, 37*, 1005–1027.

Thompson, C., Barresi, J., & Moore, C. (1997). The development of future-oriented prudence and altruism in preschoolers. *Cognitive Development, 12*, 199–212.

Tranel, D., Anderson, S. W., & Benton, A. L. (1994). Development of the concept of "executive function" and its relationship to the frontal lobes. In F. Boller & J. Grafman (Eds.), *Handbook of neuropsychology* (Vol. 9, pp. 125–148). Amsterdam: Elsevier.

Vogeley, K., Bussfeld, P., Newen, A., Herrmann, S., Happé, F., Falkai, P., Maier, W., Shah, N. J., Fink, G. R., & Zilles, K. (2001). Mind reading: Neural mechanisms of theory of mind and self-perspective. *NeuroImage, 14*, 170–181.

Waltz, J. A., Knowlton, B. J., Holyoak, K. J., Boone, K. B., Mishkin, F. S., de Menezes Santos, M., Thomas, C. R., & Miller, B. L. (1999). A system for relational reasoning in human prefrontal cortex. *Psychological Science, 10*, 119–125.

Wellman, H. M., Cross, D., & Watson, J. (2001). Meta-analysis of theory-of-mind development: The truth about false belief. *Child Development, 72*, 655–684.

Wimmer, H., & Perner, J. (1983). Beliefs about beliefs: Representation and constraining function of wrong beliefs in young children's understanding of deception. *Cognition, 13*, 103–128.

Wise, S. P., Murray, E. A., & Gerfen, C. R. (1996). The frontal cortex-basal ganglia system in primates. *Critical Reviews in Neurobiology, 10*, 317–356.

Zelazo, P. D., Carter, A., Reznick, J. S., & Frye, D. (1997). Early development of executive function: A problem-solving framework. *Review of General Psychology, 1*, 1–29.

Zelazo, P. D., Craik, F. I. M., & Booth, L. (2004). Executive function across the life span. *Acta Psychologica, 115*, 167–187.

Zelazo, P. D., & Frye, D. (1998). II. Cognitive complexity and control: The development of executive function. *Current Directions in Psychological Science, 7*, 121–126.

Zelazo, P. D., Helwig, C. C., & Lau, A. (1996). Intention, act, and outcome in behavioral prediction and moral judgment. *Child Development, 67*, 2478–2492.

Zelazo, P. D., & Müller, U. (2002). Executive function in typical and atypical development. In U. Goswami (Ed.), *Handbook of childhood cognitive development* (pp. 445–469). Oxford, UK: Blackwell.

Zelazo, P. D., & Sommerville, J. (2001). Levels of consciousness of the self in time. In C. Moore, & K. Lemmon (Eds.), *The self in time: Developmental issues* (pp. 229–252). Mahwah, NJ: Lawrence Erlbaum Associates.

Zelazo, P. D., Sommerville, J. A., & Nichols, S. (1999). Age-related changes in children's use of external representations. *Developmental Psychology, 35*, 1059–1071.

Zhang, J., & Hedden, T. (2003). Two paradigms for depth of strategic reasoning in games. *Trends in Cognitive Sciences, 7*, 4–5.

Chapter 5

Theory of Mind—The Case for Conceptual Development

Beate Sodian
University of München

Theory of mind is a label for the commonsense psychological concepts we use to attribute mental states to ourselves and others (i.e., what we know, want, think, feel). Borrowed from philosophy of mind (Fodor, 1978), the term was used by Premack and Woodruff (1978) to address one of the key questions of primate cognition: "Does the chimpanzee have a theory of mind?" These authors argued that the ability to attribute mental states to oneself and others requires theoretical knowledge because mental states are unobservable and are inferred, like theoretical terms in the sciences. Because the attribution of mental states improves our everyday predictions and explanations of human behavior, the conceptual system underlying these attributions has the explanatory power of a theory. In current research on the development of mental state attribution in children, the term *theory* is often used loosely, in the sense of a coherent body of conceptual knowledge. Over the last 20 years, theory of mind research has become a highly productive area in conceptual development (see Astington, 1993; Astington, Harris, & Olson, 1988; Baron-Cohen, Tager-Flusberg, & Cohen, 2000; Flavell, 1999, 2000; Lee & Homer, 1999; Lewis & Mitchell, 1994; Mitchell & Riggs, 2000; Moore, 1996; Perner, 1991, 1999a; Taylor, 1996; Wellman, 1990, 2002, for books and overview chapters).

Theory of mind is not the first research tradition to address children's developing understanding of the psychological world. Piaget's description of the preoperational child as fundamentally egocentric (Piaget & Inhelder, 1956) led to systematic investigations of perspective-taking abilities in young children (Lempers, Flavell, & Flavell, 1977). Studies of epistemic perspective-taking abilities (Marvin, Greenberg, & Mossler, 1976) are directly relevant to the development of mental state attribution. However, the focus was on nonegocentric perspective taking rather than on a systematic investigation of children's understanding of the mind. Other relevant precursors to theory of mind research are psycholinguistic studies of children's understanding of mental verbs (Wellman & Johnson, 1979), as well as research into children's comprehension of narratives that entails an understanding of story figures' emotions, motives, and beliefs (Stein & Trabasso, 1982; Wimmer, 1982).

A related area that partially overlaps with theory of mind is the development of metacognition, which addresses children's knowledge about person, task, and strategy variables relevant to the mastery of cognitive tasks, as well as their ability to monitor and control their own cognitive processes. Whereas metacognition focuses primarily on the contributions of metacognitive knowledge and metacognitive monitoring to cognitive achievements (e.g., memorizing), theory of mind research addresses the conceptual underpinnings of such abilities. Flavell (2000) points out parallels and convergences between the two research traditions and argues for a stronger integration.

The most important feature of theory of mind research is its focus on conceptual analysis (Perner, 1999a). Philosophical analyses of our commonsense mentalism as a representational theory of mind (Fodor, 1978) have emphasized that our intuitive psychological knowledge is knowledge about psychological relations between individuals and the world (or knowledge about the way individuals represent the world), rather than first-order knowledge about the world. This distinction became important when Premack and Woodruff (1978) found that chimpanzees were able to choose correct solutions for certain problem situations (e.g., chose the picture of keys among a number of alternatives when shown an agent who was trying to open the door of a cage) and proposed that such correct performance may indicate an ability to attribute mental states to agents. Dennett (1978) pointed out that the chimpanzees could arrive at the correct solutions by simply representing the problem situation (the world) rather than representing the agent's mental state (her or his desire to leave the cage). Therefore, the representation of a person's wrong beliefs about a state of the world is critical for mental state attribution because action prediction in this case requires representation of the person's belief, whereas action prediction can be successful solely based on a representation of the world, if the agent's beliefs about the world are true.

Based on this analysis, Wimmer and Perner (1983) developed a paradigm for the study of children's ability to represent false belief. A story is enacted with puppets in front of the child in which a story figure (Maxi) puts a piece of chocolate in location A, then leaves. In his absence, a second figure (Mom) transfers the chocolate from location A to location B and subsequently leaves. Maxi returns. The child is asked where Maxi will look for the chocolate. Almost all children younger than 3 years of age answer that Maxi will look in location B (i.e., where the chocolate actually is). Around the age of 3.5 to 4 years, children begin to base their action prediction on the story figure's false belief. Over the last 20 years, this developmental phenomenon has been addressed in several hundred empirical studies (see the section on the concept of belief below; see Wellman, Cross, & Watson, 2001, for a meta-analysis).

In our commonsense psychology, inner experience is a source of knowledge about the mental world, mental states function as theoretical terms in an intuitive theory of behavior, and mental states are characterized by intentionality (Churchland, 1984; Perner, 1991). The idea that the attribution of mental states plays a causal explanatory role in an intuitive theory of behavior can be traced back to Aristotle's practical syllogism, in which a behavioral prediction is derived from two premises, a desire attribution and a belief attribution: "Max wants to play soccer with the boys. Max believes that the boys play soccer in the park. Max goes to the park." The most important feature of mental state attribution is intentionality: In the sentence "Max thinks of a dog," the word *dog* refers to an intentional object. An intentional object differs from a physical object in aspectuality, nonexistence, and misrepresentation: Max can think of a dog that does not exist in reality but is only imagined. If Max knows that his dog barked at a postman, and the postman is 35 years old, it does not follow that Max knows that his dog barked at a 35-year-old man, although the descriptions "the postman" and "the 35-year-old man" refer to the same individual. Intentional acts, unlike physical events, refer to certain aspects of an object. Finally, intentional acts can misrepresent the target object: Max can believe that the dog chases a bird, while he really chases a cat. Propositions involving intentional acts such as "X wants to get the car" and "Z believes the chocolate is in the cupboard" are called propositional attitudes because they relate an organism to a proposition. The proposition expresses how the organism represents the world, whereas the propositional attitude indicates the psychological relation between the organism and the world. The key to understanding false beliefs is to recognize that propositions can be evaluated in different ways by different individuals (e.g., Maxi believes that the proposition "the chocolate is in the cupboard" is true, whereas I believe that this proposition is false) (Perner, 2000).

How do children come to understand the relation between organisms, propositions, and the world? It has become clear that an account of how children come to grasp the concept of belief is central to answering this question. Sections in this chapter focus on the concept of belief and related concepts, advanced theory of mind development (beyond the false belief problem), and the main current theoretical accounts of theory of mind development. In the last few years, the origins of an understanding of the psychological domain in infancy have become a particularly fruitful area of research (see Gergely, 2002; Poulin-Dubois, 1999; Sodian & Thoermer, in press b; Tomasello & Rakoczy, 2003, for reviews). Because of space limitations, this chapter contains only a very brief overview of this literature, focusing on the question of what the work on infants' representation of the psychological domain tells us about mental state representation as defined previously by the criteria of inner experience, a mentalistic theory of behavior, and intentionality.

MENTAL STATE REPRESENTATION BEFORE BELIEF

From birth, infants show a special sensitivity to and preference for the human face (Johnson & Morton, 1991), and in the first months of life they identify important sources of social information, such as eye movements, voice, and facial expression of emotion (Hood, Willen, & Driver, 1998; Walker-Andrews & Lennon, 1991). The newborn's ability to imitate some facial movements requires an ability to cross-modally detect an equivalence between perceived body motion in the other and the proprioceptive experience of one's own action and is thus the basis for perceiving the other person as "like me" (Meltzoff, 2002; Meltzoff & Gopnik, 1993). Even newborns discriminate between humans and inanimate objects by imitating human facial motion, not similar movements of inanimate objects (Legerstee, 1991), and there is ample evidence for such discriminative abilities in the first months of life, for example, from infants' affective responses and communicative signals (see Legerstee, 1992, for a review). The bidirectional affective interactions of 2- to 9-month-old infants with their caregivers show a protoconversational structure. Specific expectations of contingency in social interaction with their caregivers have been shown in infants as young as 10 weeks (Nadel & Tremblay-Leveau, 1999). Rich interpretations of infant social sensitivity have attributed an ability to gain access to one's own and others' mental states (in the sense of inner experiences) to the infant even in the first months of life (Trevarthen, 1979). However, there is little evidence for such a rich interpretation. Rather, early affective and imitative interactions between infant and caregiver may serve important evolutionary functions but do not require the infant to gain introspective access to their own affective states or to ascribe such states to others (Gergely, 2002).

The origins of the ability to represent psychological relations, such as "Max wants the chocolate," "Peter sees the thief," or "Eva hates Martin," have been located in the development of joint attention around the age of 9 to 12 months. Infants follow adults' gaze and point toward specific referents, they use adults' emotional expression to guide their own action, they learn to manipulate objects by imitating the way adults manipulate them, and they actively use communicative signals to direct adults' attention. These communicative competencies develop in intraindividual synchrony and in an interindividually consistent sequence and have been interpreted as indicating the infant's representation of people as intentional agents (Carpenter, Nagell, & Tomasello, 1998). Recent research on infants' expectations about object-directed actions supports the view that, by the end of the first year, infants encode communicative actions (looking at or pointing at a specific object) as goal directed (Woodward, 2003; Woodward & Guajardo, 2002), that they interpret whole action sequences as directed toward an overarching action goal (Woodward & Sommerville, 2000), that they parse an ongoing stream of action in an intentionally meaningful way (Baird & Baldwin, 2001), and that they can predict subsequent action from information on a person's action goal (Phillips, Wellman, & Spelke, 2002; Sodian & Thoermer, 2004). Furthermore, 9- to 12-month-old infants have principled expectations about the way agents approach their goals that are consistent with the assumption that agents choose rational means to approach their goals (Gergely, Nadasdy, Csibra, & Birò, 1995).

Interpretations of these social cognitive abilities emerging around the first birthday differ in the kinds of action representation they attribute to the infant. Tomasello (1999) relates means-ends understanding, developing around the age of 8 to 12 months, to infants' ability to adopt the intentional stance with regard to human action and argues that an understanding of people as intentional agents involves a rudimentary mentalism because it requires the differentiation of the actors' means (actions) from their mentally represented goal (Tomasello & Rakoczy, 2003). In contrast, Gergely and Csibra (1997) (see Gergely, 2002) account for the 1-year-olds' competencies in terms of a teleological (nonintentional) interpretaion of behavior that generates representations of goal-directed actions that are neither mentalistic nor causal explanatory. Whereas the older child and the adult interpret goal-directed actions in causal-mentalistic terms ("he jumps over the barrier because he wants to get to the other side and believes he cannot remove the obstacle"), a teleological perspective generates a description such as "he jumps over the barrier to get to the other side." Other theories make assumptions about a developmental sequence of representing and interpreting the relational structure of psychological states. Moore (1996; Barresi & Moore, 1996) argues that the ability to engage in joint attention and to establish reference may at first function as a source of information for the infant with regard to the relational structure of mental states, rather than being driven by a preexisting understanding of intentional agency. Meltzoff (2002) proposes a three-step process: Based on the innate ability to recognize equivalences between self-produced and observed actions, infants begin to learn about systematic relations between motor behavior and mental experiences (e.g., emotions) during the 1st year of life. Eventually, infants conceptualize others in analogy to themselves, by matching others' observed behaviors with the representation of their own matching behaviors and by attributing the appropriate mental state from self to other.

Whereas the social-cognitive competencies at the end of the 1st year do not warrant the conclusion that these young infants conceptualize people as mental agents, a number of developmental phenomena emerging around the age of 18 months do indicate that children differentiate between their own and other's mental states and construe the others' inner experiences in terms of their own equivalent mental states (see Poulin-Dubois, 1999, for a review). Empathy, intention reading (in particular, the representation of prior intentions and of failed intentions in the age range between 18 and 24 months; Carpenter, Call, & Tomasello, 2002; Meltzoff, 1995), a beginning understanding of the subjectivity of desires (Repacholi & Gopnik, 1997), and a preverbal sensitivity for the seeing = knowing relation (Poulin-Dubois, Tilden, Sodian, Metz, & Schoeppner, 2003) indicate that mental states are represented as inner experiences and play a role in children's intuitive interpretations of behavior. However, these phenomena do not indicate an understanding of intentionality in the sense of propositional attitudes. Perner (1991) distinguishes between the young child's ability to construct and mentally manipulate multiple models, and the 4-year-old's understanding of the representational relation between a model and reality. For instance, in the case of empathy, the 2-year-old builds a hypothetical model of being in an emotionally upsetting situation and thereby draws inferences about the other's emotional state. To do so, it is not necessary to understand the representational relation between the model and reality. Similarly, pretend play, emerging around the age of 18 months, can be interpreted as an ability to construct fictional worlds that are not confounded with reality (Harris & Kavanaugh, 1993) rather than as an understanding of the representational relation between the pretend world and the real world (see next section).

Commonsense mentalistic action explanations are based on belief-desire reasoning. Developmentally, desire reasoning precedes a full belief-desire interpretation of behavior. Two-year-olds spontaneously talk about their own and others' desires and intentions (Bartsch & Wellman, 1995); 2.5- to 3-year-olds explicitly relate desire, action outcome, and emotional reactions (Wellman & Woolley, 1990; Yuill, 1984) and can explain emotions by referring to a story figure's preexisting desire (Wellman & Banerjee, 1991). Moreover, 2- to 3-year-olds have an explicit understanding of the relation between desire and action: A person who finds the desired object will stop searching, whereas a person who finds another object will continue his or her search (Wellman & Woolley, 1990). Three-year-olds can predict behavior based on a person's desires and report about their own past desires and their fulfillment, but they have difficulty talking about past beliefs (Gopnik & Slaughter, 1991). Furthermore, there is evidence for an explicit, declarative understanding of the subjectivity of desires and thus an understanding of differences between personal tastes and preferences in 3-year-olds (Flavell, Mumme, Green, & Flavell, 1992). This is consistent with 3-year-olds' ability to explicitly distinguish between the mental and the physical (e.g., between a real dog and an imagined dog) (Wellman & Estes, 1986).

A naïve understanding of desires and intentions treats these mental states as relations between a person and a situation (a goal state). A more sophisticated understanding of desires implies an understanding of a desire as a mental representation of the desired situation. Theory of mind research indicates that 2- and 3-year-olds give mentalistic action explanations based on a nonrepresentational understanding of desire, whereas a representational understanding of desire develops around the age of 4 years in conjunction with an understanding of misrepresentation (Astington, 1999; Perner, 1991). Moreover, 4-year-olds, but not 3-year-olds, distinguish between desires and intentions and understand intentions as mental states with causal efficacy (Feinfield, Lee, Flavell, Green, & Flavell, 1999). Consistent with these findings is 3-year-olds' (and even many 4-year-olds') failure to understand reflex movements (the knee-jerk reflex) as lacking intention (Shultz, Wells, & Sarda, 1980). A concept of action being caused by an internal intention should be related to the capacity for self-control. In fact, children's understanding of the knee-jerk reflex has been shown to be significantly correlated with executive function tasks, and, even more important, a strong correlation was obtained between false belief understanding and understanding of the knee-jerk reflex, which could not be explained with executive components (Perner & Lang, 2000). Rather, the relationship appears to reflect the conceptual advantage of understanding the causal significance of mental states.

In sum, there is evidence for an understanding of mental states as subjective psychological experiences and for a use of these constructs for the prediction and explanation of action in 2- and 3-year-olds. However, there is lack of evidence among this age group to satisfy the third criterion for mental state understanding: an understanding of intentionality.

THE CONCEPT OF BELIEF AND RELATED CONCEPTS

Belief

The ability to distinguish beliefs from reality is critical for the development of a theory of mind. Therefore, the primary focus of theory of mind research has been on the concept of belief. In the first systematic investigation of children's understanding of false belief, Wimmer and Perner (1983) found that 40% of the 4-year-olds and 90% of the 6- to 7-year-olds correctly predicted a story protagonist's action based on his or her false belief (Maxi was absent while the chocolate was transferred from cupboard A to cupboard B. Where will Maxi look for the chocolate?). When informational access (or lack thereof) was made salient—that is, when it was emphasized that Maxi was absent while the chocolate was transferred and could not see where his mother put the chocolate—even 50% of the older 3-year-olds gave belief-based answers to the test question. Children below the age of 3.5 years, however, did not benefit from the salience of informational access.

A similar developmental trend was found in a false belief task that does not require story processing but only simple factual knowledge about the typical contents of highly familiar containers. The child is shown, for instance, a Smarties candy box and guesses that this box contains Smarties. Then the box is opened, and the child sees that it has unexpected contents, for example, a pencil. Then the box is closed again, and the child is asked what another child, who has not looked into the box, will think about its contents. Children younger than the age of 3.5 years typically say that an uninformed child will think (or say) there is a pencil in the box (Hogrefe, Wimmer, & Perner, 1986). Moreover, they also say that they believed (or said) there was a pencil in the box when they first saw the box, before it was opened (Gopnik & Astington, 1988). This inability to represent one's own previous false belief is not attributable to memory problems or to a reluctance to admit mistakes (Wimmer & Hartl, 1991). These findings support the interpretation that an understanding of wrong beliefs is not only a problem of taking another's perspective but that the representation of one's own false beliefs is based on the same conceptual system as the representation of others' beliefs and that this conceptual system undergoes developmental change in the age range between 3 and 4 years (Gopnik, 1993). The finding that young 3-year-olds consistently fail different types of false belief tasks supports the view that there is a conceptual deficit in young children's understanding of the mind (Perner, Leekam, & Wimmer, 1987). This view has been heavily criticized and has led to a series of attempts to demonstrate early competence under simplified task conditions, which will be briefly reviewed here.

Siegal and Beattie (1991) argued that the standard test questions in false belief tasks violate children's presuppositions about conversational rules. The test question "Where will Maxi look for the chocolate?" in unexpected transfer tasks could, for instance, be misinterpreted as "Where should he look?" or "Where will he look and find the chocolate?" When 2- and 3-year-olds were asked instead "Where will Maxi *first* look for his chocolate when he comes back from the playground?", Siegal and Beattie found a significant increase of belief-based responses compared with the standard condition. This finding has proved difficult to replicate. Clements and Perner (1994) found only minimal differences between the test conditions. Similarly, Perner (2000) failed to replicate the facilitating effect of modifying the test question in the Smarties task ("Before I opened the box, what did you think was in it?" instead of "When I opened the box, what did you think was in it?"), which Lewis and Osborne (1990) had observed.

Another line of reasoning concerns the salience of reality compared to the salience of the false belief. Mitchell and LaCohee (1991) and Zaitchik (1991) found that young 3-year-olds benefited from increasing the salience of the false belief by depicting it in a drawing. However, it can be argued that increasing the salience of the false belief increases the probability of children responding with the content of the false belief instead of the content of reality, even if they do not understand the propositional attitude (Perner, 2000).

A similar argument can be applied to Saltmarsh, Mitchell, and Robinson (1995) who showed that 3-year-olds' performance in the Smarties task improves when the children witness the exchange of the typical content (Smarties) for the new one (pencils) and have to judge an ignorant doll's belief, rather than being confronted with the unexpected content right away. Perner (2000) argues that children who are not sure which context the test question about the doll's belief refers to have a higher probability of giving the correct, belief-based answer (Smarties) when Smarties were in fact in the box at a certain point in time.

False positives—that is, correct answers to test questions not based on belief understanding—were also demonstrated in an explanation version of the Smarties task by Moses and Flavell (1990). These authors failed to replicate Bartsch and Wellman's (1989) finding that explanation was easier for young 3-year-olds than action prediction based on a false belief, and they found that many 3-year-olds gave the same answer, "Smarties," when asked what the story figure believed was in the container before it was opened and after it was opened, that is, when the story figure had access to the truth.

In sum, the findings from studies attempting to show belief understanding in young children under simplified task conditions indicate that correct performance can be found in children younger than the age of 3 years, 6 months under some task conditions, although in many cases there is reason to doubt that the correct answers are based on a genuine understanding of belief. A recent statistical meta-analysis of more than 500 studies investigating the development of false belief understanding (Wellman et al., 2001) showed that, despite various procedural differences, there is a robust developmental trend in belief understanding: Although 2.5- and young 3-year-olds tend to give reality-based responses, an increase in the proportion of correct (i.e., belief-based) answers with age is found above the age of 3.5 years. This developmental trend was independent of whether the test question referred to mental states (what does x think) or to behavior (where will x look) and of whether the target person was a story figure, a person in a video, a doll, a child, an adult, or the subject. Corroborating evidence comes from the study of children's spontaneous use of mentalistic speech (Bartsch & Wellman, 1995): whereas wish and emotion terms emerge toward the end of the 2nd year and are used to refer to internal mental states in the 3rd year, epistemic terms (*know, think*) typically are not observed before the 3rd birthday, except in set phrases, such as "don't know."

Despite the evidence for a conceptual deficit in young children's understanding of belief, it can be argued that explicit mental state attribution in experimental tasks as well as in natural conversations poses high verbal demands and is therefore likely to lead to an underestimation of young children's competencies. In contrast, goal-directed social interaction provides a much better context for children to apply their mental state understanding. Children can use their mental state understanding to their advantage by inducing a false belief in another person; therefore, acts of deception provide insight into the early development of belief understanding (Chandler, Fritz, & Hala, 1989). Because only intentional deception can be interpreted as evidence for belief understanding, young children's seemingly deceptive acts are often hard to interpret. The child could merely have used a well-worn strategy to obtain a reward or to avoid negative consequences, without any inferences about an opponent's beliefs, for example, when denying to have committed a transgression (Lewis, Stanger, & Sullivan, 1989; Polak & Harris, 1999; Stern & Stern, 1909). Therefore, recent systematic investigations of lying and deception in children have employed tasks that require the child to use a novel deceptive strategy. Peskin (1992) studied children's ability to hide their intentions in a laboratory task, similar to naturally occurring competitive situations: A competitor, who can choose first among a number of alternatives, always chooses the object that the child wants; therefore, the child can win only by deceiving the competitor about his or her preferences. Almost all 3- and 4-year-olds truthfully informed the competitor about their preference, whereas most 5-year-olds indicated an object that they disliked. With experience, 4-year-olds discovered the deceptive strategy, whereas 3-year-olds did not. The interpretation that 3-year-olds' deficit is a conceptual one is supported by their performance in a control condition in which they could decide whether a cooperative or a competitive puppet was allowed to choose first. Similarly, Sodian (1991) found marked developmental progress between 3 and 5 years in a strategic deception game modeled after Premack and Woodruff's (1978) study of deception in chimpanzees. Whereas children below the age of 3.5 years almost never attempted to deceive an opponent by indicating an empty container, most 4-year-olds did so spontaneously. In a similar task, Russell, Mauther, Sharpe, and Tidswell (1991) found that 3-year-olds did not learn from experience: Even after 20 trials, they did not deceive the opponent, despite their mounting frustration about the loss of the reward. Again, 3-year-olds' ability to pass a control condition in which the opponent could be hindered from obtaining the reward by physical obstruction supports the conceptual deficit interpretation (Ruffman, Olson, Ash, & Keenan, 1993; see also Sodian, 1991).

In contrast, two studies by Chandler et al. (1989) and Hala, Chandler, and Fritz (1991) did not yield an age trend in children's application of deceptive strategies (lay false tracks, wipe out tracks) in a competitive game. Even the youngest age group demonstrated competence, a finding inconsistent with a conceptual deficit view. However, the finding could not be replicated under controlled conditions: Three-year-olds did not distinguish in their strategic behaviors between hindering an opponent and helping a friend, whereas 4-year-olds did (Sodian, Taylor, Harris, & Perner, 1991). These findings suggest that 3-year-olds sometimes produce deceptive effects without understanding the effects of their actions on an opponent's epistemic state. This view is also supported by 3-year-olds' failure to understand trickery. Sullivan and Winner (1993) argued that deceptive contexts should be particularly suitable to demonstrate an early and as yet unstable concept of belief. Support for their assumption came from a study of false belief understanding in the context of trickery. When the exchange of a typical content (Smarties) for a neutral content (pencils) was embedded in a conspiratorial context in which the child was involved in playing a trick on an absent person, 3-year-olds gave significantly more belief-based answers to the test question than in the standard condition.

Sodian, Hülsken, and Thoermer (1999) showed, however, that there was no difference between 3-year-olds in the trick condition compared with those in the control (pseudotrick) condition, which was parallel to the trick condition except that the person who was supposed to be tricked was present, observing the Smarties being exchanged for the pencil.

Two recent studies investigated the development of children's lies longitudinally in the home environment in the age range between 2 and 6 years (Newton, Reddy, & Bull, 2000; Wilson, Smith, & Ross, 2003). Both found an increase in the frequency of lies and other deceptive acts with age but multiple instances of deceptive acts in children younger than age 4 years. Newton et al. found no correlation between children's lies, as reported by their mothers, and children's performance on a battery of false belief tests. The authors of both studies conclude that deceptive acts by children younger than age 4 years are too frequent and too creative to be interpreted as mere behavioral manipulations, such as the use of standard strategies to obtain a goal. It remains difficult, however, to convincingly demonstrate genuine deception, that is, the deceiver's insight into the opponent's mental state on the basis of everyday observations. Newton et al. do not interpret early lies and deceptive acts as evidence for the early onset of a theory of mind but rather as socially adaptive behaviors that are driven by pragmatic factors and other situational constraints; the deceptive acts can contribute to a developing insight into mental states, rather than being the product of such an insight. We therefore conclude that neither experimental studies nor naturalistic observations of lies and deception provide conclusive evidence for the emergence of a concept of belief in children younger than age 3.5 years.

It appears that an implicit understanding of belief developmentally precedes a full or explicit one. Clements and Perner (1994, 2001) found evidence for a dissociation between implicit and explicit understanding of belief in the age range between 2 years, 11 months, and 3 years, 6 months. Children in this age range anticipated a story figure's belief-based search in their looking behavior but gave reality-based responses when asked for an explicit judgment (pointing at a location). Garnham and Ruffman (2001) were able to rule out that anticipatory looking behavior was due to an associative bias. Thus, an implicit understanding of belief appears to precede an explicit understanding by about half a year. Recent findings by Carpenter, Call, and Tomasello (2003) suggest that young 3-year-olds may also be able to take another person's false belief into account when complying with requests in social interaction. Between one third and two thirds of young 3-year-olds took an adult's false belief into account when complying with the adult's request to bring him or her a desired object. Control conditions and additional measures (response latencies, ratings of uncertainty) rule out more reductionist interpretations. Young children's success in this task cannot be attributed to the nonverbal format of the task per se because Call and Tomasello (1999) found that a carefully controlled nonverbal false belief task was mastered only by children who also passed a standard verbal false belief task. Rather, cooperation in natural communicative interaction may be a supportive context for an early understanding of mental states. Thus, implicit understanding appears to precede explicit understanding of belief by about half a year.[1] Implicit understanding may also be the basis for young 3-year-olds' beginning ability to take another person's wrong belief into account in some communicative exchanges.

Although belief understanding is at the core of our theory of mind, the view that a theory of mind develops around the age of 4 years is based not only on the false belief phenomenon. Rather, there is evidence for the acquisition of a whole set of related concepts in the same age range and for conceptual coherence in children's developing understanding of the mental domain.

Knowledge

Belief understanding implies an understanding of the relation between a person's access to information, his or her knowledge or belief, and his or her action. Four-year-olds who pass the false belief task also pass tasks that require them to answer questions about the source of their knowledge (i.e., how they know about a simple state of affairs, such as the content of a box; Wimmer, Hogrefe, & Perner, 1988). In contrast, 3-year-olds fail to respond correctly to "how do you know?" questions, although they are able to answer parallel "why" questions about nonepistemic but internal states (e.g., about the causes of being hungry; Perner & Ogden, 1988). Three-year-olds do associate informational access with knowledge and lack of informational access with ignorance in simple forced-choice procedures (Pratt & Bryant, 1990). However, almost all 3-year-olds and even some 4-year-olds fail to understand how information acquired through different sensory modalities leads to knowledge about object properties (e.g., that feeling an object leads to knowledge about its texture, and seeing, about its color; O'Neill, Astington, & Flavell, 1992). Moreover, 3- to 4-year-olds have difficulty distinguishing between knowledge acquired through communication (from others) and self-generated knowledge acquired by perceptual access or through inferential reasoning (Gopnik & Graf, 1988). The ability to represent sources of knowledge is important for memory development. Marked improvement in free recall as well as in source monitoring, and decreased suggestibility, have been related to theory of mind development (Perner, 2000).

There is evidence for an implicit understanding of the relation between access to information and knowledge in 2-year-olds' communication:

---

[1]This view may in the future be challenged by research on infants' representation of epistemic states. Onishi and Baillargeon (2002) found looking-time patterns consistent with the assumption that 15.5-month-old infants represent false belief in a nonverbal version of an unexpected transfer task. Future research will have to demonstrate that success in this task is based on a genuine understanding of belief. A simpler heuristic for the infant could be, for instance, to encode the target person's presence or absence at each object motion and to predict his or her subsequent action based on an important situational cue—the person's presence or absence at a critical event.

O'Neill (1996) showed that 27- and 31-month-old children adapted their messages to their mother's informational access, providing more specific clues about an object's location when the mother had not been present during its transfer than when she had. Findings by Dunham, Dunham, and O'Keefe (2000) indicate that only older 2-year-olds (33-month-olds) do so on the basis of an understanding of informational access, whereas younger children do not differentiate between absence during a critical event and absence at some other point in time.

Recent research on infants' mental state representation indicates that a basic sensitivity to the seeing–knowing relation may develop in the 2nd year of life. Tomasello and Haberl (2003) found that 12- to 18-month-old children showed a new toy significantly more often to a person when the person was absent while the new toy was introduced than when the person was in the room but not participating in the game. Using a preferential looking procedure, Poulin-Dubois et al. (2003) found that 18- and 24-month-old (but not 14-month-old) infants based their expectations about a person's search for a hidden object on the person's prior access to (visual) information, looking longer at incorrect searching when the person had seen where the target was hidden and at correct searching when the person had not seen where it was hidden. Although these expectations need not be based on a causal understanding of the relations among seeing, knowing, and correct action, a beginning sensitivity to relevant situational cues may help children acquire an understanding of knowledge acquisition.

The Appearance-Reality Distinction

The distinction between appearance and reality—that is, an understanding that one and the same entity can appear to be x (e.g., an apple), but really be y (e.g., a candle)—requires an understanding of mental processes because one's own perception is the source of the apparent identity of the entity. The distinction is similar to the belief-reality distinction because it requires one to simultaneously mentally manipulate two conflicting representations of an entity (its real and its apparent identity). John Flavell and his colleagues (Flavell, Flavell, & Green, 1983, 1987; Flavell, Green, & Flavell, 1986) systematically studied the development of the appearance-reality distinction in children. In some of the experiments, children were shown fake objects, such as a sponge that looks like a rock. The child was first acquainted with the real identity of the object. Then the child was questioned about the real and the apparent identity of the object (What is it really? Is it really a sponge or is it really a rock? What does this look like? Does it look like a sponge, or does it look like a rock?). The majority of the 4-year-olds answered both pairs of questions correctly, whereas most 3-year-olds failed to differentiate—that is, they committed realistic or phenomenistic errors. Flavell, Zhang, Zou, Dong, and Qi (1983) found evidence for intercultural universality of the appearance-reality differentiation in Chinese children. Three-year-olds' difficulty with the distinction cannot be attributed to the syntactic or semantic complexity of the test questions because parallel question pairs requiring the distinction between pretend identity and real identity are answered correctly by the majority of 3-year-olds (Flavell et al., 1987; Sodian, Hülsken, Ebner, & Thoermer, 1998). Several recent studies showed that 3-year-olds, and sometimes even 2-year-olds, are able to make some differentiation between appearance and reality in particularly compelling contexts. For instance, Rice, Koinis, Sullivan, Tager-Flusberg, and Winner (1997) demonstrated a nonverbal differentiation in 3-year-olds who were asked by the experimenter to bring her an object that served a certain function (e.g., something to wipe the floor with, something that looks like a rock on a photo). However, it can be argued that these tasks avoid the problem of dual coding because they typically allow one to map the distinction onto two different reference objects or onto two different observer perspectives. In sum, it appears that the development of the appearance-reality distinction, as well as the belief-reality distinction, reflect children's developing understanding of misrepresentation. The two distinctions are not only correlated, but training 3-year-olds to distinguish appearance from reality has effects on their belief understanding, supporting the view that children's naïve psychological understanding is a coherent conceptual system (Hülsken, 2001; Slaughter & Gopnik, 1996).

Pretense

If the belief-reality and appearance-reality differentiations develop late, around the age of 4 years, how can children engage in metarepresentational activities, such as pretend play, so much earlier (beginning between 18 and 24 months)? This relation between pretend play and theory of mind development was pointed out by Alan Leslie (1987, 1994), who argued that a common, early-maturing metarepresentational mechanism underlies both the development of pretend play and the development of a theory of mind. This metarepresentational mechanism enables the 2-year-old to decouple a fictional identity of an object, a person, or an action temporarily from its permanent real identity. If this capacity is indeed metarepresentational[2] and functionally equivalent with the metarepresentational demands of belief-reality and appearance-reality differentiations, then the developmental lag appears to be attributable to task demands. Perner (1991) argued that the crucial difference between belief and pretense is truth functionality: Beliefs are representations of reality that the person who holds the belief assumes to be true, whereas pretense involves the creation of counterfactual states of affairs that the persons engaged in sym-

---

[2]German and Leslie (2000) clarified that the metarepresentational capacity assumed to underlie pretend play was not conceptualized as an explicit understanding of the representational relation between mind and world and should therefore rather be called M-representation. However, this does not appear to clarify the representational properties of M-representations.

bolic play do not believe to be true. Thus, understanding a person's false belief involves understanding that another person (or oneself in the past) misrepresents reality, whereas pretend play merely requires the child to distinguish between reality and fiction, rather than representing the representational relation between the two (see Harris, 1994, for a similar view). In fact, developmental studies have shown that children younger than age 4 or 5 years, despite their competencies in engaging in pretend play, have a very limited understanding of pretense as a representational activity (see Lillard, 2001, for an overview). Lillard (1993) found that most 4-year-olds and even some 5-year-olds believe that a story figure could pretend to be x (e.g., a rabbit) without knowing anything about x. Many preschoolers classify pretense as a physical activity (like clapping hands), not a mental activity (like thinking). Three-year-olds do understand, however, that pretend play is subjective, and they distinguish between pretend and realistic activities. In a recent imitation study, 3-year-olds (but not 2-year-olds) differentiated between actions that were introduced as "trying to do x" and actions that were labeled as "pretending to do x" (Rakoczy, Tomasello, & Striano, 2004). This is consistent with findings by Bruell and Woolley (1998), who showed that 3-year-olds can infer the symbolic play intentions of other people. Based on an early understanding of pretend play as an intentional activity, an explicit understanding of the representational relation between mind and world appears to develop late, around the age of 5–7 years.

Theory of Mind Impairments

Selective impairments in theory of mind development in children with developmental disorders or disabilities are of major importance for theoretical explanations of theory of mind development in normally developing children. Therefore, the finding that autistic children with a verbal mental age significantly older than 4 years do not have a concept of belief (Baron-Cohen, Leslie, & Frith, 1985) has sparked a whole area of autism research (see Frith, 2003, for a review). There is converging evidence from numerous studies comparing autistic children with a verbal mental age of at least 4 years with a clinical control group (often children with Down syndrome) and normally developing children, indicating that autistic children, adolescents, and adults suffer from a broad and specific mind-reading deficit concerning ontological distinctions (mental vs. physical); understanding of epistemic states, deception, appearance-reality differentiation; attribution of belief-based emotions, as well as developmental precursors to a theory of mind such as pretend play and joint attentional skills. The specificity of the deficit is well documented through experimental controls: Autistic children fail false belief tasks but pass parallel false photos tasks (a task that requires an understanding of nonmental misrepresentation) (Leslie & Thaiss, 1992); they fail deception tasks but pass parallel physical obstruction (sabotage) tasks (Sodian & Frith, 1992); they can make sense of behavioral but not of mentalistic action sequences (Baron-Cohen, Leslie,

& Frith, 1986), to mention just a few findings. Some autistic persons do develop a theory of mind (first-order false belief and related concepts) with a gross delay, but deficits in more complex tasks persist even in adulthood (Happé, 1994).

A delay of about 3 years in the acquisition of a theory of mind has been found in verbally taught deaf children (deVilliers, in press; Gale, de Villiers, de Villiers, & Pyers, 1996; Peterson & Siegal, 1999; Woolfe, Want, & Siegal, 2002), whereas deaf children of signing parents who received early and rich input in sign language were not delayed. These findings highlight the role of language in the development of a theory of mind (see next section).

Williams syndrome, a rare neurological disorder characterized by mental retardation, with some unimpaired cognitive abilities, such as vocabulary, face recognition, and rote memory, has been studied for possible islets of ability in mind reading. The findings are best compatible with a theory proposed by Tager-Flusberg and Sullivan (2000), who distinguished a social-perceptual component of mind reading that serves person perception and online representation of mental states based on facial expression, gestures, or posture from a higher order social cognitive component that requires inferences about mental states and processes. It appears that only the social-perceptual component may be selectively unimpaired in Williams syndrome patients.

Individual Differences in Theory of Mind Development

Individual differences in theory of mind development in normally developing children were initially related to family size. Perner, Ruffman, and Leekam (1994) found that children with siblings passed false belief tasks earlier than did only children. Jenkins and Astington (1996) replicated this finding but found that the effect was less pronounced in children with high verbal abilities. In a study with a large sample, Ruffman, Perner, Naito, Parkin, and Clements (1998) found the sibling effect only for older but not for younger siblings. However, two studies with lower class families did not replicate the sibling effect (Cole & Mitchell, 2000; Cutting & Dunn, 1999), indicating that theory of mind development is mediated by the quality of social interaction in the family, not by family size per se. Studies of familial interaction indicate that the frequency and the way in which parents highlight mental states in conversation with their children, as well as parental mind mindedness in general, predict children's mastery of the false belief task (Brown, Donelan-McCall, & Dunn, 1996; Meins, Fernyhough, Russell, & Clark, 1998). In longitudinal studies, within-child relations were found between frequency of fantasy play (pretend play, frequent engagement in fantasy, imaginary companions) and later theory of mind development (Taylor & Carlson, 1997). It should be noted, however, that measures of language acquisition have been shown to be by far the best predictor of theory of mind development, with language competence predicting later theory of mind, not theory of mind competencies predicting later language abilities (Astington & Jenkins, 1999; Jenkins & Astington, 1996).

Is theory of mind development important for the development of real-world social competencies? Several longitudinal studies addressed the complex web of conceptual development, language acquisition, and the development of social and cognitive competencies during the preschool and early elementary school years (Astington & Jenkins, 1995; Cutting & Dunn, 1999; Dunn & Hughes, 1998). In general, theory of mind appears to be important for the development of social competencies (e.g., as rated by teachers), even when language abilities are taken into account. Astington (2003) concludes from a review of the complex patterns of findings that theory of mind development is necessary for the development of a number of social competencies, primarily as far as conflict management, imaginative abilities, and communicative competencies are concerned. However, variation in theory of mind abilities does not, of course, account for a large proportion of the variance in social competencies and social behaviors. It should also be noted that some findings indicate that emotion understanding predicts social competence for the most part independently of general theory of mind development.

ADVANCED THEORY OF MIND DEVELOPMENT

Although there is consensus that children's understanding of the mental domain continues to develop after the age of 4 or 5 years, much less research has been devoted to these later developments than to first-order theory of mind development. One of the core developments in building on a first-order theory of mind is second-order belief understanding ("Peter believes that Max believes that . . .").

Perner and Wimmer (1985) conducted the first systematic investigation of children's understanding of second-order false belief and found that children did not correctly infer higher order beliefs until the age of 7 to 8 years. More recent studies employing simplified tasks found competence in children as young as 5 to 6 years (Sullivan, Zaitchik, & Tager-Flusberg, 1994). Still, there is a developmental sequence from first- to second-order belief understanding. Second-order belief understanding is necessary for understanding complex speech acts, such as irony, which, like lies, are intentionally false utterances, but differ from lies in that the speaker does not intend the listener to believe the lie or the joke (Winner & Leekam, 1991). A related conceptual problem concerns the understanding of commitments (Mant & Perner, 1988). Younger children tend to think that all deviations from a previously uttered plan of action are a breach of commitment. Their ability to take another person's mental state into account appears to develop earlier than their understanding that this mental state needs to be influenced in certain situations, for instance, through a white lie (Broomfield, Robinson, & Robinson, 2002).

Advanced theory of mind development is further characterized by a growing insight into inferential and interpretive mental processes. While 4-year-olds, in judging people's knowledge state, employ the simple rule seeing = knowing and neglect inference as a source of knowledge, 6-year-olds take simple inference into account when making knowledge attributions (Ruffman, 1996; Sodian & Wimmer, 1987). The development of an understanding of the role of inference in knowledge acquisition is also reflected in an increased understanding of retrieval cues in memory tasks (Sodian & Schneider, 1990). Although preschoolers can memorize facts, they often fail to represent the temporal and situational context features of learning events: Only around the age of 5 years do children retrieve such contextual information correctly; younger children often claim that they knew all along facts that they were taught during the experiment (Taylor, Esbensen, & Bennett, 1994).

Increasing insight into knowledge acquisition as a constructive process is reflected in children's developing understanding of verbal communication. Whereas 4-year-olds falsely attribute knowledge to the recipient of ambiguous messages in referential communication, 6-year-olds distinguish between the epistemic consequences of ambiguous and unambiguous messages (Sodian, 1988). Six-year-olds, but not 4-year-olds, take a speaker's false belief into account when interpreting his or her messages (Mitchell, Robinson, & Thompson, 1999). A beginning understanding of speech acts as products of mental activity is also indicated by 5- to 6-year-old children's ability to revise their first interpretations of ambiguous messages when presented with conflicting information (Beck & Robinson, 2001).

Even 6-year-olds have only a limited understanding of knowledge representation in the human mind. They fail to understand referential opacity—that is, they believe that a person who knows a description X of an object also knows the object under the description Y (Apperly & Robinson, 1998). Hulme, Mitchell, and Wood (2003) argue that children's deficient understanding of referential opacity indicates a failure to understand intensional contexts and, thus, a limited understanding of mental representation in early elementary school age. German and Leslie (2001), who found a limited ability to draw inferences from "know" to "think" in 6-year-olds, similarly argue that elementary-school children's intuitive understanding of mental representation is very limited.

A theory of mind is not only a cognitive tool that can be used for action prediction and explanation but also a system of ideas about mental states and activities. Flavell, Green, and Flavell (1993, 1995) investigated children's understanding of mental activity, asking, for instance, about mental activity in persons who did not show any physical activity (but were simply sitting still); preschoolers tended to conceptualize thinking as a momentary activity that is under voluntary control. The idea of a continuous and partly uncontrollable mental activity, in the sense of a stream of consciousness, doesn't develop until around the age of 8 years. Similarly, concepts such as inner speech and a notion of the unconscious first develop in school-age children (Flavell, Green, Flavell, & Lin, 1999). Thus, children's intuitive ideas about cognitive processes appear to develop in close conjunction with their beginning ability to introspect.

The development of an advanced theory of mind has been character-ized as the understanding of the mind as an active interpreter of infor-mation (Lalonde & Chandler, 2002). Although even 4-year-olds under-stand that misinterpretation arises from insufficient information (Perner & Davies, 1991), preschoolers fail to understand that one and the same piece of information can be interpreted differently from different view-points or interpretive stances. The first signs of a more sophisticated view of the interpretive mind can be found in young elementary-school chil-dren who begin to understand the workings of social prejudices or ste-reotypes (Pillow, 1991; Pillow & Weed, 1995). Similarly, around the age of 6 years, children begin to conceive of traits as psychological constructs and use such constructs not only to predict behavior across various situa-tions but also to predict mental states (emotions) (Yuill & Pearson, 1998). A concept of interpretive frameworks is particularly important for sci-entific reasoning (Kuhn & Pearsall, 2000). Whereas an explicit metacon-ceptual understanding of the role of theories in the construction of scien-tific knowledge is rare even in adults (Thoermer & Sodian, 2002), young elementary school children begin to understand how empirical evidence can be brought to bear on beliefs (hypotheses) about the world (Ruffman, Perner, Olson, & Doherty, 1993; Sodian, Zaitchik, & Carey, 1991). Asting-ton, Pelletier, and Homer (2002) found that 6-year-olds' understanding of what constitutes evidence for a belief is correlated with their understand-ing of second-order belief, indicating conceptual coherence in the develop-ment of an advanced theory of mind.

Further evidence for a growing understanding of mental construc-tion and interpretation comes from studies of children's understanding of mental verbs. While fundamental features of the semantics of verbs such as *think, know, guess,* and *forget* are mastered by 4- to 5-year-olds (Johnson & Wellman, 1980), the developmental process continues throughout the ele-mentary school years (Astington, 2000). Analyses of the cognitive orga-nization of mental verbs indicate a growing understanding of the role of memory and an increasing differentiation between degrees of certainty as expressed by different mental verbs (Schwanenflugel, Henderson, & Fabricius, 1998). Positive correlations have been found between metacog-nitive monitoring and the semantic differentiation among mental verbs (Schwanenflugel, Fabricius, & Noyes, 1996).

Kuhn (2000) advocates the integration of theory of mind research with research on metacognition into research on the development of metaknowl-edge across the life span. The development of epistemological views and their relation to (scientific) reasoning skills is an example of a research field with a life span perspective that is related to theory of mind research (see Chandler, Hallett, & Sokol, 2002, for a review of conflicting descrip-tions of developmental progress in intuitive epistemologies). To date, only a few studies have addressed theory of mind development in old age.

Whereas Happé, Winner, and Brownell (1998) found that theory of mind reasoning was spared in older adults, compared with their performance in control tasks, Maylor, Moulson, Muncer, and Taylor (2002) found deficits in elderly adults (over 75 years), even when memory demands, vocabulary, and speed of information processing were controlled for. Similarly, Sullivan and Ruffman (2004) found performance deficits in older adults in theory of mind tasks as well as in emotion recognition and other social cognitive tasks.

THEORETICAL EXPLANATIONS OF THEORY OF MIND DEVELOPMENT

As was argued previously, there is ample evidence for the view that first-order theory of mind development is a genuine developmental phenomenon. Similarly, there is evidence for developmental progress in children's understanding of the mind beyond preschool age, although it is less clear how to give a unifying description of the developmental phenomena in question. What is theory of mind development the development of? Domain-specific theories account for theory of mind development in terms of specific perceptual and conceptual principles or information-processing systems dedicated to processing information about the mental domain. Domain-general accounts do not deny the domain specificity of conceptual knowledge about the mind but try to account for domain-specific cognition in terms of domain-general cognitive processes, such as working memory, executive function, or reasoning abilities.

Domain-Specific Theories

Domain-specific theories of the development of social information processing posit specialized information-processing systems, operating at birth, as well as domain-specific learning mechanisms. An example is Meltzoff's (2002) theory of a social learning mechanism based on the human ability to imitate. Theories of theory of mind development face a more specific task than do theories of the development of social knowledge in general: How does the child acquire an understanding of intentional states? Three proposals are currently being discussed: (1) theory of mind development as conceptual change in a theorylike conceptual system; (2) theory of mind development as the developing ability to simulate others' mental states, based on one's own introspectively accessible experience; and (3) theory of mind development as the maturation of a specialized conceptual module.

The Theory Theory

Our commonsense intuitive psychology can be described as an (intuitive) theory because it is based on ontological commitments (about the entities and processes considered to be mental), it posits domain-specific psychological explanations for the phenomena in question, and it consists of a coherent system of concepts that function like theoretical terms in everyday predictions and explanations of behavior (Flavell, 1999; Gopnik & Meltzoff, 1997; Premack & Woodruff, 1978; Wellman & Gelman, 1998). Gopnik and Wellman (1994) draw an analogy between theory change in the sense of paradigm change in the history of science and theory change in the child's understanding of the mind, arguing that children initially conceive of human behavior in terms of desires and emotions and only later incorporate the concept of belief into their mentalistic action explanation system, which eventually becomes central for the new—representational—theory of mind. Theory theorists assume that information acquired in social interaction is crucial for processes of theory change to occur, but they have not been specific about the kinds of mechanisms underlying conceptual change.

Although theory theorists differ in their views about the exact nature of restructuring occurring in the child's conceptual understanding of the mind between the ages of about 2 and 5 years, there is agreement about the central role of the emergence of an understanding of mental representation. The most elaborate account of a developing understanding of the mind as representational has been proposed by Perner (1991). Perner describes the 4-year-old's (and the adult's) intuitive understanding of the mind as representational because an understanding of false belief implies an understanding of misrepresentation. The content of a false belief is not only a false proposition about a state of reality, but it is also a false proposition that a person assumes to be true. Thus, an understanding of false belief not only requires the ability to distinguish between true and false propositions about the world, but it also implies the insight that a false proposition can be believed to be true. Because this insight into the nature of beliefs requires an understanding of how false beliefs arise from false or insufficient information, and entails an understanding of the consequences false beliefs have for action, a representational theory of mind is a genuine causal explanatory account of mental processes. In contrast, the young child's (i.e., the 2- to 3-year-old's) understanding of the mind can be characterized as a pretheoretical understanding of situations (Perner, 1991): People act according to their goals and can pursue their goals not only in the real world but also in fictional contexts. Because the young situation theorist cannot account for people's actions in terms of their beliefs, he or she fails to understand mistakes that are based on false beliefs. Perner makes two proposals about the cognitive changes occurring around the age of 4 years.

1. Whereas the 2- and 3-year-old can build and mentally manipulate models of reality as well as fictional situation models, the 4-year-old understands models (i.e., beliefs, thoughts, images) as models about reality (i.e., understands aboutness); that is, the 4-year-old and the adult not only use representations but also understand the representational relation between a model and reality.

2. A representational understanding of beliefs implies an understanding of the causal impact of mental representations. False beliefs lead to false actions; it is the subjective representation of reality, not the state of reality itself, that determines human action.

Perner's theory has been criticized as implausible because it is highly unlikely that 4-year-old children or even adults make everyday predictions or explanations of human behavior based on an explicit understanding of concepts such as proposition, truth, or representation. In fact, German and Leslie (2000), among others, empirically demonstrated severe limitations of the young child's understanding of representation. Perner (2000) makes clear that an implicit, possibly subconceptual understanding of the concept of representation, not a highly explicit one, is assumed to underlie our understanding of the mind.

Simulation Theory

Simulation theorists assume that our intuitive psychological interpretations of human behavior are based on our experience of our own thoughts and feelings. This view can be traced back to Descartes's theorizing about humans having immediate access to their own psychological processes: Being human, we have mental states, and these mental states are accessible to conscious experience. Such an access is thought to be preconceptual, not based on conceptual knowledge. The attribution of mental states to other people is thought to be based on a simulation process. We project ourselves into the other's situation, imagine what we would think and feel in the person's situation, and attribute these simulated mental experiences onto the other person (Goldman, 1992; Gordon, 1986; Harris, 1991). Harris (1992) proposed a theory of theory of mind development, based on the simulation view. The more default assumptions have to be reset, the more difficult the simulation. To simulate another person's mental state that differs from one's own mental state, one has to set aside one's own mental state (the default setting) to simulate the other's mental state under the critical conditions. In the case of another's false belief, the child not only has to set aside his or her own mental state but also the state of reality to simulate the mental state of the person who holds a false belief. Thus, belief understanding is more difficult than simply understanding differences between one's own and another's mental state (e.g., in the case of empathy) because the default settings have to be changed.

Simulation theory and theory theory differ in their predictions about the developmental relation of understanding one's own and others' mental states. Whereas simulation theory predicts that children would have immediate access to their own mental states, with the difficulty lying in inferring the other's mental states, theory theory predicts that one's own and others' mental states should be understood at about the same time because both are based on the same conceptual system. The empirical evidence supports the theory view because 3-year-old children find it equally difficult to represent their own false beliefs as to represent another person's false beliefs (Gopnik & Astington, 1988). Moreover, Perner and Howes (1992) showed that patterns of findings that theory theory explains by making the distinction between first- and second-order belief are hard to account for by simulation theory. Perner (1999b) shows how a nonintrospective variation of simulation theory can avoid these problems. Similarly, recent philosophical analyses conclude that our everyday psychology uses both simulation (primarily for belief fixation) and theory-based knowledge (for action prediction).

Modular Theories

Modular theories assume that development of a theory of mind is based on information processing in a specialized conceptual module. Leslie (1994) assumes three successively maturing domain-specific modular mechanisms for representing agency. In the first half year, ToBy (theory of body mechanism) enables the infant to distinguish between agents and nonagents on the basis of a number of criteria, for instance, self-propelled motion. Two theory of mind mechanisms begin to operate successively in the 1st and 2nd year: TOMM1 supports the representation of intentional agents at the end of the 1st year of life, and TOMM2 comes online around the age of 18 months and supports the development of metarepresentation. Leslie (1994; see also Scholl & Leslie, 1999) assumes that a metarepresentational understanding of belief is present long before children solve false belief tasks. Children younger than age 3.5 years fail false belief tasks not because they lack the metarepresentational capacities but because they fail to infer the content of a person's false belief. This latter ability requires selection processing (i.e., inhibiting competing contents) and is a performance rather than a competence problem. Modular theories can account for dissociations between theory of mind development and other areas of cognitive development, as is the case in autism, but they have difficulty accounting for findings showing the influence of social experience, such as the developmental delay of orally taught deaf children (as compared with deaf children of signing parents; de Villiers, in press).

Social Constructivist Theories and the Role of Language in Theory of Mind Development

Critics of the cognitive theories of theory of mind development argue that these theories neglect the role of social experience and communicative interaction (Carpendale & Lewis, in press). Although the theory theory is a constructivist account of conceptual development, it is unspecific with regard to the precise ways in which social experiences influence theory construction and revision. Carpendale and Lewis present a general framework of a social interactionist, constructivist theory of theory of mind development, based on the assumption of active theory construction in social interaction, not passive enculturation into the practice of mentalistic interpretation.

This general framework of a social constructivist theory can accommodate recent research on the role of language in theory of mind development (see Astington & Baird, in press). The close association of language and theory of mind development has been documented both cross-sectionally and longitudinally with language as a predictor for theory of mind (e.g., Astington & Jenkins, 1995). It is unlikely that this association merely reflects verbal task demands because nonverbal tasks are as difficult as verbal tasks (Call & Tomasello, 1999). Language can facilitate theory of mind development by focusing the child's attention on mentalistic explanation of behavior. Language becomes a major source of information about the mental domain for the child. Therefore, the acquisition of mental terms (e.g., epistemic verbs) plays an important role in the acquisition of mental concepts (Astington & Jenkins, 1995; Bartsch & Wellman, 1995).

A specific theory about the relation between the acquisition of syntax and theory of mind development was proposed by de Villiers and de Villiers (2000): Linguistic complement structures serve as the representational structure for embedded propositions, such as "Peter believes that the chocolate is in the cupboard." Verbs of desire and communication (say, ask), as well as epistemic verbs, govern complement sentences. To understand complement sentences, it is critical to understand that the embedded complement sentence can be false while the matrix sentence is true (it can be true that Peter believes that the chocolate is in the cupboard when the chocolate really is not in there). This hypothesis is supported by close correlations between the mastery of the syntax of complement sentences and the mastery of false belief tasks (de Villiers & de Villiers, 2000). Moreover, training studies showed that experience in complement clauses had effects on 3-year-olds' mastery of false belief tasks (Hale & Tager-Flusberg, 2003; Lohmann & Tomasello, 2003). However, a strict linguistic determinism as suggested by de Villiers and de Villiers is inconsistent with findings by Perner, Sprung, Zauner, and Haider (2003), who showed that German-speaking children understood desire propositions better than belief propositions, although in German, unlike in English, the syntax of verbs of desire is identical to the syntax of epistemic verbs.

Other accounts of the role of language in theory of mind development focus on discourse. Harris (1999) argues that discourse is important for highlighting perspective differences. Lohmann and Tomasello (2003) experimentally highlighted such perspective differences in a training condition. This training condition had effects on belief understanding, and these effects were almost completely independent of those of syntax training. These findings indicate that various aspects of natural discourse (disagreements, misunderstandings, perspective change) contribute to the development of the concept of belief in conjunction with the acquisition of the syntactic means for mental state attribution (Tomasello & Rakoczy, 2003).

Domain-General Theories: Perspectives, Frames of Reference, and Action Control

Theoretical accounts of the role of language and discourse in theory of mind development are domain specific in the broader sense of operating within the social domain. However, theories about complement structures and perspective representation underlying theory of mind development can also be thought of as domain general because they account for theory of mind development in terms of broader cognitive changes that occur in the critical age range. This approach has been taken further in relating theory of mind development to the representation of perspectives or frames of reference. Perner, Brandl, and Garnham (2003) define perspective problems as situations in which the concept of a perspective is required to integrate information—that is, situations in which different representations of one and the same state of affairs have to be represented on a metalevel as different representations of the same state of affairs. Metarepresentation is required for perspective problems of different kinds, not only in the social domain. For instance, object names that individuate objects in different ways can be understood as perspective problems in the sense outlined previously. To label the same object "a rabbit" or "an animal" is to use different perspectives or frames of reference. An explicit representation of perspectives is necessary to explicitly understand the possibility of multiple labels for single objects. In fact, a close developmental relation has been shown between the mastery of naming tasks (in which the child is required, after some training, to produce or judge an alternative label for a specific entity) and the mastery of the false belief problem, even when age and working memory demands were controlled for (Perner, Stummer, Sprung, & Doherty, 2002).

Bischof-Köhler (2000) proposes a similar theory derived from the notion of a frame of reference (Bezugssystem) in German Gestalt psychology (Metzger, 1954). Theory of mind development becomes possible around the age of 4 years as a result of the child's developing ability to reflect on frames of reference. This reflective (or metarepresentational) ability is particularly important for seeing the same entity in different frames of reference (e.g., different epistemic perspectives), especially when these frames of reference are incongruent. Bischof-Köhler further assumes that this ability to reflect on frames of reference has far-reaching consequences for cognitive as well as motivational development. In particular, the representation of time that we need to plan action sequences requires the reflection of time as a frame of reference. When putting, for instance, different errands that one plans to do in a temporal order, one has to estimate the time duration of each individual errand. In particular, the reflection of time as a frame of reference is necessary to represent past and future desires and motives independently of one's present motivational state. In an empirical study with more than 100 children between ages 36 and 58 months, Bischof-Köhler studied the developmental relations of theory of mind, representation of time, delay of gratification, and action planning and found a high correlation between theory of mind and time representation independent of age, as well as evidence for the proposed relations between delay of gratification and action planning developing in close conjunction with time representation and theory of mind. The patterns of data were consistent with the view that simultaneous developments in theory of mind and time representation jointly contribute to the development of the ability to organize and control one's actions.

Developmental relations between various aspects of action planning and control and theory of mind have been found in research on the relations between executive functions and theory of mind, which are the main focus of this volume and will thus not be repeated here. Several theoretical accounts of this relationship were based on the assumption that executive abilities play a critical role in the development of children's theory of mind. Russell (1997) and Pacherie (1997) argue that simple forms of action monitoring and action control are prerequisites for self-awareness, which in turn is necessary for the development of mental concepts. Thus, a certain level of executive control is necessary to gain insight into the intentional nature of human action and to conceptualize intentional states. This theory is consistent with the close association of executive functions and theory of mind in normal development, as well as with autistic children's impairments in both areas. It is not consistent, however, with the finding that children with severe impairments in executive functions (inhibitory control in children with attention deficit hyperactivity disorder [ADHD]) are apparently unimpaired in theory of mind development (see, however, Sodian & Hülsken, this volume, for findings on specific impairments in ADHD children's advanced theory of mind). Wimmer (1989) and Perner (1998) developed an alternative theory of the relation between executive functions and theory of mind, arguing that theory of mind leads to improved self-control, based on the child's insight into the causal impact of beliefs on action. This theory is also supported by correlational findings in normal development (Lang & Perner, 2002). However, the finding that verbally taught deaf children suffer from a severe delay in theory of mind, but no comparable delays in executive functions, is inconsistent with this theory (de Villiers, in press). Therefore, current theories of functional relations between executive functions and theory of mind focus on specific relations, differentiating between various components of executive function (see Moses, Carlson, & Sabbagh, this volume). Moreover, the possibility of functional independence between executive functions and theory of mind is also considered. The two cognitive abilities appear to be supported by neighboring regions of the prefrontal cortex that mature at a similar rate, without necessarily being functionally interdependent (Ozonoff, Pennington, & Rogers, 1991).

CONCLUSIONS

Theory of mind research has contributed in important ways to our understanding of cognitive development. First, it highlights the importance of conceptual analysis for the developmental study of domain-specific knowl-edge. Theory of mind research got off the ground only by taking phil-osophical analyses of commonsense mentalism seriously. Second, it has contributed in important ways to our understanding of conceptual change in childhood. Conceptual change accounts of theory of mind development have centered on the concept of mental representation and have certainly contributed to our understanding of what it means to grasp this concept. The debate between simulation and conceptual change accounts has been productive in generating nonintrospectionist simulation accounts and models that can accommodate both conceptual development and simula-tion. Finally, theoretical explanations of theory of mind development have addressed the interplay between conceptual development and the devel-opment of other cognitive functions, as well as the development of action control. Although a certain level of action control appears to be necessary for children to express their conceptual understanding of the mind, action monitoring and action control also contribute to the emergence of men-talistic concepts, and conceptual development (understanding the causal impact of beliefs) may in turn contribute to the development of behavioral regulation. Although the developmental relations between theory of mind, language, memory, understanding perspectives or frames of reference as well as planning and action control are far from being fully understood, it has certainly become clear that these areas are related in meaningful ways on a conceptual level, not just on the superficial level of task demands.

REFERENCES

Apperly, I. A., & Robinson, E. J. (1998). Children's mental representation of referential rela-tions. *Cognition, 67*, 287–309.

Astington, J. W. (1993). *The child's discovery of the mind*. Cambridge, MA: Harvard Univer-sity Press.

Astington, J. W. (1999). The language of intention: Three ways of doing it. In P. D. Zelazo & J. W. Astington (Eds.), *Developing theories of intention: Social understanding and self-control* (pp. 295–315). Mahwah, NJ: Lawrence Erlbaum Associates.

Astington, J. W. (2000). Language and metalanguage in children's understanding of mind. In J. W. Astington (Ed.), *Minds in the making: Essays in honor of David R. Olson* (pp. 267–284). Malden, MA: Blackwell.

Astington, J. W. (2003). Sometimes necessary, never sufficient: False-belief understanding and social competence. In B. Repacholi & V. Slaughter (Eds.), *Macquarie Monographs in Cognitive Science Series: Individual differences in theory of mind: Implications for typical and atypical development* (pp. 13–38). New York: Psychology Press.

Astington, J. W., & Baird, J. (Eds.). (in press). *Why language matters for theory of mind*. Oxford, UK: Oxford University Press.

Astington, J. W., Harris, P. L., & Olson, D. R. (Eds.). (1988). *Developing theories of mind*. New York: Cambridge University Press.

Astington, J. W., & Jenkins, J. M. (1995). Theory of mind development and social under-standing. *Cognition and Emotion, 9*, 151–165.

Astington, J. W., & Jenkins, J. M. (1999). A longitudinal study on the relation between lan-guage and theory of mind development. *Developmental Psychology, 35*, 1311–1320.

Astington, J. W., Pelletier, J., & Homer, B. (2002). Theory of mind and epistemological development: The relation between children's second-order false-belief understanding and their ability to reason about evidence. *New Ideas in Psychology, 20*, 131–144.

Baird, J. A., & Baldwin, D. A. (2001). Making sense of human behavior: Action parsing and intentional inference. In B. F. Malle, L. J. Moses, & D. A. Baldwin (Eds.), *Intentions and intentionality. Foundations of social cognition* (pp. 193–206). Cambridge, MA: MIT Press.

Baron-Cohen, S., Leslie, A. M., & Frith, U. (1985). Does the autistic child have a "theory of mind"? *Cognition, 21,* 37–46.

Baron-Cohen, S., Leslie, A. M., & Frith, U. (1986). Mechanical, behavioural and intentional understanding of picture stories in autistic children. *British Journal of Developmental Psychology, 4,* 113–125.

Baron-Cohen, S., Tager-Flusberg, H., & Cohen, D. (Eds.). (2000). *Understanding other minds: Perspectives from developmental cognitive neuroscience* (2nd ed.). Oxford, UK: Oxford University Press.

Barresi, J., & Moore, C. (1996). Intentional relations and social understanding. *Behavioral and Brain Sciences, 19,* 197–154.

Bartsch, K., & Wellman, H. M. (1989). Young children's attributions of actions to beliefs and desires. *Child Development, 60,* 946–964.

Bartsch, K., & Wellman, H. M. (1995). *Children talk about the mind.* Oxford, UK: Oxford University Press.

Beck, S. R., & Robinson, E. J. (2001). Children's ability to make tentative interpretations of ambiguous messages. *Journal of Experimental Child Psychology, 79,* 95–114.

Bischof-Köhler, D. (2000). *Kinder auf Zeitreise. Theory of mind, Zeitverständnis und Handlungsorganisation* [Theory of mind, understanding of time, and action planning]. Bern, Switzerland: Huber.

Broomfield, K. A., Robinson, E. J., & Robinson, W. P. (2002). Children's understanding about white lies. *British Journal of Developmental Psychology, 20,* 47–65.

Brown, J. R., Donelan-McCall, N., & Dunn, J. (1996). Why talk about mental states? The significance of children's conversations with friends, siblings and mothers. *Child Development, 67,* 836–849.

Bruell, M. J., & Woolley, J. D. (1998). Young children's understanding of diversity in pretense. *Cognitive Development, 13,* 257–277.

Call, J., & Tomasello, M. (1999). A nonverbal false belief task: The performance of children and great apes. *Child Development, 70,* 381–395.

Carpendale, J. I., & Lewis, C. (in press). Constructing an understanding of mind: The development of children's social understanding within social interaction. *Behavioral and Brain Sciences.*

Carpenter, M., Call, J., & Tomasello, M. (2002). Understanding "prior intentions" enables two-year-olds to imitatively learn a complex task. *Child Development, 73,* 1431–1441.

Carpenter, M., Call, J., & Tomasello, M. (2003). A new false belief test for 36-month-olds. *British Journal of Developmental Psychology, 20,* 393–420.

Carpenter, M., Nagell, K., & Tomasello, M. (1998). Social cognition, joint attention, and communicative competence from 9 to 15 months af age. *Monographs of the Society for Research in Child Development, 63*(4, Serial No. 255), 1–166.

Chandler, M., Fritz, A. S., & Hala, S. (1989). Small scale deceit: Deception as a marker of 2-, 3-, and 4-year-olds' early theories of mind. *Child Development, 60,* 1263–1277.

Chandler, M., Hallett, D., & Sokol, B. W. (2002). Competing claims about competing knowledge claims. In B. K. Hofer, & P. R. Pintrich (Eds.), *Personal epistemology: The psychology of beliefs about knowledge and knowing* (pp. 145–168). Mahwah, NJ: Lawrence Erlbaum Associates.

Churchland, P. M. (1984). *Matter and consciousness: A contemporary introduction to the philosophy of mind.* Cambridge, MA: MIT Press.

Clements, W. A., & Perner, J. (1994). Implicit understanding of belief. *Cognitive Development, 9,* 377–395.

Clements, W. A., & Perner, J. (2001). When actions really do speak louder than words? But only implicitly: Young children's understanding of false belief in action. *British Journal of Developmental Psychology, 19,* 413–432.

Cole, K., & Mitchell, P. (2000). Siblings in the development of executive control and a theory of mind. *British Journal of Developmental Psychology, 18,* 279–295.

Cutting, J., & Dunn, J. (1999). Theory of mind, emotion understanding, language, and family background: Individual differences and interrelations. *Child Development, 70*, 853–865.

de Villiers, P. (in press). The role of language in theory of mind development: What deaf children tell us. In J. W. Astington & J. Baird (Eds.), *Why language matters for theory of mind.* Oxford: Oxford University Press.

de Villiers, J. G., & de Villiers, P. A. (2000). Linguistic determinism and the understanding of false beliefs. In P. Mitchell & K. J. Riggs (Eds.), *Children's reasoning and the mind* (pp. 191–228). Hove, UK: Psychology Press.

Dennett, D. C. (1978). Beliefs about beliefs. Commentary on D. Premack & G. Woodruff "Does the chimpanzee have a theory of mind?" *Behavioral and Brain Sciences, 1*, 568–570.

Dunham, P., Dunham, F., & O'Keefe, C. (2000). Two-year-olds' sensitivity to a parent's knowledge state: Mind reading or contextual cues? *British Journal of Developmental Psychology, 18*, 519–532.

Dunn, J., & Hughes, C. (1998). Young children's understanding of emotions within close relationships. *Cognition and Emotion, 12*, 171–190.

Feinfield, K. A., Lee, P. P., Flavell, E. R., Green, F. L., & Flavell, J. H. (1999). Young children's understanding of intention. *Cognitive Development, 14*, 463–486.

Flavell, J. H. (1999). Cognitive development: Children's knowledge about the mind. *Annual Review of Psychology, 50*, 21–45.

Flavell, J. H. (2000). Development of children's knowledge about the mental world. *International Journal of Behavioral Development, 24*, 15–23.

Flavell, J. H., Flavell, E. R., & Green, F. L. (1983). Development of the appearance-reality distinction. *Cognitive Psychology, 15*, 95–120.

Flavell, J. H., Flavell, E. R., & Green, F. L. (1987). Young children's knowledge about the apparent-real and pretend-real distinctions. *Developmental Psychology, 23*, 816–822.

Flavell, J. H., Green, F. L., & Flavell, E. R. (1986). Development of knowledge about the appearance-reality distinction. *Monographs of the Society for Research in Child Development, 51*(1, Serial No. 212).

Flavell, J. H., Green, F. L., & Flavell, E. R. (1993). Children's understanding of the stream of consciousness. *Child Development, 64*, 387–398.

Flavell, J. H. Green, F. L., & Flavell, E. R. (1995). Young children's knowledge about thinking. *Monographs of the Society for Research in Child Development, 60*(1, Serial No. 243), 39–47.

Flavell, J. H., Green, F. L., & Flavell, E. R., & Lin, N. T. (1999). Development of children's knowledge about unconsciousness. *Child Development, 70*, 396–412.

Flavell, J. H., Mumme, D. L, Green, F. L., & Flavell, E. R. (1992). Young children's understanding of moral and other beliefs. *Child Development, 63*, 960–977.

Flavell, J. H., Zhang, X.-D., Zou, H., Dong, Q., & Qi, S. (1983). A comparison between the development of the appearance reality distinction in the People's Republic of China and the United States. *Cognitive Psychology, 15*, 459–466.

Fodor, J. A. (1978). Propositional attitudes. *Monist, 61*, 501–523.

Frith, U. (2003). *Autism: Explaining the enigma* (2nd ed.). Malden, MA: Blackwell.

Gale, E., de Villiers, P., de Villiers, J., & Pyers, J. (1996). Language and theory of mind in oral deaf children. In A. Stringfellow, D. Cahana-Amitay, E. Hughes, & A. Zukowski (Eds.), *Proceedings of the 20th annual Boston University Conference on Language Development. Volume 1.* Somerville, MA: Cascadilla Press.

Garnham, W. A., & Ruffman, T. (2001). Doesn't see, doesn't know: Is anticipatory looking really related to understanding of belief? *Developmental Science, 4*, 94–100.

Gergely, G. (2002). The development of understanding self and agency. In U. Goswami (Ed.), *The Blackwell handbook of childhood cognitive development* (pp. 26–46). Oxford, UK: Blackwell.

Gergely, G., & Csibra, G. (1997). Teleological reasoning in infancy: The infant's naive theory of rational action. A reply to Premack and Premack. *Cognition, 63*, 227–233.

Gergely, G., Nadasdy, Z., Csibra, G., & Bíró, S. (1995). Taking the intentional stance at 12 months of age. *Cognition, 56*, 165–193.

German, T. P., & Leslie, A. M. (2000). Attending to and learning about mental states. In P. Mitchell & K. L. Riggs (Eds.), *Children's reasoning and the mind* (pp. 229–252). Hove, UK: Psychology Press.

German, T. P., & Leslie, A. M. (2001). Children's inferences from "knowing" to "pretending" and "believing." *British Journal of Developmental Psychology, 19,* 59–83.

Goldman, A. I. (1992). In defense of the simulation theory. *Mind and Language, 7,* 104–119.

Gopnik, A. (1993). How we know our minds: The illusion of first-person knowledge of intentionality. *Behavioral and Brain Sciences, 16,* 1–14.

Gopnik, A., & Astington, J. W. (1988). Children's understanding of representational change and its relation to the understanding of false belief and the appearance-reality distinction. *Child Development, 59,* 26–37.

Gopnik, A., & Graf, P. (1988). Knowing how you know: Young children's ability to identify and remember the sources of their beliefs. *Child Development, 59,* 1366–1371.

Gopnik, A., & Meltzoff, A. N. (1997). *Words, thoughts, and theories.* Cambridge, MA: MIT Press.

Gopnik, A., & Slaughter, V. (1991). Young children's understanding of changes in their mental states. *Child Development, 62,* 98–110.

Gopnik, A., & Wellman, H. M. (1994). The theory theory. In L. A. Hirschfeld & S. A. Gelman (Eds.), *Mapping the mind—Domain specificity in cognition and culture* (pp. 257–293). Cambridge, UK: Cambridge University Press.

Gordon, R. M. (1986). Folk psychology as simulation. *Mind and Language, 1,* 158–171.

Hala, S., Chandler, M., & Fritz, A. S. (1991). Fledgling theories of mind: Deception as a marker of three-year-olds' understanding of false belief. *Child Development, 62,* 83–97.

Hale, C. M., & Tager-Flusberg, H. (2003). The influence of language on theory of mind: A training study. *Developmental Science, 6,* 346–359.

Happé, F. (1994). An advanced test of theory of mind: Understanding of story characters' thoughts and feelings by able autistic, mentally handicapped, and normal children and adults. *Journal of Autism and Developmental Disorders, 24,* 129–154.

Happé, F., Winner, E., & Brownell, H. (1998). The getting of wisdom: Theory of mind in old age. *Developmental Psychology, 34,* 358–362.

Harris, P. L. (1991). The work of the imagination. In A. Whiten (Ed.), *Natural theories of mind: Evolution, development and simulation of everyday mindreading* (pp. 283–304). Oxford, UK: Basil Blackwell.

Harris, P. L. (1992). From simulation to folk psychology: The case for development. *Mind and Language, 7,* 120–144.

Harris, P. L. (1994). Understanding pretending. In M. Lewis & P. Mitchell (Eds.), *Children's early understanding of mind. Origins and development* (pp. 235–260). Hove, UK: Lawrence Erlbaum Associates.

Harris, P. L. (1999). Acquiring the art of conversation: Children's developing conception of their conversation partner. In M. Bennett (Ed), *Developmental psychology: Achievements and prospects* (pp. 89–105). Philadelphia: Psychology Press.

Harris, P. L., & Kavanaugh, R. D. (1993). Young children's understanding of pretense. *Monographs of the Society for Research in Child Development, 58*(1, Serial No. 231).

Hogrefe, G. J., Wimmer, H., & Perner, J. (1986). Ignorance vs. false belief: A developmental lag in attribution of epistemic states. *Child Development, 57,* 567–582.

Hood, B. M., Willen, J. D., & Driver, J. (1998). Adults' eyes trigger shifts of visual attention in human infants. *Psychological Science, 9,* 53–56.

Hülsken, C. (2001). *Training in der theory-of-mind-Forschung: Die Rolle von Kohärenz und Feedback in der Entwicklung einer naiven Alltagspsychologie* [Training in theory of mind research. The role of coherence and feedback in the development of an understanding of the world]. Aachen, Germany: Shaker Verlag.

Hulme, S., Mitchell, P., & Wood, D. (2003). Six-year-olds' difficulties handling intensional contexts. *Cognition, 87,* 73–99.

Jenkins, J. M., & Astington, J. W. (1996). Cognitive factors and family structure associated with theory of mind development in young children. *Developmental Psychology, 32,* 70–78.

Johnson, M. H., & Morton, J. (1991). *Biology and cognitive development: The case of face recognition.* Oxford, UK: Basil Blackwell.

Johnson, C. N., & Wellman, H. M. (1980). Children's developing understanding of mental verbs: Remember, know, and guess. *Child Development, 51,* 1095–1102.

Kuhn, D. (2000). Theory of mind, metacognition, and reasoning: A life-span perspective. In P. Mitchell & K. J. Riggs (Eds.), *Children's reasoning and the mind* (pp. 301–326). Hove, UK: Psychology Press.

Kuhn, D., & Pearsall, S. (2000). Developmental origins of scientific thinking. *Journal of Cognition and Development, 1,* 113–129.

Lalonde, C. E., & Chandler, M. J. (2002). Children's understanding of interpretation. *New Ideas in Psychology, 20,* 163–198.

Lang, B., & Perner, J. (2002). Understanding of intention and false belief and the development of self control. British Journal of Developmental Psychology, 20, 67–76.

Lee, K., & Homer, B. (1999). Children as folk psychologists: The developing understanding of the mind. In A. Slater & D. Muir (Eds.), *The Blackwell reader in developmental psychology* (pp. 228–252). Oxford, UK: Blackwell.

Legerstee, M. (1991). The role of person and object in eliciting early imitation. *Journal of Experimental Child Psychology, 51,* 423–433.

Legerstee, M. (1992). A review of the animate-inanimate distinction in infancy: Implications for models of social and cognitive knowing. *Early Development and Parenting, 1,* 59–67.

Lempers, J. D., Flavell, E. R., & Flavell, J. H. (1977). The development in very young children of tacit knowledge concerning visual perception. *Genetic Psychology Monographs, 95,* 3–53.

Leslie, A. M. (1987). Pretense and representation: The origins of a "theory of mind." *Psychological Review, 94,* 412–426.

Leslie, A. M. (1994). ToMM, ToBy, and agency: Core architecture and domain specificity in cognition and culture. In L. A. Hirschfeld & S. A. Gelman (Eds.), *Mapping the mind: Domain specificity in cognition and culture* (pp. 119–148). New York: Cambridge University Press.

Leslie, A. M., & Thaiss, L. (1992). Domain specificity in conceptual development: evidence from autism. *Cognition, 43,* 225–251.

Lewis, C., & Mitchell, P. (Eds.). (1994). *Children's early understanding of mind.* Hillsdale, NJ: Lawrence Erlbaum Associates.

Lewis, C., & Osborne, A. (1990) Three-year-olds' problems with false belief: Conceptual deficit or linguistic artifact? *Child Development, 61,* 1514–1519.

Lewis, M., Stanger, C., & Sullivan, M. W. (1989). Deception in 3-year-olds. *Developmental Psychology, 25,* 439–443.

Lillard, A. S. (1993). Pretend play skills and the child's theory of mind. *Cognitive Development, 64,* 348–371.

Lillard, A. S. (2001). Pretend play as twin earth: A social-cognitive analysis. *Developmental Review, 21,* 495–531.

Lohmann, H., & Tomasello, M. (2003). The role of language in the development of false belief understanding: A training study. *Child Development, 74,* 1130–1144.

Mant, C. M., & Perner, J. (1988). The child's understanding of commitment. *Developmental Psychology, 24,* 343–351.

Marvin, R. S., Greenberg, M. T., & Mossler, D. G. (1976). The early development of conceptual perspective taking: Distinguishing among multiple perspectives. *Child Development, 47,* 511–514.

Maylor, E. A., Moulson, J. M., Muncer, A. M., & Taylor, L. A. (2002). Does performance on theory of mind tasks decline in old age? *British Journal of Psychology, 93,* 465–485.

Meins, E., Fernyhough, C., Russell, J., & Clark, C.D. (1998). Security of attachment as a predictor of symbolic and mentalising abilities: A longitudinal study. *Social Development, 7,* 1–24.

Meltzoff, A. N. (1995). Understanding the intentions of others: Re-enactment of intended acts by 18-month-old-children. *Developmental Psychology, 31,* 838–850.

Meltzoff, A. N. (2002). Elements of a developmental theory of imitation. In A. N. Meltzoff

& W. Prinz (Eds.), *The imitative mind: Development, evolution, and brain bases* (pp. 19–41). Cambridge, UK: Cambridge University Press.

Meltzoff, A. N., & Gopnik, A. (1993). The role of imitation in understanding persons and developing a theory of mind. In S. Baron-Cohen, H. Tager-Flusberg, & D. J. Cohen (Eds.), *Understanding other minds. Perspective from autism* (pp. 335–366). New York: Oxford University Press.

Metzger, W. (1954). Grundbegriffe der Gestaltpsychologie [Basic concepts of gestalt psychology]. *Beiheft zur Schweizerischen Zeitschrift für Psychologie und ihre Anwendungen, 24,* 3–15.

Mitchell, P., & LaCohee, H. (1991). Children's early understanding of false belief. *Cognition, 39,* 107–127.

Mitchell, P., & Riggs, K. J. (Eds.). (2000). *Children's reasoning and the mind.* Hove, UK: Psychology Press.

Mitchell, P., Robinson, E. J., & Thompson, D. E. (1999). Children's understanding that utterances emanate from minds: Using speaker belief to aid interpretation. *Cognition, 72,* 45–66.

Moore, C. (1996). Theories of mind in infancy. *British Journal of Developmental Psychology, 14,* 19–40.

Moses, L. J., & Flavell, J. H. (1990). Inferring false beliefs from actions and reactions. *Child Development, 61,* 929–945.

Nadel, J., & Tremblay-Leveau, H. (1999). Early perception of social contingencies and interpersonality: Dyadic and triadic paradigms. In P. Rochat (Ed.), *Early social cognition. Understanding others in the first months of life* (pp. 189–212). Mahwah, NJ: Lawrence Erlbaum Associates.

Newton, P., Reddy, V., & Bull, R. (2000). Children's everyday deception and performance on false belief tasks. *British Journal of Developmental Psychology, 18,* 297–317.

O'Neill, D. (1996). Two-year-olds' sensitivity to a parent's knowledge state when making requests. *Child Development, 67,* 659–677.

O'Neill, D., Astington, J. W., & Flavell, J. H. (1992). Young children's understanding of the role that sensory experiences play in knowledge acquisition. *Child Development, 63,* 474–490.

Onishi, K., & Baillargeon, R. (2002, April). *15-month-old infants' understanding of belief.* Presented at XIIIth International Conference on Infant Studies, Toronto, Canada.

Ozonoff, S., Pennington, B. F., & Rogers, S. J. (1991). Executive function deficits in high-functioning autistic individuals: Relationship to theory of mind. *Journal of Child Psychology and Psychiatry, 32,* 1081–1105.

Pacherie, E. (1997). Motor-images, self consciousness and autism. In J. Russell (Ed.), *Autism as an executive disorder* (pp. 215–255). Oxford, UK: Oxford University Press.

Perner, J. (1991). *Understanding the representational mind.* Cambridge, MA: MIT Press.

Perner, J. (1998). The meta-intentional nature of executive functions and theory of mind. In P. Carruthers & J. Boucher (Eds.), *Language and thought: Interdisciplinary themes* (pp. 270–283). Cambridge, UK: Cambridge University Press.

Perner, J. (1999a). Theory of mind. In M. Bennett (Ed.), *Developmental psychology. Achievements and prospects* (pp. 205–230). Hove, UK: Psychology Press.

Perner, J. (1999b). Metakognition und introspektion in entwicklungspsychologischer Sicht: Studien zur "theory of mind" und "simulation" [Developmental perspectives on metacognition and introspection: Studies in theory of mind and simulation]. In W. Janke & W. Schneider (Eds.), *Hundert Jahre Institut für Psychologie und Würzburger Schule der Denkpsychologie* (pp. 411–431). Göttingen, Germany: Hogrefe.

Perner, J. (2000). About + belief + counterfactual. In P. Mitchell & K. L. Riggs (Eds.), *Children's reasoning and the mind* (pp. 367–401). Hove, UK: Psychology Press.

Perner, J., Brandl, J., & Garnham, A. (2003). What is a perspective problem? Developmental issues in understanding belief and dual identity. *Facta Philosophica, 5,* 355–378.

Perner, J., & Davies, C. (1991). Understanding the mind as an active information processor: Do young children have a "copy theory of mind"? *Cognition, 39,* 51–69.

Perner, J., & Howes, D. (1992). "He thinks he knows": And more developmental evidence against the simulation (role taking) theory. *Mind and Language, 7,* 72–86.

Perner, J., & Lang, B. (2000). Theory of mind and executive function: Is there a developmental relationship? In S. Baron-Cohen, H. Tager-Flusberg, & D. J. Cohen (Eds.), *Under-standing other minds: Perspectives from developmental cognitive neuroscience* (2nd ed., pp.150–181). Oxford, UK: Oxford University Press.

Perner, J., Leekam, S. R., & Wimmer, H. (1987). Three-year olds' difficulty with false belief: The case for a conceptual deficit. *British Journal of Developmental Psychology, 5,* 125–137.

Perner, J., & Ogden, J. E. (1988). Knowledge for hunger: Childrens's problem with represen-tation in imputing mental states. *Cognition, 29,* 47–61.

Perner, J., Ruffman, T., & Leekam, S. R. (1994). Theory of mind is contagious: You catch it from your sibs. *Child Development, 65,* 1228–1238.

Perner, J., Sprung, M., Zauner, P., & Haider, H. (2003). Want-that is understood well before think-that, say-that, and false belief: A test of deVilliers' linguistic determinism on German speaking children. *Child Development, 74,* 179–188.

Perner, J., Stummer, S., Sprung, M., & Doherty, M. (2002). Theory of mind finds its Piage-tian perspective: Why alternative naming comes with understanding belief. *Cognitive Development, 17,* 1451–1472.

Perner, J., & Wimmer, H. (1985). "John thinks that Mary thinks that": Attribution of second order beliefs by 5- to 10-year-old children. *Journal of Experimental Psychology, 39,* 437–471.

Peskin, J. (1992). Ruse and representations: On children's ability to conceal information. *Developmental Psychology, 28,* 84–89.

Peterson, C. C., & Siegal, M. (1999). Representing inner worlds: Theory of mind in autistic, deaf, and normal hearing children. *Psychological Science, 10,* 126–129.

Phillips, A. T., Wellman, H. M., & Spelke, E. S. (2002). Infants' ability to connect gaze and emotional expression to intentional action. *Cognition, 85,* 53–78.

Piaget, J., & Inhelder, B. (1956). *The child's conception of space.* London: Routledge & Kegan Paul.

Pillow, B. H. (1991). Children's understanding of biased social cognition. *Developmental Psy-chology, 27,* 539–551.

Pillow, B. H., & Weed, S. T. (1995). Children's understanding of biased interpretation: Gen-erality and limitations. *British Journal of Developmental Psychology, 13,* 347–366.

Polak, A., & Harris, P. L. (1999). Deception by young children following noncompliance. *Developmental Psychology, 35,* 561–568.

Poulin-Dubois, D. (1999). Infants' distinction between animate and inanimate objects: The origins of naive psychology. In P. Rochat (Ed.), *Early social cognition. Understanding others in the first months of life* (pp. 281–297). Mahwah, NJ: Lawrence Erlbaum Associates.

Poulin-Dubois, D., Tilden, J., Sodian, B., Metz, U., & Schoeppner, B. (2003). *Implicit under-standing of the seeing-knowing relation in 14- to 24-month-olds.* Manuscript submitted for publication.

Pratt, C., & Bryant, P. (1990). Young children understand that looking leads to knowing (so long as they are looking into a single barrel). *Child Development, 61,* 973–982.

Premack, D., & Woodruff, G. (1978). Does the chimpanzee have a theory of mind? *Behav-ioral and Brain Sciences, 1,* 515–526.

Rakoczy, J., Tomasello, M., & Striano, T. (2004). Young children know that trying is not pretending—A test of the "behaving-as-if" construal of children's early concept of "pre-tense." *Developmental Psychology, 40,* 388–399.

Repacholi, B. M., & Gopnik, A. (1997). Early reasoning about desires: Evidence from 14- and 18-month-olds. *Developmental Psychology, 33,* 12–21.

Rice, C., Koinis, C., Sullivan, K., Tager-Flusberg, H., & Winner, E. (1997). When 3-year-olds pass the appearance-reality test. *Developmental Psychology, 33,* 54–61.

Ruffman, T. (1996). Do children understand the mind by means of simulation or theory? Evidence from their understanding of inference. *Mind and Language, 11,* 388–414.

Ruffman, T., Perner, J., Naito, M., Parkin, L., & Clements, W. A. (1998). Older (but not younger) siblings facilitate false belief understanding. *Developmental Psychology, 34,* 161–174.

Ruffman, T., Olson, D. R., Ash, T., & Keenan, T. (1993). The ABCs of deception: Do young children understand deception in the same way as adults? *Developmental Psychology, 29,* 74–87.

Ruffman, T., Perner, J., Olson, D. R., & Doherty, M. (1993). Reflecting on scientific thinking: Children's understanding of the hypothesis-evidence relation. *Child Development, 64,* 1617–1636.

Russell, J. (1997). How executive disorders can bring about an inadequate theory of mind. In R. Russell (Ed.), *Autism as an executive disorder* (pp. 256–304). Oxford, UK: Oxford University Press.

Russell, J., Mauther, N., Sharpe, S., & Tidswell, T. (1991). The "windows task" as a measure of strategic deception in preschoolers and autistic subjects. *British Journal of Developmental Psychology, 9,* 331–349.

Saltmarsh, R., Mitchell, P., & Robinson, E. J. (1995). Realism and children's early grasp of mental representation: Belief-based judgments in the state change task. *Cognition, 57,* 297–325.

Scholl, B. J., & Leslie, A. M. (1999). Modularity, development and "theory of mind." *Mind and Language, 14,* 131–153.

Schwanenflugel, P. J., Fabricius, W. V., & Noyes, C. R. (1996). Developing organization of mental verbs: Evidence for the development of a constructivist theory of mind in middle childhood. *Cognitive Development, 11,* 265–294.

Schwanenflugel, P. J., Henderson, R. L., & Fabricius, W. F. (1998). Developing organization of mental verbs and theory of mind in middle childhood: Evidence from extensions. *Developmental Psychology, 34,* 512–524.

Shultz, T. R., Wells, D., & Sarda, M. (1980). Development of the ability to distinguish intended actions from mistakes, reflexes, and passive movements. *British Journal of Social and Clinical Psychology, 19,* 301–310.

Siegal, M., & Beattie, K. (1991). Where to look first for children's understanding of false beliefs. *Cognition, 38,* 112.

Slaughter, V., & Gopnik, A. (1996). Conceptual coherence in the child's theory of mind: Training children to understand belief. *Child Development, 67,* 2967–2988.

Sodian, B. (1988). Children's attributions of knowledge to the listener in a referential communication task. *Child Development, 59,* 378–385.

Sodian, B. (1991). The development of deception in young children. *British Journal of Developmental Psychology, 9,* 173–188.

Sodian, B., & Frith, U. (1992). Deception and sabotage in autistic, retarded, and normal children. *Journal of Child Psychology and Psychiatry, 33,* 591–606.

Sodian, B., Hülsken, C., Ebner, C., & Thoermer, C. (1998). Die begriffliche Unterscheidung von Mentalität und Realität im kindlichen Symbolspiel—Vorläufer einer Theory of mind? [The conceptual differentiation of mentality and reality in pretend play—Precursor to a theory of mind?] *Sprache und Kognition, 17,* 199–213.

Sodian, B., Hülsken, C., & Thoermer, C. (1999). Young children's understanding of deception. *Enfance, 51,* 215–224.

Sodian, B., & Schneider, W. (1990). Children's understanding of cognitive cuing: How to manipulate cues to fool a competitor. *Child Development, 61,* 697–704.

Sodian, B., Taylor, C., Harris, P. L., & Perner, J. (1991). Early deception and the child's theory of mind: False trails and genuine markers. *Child Development, 62,* 468–483.

Sodian, B., & Thoermer, C. (2004). Infants' understanding of looking, pointing and reaching as cues to goal-directed action. *Journal of Cognition and Development, 5,* 289–316.

Sodian, B., & Thoermer, C. (in press). Theory of mind. In W. Schneider & B. Sodian (Eds.), *Enzyklopädie der Psychologie. Kognitive Entwicklung.* Göttingen, Germany: Hogrefe.

Sodian, B., & Wimmer, H. (1987). Children's understanding of inference as a source of knowledge. *Child Development, 58,* 424–433.

Sodian, B., Zaitchik, D., & Carey, S. (1991). Young children's differentiation of hypothetical beliefs from evidence. *Child Development, 62,* 753–766.

Stein, N. L., & Trabasso, T. (1982). What's in a story: Critical issues in comprehension and instruction. In R. Glaser (Ed.), *Advances in instructional psychology* (Vol. 2, pp. 213–267). Hillsdale, NJ: Lawrence Erlbaum Associates.

Stern, C., & Stern, W. (1909). *Erinnerung, Aussage und Lüge in der ersten Kindheit* [Memory, narrative, and lie in early childhood]. Leipzig, Germany: Barth.

Sullivan, S., & Ruffman, T. (2004). Social understanding: How does it fare with advancing years? *British Journal of Psychology, 95,* 1–18.

Sullivan, K., & Winner, E. (1993). Three-year-olds' understanding of mental states: The influence of trickery. *Journal of Experimental Child Psychology, 56*, 135–148.

Sullivan, K., Zaitchik, D., & Tager-Flusberg, H. (1994). Preschoolers can attribute second order beliefs. *Developmental Psycholgy, 30*, 395–402.

Tager-Flusberg, H., & Sullivan, K. (2000). A componential view of theory of mind: Evidence from Williams syndrome. *Cognition, 76*, 59–89.

Taylor, M. (1996). A theory of mind perspective on social-cognitive development. In R. Gelman & T. Kit-Fong Au (Eds.), *Perceptual and cognitive development: Handbook of perception and cognition* (2nd ed., pp. 283–329). San Diego, CA: Academic Press.

Taylor, M., & Carlson, S. (1997). The relation between individual differences in fantasy and theory of mind. *Child Development, 68*, 436–455.

Taylor, M., Esbensen, B. M., & Bennett, R. T. (1994). Children's understanding of knowledge acquisition: The tendency for children to report that they have always known what they have just learned. *Child Development, 65*, 1581–1604.

Thoermer, C., & Sodian, B. (2002). Science undergraduates' and graduates' epistemologies of science: The notion of interpretive frameworks. *New Ideas in Psychology, 20*, 263–283.

Tomasello, M. (1999). Social cognition before the revolution. In P. Rochat (Ed.), *Early social cognition* (pp. 301–314). Mahwah, NJ: Lawrence Erlbaum Associates.

Tomasello, M., & Haberl, K. (2003). Understanding attention: 12- and 18-month-olds know what's new for other persons. *Child Development, 39*, 906–912.

Tomasello, M., & Rakoczy, H. (2003). What makes human cognition unique? From individual to shared to collective intentionality. *Mind and Language, 18*, 121–147.

Trevarthen, C. (1979). Communication and cooperation in early infancy: A description of primary intersubjectivity. In M. Bullowa (Ed.), *Before speech: The beginning of human communication* (pp. 321–247). Cambridge, UK: Cambridge University Press.

Walker-Andrews, A. S., & Lennon, E. (1991). Infants' discrimination of vocal expressions: Contributions of auditory and visual information. *Infant Behavior and Development, 14*, 131–142.

Wellman, H. M. (1990). *The child's theory of mind.* Cambridge, MA: MIT Press.

Wellman, H. M. (2002). Understanding the psychological world: Developing a theory of mind. In U. Goswami (Ed.), *The Blackwell handbook of childhood cognitive development* (pp. 167–187). Oxford, UK: Blackwell.

Wellman, H. M., & Banerjee, M. (1991). Mind and emotion: Children's understanding of the emotional consequences of beliefs and desires. *British Journal of Developmental Psychology, 9*, 191–214.

Wellman, H. M., Cross D., & Watson, J. (2001). A meta-analysis of theory of mind development: The truth about false belief. *Child Development, 72*, 655–684.

Wellman, H. M., & Estes, D. (1986). Early understanding of mental entities: A reexamination of childhood realism. *Child Development, 57*, 910–923.

Wellman, H. M., & Gelman, S. A. (1998). Knowledge acquisition in foundational domains. In D. Kuhn & R. S. Siegler (Eds.), *Cogniton, perception and language: Handbook of child psychology* (5th ed., Vol. 2, pp. 523–573). New York: Wiley.

Wellman, H. M., & Johnson, C. N. (1979). Understanding of mental processes: A developmental study of "remember" and "forget." *Child Development, 50*, 79–80.

Wellman, H. M., & Woolley, J. D. (1990). From simple desires to ordinary beliefs: The early development of everyday psychology. *Cognition, 57*, 245–275.

Wilson, A. E., Smith, M. D., & Ross, H. S. (2003). The nature and effects of young children's lies. *Social Development, 12*, 21–45.

Wimmer, H. (1982). *Zur Entwicklung des Verstehens von Erzählungen* [The development of children's comprehension of narratives]. Bern, Switzerland: Hans Huber.

Wimmer, H. (1989). Common-sense mentalismus und emotion: Einige entwicklungspsychologische Implikationen [Common-sense mentalism and emotion: Some developmental implications]. In E. Roth (Ed.), *Denken und Fühlen* (pp. 56–66). Berlin: Springer.

Wimmer, H., & Hartl, M. (1991). Against the Cartesian view on mind: Young children's difficulty with own false beliefs. *British Journal of Developmental Psychology, 9*, 125–138.

Wimmer, H., Hogrefe, G.-J., & Perner, J. (1988). Children's understanding of informational access as a source of knowledge. *Child Development, 59*, 386–396.

Wimmer, H., & Perner, J. (1983). Beliefs about beliefs: Representation and constraining function of wrong beliefs in young children's understanding of deception. *Cognition, 13,* 103–128.

Winner, E., & Leekam, S. (1991). Distinguishing irony from deception: Understanding the speaker's second-order intention. *British Journal of Developmental Psychology, 9,* 257–270.

Woodward, A. L. (2003). Infants' developing understanding of the link between looker and object. *Developmental Science, 6,* 297–311.

Woodward, A. L., & Guajardo, J. J. (2002). Infants' understanding of the point gesture as an object-directed action. *Cognitive Development, 17,* 1061–1084.

Woodward, A. L., & Sommerville, J. A. (2000). Twelve-month-old infants interpret action in context. *Psychological Science, 11,* 73–77.

Woolfe, T., Want, S., & Siegal, M. (2002). Signposts to development: Theory of mind in deaf children. *Child Development, 73,* 768–778.

Yuill, N. (1984). Young children's coordination of motive outcome in judgements of satisfaction and morality. *British Journal of Developmental Psychology, 2,* 73–81.

Yuill, N., & Pearson, A. (1998). The development of bases for trait attribution: Children's understanding of traits as causal mechanisms based on desire. *Developmental Psychology, 34,* 574–586.

Zaitchik, D. (1991). Is seeing really believing? Sources of true belief in the false belief task. *Cognitive Development, 6,* 91–103.

Chapter 6

On the Specificity of the Relation Between Executive Function and Children's Theories of Mind

Louis J. Moses
University of Oregon

Stephanie M. Carlson
University of Washington

Mark A. Sabbagh
Queens University

The preschool years herald the onset of decisive changes in children's theories of mind (ToM). At the beginning of this period, children's ability to negotiate different perceptual and cognitive perspectives is at best limited. By the time they are 5 or 6 years old, however, a dawning appreciation of the subjectivity of mental life has begun to emerge, generating increasingly adept skill at recognizing perspectival diversity (Flavell & Miller, 1998; Wellman, 2002). Numerous theories have been offered as explanations of these landmark changes including, for example, appeals to theory change (Flavell, 1988; Gopnik & Wellman, 1994; Perner, 1991), simulative capacity (Goldman, 2001; Harris, 2000), maturation of cognitive modules (Baron-Cohen, 1995; Leslie, 1994), and advances in syntactic ability (deVilliers & deVilliers, 1999). In this chapter, we discuss an alternative perspective that either contrasts with or, in some cases, complements these explanations and emphasizes the role of executive functioning in the early development of ToM.

The executive functions (EF) embrace a heterogeneous set of cognitive skills that are believed to be related to the functioning of the prefrontal cortex (Luria, 1973). These skills include inhibition, working memory, cognitive flexibility, planning, error correction and detection, and many other capacities that are implicated in the monitoring and control of thought and action (Welsh, Pennington, & Groisser, 1991; Zelazo, Carter, Reznick, & Frye, 1997). There are good reasons to suspect that executive functioning might impinge in some way on theory of mind development. As with theory of mind, children make impressive strides in their executive skills in the preschool years (Diamond, 2002; Kochanska, Coy, & Murray, 2001; Zelazo, Müller, Frye, & Marcovitch, 2003). Moreover, just as prefrontal functioning underpins executive skills, recent brain imaging studies suggest that it may also be central to ToM (Siegal & Varley, 2002; Stuss, Gallup, & Alexander, 2001). In addition, the well-known deficits in ToM that are found in autism are accompanied by profound executive deficits as well (Ozonoff, Pennington, & Rogers, 1991; Russell, 1997). Finally, even a cursory analysis of ToM tasks makes clear that some level of executive skill is at least necessary for successful task performance. On the standard false belief task (Wimmer & Perner, 1983), for example, children must hold in mind both their own and the story protagonist's perspective (hence implicating the need for working memory), and they must suppress their own accurate perspective to focus instead on the flawed perspective of the protagonist (hence implicating the need for inhibition).

More direct evidence of a link between these two cognitive capacities comes from a recent series of correlational studies all reporting moderately high correlations between various measures of EF and ToM tasks, such as false belief, deception, and appearance reality (Carlson & Moses, 2001; Carlson, Moses, & Breton, 2002; Carlson, Moses, & Claxton, 2004; Davis & Pratt, 1996; Frye, Zelazo, & Palfai, 1995; Gordon & Olson, 1998; Hala, Hug, & Henderson, 2003; Hughes, 1998a, 1998b; Keenan, Olson, & Marini, 1998; Perner & Lang, 2000; Perner, Lang, & Kloo, 2002). In a meta-analysis of many of these studies Perner and Lang (1999) reported a strong effect size.

Nonetheless, such relations, no matter how strong, could be by-products of more general maturational or cognitive processes. In that regard, however, relations between EF and ToM typically remain significant when age, verbal ability, or general intelligence, or all three, are held constant (e.g., Carlson & Moses, 2001; Carlson et al., 2002; Davis & Pratt, 1996). Moreover, in the Carlson and Moses study, the relation held up when still other factors that relate (or might relate) to either EF, ToM, or both, were controlled. These factors included a measure of symbolic play, the number of siblings present in the family, and mental state control tasks designed to be similar to ToM tasks in their processing demands. These various findings make clear that the relation between EF and ToM is quite robust. Further, although some extraneous factor or factors might yet be found responsible for the relation, a number of the most likely candidates in this respect have now been tested and ruled out.

WHAT ASPECTS OF EXECUTIVE FUNCTION UNDERLIE THE EF-ToM RELATION?

As noted earlier, EF is a rather heterogeneous construct, and any number of its various facets might be implicated in ToM development. That said, a small set of potentially relevant dimensions of EF have been isolated that are believed to be central to most executive skills: working memory, inhibitory control, and set shifting (Hughes, 1998a; Pennington, 1997; Welsh et al., 1991). Two of these dimensions in particular have been argued to be critical for ToM development: working memory and inhibitory control. Working memory refers to the ability to hold information in mind while pursuing some relevant goal (Baddeley, 1986). Inhibitory control is the ability to suppress thoughts or actions that are irrelevant to the goal at hand (Rothbart & Posner, 1985).

These two executive skills might facilitate either the expression or the emergence of children's ToM (Olson, 1993; Moses, 2001; Russell, 1996). With respect to expression, EF might affect children's ability to translate already-present conceptual knowledge into successful task performance. For example, even with the relevant conceptual understanding in place, children might nonetheless fail a false belief task either because they lack the working memory capacity to hold in mind their own belief and the mistaken belief of the protagonist or because they lack the inhibitory capacity to suppress the prepotent true state of affairs. With respect to emergence, EF might be necessary for the acquisition of the mental state concepts themselves. For example, without an ability to hold in mind more than one perspective, it is difficult to envisage how children could ever come up with the insight that multiple perspectives on the world are in principle possible. Similarly, without some ability to suppress irrelevant stimuli, children would be entirely at the mercy of whatever is most salient in the perceived behavioral stream and hence would be unable to consider the possibility of a hidden realm of mental states that generates behavior.

Given these theoretical considerations, what empirical evidence suggests that either of these constructs is specifically linked to children's ToM? With respect to working memory, several studies found moderate relations between working memory and ToM (Gordon & Olson, 1998; Hughes, 1998a; Keenan et al., 1998), and these relations remain when age and verbal ability are controlled (Davis & Pratt, 1996; Keenan, 1998). For example, Davis and Pratt examined the relation between working memory, as measured by a backward digit span task, and false belief performance. They found that the digit span task was significantly related to false belief performance ($r = .46$) and remained so when age, receptive vocabulary, and forward digit span (a measure of short-term memory span) were held constant. With respect to inhibition, a growing number of studies have found similarly strong relations with ToM (Carlson & Moses, 2001; Carlson et al., 2002, 2004; Frye et al., 1995; Hala et al., 2003; Hughes, 1998a, 1998b; Perner & Lang, 2000; Perner et al., 2002). In perhaps the largest study of this kind, Carlson and Moses gave 107 preschoolers a battery of inhibitory control and ToM tasks across two sessions. The ToM battery consisted of eight tasks, including various measures of false belief understanding, the appearance-reality distinction, and deception. The executive battery consisted of 10 measures of inhibitory control. Carlson and Moses found that the executive battery and the ToM battery were strongly correlated ($r = .66$), as were many of the individual tasks from each battery. Moreover, as noted earlier, the relations persisted over and above age, verbal ability, and a number of other relevant controls.

These findings clearly suggest potential roles for both working memory and inhibition in ToM development, but they leave wide open the exact nature of these roles. Among the possibilities are the following. First, working memory and inhibition might make entirely independent contributions to ToM. Second, their contributions might be interactive in some way. Perhaps, the two skills work together synergistically such that only when children have developed beyond a certain threshold level of each skill can they begin to acquire ToM concepts (or successfully apply such concepts). Finally, the contribution of one skill might subsume that of the other. Perhaps working memory tasks relate to ToM only in virtue of the inhibitory demands they also impose, or perhaps inhibitory tasks relate to ToM only in virtue of the working memory demands they also impose.

Other findings begin to tease apart these alternatives. For example, in their executive battery, Carlson and Moses (2001) included two kinds of inhibitory measures: conflict tasks and delay tasks. The distinction between these tasks was subsequently confirmed in a principal component analysis. Conflict tasks require children to choose between competing responses across a series of trials in a context in which one type of response is dominant. In contrast, delay tasks, as the name implies, require children to wait before executing a dominant response. An example of a conflict measure is the bear/dragon task (Reed, Pien, & Rothbart, 1984; Kochanska, Murray, Jacques, Koenig, & Vandegeest, 1996). In this task children are asked to respond to the commands of a nice bear puppet (e.g., "Touch your ears") but not to respond to the commands of mean dragon puppet (e.g., "Touch your tummy"). Preschool children frequently err on this task by responding to the commands of both puppets. An example of a delay measure is the gift delay task (Kochanska et al., 1996), in which children are asked to turn away for a period of 60 s while an experimenter noisily wraps a gift for them. On this task many preschoolers have a very difficult time resisting peeking.

Interestingly, Carlson and Moses (2001) found that, although both conflict and delay tasks were related to ToM, the correlations were substantially larger for the conflict tasks. Moreover, in a regression analysis the conflict battery predicted ToM over and above the delay battery and control variables, but the delay battery did not do so in a corresponding analysis. Carlson and Moses hypothesized that the conflict tasks imposed substantial loads on both working memory and inhibitory capacity, whereas the delay tasks imposed a substantial inhibitory load but only minimal working memory demands. On a conflict task such as the bear/ dragon, for example, children not only need to inhibit the prepotent tendency to respond to both puppets, but they also need to simultaneously keep in mind a pair of rules (respond to the bear but do not respond to the dragon). In contrast, on a delay task such as the gift delay measure children again need to inhibit a prepotent tendency (to immediately peek), but they only need to hold in mind a single rule (wait).

Support for the Carlson and Moses (2001) hypothesis was obtained in a follow-up study (Carlson et al., 2002) in which children were given working memory tasks as well as a subset of the inhibitory and ToM tasks from the original study. The working memory tasks included a backward digit span task, a backward word span task, and a counting and labeling task in which children were required to simultaneously count and label a set of objects. The latter task, like the digit span task, had previously been found to relate to ToM with age controlled (Gordon & Olson, 1998). In their follow-up study Carlson et al. again found a different pattern for conflict and delay. The conflict tasks correlated with ToM over age and intelligence. In contrast, the correlation for delay was much smaller, and this time it was in fact not significant at all. Moreover, working memory was significantly correlated with the conflict tasks but not with delay. As hypothesized, then, the conflict tasks imposed a substantial working memory load, whereas the delay task did not.

Although this finding is certainly consistent with the view that both working memory and inhibition are implicated in the EF–ToM relation, it is also compatible with another more straightforward account. Specifically, it may be that inhibition is not part and parcel of the EF–ToM relation at all. Instead, perhaps conflict tasks correlate with ToM only in virtue of their working memory demands. However, if this were the case, then one would expect to find in the Carlson et al. (2002) study that the working memory tasks correlate with ToM. And, although this was the case for the raw correlations, the relation between working memory and ToM did not remain significant when age and verbal ability were held constant. Moreover, in a regression analysis, the conflict inhibition tasks remained significant predictors of ToM even when age, verbal ability, *and* working memory were controlled. Hence, the data suggested that simple inhibition (as in the delay task) or simple working memory (as in the span tasks) could not account for the EF–ToM relation. In contrast, a model emphasizing the combination of both inhibition and working memory fits the pattern of findings very well. That this is so should not be surprising: Effective social cognition requires both the ability to hold in mind competing perspectives as well as the ability to suppress those perspectives that are irrelevant when a specific mental state attribution is required.

Importantly, these findings have recently been replicated with a substantially different set of executive tasks. Hala et al. (2003) gave preschoolers two delay tasks: the gift delay measure described earlier and a similar snack delay task (Kochanska et al., 1996). Children were also given two conflict tasks: the day/night task (Gerstadt, Hong, & Diamond,

1994), in which children are required to respond "day" to a picture of the moon and stars and "night" to a picture of the sun, and a version of Luria's tapping task (Diamond & Taylor, 1996), in which children are asked to tap twice when the experimenter tapped once, and once when the experimenter tapped twice. Finally, children received two working memory tasks: a control version of the day/night task (Gerstadt et al., 1994), in which the pictures were two abstract designs bearing an arbitrary relation to the responses required of children, and the six boxes scrambled task (Diamond, Prevor, Callender, & Druin, 1997), in which children were invited to find stickers hidden in six boxes (the boxes were scrambled after each choice, hence requiring that children hold in mind the type of boxes they had previously looked in across trials). Hala et al.'s findings were very similar to those of Carlson et al. (2002). The conflict tasks, but not the delay tasks, correlated with working memory; only weak relations were found between the delay tasks and children's false belief performance and between the working memory tasks and false belief performance. In stark contrast, the two conflict tasks—imposing both working memory and inhibitory demands—correlated strongly with false belief performance over and above age and verbal ability.

Two other lines of inquiry speak against a simple working memory account. In the first, Moses, Carlson, Stieglitz, and Claxton (2003) examined how inhibitory tasks related to children's understanding of various mental states. Children were given an executive battery consisting of both conflict and delay tasks, as well as tasks assessing their understanding of beliefs, desires, and pretense. In closely matched tasks adapted from Lillard and Flavell (1992), children were told that a story protagonist either thought, wanted, or pretended that X was the case but that in fact Y was the case. They were then simply asked what the protagonist thought, wanted, or pretended. In an analogous set of tasks adapted from Gopnik and Slaughter (1991), children themselves initially thought, wanted, or pretended X but then changed to thinking, wanting, or pretending Y. They were then asked what they first thought, wanted, or pretended. In both types of tasks the working memory demands would seem to be equivalent across the different mental state variants. Children either need to hold in mind a mental state and an actual state of affairs or a formerly held mental state and a currently held mental state. If working memory alone were responsible for the EF–ToM relation, then one would expect comparably high correlations between executive tasks and tasks assessing children's understanding of each of these mental states. But that was not the case. In raw correlations, only the belief and desire tasks were related to the executive battery, and, when age and verbal ability were controlled, only the belief tasks remained significant.

Of course, one might reasonably suppose that the inhibitory demands, as well as the working memory demands, were equivalent across the different mental state tasks. After all, in each case children needed to suppress their knowledge of the actual state of affairs (or their current mental state, or both) to make successful attributions about the protagonist's mental state or their own former mental state. However, we would argue that the equivalence of inhibitory demands across these tasks is more apparent than real. In fact, Moses et al. (2003) were testing the a priori hypothesis that these demands are in fact quite different (see Moses, 1993). Specifically, they argued that the relation between belief and reality varies across each of these mental states. In the case of belief, the very point of the mental state is to correspond with reality. We place a high premium on holding beliefs that are true. Hence, the actual state of affairs is likely to be prepotent when reasoning about beliefs. In contrast, in the case of pretense, the very point is to create an interesting counterfactual situation— the true state of affairs is largely irrelevant to pretense, so it is less likely to be prepotent when reasoning about pretense. Finally, the case of desire is perhaps somewhat intermediate. Although one might like (some of) one's desires to be fulfilled (and hence to match reality), the pressure for change is mostly on the world rather than our desires (see Searle, 1983). That is, in contrast to belief, we for the most part try to change the world to meet our desires rather than the other way around. Given this analysis, we would expect that the inhibitory demands of belief tasks should be strong, those of desire tasks intermediate, and those of pretense tasks relatively weak. And this, of course, was precisely what Moses et al. found.

In a second, and in some ways related, line of research Sabbagh, Moses, and Shiverick (2004) examined the relation between EF and reasoning about both false beliefs and "false" photographs. False photograph tasks are designed to be structurally identical to false belief tasks. After some experience with the workings of a Polaroid camera, children watch as a photograph is taken of character A in location X. After the photo has been taken, character A is replaced by character B at X. Children are then questioned concerning who is at location X in the photo. Children's performance on tasks like this roughly parallels their performance on false belief tasks: The tasks are difficult for 3-year-olds but easier for 4- and 5-year-olds (Davis & Pratt, 1996; Leslie & Thaiss, 1992; Zaitchik, 1990). Such findings initially suggested the hypothesis that what might be developing in the preschool years is not a specific concept of mental representation but rather a concept of representation in general (Perner, 1991; Zaitchik, 1990). Against that, however, it turned out that false belief performance and false photo performance are typically uncorrelated (Davis & Pratt, 1996; Slaughter, 1998), suggesting that different mechanisms are at play in the development of these concepts. Moreover, training children on the false photo task improves false photo task performance, but the improvement does not generalize to false belief performance (Slaughter, 1998). Similarly, there is no transfer to false photo performance from false belief training.

For present purposes, what is interesting is that the working memory demands of false belief and false photograph tasks would appear to be roughly equivalent. In the belief case, one has to hold in mind a protagonist's initially correct representation while tracking changes in a state of affairs that render the belief false. Analogously, in the photo case, one has to hold in mind an initially veridical photographic representation while tracking changes in a state of affairs that renders the photo outdated. If this analysis is correct, working memory might play some general role in the development of these concepts but could not be implicated in whatever is unique to the development of belief reasoning. Again, however, it would seem that the same line of argument might be applied with respect to the contribution of inhibitory control. Just as children need to suppress their knowledge of the true state of affairs when reasoning about false beliefs, so too would they need to suppress that knowledge when reasoning about outdated photographs. Given that, we might expect to see similarly high correlations between EF and false photograph performance as between EF and false belief reasoning. However, this was not what Sabbagh et al. (2004) found: Correlations with false belief performance were sizeable, whereas those with false photo performance were close to zero.

How can we make sense of this pattern of findings? Sabbagh et al. (2004) offer a similar analysis to that suggested earlier in relation to the inhibitory demands imposed by reasoning about different kinds of mental states. Whereas beliefs should optimally reflect current reality, there is no such expectation for photographs. Photographs should capture some aspect of the state of affairs pertaining at the time at which they were taken, but we do not expect them to bear any necessary relation to current states of affairs. And, anecdotally, children do not appear to think there should be such a relation. For example, when viewing pictures of themselves basking in the sun during the previous year's summer vacation, they do not appear disturbed by the snow currently falling outside the window. Hence, although the inhibitory demands imposed when reasoning about false beliefs may be substantial, they would seem to be relatively minimal when reasoning about false photographs.

Sabbagh et al. (2004) tested this hypothesis in a follow-up study in which they assessed the relation between EF and false beliefs, false photos, and false signs. False signs (indicating the location of objects) represent a critical test case: Like false photos, they are an example of an external, non-mental representational medium; however, unlike false photos (but like false beliefs), they are intended to accurately represent the current state of affairs (Parkin & Perner, 1996). Hence, Sabbagh et al. predicted that, in contrast to the false photo task, the EF demands of the false sign task should be just as great as those of the false belief task. And that is exactly what they found: The correlation between EF and the false photo task was again not significant, but that between EF and the false sign task was significant and just as sizeable as that between EF and the false belief task.

NEURAL BASIS OF THE EF–ToM RELATION

The finding that false photograph and false belief tasks differ in their inhibitory demands has implications for our understanding of the neural systems recruited in ToM reasoning. A number of studies have attempted to localize these systems (for reviews, see Frith & Frith, 1999; Siegal & Varley, 2002). Most relevant to the current discussion, Sabbagh and Taylor (2000) used the event-related potential (ERP) technique to differentiate the neural systems recruited when adults reason about false beliefs versus false photographs. Their findings showed that, relative to photo reasoning, reasoning about beliefs was associated with an extended frontal positivity focal to left anterior regions of the scalp. Although the ERP technique does not allow for precise localization of neural generators, this pattern likely reflects the unique contribution of medial frontal regions (e.g., Brodmann's area 6) to ToM reasoning. This region has been implicated in the majority of studies investigating the neural bases of ToM reasoning using methods that offer more precise localization of critical neural regions.

Although findings like those of Sabbagh and Taylor (2000) might be taken as evidence that ToM-based reasoning involves specialized, perhaps modular, cognitive processes, our own findings suggest a different interpretation. In particular, the domain specificity argument rests on the hypothesis that false photo and false belief tasks are matched in terms of their executive demands. As we have just seen, however, although this may be true with respect to working memory, it is unlikely to be the case with respect to inhibition. False belief tasks would appear to impose a substantially greater inhibitory burden than do false photo tasks. If that is the case, then the question arises as to whether the neural systems that are commonly found to be associated with ToM might in fact be so linked because they are implicated in inhibitory processing as opposed to mentalizing per se.

Unfortunately, the data are somewhat unclear on this issue. On the one hand, the neuropsychological evidence indicates that executive functioning is strongly impaired following acquired injury to the frontal lobes (see Miller, 2000, for a review) and that the impairments may be particularly profound when the damage is in the left hemisphere. Moreover, recent work suggests that damage to left frontal areas also causes impairments in ToM functioning (Channon & Crawford, 2000). Thus, the neuropsychological literature suggests some homology with respect to the neural systems crucial for both EF and ToM. On the other hand, methods that allow more precise localization suggest that the systems may not be overlapping. For instance, both animal lesion work and human neuroimaging work suggest that the neural systems underlying executive functioning skills, including working memory and inhibitory control, may lie in dorsal-lateral prefrontal cortex (DL-PFC; Cohen et al., 1997; Diamond, 1998). In contrast, as mentioned earlier, the neural regions most consistently associated with ToM reasoning are in the medial surface of the left frontal regions. Thus, although the regions associated with these cognitive capacities are in the same general cortical vicinity (and thus could be collaterally damaged by the same insult), they appear, nonetheless, to be dissociable. Although executive abilities may be necessary for ToM reasoning, such reasoning cannot be reduced simply to executive processing.

CAUSAL BASIS OF THE EF–ToM RELATION

We have tacitly assumed throughout this chapter that the causal direction underlying the EF–ToM relation runs from EF to ToM: Executive advances in some way promote ToM advances. In contrast, Perner (1998; Perner & Lang, 2000) argued in favor of the opposite causal direction: Theory of mind advances are responsible for advances in executive ability in the preschool period. In particular, he suggested that the ability to metarepresent, as reflected in ToM reasoning, is necessary for children to successfully inhibit inappropriate but prepotent responses to execute appropriate responses.

Although we agree that ToM likely does have an impact on the development of executive skills, there are several reasons to think that the lion's share of the causal work comes from the executive side. First, Perner's (1998) account would appear to have difficulty explaining why only some executive tasks relate to ToM. For example, despite conflict and delay tasks being about equally difficult for preschool children, conflict tasks are consistently more strongly related to ToM than are delay tasks (Carlson & Moses, 2001; Carlson et al., 2002). But if ToM is necessary for inhibiting inappropriate action tendencies, it should correlate with delay tasks as well as conflict tasks because both require the ability to inhibit prepotent responses.

Second, although the account offers a potential explanation for how ToM could impact inhibitory control, it is less clear how ToM could generate advances in working memory. As we argued earlier, however, both inhibitory control and working memory appear to be implicated in the EF–ToM relation.

Third, in a recent training study, Kloo and Perner (2003) found some evidence of bidirectionality. Children trained on executive tasks later improved their performance on false belief tasks compared with a control group receiving training on an irrelevant cognitive task, and children trained on false belief later showed improved executive performance. Nonetheless, the effects were stronger for the executive training, and the false belief training effects were difficult to interpret (e.g., false belief training improved executive performance but, surprisingly, not false belief performance).

Finally, recent longitudinal data tend to favor an EF to ToM causal account. For example, Hughes (1998b) tested children on measures of EF and ToM at a mean age of 3.11 and again at 5.0. Performance on a conflict EF task (detour reaching) significantly predicted ToM 1 year later, independent of age, verbal ability, and earlier ToM scores. There was, however, no evidence of a reciprocal relation (ToM predicting EF). Carlson, Mandell, and Williams (in press) extended these findings in an important way by showing a similar pattern of results in a much younger sample of children. They administered EF and ToM batteries to children at 24 and 39 months of age and found that although the EF–ToM relation was not apparent until 39 months, EF at 24 months significantly predicted later

ToM performance after controlling for age, sex, verbal ability, maternal education, and scores on early ToM tasks given at Time 1. In contrast, there was only limited evidence in favor of the alternative causal account: Only one of the ToM tasks given at Time 1—understanding of visual perception—predicted later EF over and above controls. Similarly, in a microgenetic study of inhibition skills and false belief task performance in preschoolers, mastery of inhibitory control (as measured by Luria's hand game and lights task) developmentally preceded successful performance on false belief tasks (Flynn, O'Malley, & Wood, 2004). Together, these findings suggest that EF plays an important role in ToM development and that a predictive relation can be traced from as early as 24 months of age.

EXPRESSION VERSUS EMERGENCE

We mentioned earlier the distinction between executive expression and executive emergence theories. In an expression account, executive abilities are implicated in online ToM task performance. In an emergence account, such abilities play a role in the emergence of ToM concepts themselves. If the expression account is correct, then task manipulations that target executive demands should systematically affect ToM performance. Certainly, there is some evidence in support of this view: Most task manipulations that have generated enhanced ToM performance in preschoolers can, in retrospect, be viewed as having altered the inhibitory or working memory demands of the tasks (see Carlson, Moses, & Hix, 1998). Moreover, some studies that have manipulated executive demands directly found predictable effects on ToM performance (e.g., Carlson et al., 1998; Hala & Russell, 2001; Leslie & Polizzi, 1998). Still, although such studies generate some improvements in ToM performance, they certainly do not come close to removing all obstacles to success on ToM tasks (and this is especially true for younger 3-year-olds—see Wellman, Cross, & Watson, 2001). Difficulties expressing existing conceptual knowledge do not appear to be the central factor in age-related changes in ToM performance.

In contrast, recent correlational studies provide stronger support for executive emergence accounts. In particular, Perner et al. (2002) found that executive tasks were just as strongly correlated with false belief prediction tasks as they were with false belief explanation tasks (see also Hughes, 1998a). Although the true state of affairs may be prepotent in a prediction task asking where the protagonist will look for the desired object, it would appear to have no impact in an explanation task asking why the protagonist looked where he or she did. Similarly, in our own work, we found that other kinds of ToM tasks, such as the sources of knowledge task (O'Neill & Gopnik, 1991) and the mental state certainty task (Moore, Pure, & Furrow, 1990), correlate just as highly with executive performance as do false belief prediction tasks (Moses et al., 2003). Yet the former tasks do not appear to impose substantial inhibitory demands—when children err on these tasks, they do not perseverate on a particular response; rather, their performance appears to be random. Hence, the correlations could not result from difficulties expressing conceptual knowledge. Instead the findings are consistent with the view that executive abilities are implicated in the emergence of the concepts themselves.

Further intriguing support for the emergence hypothesis comes from Carlson et al.'s (in press) longitudinal study. They found that one of their executive measures at Time 1 predicted ToM at Time 2 over and above EF at Time 2 (and other controls). A plausible explanation for this pattern of findings is that concurrent EF skills at Time 2 are used for online ToM reasoning. In contrast, earlier EF skills would not seem relevant to current processing (at least whatever components of those skills contribute to ToM over and above concurrent EF skills). Rather these effects look very much like emergence effects: Executive abilities at age 2 years may well be influencing the emergence of ToM concepts that appear at age 3 years.

CONCLUSION

To conclude, we argue that executive abilities play a critical role in the development of children's ToM. In particular, the evidence we presented suggests that inhibitory control and working memory are jointly implicated. These basic cognitive processes make possible the flexible deployment of attention that is central both to online reasoning about mental states and to the formation of mental state concepts themselves. Our data suggest that these executive skills may be especially relevant to mental state concept formation (i.e., emergence as opposed to expression). Awaiting further study is the mechanism through which such skills impact ToM development. Executive skills might directly facilitate concept formation as we have suggested here, or, alternatively, the relation might be indirect. For example, Hughes (Hughes, 1998b, 2002; Hughes, Dunn, & White, 1998) has argued that children with better executive skills also are likely to have good social and communication skills and thus have more opportunities for observing social interaction and learning about other people's minds. In either case, however, a well-functioning executive system appears to be crucial in enabling the development of a representational ToM.

REFERENCES

Baddeley, A. D. (1986). *Working memory.* Oxford, UK: Clarendon Press.

Baron-Cohen, S. (1995). *Mindblindness: An essay on autism and theory of mind.* Cambridge, MA: MIT Press.

Carlson, S. M., Mandell, D. J., & Williams, L. (in press). Executive function and theory of mind: Stability and prediction from age 2 to 3 years. *Child Development.*

Carlson, S. M., & Moses, L. J. (2001). Individual differences in inhibitory control and children's theory of mind. *Child Development, 72,* 1032–1053.

Carlson, S. M., Moses, L. J., & Breton, C. (2002). How specific is the relation between executive function and theory of mind? Contributions of inhibitory control and working memory. *Infant and Child Development, 11,* 73–92.

Carlson, S. M., Moses, L. J., & Claxton, L. J. (2004). Individual differences in executive functioning and theory of mind: An investigation of inhibitory control and planning ability. *Journal of Experimental Child Psychology, 87,* 299–319.

Carlson, S. M., Moses, L. J., & Hix, H. R. (1998). The role of inhibitory control in young children's difficulties with deception and false belief. *Child Development, 69,* 672–291.

Channon, S., & Crawford, S. (2000). The effects of anterior lesions on performance on a story comprehension test: Left anterior impairment on a theory of mind-type task. *Neuropsychologia, 38,* 1006–1017.

Cohen, J. D., Perlstein, W. M., Braver, T. S., Nystrom, L. E., Noll, D. C., Jonides, J., & Smith, E. E. (1997). Temporal dynamics of brain activation during a working memory task. *Nature, 386,* 604–608.

Davis, H. L., & Pratt, C. (1996). The development of children's theory of mind: The working memory explanation. *Australian Journal of Psychology, 47,* 25–31.

deVilliers, J. G., & deVilliers, P. A. (1999). Linguistic determinism and false belief. In P. Mitchell & K. Riggs (Eds.), *Children's reasoning about the mind* (pp. 191–228). Hove, UK: Psychology Press.

Diamond, A. (1998). Evidence for the importance of dopamine for prefrontal cortex functions early in life. In A. C. Roberts, T. W. Robbins, & L. Weiskrantz (Eds.), *The prefrontal cortex: Executive and cognitive functions* (pp. 144–164). Oxford, UK: Oxford University Press.

Diamond, A. (2002). Normal development of prefrontal cortex from birth to young adulthood: Cognitive functions, anatomy, and biochemistry (pp. 466–503). In D. Stuss & R. Knight (Eds.), *Principles of frontal lobe function.* New York: Oxford University Press.

Diamond, A., Prevor, M. B., Callender, G., & Druin, D. P. (1997). Prefrontal cortex cognitive deficits in children treated early and continuously for PKU. *Monographs of the Society for Research in Child Development, 62*(4, Serial No. 252).

Diamond, A., & Taylor, C. (1996). Development of an aspect of executive control: Development of the abilities to remember what I said and "Do as I say, not as I do." *Developmental Psychobiology, 29,* 315–334.

Flavell, J. H. (1988). The development of children's knowledge about the mind: From cognitive connections to mental representations. In J. W. Astington, P. L. Harris, & D. R. Olson (Eds.), *Developing theories of mind* (pp. 244–267). New York: Cambridge University Press.

Flavell, J. H., & Miller, P. H. (1998). Social cognition. In W. Damon (Gen. Ed.), D. Kuhn, & R. Siegler (Vol. Eds.), *Handbook of child psychology: Vol. 2. Cognition, perception, and language* (5th ed., pp. 851–898). New York: Wiley.

Flynn, E., O'Malley, C., & Wood, D. (2004). A longitudinal, microgenetic study of the emergence of false belief understanding and inhibition skills. *Developmental Science, 7,* 103–115.

Frith, C. D., & Frith, U. (1999). Interacting minds—A biological basis. *Science, 286,* 1692–1695.

Frye, D., Zelazo, P. D., & Palfai, T. (1995). Theory of mind and rule-based reasoning. *Cognitive Development, 10,* 483–527.

Gerstadt, C. L., Hong, Y. J., & Diamond, A. (1994). The relationship between cognition and action: Performance of children 3.5–7 years old on a Stroop-like day-night test. *Cognition, 53,* 129–153.

Goldman, A. I. (2001). Desire, intention, and the simulation theory. In B. F. Malle, L. J. Moses, & D. A. Baldwin (Eds.), *Intentions and intentionality: Foundations of social cognition* (pp. 207–224). Cambridge, MA: MIT Press.

Gopnik, A., & Slaughter, V. (1991). Young children's understanding of changes in their mental states. *Child Development, 62,* 98–110.

Gopnik, A., & Wellman, H. M. (1994). The theory theory. In L. Hirschfeld & S. Gelman (Eds.), *Mapping the mind: Domain specificity in cognition and culture* (pp. 257–293). New York: Cambridge University Press.

Gordon, A. C. L., & Olson, D. R. (1998). The relation between acquisition of a theory of mind and the capacity to hold in mind. *Journal of Experimental Child Psychology, 68,* 70–83.

Hala, S., Hug, S., & Henderson, A. (2003). Executive functioning and false belief understanding in preschool children: Two tasks are harder than one. *Journal of Cognition and Development, 4,* 275–298.

Hala, S., & Russell, J. (2001). Executive control within strategic deception: A window on early cognitive development? *Journal of Experimental Child Psychology, 80,* 112–141.

Harris, P. L. (2000). *The work of the imagination.* Oxford, UK: Blackwell.

Hughes, C. (1998a). Executive function in preschoolers: Links with theory of mind and verbal ability. *British Journal of Developmental Psychology, 16,* 233–253.

Hughes, C. (1998b). Finding your marbles: Does preschoolers' strategic behavior predict later understanding of mind? *Developmental Psychology, 34,* 1326–1339.

Hughes, C. (2002). Executive functions and development: Emerging themes. *Infant and Child Development, 11,* 201–209.

Hughes, C., Dunn, J., & White, A. (1998). Trick or treat? Uneven understanding of mind and emotion and executive dysfunction in "hard-to-manage" preschoolers. *Journal of Child Psychology and Psychiatry, 39,* 981–994.

Keenan, T. (1998). Memory span as a predictor of false belief understanding. *New Zealand Journal of Psychology, 27,* 36–43.

Keenan, T., Olson, D. R., & Marini, Z. (1998). Working memory and children's developing understanding of mind. *Australian Journal of Psychology, 50,* 76–82.

Kloo, D., & Perner, J. (2003). Training transfer between card sorting and false belief understanding: Helping children apply conflicting descriptions. *Child Development, 74,* 1823–1839.

Kochanska, G., Coy, K. C., & Murray, K. T. (2001). The development of self-regulation in the first four years of life. *Child Development, 72,* 1091–1111.

Kochanska, G., Murray, K., Jacques, T. Y., Koenig, A. L., & Vandegeest, K. A. (1996). Inhibitory control in young children and its role in emerging internalization. *Child Development, 67,* 490–507.

Leslie, A. M. (1994). ToMM, ToBY, and agency: Core architecture and domain specificity. In L. A. Hirschfeld & S. A. Gelman (Eds.), *Mapping the mind: Domain specificity in cognition and culture* (pp. 119–148). New York: Cambridge University Press.

Leslie, A. M., & Polizzi, P. (1998). Inhibitory processing in the false belief task: Two conjectures. *Developmental Science, 1,* 247–253.

Leslie, A. M., & Thaiss, L. (1992). Domain specificity in conceptual development: Neuropsychological evidence from autism. *Cognition, 43,* 225–251.

Lillard, A. S., & Flavell, J. H. (1992). Young children's understanding of different mental verbs. *Developmental Psychology, 28,* 626–634.

Luria, A. R. (1973). *The working brain: An introduction to neuropsychology.* New York: Basic Books.

Miller, E. K. (2000). The prefrontal cortex and cognitive control. *Nature Reviews Neuroscience, 1,* 59–65.

Moore, C., Pure, K., & Furrow, D. (1990). Children's understanding of the modal expression of certainty and uncertainty and its relation to the development of a representational theory of mind. *Child Development, 61,* 722–730.

Moses, L. J. (1993). Young children's understanding of belief constraints on intention. *Cognitive Development, 8,* 1–25.

Moses, L. J. (2001). Executive accounts of theory of mind development. *Child Development, 72,* 688–690.

Moses, L. J., Carlson, S. M., Stieglitz, S., & Claxton, L. J. (2003). *Executive function, prepotency, and children's theories of mind.* Manuscript in preparation, University of Oregon.

Olson, D. R. (1993). The development of representations: The origins of mental life. *Canadian Psychology, 34,* 293–306.

O'Neill, D. K., & Gopnik, A. (1991). Young children's ability to identify the sources of their beliefs. *Developmental Psychology, 27,* 390–397.

Ozonoff, S., Pennington, B. F., & Rogers, S. J. (1991). Executive function deficits in high-functioning autistic individuals: Relationship to theory of mind. *Journal of Child Psychology and Psychiatry and Allied Disciplines, 32,* 1081–1105.

Parkin, L. J., & Perner, J. (1996). *Wrong directions in children's theory of mind: What it means to understand belief as representation*. Unpublished manuscript, University of Sussex.

Perner, J. (1991). *Understanding the representational mind*. Cambridge, MA: MIT Press.

Perner, J. (1998). The meta-intentional nature of executive functions and theory of mind. In P. Carruthers & J. Boucher (Eds.), *Language and thought* (pp. 270–283). Cambridge, UK: Cambridge University Press.

Perner, J., & Lang, B. (1999). Development of theory of mind and executive control. *Trends in Cognitive Sciences, 3*, 337–344.

Perner, J., & Lang, B. (2000). Theory of mind and executive function: Is there a developmental relationship? In S. Baron-Cohen, H. Tager-Flusberg, & D. Cohen (Eds.), *Understanding other minds: Perspectives from autism and developmental cognitive neuroscience* (pp. 150–181). Oxford, UK: Oxford University Press.

Perner, J., Lang, B., & Kloo, D. (2002). Theory of mind and self control: More than a common problem of inhibition. *Child Development, 73*, 752–767.

Reed, M., Pien, D. L., & Rothbart, M. K. (1984). Inhibitory self-control in preschool children. *Merrill Palmer Quarterly, 30*, 131–147.

Rothbart, M. K., & Posner, M. I. (1985). Temperament and the development of self-regulation. In L. Hartlage & C. F. Telzrow (Eds.), *The neuropsychology of individual differences: A developmental perspective* (pp. 93–123). New York: Plenum.

Russell, J. (1996). *Agency: Its role in mental development*. Hove, UK: Psychology Press.

Russell, J. (Ed.). (1997). *Autism as an executive disorder*. New York: Oxford University Press.

Sabbagh, M. A., Moses, L. J., & Shiverick, S. M. (2004). *Executive functioning and preschoolers' understanding of false beliefs, false photographs, and false signs*. Manuscript submitted for publication.

Sabbagh, M. A., & Taylor, M. (2000). Neural correlates of theory-of-mind reasoning: An event-related potential study. *Psychological Science, 11*, 46–50.

Searle, J. (1983). *Intentionality*. Cambridge, UK: Cambridge University Press.

Siegal, M., & Varley, R. (2002). Neural systems involved in "theory of mind." *Nature Reviews Neuroscience, 3*, 463–471

Slaughter, V. (1998). Children's understanding of pictorial and mental representations. *Child Development, 69*, 321–332.

Stuss, D. T., Gallup, G. G., Jr., & Alexander, M. P. (2001). The frontal lobes are necessary for "theory of mind." *Brain, 124*, 279–286.

Wellman, H. M. (2002). Understanding the psychological world: Developing a theory of mind. In U. Goswami (Ed.), *Blackwell handbook of childhood cognitive development* (pp. 167–187). Malden, MA: Blackwell.

Wellman, H. M., Cross, D., & Watson, J. (2001). Meta-analysis of theory of mind development: The truth about false belief. *Child Development, 72*, 655–684.

Welsh, M. C., Pennington, B. F., & Groisser, D. B. (1991). A normative-developmental study of executive function: A window on prefrontal function in children. *Developmental Neuropsychology, 7*, 131–149.

Wimmer, H., & Perner, J. (1983). Beliefs about beliefs: Representation and constraining function of wrong beliefs in young children's understanding of deception. *Cognition, 13*, 103–128.

Zaitchik, D. (1990). When representations conflict with reality: The preschooler's problem with false beliefs and "false" photographs. *Cognition, 35*, 41–68.

Zelazo, P. D., Carter, A., Reznick, J. S., & Frye, D. (1997). Early development of executive function: A problem-solving framework. *Review of General Psychology, 1*, 1–29.

Zelazo, P. D., Müller, U., Frye, D., & Marcovitch, S. (2003). The development of executive function in early childhood. *Monographs of the Society for Research in Child Development, 89*(3, Serial No. 274).

Chapter 7

The Evolution of Theory of Mind: Big Brains, Social Complexity, and Inhibition

David F. Bjorklund
Christopher A. Cormier
Justin S. Rosenberg
Florida Atlantic University

Theory of mind (ToM) has been one of the most investigated topics in developmental psychology since the publication of the first child developmental study on the issue (Wimmer & Perner, 1983), and deservedly so. The ontogeny of the ability to reflect on one's own knowledge and the knowledge of others is fundamental to the type of symbolic representation that sets humans apart from all other species and affords *Homo sapiens* the supremacy over its environs that, for better or worse, it currently holds. Perhaps of greatest significance is the manner in which possessing ToM changes social dynamics, permitting more complex social interactions to take place, including advanced forms of social competition and cooperation, and political machinations unimaginable in even the most socially sophisticated nonhuman primates. Given the undeniable importance, phylogenetic uniqueness, and relative recency of the emergence of capacities associated with ToM (and other advanced forms of social cognition), it is not surprising that evolutionarily oriented scholars have directed a great deal of effort to the task of illuminating these phenomena. In fact, numerous scientists have proposed that the social complexity of ancient hominid groups was the principle selective pressure for the evolution of the modern human mind (e.g., Alexander, 1989; Bjorklund & Harnishfeger, 1995; Byrne & Whiten, 1988; Dunbar, 1992; Humphrey, 1976).

In this chapter we examine the evolution of human social cognitive abilities, particularly ToM, looking at hypotheses and evidence suggesting that, although related species possess substantial social cognitive prowess, ToM, as reflected in the thinking of most 5-year-old children, is a species-unique capacity. We examine the possible origins of this ability and make the claim that an increase in domain-general processing abilities (as a direct result of increased brain size) made more complex social relations possible and permitted the evolution of relatively domain-specific mental operations associated with social cognition.

In the following sections, we first outline how the field of evolutionary psychology views ToM, followed by a brief examination of the development of ToM in children and factors associated with its development during the preschool years. We then examine the evolution of ToM, starting with a look at the evolution of the human brain, followed by an examination of the social-cognitive abilities of our closet genetic cousins, chimpanzees (*Pan troglodytes*). We then examine more closely arguments that social cognition played the central role in the evolution of the modern human mind. We conclude by proposing that increased inhibition abilities were primarily responsible for the enhanced social-cognitive skills of our ancestors and that such skills permitted the evolution of other more domain-specific abilities, some of which were associated with what we refer to as ToM.

EVOLUTIONARY PSYCHOLOGY

Evolutionary psychology has emerged as a cohesive and unique approach to the study of evolved species-typical psychological characteristics (e.g., Barkow, Cosmides, & Tooby 1992; Buss, 1995, in press; Cosmides & Tooby, 2002; Daly & Wilson, 1988; Pinker, 1997), as well as, more recently, to processes associated with human ontogeny (e.g., Bjorklund & Pellegrini, 2000, 2002; Bugental, 2000; Geary & Bjorklund, 2000; Hernández Blasi & Bjorklund, 2003). Its power and ultimate value derive from its potential to provide an overarching and potent metatheoretical framework through which not only are entirely new avenues of scientific exploration made possible, but also the frequently disparate and otherwise ostensibly superficial findings generated within the various branches and subdisciplines of psychology may be integrated and grounded in the deepest of theoretical bedrock (Buss, 1995). Even more recently, and in a manner not dissimilar to that proposed for psychology, the tenets of evolutionary theory have been proposed as a guiding top-down metatheory for the cognitive neurosciences (e.g., Gazzaniga, 2000) and have also been productively applied to the study of processes inherent in modern academic schooling (e.g., Geary, 2002).

Evolutionary psychology applies the basic tenets of Darwin's theory of evolution, namely natural selection, to understand the adaptive function of a diverse range of species-universal behaviors. A central assumption of evolutionary psychology is that what evolved are networks of domain-specific information-processing mechanisms that were used to solve recurrent problems faced by our ancestors in what has been termed the environment of evolutionary adaptedness, generally defined as the Pleistocene (1.8 million years ago until approximately 10,000 years ago), during which time our ancestors lived as nomadic hunters and gatherers.

For our purposes, the most critical assumption of evolutionary psychology is that what underlies adaptive thought and behavior are domain-specific cognitive mechanisms, in contrast to more domain-general mechanisms (e.g., Buss, 1995; Tooby & Cosmides, 1992). Evolutionary psychology sees the human mind as being modular in nature, much like the human body. According to this perspective, individual organs of the body did not evolve to embody domain-general processes such as "maintain good health" or "perceive the environment." Instead, what evolved are biological structures whose functions manifest specific processes such as "extract oxygen from the atmosphere" (lungs) and "neurally encode a specific range of electromagnetic frequencies in the environment" (eyes). Similarly, the mind has not evolved to produce general behaviors such as "be successful" or even "stay alive." Rather, the mind consists of specific (information-processing) mechanisms that have historically produced successful responses to specific aspects of evolutionarily recurrent challenges and problems associated with the more general issues of survival and reproduction (e.g., food acquisition, mate section, predator avoidance, parenting).

This modular view of the human mind has been applied to important aspects of social cognition, including ToM (e.g., Baron-Cohen, 1995) and social reasoning (e.g., Cosmides & Tooby, 1992). For example, Baron-Cohen (1995) postulated that there are four separate processors involved in what is commonly referred to as ToM. The intentionality detector (ID) serves as a perceptual apparatus designed to interpret moving stimuli as having some intention toward an object or a person. Serving as a primitive basis for understanding volitional states, the ID helps to better understand animalistic movements: approach and avoidance. The second mechanism is that of the eye-direction detector (EDD), which works strictly through the sense of vision (whereas the ID combines vision, touch, and audition) and has three basic functions: detecting eyes or eyelike stimuli, inferring the directionality of the eyes (i.e., where are they looking), and determining that eyes that are directed toward a target actively perceive that target. The main function of the EDD is to interpret stimuli by means of what another organism sees. Baron-Cohen's third mechanism is the shared-attention mechanism (SAM) whose key function is to establish triadic representation (e.g., "He sees that I see the object" and "I see the object he sees"). Baron-Cohen provides evidence for the SAM through infants' gaze monitoring, whereby an infant checks (by looking back and forth) to make sure that someone else is looking at the same thing that he or she is seeing. Fourth and final to Baron-Cohen's hierarchical model of the neurocognitive mechanisms underlying ToM is that of the theory-of-mind mechanism (ToMM) itself, which is "a system for inferring the full range of mental states from behavior—that is, for employing a 'theory of mind' . . . It has the dual purpose of representing the set of epistemic mental states and turning all this mentalistic knowledge into a useful theory" (1995, p. 51). Lillard (1997) refers to the ToMM as a mechanism that links agents to propositions through the detection of mental attitudes. The ToMM is similar to belief–desire reasoning as proposed by Wellman (1990), which is discussed in the following section.

Evidence of the modular nature of these social-cognitive mechanisms comes from studies that document the relative absence of some of the more advanced forms of ToM abilities in people with autism. Although intellectual impairment is variable in people diagnosed with autism, one feature that appears central to the disorder is a particular type of difficulty with social relations. Baron-Cohen (1995) proposes that people with autism are unable to read others' minds (i.e., demonstrate impairment in belief–desire reasoning, at least with respect to other people), a condition he refers to as mindblindness. For example, high-functioning autists often perform well on nonsocial problem-solving tasks but nonetheless perform poorly on false belief tasks (see later discussion) and other tasks involving social reasoning. This is in contrast to people with mental retardation, such as Down syndrome, who perform false belief tasks easily but typically fail tasks involving nonsocial problems (e.g., Baron-Cohen, 1989; Baron-Cohen, Leslie, & Frith, 1985, 1986; Baron-Cohen, Wheelwright, Stone, & Rutherford, 1999; Perner, Frith, Leslie, & Leekam, 1989). Autists generally perform well on the simpler ToM tasks requiring the ID or EDD modules but fail the more complex tasks involving the SAD and especially the ToMM modules. That is, their deficit is not one of general intelligence (or lack of some other domain-general ability, such as executive function), but specific to the abilities proposed for the SAD and ToMM modules. Additional evidence for the modularity of some ToM abilities comes from neuropsychological research, which indicates the presence of processing deficits for autists in brain regions (left frontal lobe) associated with processing on ToM tasks for normal adults (e.g., Sabbagh & Taylor, 2000). Other research identified genetic influence on ToM tasks that is independent of general verbal performance, a finding consonant with the idea that ToM is not simply a function of general intellectual functioning (Hughes & Cutting, 1999).

Such findings would seem to be at odds with the major theme of this book, that theory of mind is related to domain-general abilities, such as executive function, inhibition, general intelligence, or working memory, at least in its development over the preschool years. Despite concurring with much of Baron-Cohen's (1995) interpretation of the domain specificity of ToM, we do not believe that this precludes the simultaneous influence on ToM development of the aforementioned domain-general skills. Although evolutionary psychologists have emphasized the modular nature of evolved information-processing mechanisms, such mechanisms are not totally independent of other, related mechanisms. Just as the heart is modular in nature, its functioning influences and is influenced by other structures and processes, such as the lungs, the digestive tract, and the brain. Some evolutionary psychologists have acknowledged that domain-general mechanisms may have also played a role in human cognitive evolution, as well as in the functioning of contemporary people (e.g., Bjorklund & Kipp, 2002, Bjorklund & Pellegrini, 2002; Geary, 2005; Geary & Huffman, 2002; Rakison, 2005). We later briefly review research indicating the relationship between domain-general processing abilities and ToM development in children and propose that it was the presence of increased general-processing abilities in our hominid ancestors that contributed to our species' enhanced social-cognitive abilities and resulted, eventually, in the evolution of the more domain-specific information-processing abilities as advocated by evolutionary psychology.

THEORY OF MIND IN CHILDREN

Development of Mindreading

Simply stated, ToM is the ability to attribute mental states to both oneself and to others. These mental states can include, but are certainly not limited to, beliefs, desires, volitions, and feelings. Since Premack and Woodruff (1978) first conducted experiments with chimpanzees (*Pan troglodytes*) in an attempt to determine whether or not they possessed a "theory of mind" (see later discussion), this topic has been a focal feature of the psychological literature (e.g., Astington, 1993; Baron-Cohen, 1995; Bartsch & Wellman, 1995; Frye & Moore, 1991; Heyes, 1998; Jenkins & Astington, 1996, 2000; Wellman, 1990; Wellman, Cross, & Watson, 2001) and has been studied and tested within a plethora of experimental paradigms across a multitude of psychological subdisciplines (e.g., developmental, cognitive, comparative, evolutionary).

Drawing on folk psychology (e.g., Lillard, 1997, 1998; Lillard & Flavell, 1992), ToM reflects reasoning capacities that allow an organism to infer, predict, and understand the behavior of self and others. Wellman (1990) postulated that ToM is the end product of belief-desire reasoning—that is, we predict the behavior of others based on our inferences about other people's beliefs and desires. Such belief-desire reasoning is likely to have evolved in support of social cognition (Bjorklund & Bering, 2003; Cummins, 1998).

Serving as a basis for human social cognition, children are said to possess a (somewhat) fully developed ToM by around the age of 4 years (e.g., Perner & Lang, 1999, 2000; Wellman, 1990; Wellman et al., 2001), as reflected in the passing of one of various standard false belief tasks. One variant of the false belief task, the Maxi task, includes a protagonist (Maxi) who puts an object (e.g., a cookie, toy) into one of two locations (boxes, cupboards, etc.). In Maxi's absence, another character (e.g., Maxi's mother) enters the scene, and, unbeknownst to Maxi, moves the object to a different location. Upon Maxi's return, the experimenter asks the child where Maxi will look for his object. Three-year-olds tend to report (erroneously) that Maxi will look in the new location, whereas most 4-year-olds correctly report that Maxi will look in the initial location, in recognition of the fact that Maxi will act in accord with his false belief.

Another commonly used false belief task is the Smarties task, in which an experimenter presents a child with a box (e.g., a Smarties box, a candy familiar to British children) and then asks what it contains, to which the likely response is "Smarties." The experimenter then reveals the true contents of the box to be something other than Smarties (e.g., pennies). When the child is then asked what someone else will think the box contains, children who have not fully developed a ToM (most children younger than 4 years of age) tend to erroneously report "pennies." Conversely, somewhat older children, who typically possess a more fully developed ToM generally respond correctly, indicating an understanding that others will act on the basis of a false belief in expecting the box to contain Smarties.

It would be inaccurate to suggest that ToM is an all-or-nothing phenomenon, however, because although 3-year-olds may not be able to pass standard false belief tasks, they obviously have some capacity for correctly inferring some aspects of what other people know, think, and desire. For example, Repacholi and Gopnik (1997) gave 14- and 18-month-old toddlers a choice of either Pepperidge Farm Goldfish crackers (a snack food typically liked by children) or broccoli (a food typically disliked by children), serving as a baseline condition. Children subsequently were instructed to watch as an experimenter tasted both types of food. The experimenter then indicated a preference opposite that of the child. Repacholi and Gopnik found that when the same experimenter then asked the child to pick a snack for her, there was a clear dichotomy between the responses of the 14- and 18-month olds. Whereas the 14-month-olds offered the food that they themselves preferred, the 18-month-olds appeared to realize that the experimenter had personal preferences that were different from their own and, accordingly, offered the snack for which the experimenter had displayed a personal preference in contrast to their own. Additional evidence for the presence of a rudimentary, early developing component of ToM comes from the mirror self-recognition task, which entails the surreptitious placement of a conspicuous mark on a child's forehead, just prior to viewing his or her image in a mirror. Children demonstrate self-recognition if they touch the mark on their foreheads, rather than attempting to touch the image of the mark in the mirror, which is presumed to indicate an understanding that the mark is on their own body, as opposed to the body of the "child" in the mirror. Children tend to pass mirror self-recognition tests by about 18 months of age (Brooks-Gunn & Lewis, 1984). As children's metarepresentational abilities develop further, there is a marked set of changes that take place between 3 and 5 years of age (Gopnik & Astington, 1988) that are most evident within the context of the aforementioned false belief tasks (see, e.g., Hogrefe, Wimmer, & Perner, 1986; Wimmer & Perner, 1983).

What Factors Contribute to Children's Developing ToM?

Even if one accepts that ToM is modular in nature, as suggested by Baron–Cohen (1995), its development should nonetheless be related to conditions in the environment, to other contemporaneously developing cognitive abilities, or to both. For the purposes of this chapter, we focus on two sets of correlates: the social environment and domain-general cognitive abilities.

The Social Environment.   In the environment of evolutionary adaptedness (i.e., the Pleistocene; see earlier discussion), humans are likely to have evolved a richly developed ToM to better deal with conspecifics in a socially complex environment (see later discussion). It is thus reasonable to assume that children's development of ToM might similarly be sensitive to social factors in the environment, with some factors facilitating and others perhaps retarding its development. One such factor positively related to ToM development is that of family size (e.g., Jenkins & Astington, 1996; Ruffman, Perner, Naito, Parkin, & Clements, 1998). For example, Ruffman et al. (1998) reported a positive correlation between ToM development (e.g., false belief understanding) and number of older siblings a child had; however, they found no significant relation between false belief understanding and number of younger siblings.

Why older as opposed to younger siblings? Ruffman et al. (1998) proposed that older siblings stimulate pretend play, which helps younger children represent counterfactual states of affairs, which is a necessary skill for solving false belief tasks. An alternative hypothesis takes into account the evolutionary role of social dominance (e.g., Cummins, 1998), proposing that it is the social competitive disadvantages of younger siblings (e.g., smaller size, generally less-developed cognitive faculties) in competition for valued resources (e.g., toys, parental attention, caregiving) that spurs their precocious social-cognitive development, including capacities associated with ToM and reasoning about dominance hierarchies.

Domain-General Cognitive Abilities.   Evidence has accumulated that ToM development is associated with the development of several related domain-general skills, usually collectively referred to as executive function (EF; e.g., Carlson, Moses, & Breton, 2002; Hughes, 2002a, 2002b; Perner & Lang, 1999, 2000). EF refers to "those processes in the control of behaviour, like planning, coordinating, and controlling sequences of action, that are disrupted upon frontal lobe injury" (Perner & Lang, 2000, p. 151). Developmental trends in executive functioning closely resemble those of ToM, in that children show a marked change in executive function around the age of 4 years (Perner & Lang, 1999). Most tasks evaluating EF test children's abilities to inhibit prepotent responses (behavioral, verbal, etc.) or to recall items from memory (e.g., Perner, Lang, & Kloo, 2002).

The most frequently investigated aspect of EF with respect to ToM has been inhibition (e.g., Carlson & Moses, 2001; Leslie, 2000; Perner, Stummer, & Lang, 1999; Russell, Mauthner, Sharpe, & Tidswell, 1991). For example,

Peskin (1992) conducted experiments in which young children played a game with Mean Monkey, a hand puppet controlled by the experimenter. On each trial, children were shown a set of stickers and asked to chose one for him- or herself, at which point Mean Monkey would take and keep the child's selection, thereby leaving the less-attractive option for the child. Thus, to receive the more attractive sticker, the child needed to inhibit the prepotent response of selecting the more desirable sticker and instead *deceive* Mean Monkey by indicating selection of the less-desirable sticker. Peskin found that most 3-year-old (but not 4-year-old) children had a difficult time deceiving Mean Monkey, being unable to inhibit the selection of their favored sticker and thus consistently ended up receiving the stickers they did not want.

In a similar line of research, Hala and Russell (2001) used variants of the windows task (see Russell et al., 1991) to systematically examine the relationship between EF and strategic deception. In the original task a selector (the child) and an opponent are presented with an array of windows containing variously attractive treats, unattractive treats, or nothing at all. Children are instructed to select a window (thereby indicating preference for a particular treat if one is present in the selected window), but, in a manner similar to that of the Mean Monkey task, to receive the preferred item, they must select a window that does not correspond to their actual preference (i.e., they must strategically deceive their opponent). Russell et al. (1991) found that 3-year-old children, more often than not, did not pass this test, whereas 4-year-olds were typically successful. However, the results of subsequent research (Hala & Russell, 2001) indicate that manipulation of task demands in a manner that specifically reduces load on executive functioning enables 3-year-olds to succeed. For example, Hala and Russell used artificial response mediums (e.g., a pointer) and modified the task so that it involved cooperative play or required cooperative partnership to aid children in espousing an effective strategy.

Whereas early explanations of young children's failure at tasks involving strategic deception (e.g., the Mean Monkey and windows tasks) assumed an underdeveloped ToM, Hala and Russell (2001) argue that inadequate executive control may be primary. The results of studies examining the relationship between children's performance on ToM tasks and tasks assessing EF have been generally consistent with this latter interpretation in reporting positive correlations that typically fall within the range of .30 to .60 (e.g., Carlson & Moses, 2001; Perner et al., 1999). Although one must be cautious in interpreting both the presence and direction of causality (see Perner & Lang, 2000), the clear implication is that EF and, more specifically, inhibitions propel the development of ToM during the preschool years.

THE DEVELOPMENT OF SOCIAL REASONING

ToM is foundational to more advanced forms of social cognition. One form of advanced social cognition that is characteristic of everyday human social intercourse and presumably relies on ToM involves reasoning about social exchanges—making deals—and the ability to detect people who might be violating the rules. This form of social reasoning (cheater detection) has received relatively little attention in the child developmental literature but has been studied extensively from an evolutionary psychological perspective in adults (e.g., Cosmides & Tooby, 1992). The logic of many social exchanges is similar to that found in problems of formal logic, such as the Wason (1966) task. In this task, people are shown four cards, similar to the ones displayed below, and given the following rule: "If a card has a vowel on one side, then it must have an even number on the other side."

E	K	2	5

The task is to determine if the set of cards in front of them conforms to the rule or not by turning over those cards (and only those cards) that are necessary to make this determination. This is a difficult task, one that many college students fail. (The correct answer in this example is "E" and "5.")

Despite the apparent difficulty of this task, it is solved easily if it is modified to model the elements of a social contract. For example, rather than using letters and numbers, participants are told that the cards correspond to ages of people and drinks they ordered, as shown below.

Beer	Cola	15 years old	25 years old

The rule that must now be assessed is, "If a person is drinking alcohol, then he or she must be at least 21 years old." This becomes an easy task for adults, most of whom now select the "15 years old" and "beer" cards to turn over, realizing that age is irrelevant if one is drinking cola and that a 25-year-old can drink anything desired (see Cosmides & Tooby, 1992). This pattern of findings is consistent with the idea that aspects of social reasoning are domain specific in nature. People do not rely exclusively on general reasoning or information-processing abilities to solve these problems; if they did, performance should be comparable across the different versions of the task, regardless of the problem content. Rather, they use specific social-cognitive algorithms, which presumably not only had ecological validity for our ancestors but also continue to be relevant in modern environments.

Children also seem to be similarly influenced by the nature of tasks, performing at higher levels on tasks that rely on social proscription (deontic reasoning, i.e., reasoning about what one should or ought to do) versus identical tasks that involve descriptive, or indicative, reasoning, which implies only a description of facts and no violation of social rules (e.g., Cummins, 1996; Harris & Núñez, 1996). In one study, Harris and Núñez (1996, Exp. 4) told stories to 3- and 4-year-old children, some of which involved the breaking of a proscriptive rule (deontic condition) and others that had the same content but no implications for social proscription (descriptive condition). For example, children in the deontic condition were told "One day Carol wants to do some painting. Her Mum says if she does some painting she should put her apron on." Other children were told, "One day Carol wants to do some painting. Carol says that, if she does some painting, she always puts her apron on" (descriptive condition). Children were then shown a series of four drawings, for example, Carol painting with her apron, Carol painting without her apron, Carol not painting with her apron, and Carol not painting without her apron.

Children were then told either "Show me the picture where Carol is doing something naughty and not doing what her Mum said" (deontic condition) or "Show me the picture where Carol is doing something different and not doing what she said" (descriptive condition). Consistent with the findings from adults (e.g., Cosmides & Tooby, 1992), children were more likely to select the correct picture in the deontic condition than in the descriptive condition. That is, despite the identical structure of the problems, preschoolers showed higher levels of reasoning when a social contract was being violated than when no such social obligation was involved.

THE EVOLUTION OF ToM

We believe that ToM and related social cognitive mechanisms were central to the evolution of the modern human mind. From this perspective, human intelligence emerged in response to pressures associated with the complexities of social existence (i.e., competition and cooperation). These pressures are believed to have resulted specifically in the evolution of advanced forms of social cognition, that, once attained, were coopted for use in other non-social (e.g., technical) contexts (see Alexander, 1989; Bjorklund & Kipp, 1996; Byrne & Whiten, 1988; Dunbar, 1992; Humphrey, 1976). Social complexity, of course, is not independently sufficient for the evolution of advanced forms of intelligence, otherwise such abilities would be observed in a vast array of species, including social insects. We proposed elsewhere that in addition to this factor two other conditions must exist for the evolution of ToM, specifically, that of a large brain and an extended juvenile period (Bjorklund & Bering, 2003; Bjorklund & Pellegrini, 2002; Bjorklund & Rosenberg, 2005; see also Dunbar, 1995, 2001; Geary & Flinn, 2001). The relationship of these multiple influences on intelligence and social cognition is believed to have been essentially synergistic in nature. Consequently, one factor cannot be properly viewed as causally or merely additively related to another.

How does one evaluate such evolutionary hypotheses? Obviously, we cannot go back in time and run experiments to test the validity of these claims. They must be evaluated inferentially, based primarily on an examination of the fossil record and on both naturalistic and experimental assessments of the social–cognitive abilities of our closest living relatives, chimpanzees (*Pan troglodytes*). Humans, of course, did not evolve from chimpanzees but last shared a common ancestor with chimps as recently as 5 to 8 million years ago (e.g., Sibley & Ahlquist, 1984). Paleontologists describe chimpanzees as an evolutionarily conservative species, meaning that they have not changed much since they last shared a common ancestor with humans. If our common ancestor was anything like modern chimpanzees, they had relatively large brains for their body size, lived in socially complex groups, and had an extended juvenile period. Although each of these characteristics is quite exaggerated in modern humans, they are also found in a lesser degree in chimpanzees. For example, using Jerison's (1973) encephalization quotient (see later discussion), which represents the degree to which brain size in a species corresponds to body size, chimpanzees have a brain that is 2.3 times larger than expected for an animal of its size; the corresponding value in humans is 7.6.

Moreover, chimpanzee social life is inarguably complex, with dominance and access to resources being based not simply on brute strength but also on social alliances (e.g., de Waal, 1982; Goodall, 1986). There is now clear evidence that chimpanzees possess culture, in that acquired behavioral patterns including ant and termite fishing, nut cracking, and different forms of greetings and grooming are unique to certain chimpanzee troops and are transmitted from one generation to the next via social learning (Whiten et al., 1999). Thus, the roots of complex social cognition can be found in contemporary chimpanzees and were likely found in our common ancestor. Yet, as we argue later, although chimpanzees often display impressive forms of social cognition, they only weakly approximate those shown by humans.

In the sections to follow we first examine the expansion of the human brain over hominid evolution and the developmental mechanisms seemingly responsible for such an expansion. We then explore research and theory related to ToM, and social cognition in general, in chimpanzees (*Pan troglodytes*), arguing that this species represents the best approximation to what our common ancestor may have been like. We next examine in more detail the proposal that having to deal with conspecifics in complex social groups was the primary selection pressure in human cognitive evolution and that the evolution of increased inhibition abilities permitted our ancestors to exert better intentional control over their behavior, particularly in social situations. We conclude by arguing that the enhanced social-cognitive abilities brought about by increased inhibitory control altered the ecological landscape for hominids, producing new selective pressures and resulting in the eventual emergence of more domain-specific social-cognitive abilities and subsequent advances in theory of mind.

The Evolution of the Human Brain

Modern humans did not arise fully formed 5 to 8 million years ago, of course. Although there are a variety of competing hypotheses for the course of human evolution, most concur that the immediate ancestral source of early humans was the australopithecines, which are believed to have appeared approximately 5.5 million years ago. The timing of the transition from australopithecus to humans remains a source of debate, although most accounts assume that the earliest member of the Homo lineage (usually thought to be *Homo habilis*), emerged about 2.5 million years ago, followed by *Homo erectus* (or *Homo ergaster*), which appeared as early as 1.8 million years ago, and which preceded *Homo sapiens*, who appeared approximately 300,000 years ago. It is generally believed that *Homo sapiens* spread from the African continent, perhaps in several distinct waves, and consequently replaced other archaic humans, such as the Neanderthals. Several sources of evidence, such as fossil and archaeological records, data on genetic associations, and the diversity of present-day *Homo sapiens* support this latter claim (Gabunia et al., 2000; Johanson & Edgar, 1996).

The evolution of the hominid brain has witnessed consistent and substantial increases in both absolute and relative volume over time. By way of gross comparison and outline, the australopithecine brain averaged about 420 cc and that of *Homo habilis*, 650 cc. The brain of *Homo erectus* averaged approximately 950 cc, and that of *Homo sapiens* currently averages close to 1,300 cc (Eccles, 1989). Although it is also true that body mass has displayed corresponding increases along this evolutionary timeline, growth of the brain has consistently outpaced that observed for body mass. This latter point has been demonstrated by use of the encephalization quotient (EQ; Jerison, 1973, 2002; Rilling & Insel, 1999), which reflects, for individual species, the standardized ratio of observed brain size to body size for an average extant animal, with 1.0 being the expected EQ for any species. Changes in EQ over hominid evolution have been quite drastic: *Australopithecus afarensis*, 3.1; *Homo habilis*, 4.0; *Homo erectus*, 5.5; and *Homo sapiens*, 7.6 (Tobias, 1987).

Although the human brain has shown substantial overall expansion, the greatest relative increases have occurred in the neocortex (Deacon, 1997), which is the part of the brain most associated with distinctively human thought (Fuster, 1984; Luria, 1973) as well other possibly uniquely human cognitive specializations, such as language (Bickerton, 1990) and self-consciousness (Eccles, 1989). The expansion of the neocortex (particularly the prefrontal lobes) has also resulted in quantitative enhancement of cognitive skills that are available, to a significantly lesser degree, to monkeys and apes, such as memory, problem solving, and the control of emotional reactions (i.e., behavioral inhibition). Not surprisingly, the prefrontal lobes of the neocortex are the last area of the cortex to reach full development during ontogeny, and presumably, the last to have evolved phylogenetically (see Eccles, 1989; Jerison, 1973).

Although there were surely many different evolutionary selective pressures ultimately responsible for the brain expansion and specialization observed over hominid phylogeny, the proximal cause for building bigger brains resides in the relative timing associated with the offset of neurogenesis (i.e., the production of new neurons as the result of continued stem cell division), with relatively delayed offsets resulting in the production of relatively greater numbers of neurons (and hence larger neural structures) being produced (Finlay & Darlington, 1995; Finlay, Darlington, & Nicastro, 2001). However, the steady increases in fetal neural tissue mass that are proposed to have occurred over human phylogeny must also have been associated with increased fetal skull size, resulting in problems for passage through hominid birth canals. A necessary coevolutionary response would be the evolution of premature human birth (i.e., birth that occurs relatively early in development in comparison to other mammals) and the resultant necessity that an unusually large proportion of brain development must therefore occur postnatally.

In addition to having a greater number of neurons (i.e., more brain), humans have also evolved specialized brain structures and functions relative to our ancestors (Preuss, 2001), consistent with the claims for domain specificity of evolutionary psychologists. However, we believe that the earliest cognitive gains resulting from an expansion of the neocortex were domain general in nature. Enhancements in speed of processing, working memory, and inhibition, for example, would have been applied primarily in the social realm and afforded the subsequent evolution of more domain-specific abilities that characterize modern humans (Bjorklund & Harnishfeger, 1995; Bjorklund & Kipp, 1996, 2002; Bjorklund & Pellegrini, 2002). Once brain expansion reached a certain level, bringing with it, in particular, the enhanced abilities to focus attention, keep irrelevant information out of working memory, and inhibit unwanted behavior, such capacities could be put to immediate use in dealing with fellow members of one's social group. Such abilities, that perhaps manifested themselves as self-awareness and consciousness (Bering & Bjorklund, in press), are obviously not necessary for life in a socially complex group but would have nonetheless greatly enhanced the inclusive fitness (i.e., increased odds of survival and successful reproduction of one's genes) of any individuals within the species that possessed them. This possibility is discussed in greater detail in a later section.

ToM in Great Apes

There is no denying that chimpanzees have impressive social-learning abilities. As we noted earlier, there is now solid evidence of the transmission of complex behavioral patterns across generations (Whiten et al., 1999), a defining criterion for culture. Yet there is great debate about the social-cognitive abilities of chimpanzees, with some believing that chimpanzees are almost human (e.g., de Waal, 1989; Fouts, 1997; Goodall, 1986), and others contending that chimpanzees are merely clever behaviorists, able to accomplish feats of social complexity in the absence of abstract cognitive abilities (e.g., Povinelli, 2000; Povinelli & Bering, 2002).

One ability that chimpanzees seem to possess, which would be foundational for ToM, is mirror self-recognition, discussed earlier with respect to children, who tend to "pass" such tests at around 18 months of age (Brooks–Gunn & Lewis, 1984). Chimpanzees, as well as orangutans and a few gorillas, also pass this test, although monkeys do not (Gallup, 1979;

see Suddendorf & White, 2001; Swartz, Sarauw, & Evans, 1999). There have also been observations of mother chimpanzees teaching their offspring how to crack nuts (e.g., Boesch, 1991, 1993; Greenfield, Maynard, Boehm, & Schmidtling, 2000). Successful teaching presumably requires an understanding that a learner has different knowledge and a different perspective from oneself and represents a potent factor in cultural transmission and a clear demonstration of ToM (see Tomasello, Kruger, & Ratner, 1993). However, the interpretation of such episodes in chimpanzees has been questioned, and they are rarely observed, indicating at the very least that direct teaching is not a common form of cultural transmission in chimpanzees (see Bering, 2001; Bering & Povinelli, 2003).

Seeing is Knowing. Recall from our presentation of Baron-Cohen's (1995) model that an early developing component in children's ToM is the EDD, which basically implies that one realizes that eyes possess knowledge. That is, a child possessing the EDD module understands that if person A is looking at object B, he or she sees object B and thus has knowledge about object B. Do chimpanzees behave as if they possess an EDD module? The answer is mixed. In one set of studies using a naturalistic food-competition paradigm, Hare and his colleagues (Hare, Call, Agentta, & Tomasello, 2000; Hare, Call, & Tomasello, 2001) demonstrated that subordinate chimpanzees retrieve food items only when the food is out of sight of a more dominant animal's view, a seeming indication that one animal understands what the other animal sees. However, other studies by Povinelli and his colleagues (Povinelli & Eddy, 1996; Reaux, Theall, & Povinelli, 1999) present a different picture. These researchers report that chimpanzees are just as likely to request food from a blindfolded as a sighted caregiver, apparently not realizing that the eyes have knowledge. The contradiction in findings may be due to the different contexts in which the animals were tested (food competition with a conspecific in Hare et al.'s studies vs. requesting food from a familiar human in the Povinelli studies). Regardless of the reason for the different patterns of findings, it is clear that chimpanzees' ability to interpret eye gaze is not the same as it is in human children and in fact may be restricted to specific contexts.

Deception and ToM. There is also some anecdotal evidence for deception in chimpanzees (see Whiten & Byrne, 1988). Deception is clearly an important social skill and, in many cases, would seem to involve realizing that the deceived has different beliefs and desires than does the deceiver. In their survey of primatologists, Whiten and Byrne (1988) reported differential evidence of deception in monkeys and apes. In general, apes (chimpanzees and gorillas) displayed greater levels of sophistication in the use of deception than monkeys (including baboons). For example, concealment was observed for both groups, but, as Whiten and Byrne point out, only apes demonstrated a capacity to conceal objects. Monkeys inhibited behavior (e.g., froze) to avoid attracting the attention of another (typically dominant) individual but did not display anything like the object concealments reported for chimps. As an example, a female chimpanzee named Belle would be shown the location of food and later given the opportunity to get the food. However, when the dominant chimp, Rock, was around, Belle would not go to the food until Rock left the area. (When she did, Rock would take the food for himself.) She sometimes would even move to an area without food, presumably in an effort to mislead him (Menzel, 1974).

In experimental tests of deception, chimpanzees have often not fared as well as one might expect given the anecdotal reports. For example, Boysen and Bernston (1995) examined strategic deception in two trained chimpanzees, Sarah (32 years old) and Sheba (9 years old). The chimpanzees sat on opposite sides of a partition, with one chimp acting as the selector and the other acting as the observer. An array consisting of two boxes filled with candies (one with a larger amount and one with a smaller amount) was placed in front of the selector, who, in turn, selected one of the arrays. Similar to experiments using preschool children as participants (e.g., Hala & Russell, 2001; Peskin, 1992; Russell et al., 1991), the crux of these experiments was that, for the selector to receive the larger candy display, she needed to pick the smaller one because the candy display actually selected was subsequently given to the observer. Boysen and Bernston had the chimpanzees switch roles (selector ↔ observer) and found that, regardless of which chimpanzee was the selector, they both repeatedly failed the task.

In a manner similar to that of young children, the chimps could not inhibit their prepotent response of selecting the array with the larger portion and thus consistently received the lesser quantity of food. Interestingly, when Arabic numerals replaced the food, Sheba, who had been extensively trained to associate specific quantities with specific numerals (e.g., 2 corresponds to two entities), was able to "pass" the task, consistently selecting the smaller numeral and thus getting the larger quantity. Presumably, the use of symbols made it possible for this highly trained chimpanzee to overcome her tendency to directly select the larger quantity. Thus, it appears that chimpanzees are able to inhibit prepotent responses in some circumstances, but it is difficult for them do to so, making strategic deception a seemingly rare event in chimpanzee life.

These and other feats associated with chimpanzee social intelligence are impressive (for other examples, see Whiten & Byrne, 1988) and indicate that chimpanzees are sometimes able to use deception to their benefit. However, the observed forms of deception just described do not necessarily require knowing the mind of another. The animals in these studies may have learned from past experience that not inhibiting a behavior in a certain context produces maladaptive results. Nonetheless, such behaviors are impressive, and they do reflect the appropriate inhibition of a prepotent behavior. But, other than inhibition, they say little about the social-cognitive mechanisms underlying the behaviors.

In fact, in laboratory-controlled tests of ToM, chimpanzees, similar to 3-year-old children, typically fail. Although some claim chimpanzees have passed false belief tasks (e.g., Premack & Woodruff, 1978), there is little evidence that chimpanzees understand the dynamics of false belief when proper controls are applied. For instance, in the best controlled version of a false belief task to date using chimpanzees as participants, Call and Tomasello (1999) hid food treats behind a barrier outside of an ape's view but in the view of a human communicator. The barrier was removed, and the communicator placed a marker on the container in which the treat was hidden. After learning how to perform the basic task, the false belief portion of the task began. After watching as a treat was moved from one container to another, the communicator left the room. Then the ape watched as a new person entered and moved the treat to a different container. The communicator returned and placed the marker where she had previously seen the food hidden. That is, just as in the Maxi task with children (Wimmer & Perner, 1983), the communicator had a false belief of where the treat was hidden. If the ape understands this, it should not select the container marked by the communicator. The apes in this experiment consistently failed this task, suggesting that they did not understand that the communicator had a false belief. (Interesting, most 4-year-old children also failed this task, although 5-year-olds passed it.) Call and Tomasello interpreted their findings as indicating that chimpanzees do not understand false belief, at least not in the same way as do most 5-year-old children

Social Learning.   With respect to social learning, unlike most child developmental psychologists, comparative psychologists differentiate between different types of learning by observation, based on presumed underlying mechanisms (see Tomasello, 1996, 2000; Tomasello & Call, 1997). Tomasello and his colleagues (Tomasello, 1996, 2000; Tomasello, Kruger, & Ratner, 1993) identified true imitation as the most cognitively complex form of social learning, requiring an understanding of the goals, or intentions, of a model, as well as the reproduction of important aspects of modeled behavior. In other words, true imitation involves perspective taking, a core element of ToM. Other forms of social learning include mimicry, in which an observer copies aspects of a model's behavior without understanding the goal of those behaviors, and emulation, in which an observer appreciates the general goal of a model but does not reproduce specific behaviors in attempts to attain that goal. For instance, one ape may watch another displacing a log by rolling it, and, as a result, gain access to a nest of tasty ants. The observer may then approach the same or a different log and somehow manipulate it (lift it up, jump on it) and, eventually, achieve the same outcome (exposure to ants for a snack) but without duplication of important aspects of the model's behavior. This is a cognitively complex mechanism, but not as complex, presumably, as true imitation (e.g., Tomasello & Call, 1997).

Although chimpanzees often master complicated tasks through observation of a model, there is little evidence that they engage in true imitation, at least when acting on objects, as in tool use (e.g., Tomasello,

Savage-Rumbaugh, & Kruger, 1993). Evidence of exception to these limits may exist for enculturated apes (i.e., those that are reared by humans and in a manner similar to that of human children). For example, enculturated apes have been observed to duplicate actions that have been modeled on objects, presumably displaying true imitation (e.g., Bering, Bjorklund, & Ragan, 2000; Bjorklund, Yunger, Bering, & Ragan, 2002; Tomasello, Savage-Rumbaugh, & Kruger, 1993). In one study, Tomasello, Savage-Rumbaugh, and Kruger presented mother-reared chimpanzees, enculturated chimpanzees, and 18- and 30-month-old children sets of items to explore during a baseline period. They then demonstrated some actions on the objects and, either immediately or following a 24- or 48-hour delay, gave the objects back to the participants and noted any evidence of imitation. For the more challenging delayed tasks, both groups of children and the mother-reared apes performed poorly; only the enculturated apes (two bonobos, *Pan paniscus*, and one common chimpanzee, *Pan troglodytes*) showed evidence of imitation of tool use (see also Bering et al., 2000).

In related work, Bjorklund and his colleagues (Bjorklund et al., 2002) demonstrated that enculturated chimpanzees (*Pan troglodytes*) displayed deferred imitation not only by replicating target behaviors with the modeled objects (e.g., clapping together two round, metal cymbals) but also by generalizing the behaviors to different but somewhat similar objects (e.g., clapping together two rectangular, wooden trowels). Bjorklund and his colleagues argued that the generalization of observed behaviors to different objects was good evidence that the learned behaviors were acquired via the mechanisms of true imitation rather than alternative forms of social learning, such as mimicry (in which the goal of the model is not considered) or emulation (in which behaviors other than those observed are used). Thus, although most captive chimpanzees seem not to engage in true imitation, they can apparently be induced to do so when they experience a radically different rearing environment, in this cases those involving the use of language, direct teaching, and joint-shared attention (i.e., triadic interactions). It is impossible to be certain which mechanisms of social learning chimpanzees in the wild engage in, but the data suggest that contemporary chimpanzees have the underlying ability for true imitation, even if it is expressed only in species-atypical contexts.

The literature on the social-cognitive abilities of chimpanzees is admittedly not straightforward. Although it reveals substantial social skills in these animals, both in the wild and in the laboratory, evidence for ToM comparable to that of 4-year-old children (i.e., successful performance on false belief tasks) remains elusive. If the common ancestor humans shared with chimpanzees possessed social-cognitive abilities similar to those of modern apes, it seems clear that when enhanced levels of computational power were achieved via evolutionary expansion of gross brain volume, it was in a species that was in a position to put it to good use in a complex social milieu in which sophistication in the use of both competitive and cooperative behaviors would result in clearly improved inclusive fitness.

The Social Origins of Mind

There has been no dearth of hypotheses about the origins of human intelligence. Hunting, food preparation skills, and tool use, among others, have all been proposed as the principal selective pressure in human cognitive phylogeny. Currently popular accounts, as the one favored here, focus on social pressures as being primarily responsible for the advent of the modern human mind. But theories need to be evaluated, and, although we cannot go back in time to either observe or manipulate events to prove one hypothesis and disprove others, evidence can be amassed to contrast the feasibility of different theories of human cognitive evolution.

For example, Barton and Dunbar (1997) examined multiple theories proposed to account for observed evolutionary increases in primate brain size, including ecologically based theories (which include the general class of foraging-niche hypotheses), life span theories (with longer life spans associated with greater degrees of encephalization), and social intelligence–based theories. Although theorists acknowledge that survival problems associated with an organism's ecological environment may produce cognitive adaptations, they do not believe that such adaptations account for the particularly large brains and specialized cognitive abilities of primates. In comparison to that required for the processing of ecological information, Barton and Dunbar suggest that the inherent complexity of social information implies a much heavier processing load:

> We suggest that it is the massively parallel nature of social information that requires so much brain tissue; social interactions and relationships are in a constant state of flux, demanding continuous on-line processing of rapidly changing information. The only comparable ecological processing would be the computation of optimal foraging routes simultaneously taking into account a range of resources and hazards at varying distances and trajectories relative to the individual's current position. . . . In fact, there is little, if any, evidence suggesting that the ecological problems faced by primates are particularly complex, or that primates have especially sophisticated foraging strategies" (p. 257; but see Kaplan, Hill, Lancaster, & Hurtado, 2000, for a counter argument.)

Following this argument, it would appear that for primates (including humans) the cognitive demands inherent in social existence represent the primary source of selective pressures that were responsible for the evolution of the larger brains and impressive cognitive capacities displayed by these species.

As we noted previously, other contemporary scholars posit a central role for social factors in the origins and expansion of human intelligence and brain development (e.g., Alexander, 1989; Crook, 1980; Humphrey, 1976). According to Bjorklund and Harnishfeger (1995), although traditional peoples and early hominids shared life-sustaining concerns of avoiding predators and acquiring food, and even the development and maintenance of various technologies, the most complex tasks shared by these groups, as well as by modern humans, are those that are associated with the processing of social information. Humphrey states that given an analysis of the physical demands in ancestral environments (based on examination of the lifestyles of contemporary hunter/gatherers and the paleontological record), humans are far more intelligent than would appear to be required solely to meet the demands of the physical environment. Similarly, chimpanzees display far more skill in the execution of laboratory tasks than is presumably required for survival within the merely physical aspects of their natural environments.

According to Humphrey (1976), human (and perhaps ape) technical genius becomes evident in the execution of artificial tasks. For example, a distant field anthropologist observing Albert Einstein from afar would have likely concluded that even he had a merely adequate mind. Our most impressive and frequently used intellectual skills (which are typically acquired and deployed in a largely automatic fashion) are those associated with the navigation of the human social terrain. From this perspective, the large brains and impressive intellects associated with various hominid species evolved in response to the specific selective pressures associated with the dangers and opportunities afforded by social environments, with the consequent and secondary developments of language, culture, and advanced technologies.

Byrne and Whiten (1988, 1997) refer to the unique skills required for successful navigation of the complex social environments of both apes and humans as Machiavellian intelligence. According to this hypothesis, as hominid and ape groups evolved increasingly complex social orders, selective pressures associated with intraspecific competition and the formation of cooperative alliances favored those individuals who could successfully control sexual, aggressive, and other affectively based behavioral impulses. These selective pressures also favored those individuals that could successfully engage in effective social calculation, including deception and anticipation of the behaviors of other group members. Such individuals would presumably achieve, on average, higher social rank as well as have greater access to desired resources and mates.

One clearly fundamental component underlying the successful execution of skilled social behaviors is the inhibition of prepotent responses, especially those associated with aggressive, sexual, and other affectively based impulses. It does not require much effort to recognize the dangers posed within large social groups, either human or other, of members or subgroups that are overly wont to act in unrestrained ways.

The Role of Inhibition in the Evolution of Hominid Social Cognition

A number of researchers have suggested that increased inhibition abilities, afforded by increased brain matter, played a significant role in human cognitive evolution, particularly in the emergence of human social-cognitive abilities (e.g., Bjorklund & Harnishfeger, 1995; Bjorklund & Kipp, 1996,

2002; Stenhouse, 1974). This is seen, for example, in the ability to inhibit sexual and aggressive behaviors, a point central to the perspectives of a number of early theorists (e.g., Chance, 1962; Chance & Meade, 1953; Fox, 1972). In a great number of mammalian species, competition between males for sexual access to females is substantial. Within most of these species, this competition occurs during periods of female estrus, which are associated with female sexual receptivity. The duration of periods of estrus and female receptivity vary considerably across species, with substantial extension of these periods being observed for chimpanzees and some species of monkey. A natural consequence of these factors is the extension of periods in which males are potentially in conflict. This point is highlighted by the fact that in chimpanzees, some matings occur outside of periods of estrus and therefore in response primarily to social factors.

This extension of periods of either actual or potential female sexual receptivity is most pronounced in humans, for whom the influence of social factors on mating behavior has evolved beyond that observed for any other mammal (with the possible exception of bonobos, *Pan paniscus*). Moreover, humans represent one of the few species for which female ovulation has become fully concealed, that is, not associated with any reliable external indicators, such as swollen genitals (as is the case for apes), which may otherwise serve to alert males to the onset of periods of female receptivity and ovulation. Moreover, unlike any other mammal, the human female presents permanently swollen mammaries (regardless of nursing activity), which function as constant sexual signals to males, despite their unreliability in predicting the presence of either ovulation or sexual receptivity. Theoretically, then, both men and women are potentially continuously sexually receptive.

Chance (1962) suggested that during the course of mammalian evolution, the inhibition of sexual behaviors became subject to increasing levels of cortical and, therefore, intentional, control. This neuroanatomical shift in the control of sexual behaviors was related to phylogenetic increases in relative neocortical volumes that occurred throughout mammalian evolution, a relationship recognized early on by Beach (1947), who stated, "In the course of mammalian evolution as the cerebral cortex assumed a more and more dominant role in the cortical control of all complex behavior patterns, it came to exert an increasing influence over more primitive social neural mechanisms which originally possessed sole responsibility for the mediation of sexual activities" (p. 310).

Bjorklund and Kipp (1996, 2002) speculated that enhanced inhibition skills were critical to successful parenting. Over the course of hominid evolution, the period of infant dependency likely increased and was presumably associated with greater levels of behavioral immaturity in offspring, requiring concomitant enhancements to parental skills, especially with regard to behavioral inhibition and control. The vast bulk of child care in most mammals and all contemporary groups of people falls to women, and Bjorklund and Kipp (1996) speculated that females should display greater inhibitory abilities in the behavioral and social/emotional (but not necessarily cognitive) realms than males. This is a pattern that has been reported in separate meta-analyses (Bjorklund & Kipp, 1996; Silverman, 2003; Stevenson & Williams, 2000).

The neuroanatomical basis of inhibition is located primarily in the prefrontal lobes, an area that experienced substantial expansion over primate evolution. Damage to these areas results in decrements in the inhibition of social and other affectively based impulses, as well as increased distractibility at the cognitive level. The prefrontal areas also maintain a rich set of connections with the emotion centers of the brain. Specific neural pathways that have been clearly implicated in both pleasurable (e.g., sexual) and aggressive (e.g., rage) affective responses (see MacLean, 1990) run from the septal nuclei and amygdala of the limbic system through the thalamus and on to the prefrontal lobes (Eccles, 1989). Although some have speculated that the limbic system plays a less central role in the functioning of the human brain than in nonhuman primates, the individual structures of the system have actually increased in size in humans, suggesting that its role in brain functioning should not be substantially different for human and nonhuman primates (see Armstrong, 1991). Additional support for this perspective is found in the fact that the hippocampus and amygdala (contained within the limbic system) also play a crucial role in learning and remembering, functions that are particularly highly evolved in humans. It would seem, therefore, that the heightened levels of emotional control generally displayed by humans in comparison to nonhuman primates are not the result of a diminished functional relevance of the limbic system. We remain not only highly emotional animals but arguably the most emotional of all species.

These increased levels of behavioral control most likely result from heightened levels of inhibitory capacity made possible by the expansion of the prefrontal cortex, which, as indicated previously, has displayed substantial evolutionary expansion within the hominid line. An interesting implication of the evolution of increased inhibitory capacity as a result of prefrontal expansion is the possibility of recruitment of this neural apparatus for purposes other than that for which it may have been originally selected. Specifically, neural circuitry associated with the evaluation and inhibition of affectively relevant stimuli (i.e., resulting in substantial limbic activity) may have been recruited for use within the context of other, more cognitive operations, resulting in increased resistance to interference and distractibility, ultimately resulting in enhanced levels of concentration (and perhaps more efficient use of working memory capacity) required for the development of advanced technologies (Bjorklund & Harnishfeger, 1995) as well as improved social-cognitive functioning.

Bigger Brains, Increased Inhibitory Abilities, and ToM

Our claim is that increased inhibitory abilities brought about by brain expansion over hominid evolution were adaptively applied to deal with the everyday social problems that our prehuman ancestors faced. Counter to conventional evolutionary psychological theory, these abilities were domain general in nature and could have been applied to a wide range of tasks within the ecology of early hominids.

A relationship between ToM and domain-general abilities, such as inhibition or EF more specifically, is found in contemporary children. As we noted earlier, a certain level of domain-general processing capacity (e.g., inhibition) seems to be required before children can engage successfully in standard false belief tasks (e.g., Perner & Lang, 2000). Yet children, like adults (e.g., Cosmides & Tooby, 1992), also appear to perform some social-cognitive tasks at a higher level than comparable tasks that involve non-social content, suggesting some degree of domain specificity (e.g., Harris & Núñez, 1996). We argue that human social-cognitive phylogeny may have followed a course similar to that of human social-cognitive ontogeny, with increased domain-general capacities preceding the onset of domain-specific skills, essentially playing a permissive role by setting the neurological stage for the evolution of these more modular skills, such as the SAD and ToMM modules hypothesized by Baron-Cohen (1995).

A prolonged juvenile period, which provided ample time to learn the complexities of the social group, provided a context for early humans in which increased inhibition abilities could be put to use. The increased brain expansion also influenced other related abilities, particularly consciousness and EF in general (see Bering & Bjorklund, in press). It changed the social world of the animals that possessed these skills, establishing new selective pressures (see West-Eberhard, 2003), and presumably set the stage for the evolution of domain-specific skills associated with more advanced forms of social cognition.

ACKNOWLEDGMENTS

This chapter was written while the first author was supported by a Research Award from the Alexander von Humboldt Foundation, Germany, and while working at the University of Würzburg, Germany. We wish to express our appreciation to the Humboldt Foundation and to Wolfgang Schneider for their support of this work. Correspondence should be sent to David F. Bjorklund, Department of Psychology, Florida Atlantic University, 777 Glades Road, Boca Raton, FL 33431, USA; e-mail: dbjorklu@fau.edu.

REFERENCES

Alexander, R. D. (1989). Evolution of the human psyche. In P. Mellers & C. Stringer (Eds.), *The human revolution: Behavioural and biological perspectives on the origins of modern humans* (pp. 455–513). Princeton, NJ: Princeton University Press.

Armstrong, E. (1991). The limbic system and culture: An allometric analysis of the neocortex and limbic nuclei. *Human Nature, 2,* 117–136.

Astington, J. W. (1993). *The child's discovery of the mind.* Cambridge, MA: Harvard University Press.

Barkow, J. H., Cosmides, L., & Tooby, J. (Eds.). (1992). *The adapted mind: Evolutionary psychology and the generation of culture.* New York: Oxford University Press.

Baron-Cohen, S. (1989). The autistic child's theory of mind: A case specific developmental delay. *Journal of Child Psychology and Psychiatry, 30,* 285–298.

Baron-Cohen, S. (1995). *Mindblindness: An essay on autism and theory of mind.* Cambridge, MA: MIT Press.

Baron-Cohen, S., Leslie, A., & Frith, U. (1985). Does the autistic child have a "theory of mind"? *Cognition, 21,* 37–46.

Baron-Cohen, S., Leslie, A., & Frith, U. (1986). Mechanical, behavioral, and intentional understanding of pictures and tools in autistic children. *British Journal of Developmental Psychology, 4,* 113–125.

Baron-Cohen, S., Wheelwright, S., Stone, V., & Rutherford, M. (1999). A mathematician, a physicist and a computer scientist with Asperger syndrome: Performance on folk psychology and folk physics tests. *Neurocase, 5,* 475–483.

Barton, R. A., & Dunbar, R. I. (1997). Evolution of the social brain. In A. Whiten & R. W. Byrne (Eds.), *Machiavellian intelligence II: Extensions and evaluations* (pp. 240–263). Cambridge, UK: Cambridge University Press.

Bartsch, K., & Wellman, H. M. (1995). *Children talk about the mind.* New York: Oxford University Press.

Beach, F. A. (1947). Evolutionary changes in the physiological control of mating behavior in mammals. *Psychological Review, 54,* 297–315.

Bering, J. M. (2001). Theistic percepts in other species: Can chimpanzees represent the minds of non-natural agents? *Journal of Cognition and Culture, 1,* 107–137.

Bering, J. M., & Bjorklund, D. F. (in press). The serpent's gift: Evolutionary psychology and consciousness. In P. D. Zelazo (Ed.), *Handbook of consciousness.* Cambridge, UK: Cambridge University Press.

Bering, J. M., Bjorklund, D. F., & Ragan, P. (2000). Deferred imitation of object-related actions in human-reared juvenile chimpanzees and orangutans. *Developmental Psychobiology, 36,* 218–232.

Bering, J. M., & Povinelli, D. J. (2003). Comparing cognitive development. In D. Maestripieri (Ed.), *Primate psychology* (pp. 205–233). Cambridge, MA: Harvard University Press.

Bickerton, D. (1990). *Language and species.* Chicago: University of Chicago Press.

Bjorklund, D. F., & Bering, J. M. (2003). Big brains, slow development, and social complexity: The developmental and evolutionary origins of social cognition. In M. Brüne, H. Ribbert, & W. Schiefenhövel (Eds.), *The social brain: Evolutionary aspects of development and pathology* (pp. 133–151). New York: Wiley.

Bjorklund, D. F., & Harnishfeger, K. K. (1995). The role of inhibition mechanisms in the evolution of human cognition and behavior. In F. N. Dempster & C. J. Brainerd (Eds.), *New perspectives on interference and inhibition in cognition* (pp. 141–173). New York: Academic Press.

Bjorklund, D. F., & Kipp, K. (1996). Parental investment theory and gender differences in the evolution of inhibition mechanisms. *Psychological Bulletin, 120,* 163–188.

Bjorklund, D. F., & Kipp, K. (2002). Social cognition, inhibition, and theory of mind: The evolution of human intelligence. In R. J. Sternberg & J. C. Kaufman (Eds.), *The evolution of intelligence* (pp. 27–53). Mahwah, NJ: Lawrence Erlbaum Associates.

Bjorklund, D. F., & Pellegrini, A. D. (2000). Child development and evolutionary psychology. *Child Development, 71,* 1687–1708.

Bjorklund, D. F., & Pellegrini, A. D. (2002). *The origins of human nature: Evolutionary developmental psychology.* Washington, DC: American Psychological Association.

Bjorklund, D. F., & Rosenberg, J. S. (2005). The role of developmental plasticity in human cognitive evolution. In B. J. Ellis & D. F. Bjorklund (Eds.), *Origins of the social mind: Evolutionary psychology and child development.* New York: Guilford.

Bjorklund, D. F., Yunger, J. L., Bering, J. M., & Ragan, P. (2002). The generalization of deferred imitation in enculturated chimpanzees (*Pan troglodytes*). *Animal Cognition, 5,* 49–58.

Boesch, C. (1991). Teaching among wild chimpanzees. *Animal Behaviour, 41,* 530–532.

Boesch, C. (1993). Toward a new image of culture in chimpanzees. *Behavioral and Brain Sciences, 16*, 514–515.

Boysen, S. T., & Bernston, G. G. (1995). Responses to quantity: Perceptual versus cognitive mechanisms in chimpanzees (*Pan troglodytes*). *Journal of Experimental Psychology: Animal Behavior Processes, 21*, 82–86.

Brooks-Gunn, J., & Lewis, M. (1984). The development of early self-recognition. *Developmental Review, 4*, 215–239.

Bugental, D. B. (2000). Acquisition of the algorithms of social life: A domain-based approach. *Psychological Bulletin, 126*, 187–219.

Buss, D. M. (1995). Evolutionary psychology. *Psychological Inquiry, 6*, 1–30.

Buss, D. M. (Ed.). (in press). *Evolutionary psychology handbook*. New York: Wiley.

Byrne, R., & Whiten, A. (Eds.). (1988). *Machiavellian intelligence: Social expertise and the evolution of intellect in monkeys, apes, and humans*. Oxford, UK: Clarendon.

Byrne, R.W., & Whiten, A. (1997). Machiavellian intelligence. In A. Whiten & R. W. Bryne (Eds.), *Machiavellian intelligence II: Extensions and evaluations* (pp. 1–23). Cambridge, UK: Cambridge University Press.

Call, J., & Tomasello, M. (1999). A nonverbal false belief task: The performance of children and great apes. *Child Development, 70*, 381–395.

Carlson, S. M., & Moses, L. J. (2001). Individual differences in inhibitory control and children's theory of mind. *Child Development, 72*, 1032–1053.

Carlson, S. M., Moses, L. J., & Breton, C. (2002). How specific is the relation between executive function and theory of mind? Contributions of inhibitory control and working memory. *Infant and Child Development, 11*, 73–92.

Chance, M. R. A. (1962). Social behaviour and primate evolution. In M. F. A. Montagu (Ed.), *Culture and the evolution of man* (pp. 84–130). New York: Oxford University Press.

Chance, M. R. A., & Meade, A. P. (1953). Social behavior and primate evolution. *Symposia of the Society for Experimental Biology, 7*, 395–439.

Cosmides, L., & Tooby, J. (1992). Cognitive adaptations for social exchange. In J. H. Barkow, L. Cosmides, & J. Tooby (Eds.), *The adapted mind: Evolutionary psychology and the generation of culture* (pp. 163–228). New York: Oxford University Press.

Cosmides, L., & Tooby, J. (2002). Unraveling the enigma of human intelligence: Evolutionary psychology and the multimodular mind. In R. J. Sternberg & J. C. Kaufman (Eds.), *The evolution of intelligence: Evolutionary psychology and the generation of culture* (pp. 145–198). Mahwah, NJ: Lawrence Erlbaum Associates.

Crook, J. M. (1980). *The evolution of human consciousness*. Oxford, UK: Clarendon Press.

Cummins, D. D. (1996). Evidence of deontic reasoning in 3- and 4-year-old children. *Memory and Cognition, 24*, 823–829.

Cummins, D. D. (1998). Cheater detection is modified by social rank: The impact of dominance on the evolution of cognitive functions. *Evolution and Human Behavior, 20*, 229–248.

Daly, M., & Wilson, M. (1988). *Homicide*. New York: Aldine.

Deacon, T. W. (1997). *The symbolic species: The co-evolution of language and the brain*. New York: Norton.

de Waal, F. B. M. (1982). *Chimpanzee politics: Power and sex among apes*. London: Jonathan Cape.

de Waal, F. B. M. (1989). *Peace making among primates*. Cambridge, MA: Harvard University Press.

Dunbar, R. I. M. (1992). Neocortex size as a constraint on group size in primates. *Journal of Human Evolution, 20*, 469–493.

Dunbar, R. I. M. (1995). Neocortex size and group size in primates: A test of the hypothesis. *Journal of Human Evolution, 28*, 287–296.

Dunbar, R. I. M. (2001). Brains on two legs: Group size and the evolution of intelligence. In F. B. M. de Waal (Ed.), *Tree of origins: What primate behavior can tell us about human social evolution* (pp. 173–191). Cambridge, MA: Harvard University Press.

Eccles, J. C. (1989). *Evolution of the brain: Creation of the self*. New York: Routledge.

Finlay, B. L., & Darlington, R. D. (1995). Linked regularities in the development and evolution of mammalian brains. *Science, 268*, 1579–1584.

Finlay, B. L., Darlington, R. B., & Nicastro, N. (2001). Developmental structure in brain evolution. *Behavioral and Brain Sciences, 24,* 263–308.

Fouts, R. (1997). *Next of kin: What chimpanzees have taught me about who we are.* New York: William Morrow.

Fox, R. (1972). Alliance and constraint: Sexual selection and the evolution of human kinship systems. In B. Campbell (Ed.), *Sexual selection and the descent of man 1871–1971* (pp. 282–331). Chicago: Aldine.

Frye, D., & Moore, C. (1991). *Children's theories of mind: Mental states and social understanding.* Hillsdale, NJ: Lawrence Erlbaum Associates.

Fuster, J. M. (1984). The prefrontal cortex and temporal integration. In A. Peters & E. G. Jones (Eds.), *Cerebral cortex: Vol. 4. Association and auditory cortices* (pp. 151–177). New York: Plenum.

Gabunia, L., Vekua, A., Lordkipanidze, D., Swisher, C. C., III, Ferring, R., Justus, A., Nioradze, M., Tvalchrelidze, M., Anton, S. C., Bosinski, G., Jöris, O., de Lumley, M.-A., Majsuradze, G., & Mouskhelishvili, A. (2000). Earliest Pleistocene hominid cranial remains from Dmanisi, Republic of Georgia: Taxonomy, setting, and age. *Science, 288,* 1019–11025.

Gallup, G. G., Jr. (1979). *Self-recognition in chimpanzees and man: A developmental and comparative perspective.* New York: Plenum Press.

Gazzaniga, M. S. (Ed.). (2000). *The new cognitive neurosciences* (2nd ed.). Cambridge, MA: MIT Press.

Geary, D. C. (2002). Principles of evolutionary educational psychology. *Learning and Individual Differences, 12,* 317–345.

Geary, D. C. (2005). *The origin of mind: Evolution of brain, cognition, and general intelligence.* Washington, DC: American Psychological Association.

Geary, D. C., & Bjorklund, D. F. (2000). Evolutionary developmental psychology. *Child Development, 71,* 57–65.

Geary, D. C., & Flinn, M. V. (2001). Evolution of human parental behavior and the human family. *Parenting: Science and Practice, 1,* 5–61.

Geary, D. C., & Huffman, K. (2002). Brain and cognitive evolution: Forms of modularity and functions of mind. *Psychological Bulletin, 128,* 667–698.

Gopnik, A., & Astington, J. W. (1988). Children's understanding of representational change and its relation to the understanding of false belief and the appearance-reality distinction. *Child Development, 59,* 26–37.

Goodall, J. (1986). *The chimpanzees of Gombe.* Cambridge, MA: Belknap.

Greenfield, P., Maynard, A., Boehm, C., & Schmidtling, E. Y. (2000). Cultural apprenticeship and cultural change: Tool learning and imitation in chimpanzees and humans. In S. T. Parker, J. Langer, & M. L. McKinney (Eds.), *Biology, brains, and behavior: The evolution of human development* (pp. 237–277). Santa Fe, NM: School of American Research Press.

Hala, S., & Russell, J. (2001). Executive control within strategic deception: A window on early cognitive development. *Journal of Experimental Child Psychology, 80,* 112–141.

Hare, B., Call, J., Agnetta, B., & Tomasello, M. (2000). Chimpanzees know what conspecifics do and do not see. *Animal Behaviour, 59,* 771–785.

Hare, B., Call, J., & Tomasello, M. (2001). Do chimpanzees know what conspecifics know? *Animal Behaviour, 61,* 139–151.

Harris, P. L., & Núñez, M. (1996). Understanding of permission rules by preschool children. *Child Development, 67,* 1572–1591.

Hernández Blasi, C., & Bjorklund, D. F. (2003). Evolutionary developmental psychology: A new tool for better understanding human ontogeny. *Human Development, 46,* 259–281.

Heyes, C. M. (1998). Theory of mind in nonhuman primates. *Behavioral and Brain Sciences, 21,* 101–148.

Hogrefe, G. J., Wimmer, H., & Perner, J. (1986). Ignorance versus false belief: A developmental lag in attribution of epistemic states. *Child Development, 57,* 567–582.

Hughes, C. (2002a). Executive functions and development: Emerging themes. *Infant and Child Development, 11,* 201–209.

Hughes, C. (2002b). Executive functions and development: Why the interest? *Infant and Child Development, 11,* 69–71.

Hughes, C., & Cutting, A. L. (1999). Nature, nurture, and individual differences in early understanding of mind. *Psychological Science, 10,* 429–432.

Humphrey, N. K. (1976). The social function of intellect. In P. P. G. Bateson & R. Hinde (Eds.), *Growing points in ethology* (pp. 303–317). Cambridge, UK: Cambridge University Press.

Jenkins, J. M., & Astington, J. W. (1996). Cognitive factors and family structure associated with theory of mind development in young children. *Developmental Psychology, 32,* 70–78.

Jenkins, J. M., & Astington, J. W. (2000). Theory of mind and social behavior: Causal models tested in a longitudinal study. *Merrill-Palmer Quarterly, 46,* 203–220.

Jerison, H. J. (1973). *Evolution of the brain and intelligence.* New York: Academic Press.

Jerison, H. J. (2002). On theory in comparative psychology. In R. J. Sternberg & J. C. Kaufman (Eds.), *The evolution of intelligence* (pp. 251–288). Mahwah, NJ: Lawrence Erlbaum Associates.

Johanson, D., & Edgar, B. (1996). *From Lucy to language.* New York: Simon & Schuster.

Kaplan, H., Hill, K., Lancaster, J., & Hurtado, A. M. (2000). A theory of human life history evolution: Diet intelligence, and longevity. *Evolutionary Anthropology, 9,* 156–185.

Leslie, A. M. (2000). "Theory of mind" as mechanism of selective attention. In M. S. Gazzaniga (Ed.), *The new cognitive neurosciences* (2nd ed., pp. 1235–1247). Cambridge, MA: MIT Press.

Lillard, A. S. (1997). Other folk's theories of mind and behavior. *Psychological Science, 8,* 268–274.

Lillard, A. S. (1998). Ethnopsychologies: Cultural variations in theories of mind. *Psychological Bulletin, 123,* 3–32.

Lillard, A. S., & Flavell, J. H. (1992). Young children's understanding of different mental states. *Developmental Pyschology, 28,* 626–634.

Luria, A. R. (1973). *The working brain: An introduction to neuropsychology.* New York: Liveright.

MacLean, P. D. (1990). *The triune brain in evolution: Role in paleocerebral functions.* New York: Plenum.

Menzel, E. W., Jr. (1974). A group of young chimpanzees in a 1-acre field: Leadership and communication. In A. M. Schrier & F. Stollnitz (Eds.), *Behavior of nonhuman primates* (Vol. 5, pp. 83–153). New York: Academic Press.

Perner, J., Frith, U., Leslie, A., & Leekam, S. (1989). Exploration of the autistic child's theory of mind: Knowledge, belief, and communication. *Child Development, 60,* 689–700.

Perner, J., & Lang, B. (1999). Development of theory of mind and executive control. *Trends in Cognitive Sciences, 3,* 337–344.

Perner, J., & Lang, B. (2000). Theory of mind and executive function: Is there a developmental relationship? In S. Baron-Cohen, H. Tager-Flusberg, & D. Cohen (Eds.), *Understanding other minds: Perspectives from autism and developmental cognitive neuroscience* (2nd ed., pp. 150–181). Oxford, UK: Oxford University Press.

Perner, J., Lang, B., & Kloo, D. (2002). Theory of mind and self-control: More than a common problem of inhibition. *Child Development, 73,* 752–767.

Perner, J., Stummer, S., & Lang, B. (1999). Executive functions and theory of mind: Cognitive complexity or functional dependence? In P. D. Zelazo, J. W. Astington, & D. R. Olson (Eds.), *Developing theories of intention: Social understanding and self control* (pp. 133–152). Mahwah, NJ: Lawrence Erlbaum Associates.

Peskin, J. (1992). Ruse and representations: On children's ability to conceal information. *Developmental Psychology, 28,* 84–89.

Pinker, S. (1997). *How the mind works.* New York: Norton.

Povinelli, D. J. (2000). *Folk physics for apes: The chimpanzee's theory of how the world works.* Oxford, UK: Oxford University Press.

Povinelli, D. J., & Bering, J. M. (2002). The mentality of apes revisited. *Current Directions in Psychological Science, 11,* 115–119.

Povinelli, D. J., & Eddy, T. J. (1996). What young chimpanzees know about seeing. *Monograph of the Society for Research in Child Development, 61*(3, Serial No. 247).

Premack, D., & Woodruff, G. (1978). Does the chimpanzee have a theory of mind? *Behavioral and Brain Sciences, 1,* 515–526.

Preuss, T. M. (2001). The discovery of cerebral diversity: An unwelcome scientific revolution. In D. Falk & K. Gibson (Eds.), *Evolutionary anatomy of the primate cerebral cortex* (pp. 138–164). Cambridge, UK: Cambridge University Press.

Rakison, D. (2005). Infant perception and cognition: An evolutionary perspective on early learning. In. B. J. Ellis & D. F. Bjorklund (Eds.), *Origins of the social mind: Evolutionary psychology and child development.* New York: Guilford.

Reaux, J. E., Theall, L. A., & Povinelli, D. J. (1999). A longitudinal investigation of chimpanzee's understanding of visual perception. *Child Development, 70,* 275–290.

Repacholi, B. M., & Gopnik, A. (1997). Early reasoning about desires: Evidence from 14- and 18-month olds. *Developmental Psychology, 33,* 12–21.

Rilling, J. K., & Insel, T. R. (1999). The primate neocortex in comparative perspective using magnetic resonance imaging. *Journal of Human Evolution, 37,* 191–223.

Ruffman, T., Perner, J., Naito, M., Parkin, L., & Clements, W. A. (1998). Older (but not younger) siblings facilitate false belief understanding. *Developmental Psychology, 34,* 161–174.

Russell, J., Mauthner, N., Sharpe, S., & Tidswell, T. (1991). The "windows tasks" as a measure of strategic deception in preschoolers and autistic subjects. *British Journal of Developmental Psychology, 9,* 331–349.

Sabbagh, M. A., & Taylor, M. (2000). Neural correlates of theory-of-mind reasoning: An event-related potential study. *Psychological Science, 11,* 46–50.

Sibley, C. G., & Ahlquist, J. E. (1984). The phylogeny of the hominoid primates, as indicated by DNA-DNA hybridization. *Journal of Molecular Evolution, 20,* 2–15.

Silverman, I. (2003). Gender differences in resistance to temptation: Theories and evidence. *Developmental Review, 23,* 219–259.

Stenhouse, D. (1974). *The evolution of intelligence.* New York: Barnes & Noble.

Stevenson, J. C., & Williams, D. C. (2000). Parental investment, self-control, and sex differences in the expression of ADHD. *Human Nature, 11,* 405–422.

Suddendorf, T., & Whiten, A. (2001). Mental evolution and development: Evidence for secondary representation in children, great apes and other animals. *Psychological Bulletin, 127,* 629–650.

Swartz, K. B., Sarauw, D., & Evans, S. (1999). Cognitive aspects of mirror self-recognition in great apes. In S. T. Parker, R. W. Mitchell, & H. L. Miles (Eds.), *The mentalities of gorillas and orangutans: Comparative perspectives* (pp. 283–294). Cambridge, UK: Cambridge University Press.

Tobias, P. V. (1987). The brain of *Homo habilis:* A new level of organization in cerebral evolution. *Journal of Human Evolution, 16,* 741–761.

Tomasello, M. (1996). Do apes ape? In C. Heyes & B. Galef (Eds.), *Social learning in animals: The role of culture* (pp. 319–346). San Diego, CA: Academic Press.

Tomasello, M. (2000). Culture and cognitive development. *Current Directions in Psychological Science, 9,* 37–40.

Tomasello, M., & Call, J. (1997). *Primate cognition.* New York: Oxford University Press.

Tomasello, M., Kruger, A. C., & Ratner, H. H. (1993). Cultural learning. *Behavioral and Brain Sciences, 16,* 495–511.

Tomasello, M., Savage-Rumbaugh, S., & Kruger, A. C. (1993). Imitative learning of actions on objects by children, chimpanzees, and enculturated chimpanzees. *Child Development, 64,* 1688–1705.

Tooby, J., & Cosmides, L. (1992). The psychological foundations of culture. In J. H. Barkow, L. Cosmides, & J. Tooby (Eds.), *The adapted mind: Evolutionary psychology and the generation of culture* (pp. 19–139). New York: Oxford University Press.

Wason, P. (1966). Reasoning. In B. M. Foss (Ed.), *New horizons in psychology* (pp. 135–151). London: Penguin.

West-Eberhard, M. J. (2003). *Developmental plasticity and evolution.* Oxford, UK: Oxford University Press.

Wellman, H. M. (1990). *The child's theory of mind.* Cambridge, MA: MIT Press.

Wellman, H. M., Cross, D., & Watson, J. (2001). Meta-analysis of theory-of-mind development: The truth about false belief. *Child Development, 72,* 655–684.

Whiten, A., & Byrne, R. W. (1988). The manipulation of attention in primate tactical deception. In R. W. Byrne & A. Whiten (Eds.), *Machiavellian intelligence: Social expertise and the evolution of intellect in monkeys, apes, and humans* (pp. 211–223). Oxford, UK: Clarendon Press.

Whiten, A., Goodall, J., McGrew, W. C., Nishida, T., Reynolds, V., Sugiyama, Y., Tutin, C. E. G., Wrangham, R. W., & Boesch, C. (1999). Cultures in chimpanzees. *Nature, 399,* 682–685.

Wimmer, H., & Perner, J. (1983). Beliefs about beliefs: Representation and constraining function of wrong beliefs in young children's understanding of deception. *Cognition, 13,* 103–128.

Chapter 8

The Developmental Relation of Theory of Mind and Executive Functions: A Study of Advanced Theory of Mind Abilities in Children With Attention Deficit Hyperactivity Disorder

Beate Sodian
Christian Hülsken
University of München

Executive accounts of theory of mind (ToM) development have recently emerged as competition to conceptual change accounts (Carlson & Moses, 2001; Frye, Zelazo, & Palfai, 1995; Hughes, 1998a; Russell, 1996, 1997). Executive functions (EF), broadly defined, refer to the cognitive functions that underlie goal-directed behavior. The main dimensions of EF include inhibitory control, working memory and attentional flexibility (Welsh, Pennington, & Groissier, 1991; Pennington et al., 1997). Recent developmental research indicates significant advances in EF between the ages of 3 and 6 years (Diamond, Prevor, Callender, & Druin, 1997; Hughes, 1998a; Kochanska, Murray, & Coy, 1997; Zelazo, Carter, Reznick, & Frye, 1997). This period coincides with the emergence of a ToM in children. Thus, at about the same age as children gain insight into their own and others' representational mental states, they also show marked improvement in a variety of measures of EF. A robust association has been found in numerous studies between performance on EF tests and on tests of ToM ability (primarily the mastery of first-order false belief tasks) both in normally developing children (Carlson & Moses, 2001; Carlson, Moses, & Hix, 1998; Frye et al., 1995) and in children with autism (Ozonoff, Pennington, & Rogers, 1991; see Perner & Lang, 1999, 2000, for reviews). Significant correlations persist when age and IQ are controlled for. In a recent study employing comprehensive test batteries for both EF and ToM in 40- to 60-month-old preschoolers, Carlson, Moses, and Breton (2002) found that after IQ and age were partialled out first-order false belief understanding remained significantly correlated with inhibitory control. There is evidence that both inhibitory control and working memory components of EF are implicated in mastery of the false belief task: Hala, Hug, and Henderson (2003) found that performance on EF tasks that combined working memory and inhibitory demands was highly predictive of performance on first-order false belief tasks. Moreover, a longitudinal study of normally developing preschoolers showed that progress in EF predicted developmental changes in ToM, but not the reverse (Hughes, 1998b). Research on the relation between advanced ToM development (advances in the understanding of the mind beyond the age of 5 years) and EF indicates that, among normally developing children, second-order ToM performance (second-order belief, introspective skills) may be as strongly correlated with performance on a range of EF tasks as is first-order performance (Perner, Kain, & Barchfeld, 2002).

One interpretation of these findings is that the association between the development of EF and ToM development is due to the executive demands of the ToM tasks. Thus, it is possible that young children already have a concept of belief but are unable to express it in standard tasks because they cannot inhibit their knowledge of the true state of affairs. However, significant correlations between ToM and EF have been demonstrated even for ToM tasks that pose minimal executive demands: The explanation version of the false belief task does not require the inhibition of a wrong but prepotent answer strategy, yet correlations between explanation versions of the false belief task and executive tasks were as high as between prediction versions and executive tasks (Hughes, 1998a, 1998b; Perner & Lang, 1999; Perner, Lang & Kloo, 2002). Moreover, children at risk of attention deficit hyperactivity disorder (ADHD) who had deficits in various EF tasks had intact second-order ToM in a study by Perner et al. (2002). This dissociation between ToM performance and EF also poses a problem for more sophisticated versions of an executive account of ToM development, as proposed by Russell (1997) and Pacherie (1997). In this view, an increase in executive control leads to improvements in ToM through self-monitoring of action and increasing insight into the intentional nature of action. Thus, a certain level of executive ability is required to gain insight into thought and action and to construct a belief concept. It is inconsistent with this view that children with severe deficits in executive ability should have an unimpaired understanding of the mind. Thus, it appears that ToM development cannot be accounted for by the maturation of EF.

Conceptual change accounts of ToM development have also proposed explanations for the association between ToM development and EF. These theories claim that improved EF is the consequence, rather than the antecedent, of ToM development. Such a proposal was made by Wimmer (1989) and Perner (1998), who argued that the acquisition of a ToM leads to improved self-control because a ToM entails insight into the causal consequences of belief and, therefore, improves self-insight. Consistent with the view that an understanding of mental states as representations with causal efficacy is important for the ability to inhibit interfering action tendency, Lang and Perner (2002) found that the relationship between false belief and executive control also extends to children's understanding of reflex movements as nonintentional actions. Perner's (1998) theory is consistent with the finding that a ToM deficit is accompanied by an EF deficit in autistic children, as well as the finding that there is a dissociation between unimpaired ToM and executive dysfunction in hyperactive children because Perner's theory allows for intact ToM with impaired EF, ToM being necessary but not sufficient for the development of EF, not for the reverse pattern. However, the reverse pattern that is, delayed ToM development in children with intact EF—has been observed in verbally taught deaf children (deVilliers, 2001). Thus, ToM development may be neither necessary nor sufficient for the development of executive control.

In sum, research on the developmental relation between ToM and EF indicates that ToM development cannot be directly accounted for by developmental changes in EF and that executive control does not appear to be a direct consequence of ToM development. Similarly, theories that attempt to explain the synchrony between ToM and executive development around the age of 4 years by analyzing the relevant tasks in terms of a common logical structure (Frye et al., 1995) have been unable to account for correlations of EF with ToM tasks that cannot be analyzed in terms of double-embedded conditionals (Perner & Lang, 1999; Perner et al., 2002; Hughes, 2002). At present, the view that ToM and EF are supported by closely related brain structures that mature at a similar rate (Ozonoff et al., 1991) can accommodate best the observed correlations and dissociations (Perner et al., 2002). Hughes (2002) concludes from a review of the research that functional relations between ToM and EF, if they exist on the cognitive level, are probably more specific (requiring a distinction between different aspects of executive functions) and less direct (i.e., moderated by other cognitive factors) than was previously assumed.

THE ROLE OF EF IN ADVANCED ToM DEVELOPMENT: A CLOSER LOOK AT ADHD CHILDREN'S ToM

In the present study, we focus on the role of EF in the acquisition of an advanced ToM. Previous research primarily addressed developmental relations between EF and ToM in children between the ages of 3 and 6 years. However, as has become clear from the literature reviewed in the previous section, abnormal populations with a dissociation between ToM and EF are critical to evaluating competing theoretical accounts of functional relations between the two cognitive capacities. Because important gains in self-control occur in children between ages 3 and 6 years in normal development, developmental disorders in the acquisition of self-control first become apparent around the age of 5 or 6 years. Previous research on ToM in children with EF deficits was primarily conducted with younger children who were considered at risk of ADHD, not with children diagnosed with ADHD. Moreover, the theoretically important conclusion that poor executive control does not lead to deficits in higher order ToM reasoning (Perner et al., 2002) rests on a small sample of advanced ToM tasks that were included in the few studies that have addressed ADHD children's understanding of the mind. Perner et al. (2002), who conducted the most comprehensive assessment of advanced ToM reasoning in children with poor executive control, found no impairment in 4.5 to 6.5-year-old children at risk of ADHD on four advanced ToM tasks: second-order belief, distinction between joke and lie, understanding own thoughts, and understanding consciousness. Charman, Carroll, and Sturge (2001) used Happé's strange stories (a task testing an understanding of nonliteral speech) and found no difference between 6- to 10-year-old ADHD children and normal controls in advanced ToM reasoning. Similarly, Happé and Frith (1996) found no difference between 6- to 12-year-old children with conduct disorder (often comorbid with ADHD) and normal children on second-order false belief tasks. To date, only one study (Buitelaar, van der Wees, Swaab-Barneveld, & van der Gaag, 1999) reports a significant deficit in second-order belief tasks, in a sample of only nine ADHD children (as compared to psychiatric control children).

These studies of advanced ToM reasoning in children with poor executive control were not based on analyses of possible interactions between the conceptual content of the ToM tasks and their inhibitory demands. Inhibitory demands of ToM tasks should be especially high when mental states have to be inferred while faced with a conflicting state of reality or a conflicting behavioral outcome. This is the case, for instance, when a person responds correctly to a question about a state of affairs—for example, the content of a box—without having had access to relevant information (i.e., guesses correctly). Thus, the ability to assess one's own or another person's certainty should be difficult for children with executive problems because it requires a judgment of a mental state, based on an assessment of one's own or another's access to information, while inhibiting a conflicting behavioral outcome (e.g., in the case of guessing correctly, one's own or the other person's ability to give a correct response). In contrast, the inhibitory demands of explanation tasks such as Happé's strange stories should be relatively low.

The theory about possible effects of executive impairments on advanced mental state representation proposed here is an expression account (Moses,

Carlson, & Sabbagh, this volume), assuming that children with executive problems possess more or less intact mental state concepts but encounter difficulty expressing them in situations with high inhibitory demands. This view is consistent with previous research showing that ADHD children have no deficits in second-order belief or other advanced ToM tasks but do show impairments in the online representation of social situations (Milch-Reich, Campbell, Pelham, Connelly, & Geva, 1999) as well as in metacognitive monitoring and strategy use (Douglas & Benezra, 1990; Seidel & Joschko, 1990). We propose, thus, that the development of executive control does have effects on the ability to adequately apply advanced mental state knowledge in social and nonsocial (e.g., metacognitive monitoring) situations. We therefore predict that children with EF impairment will tend to neglect mental states in situations with high inhibitory demands. This view implies the assumption of a bidirectional functional relation between ToM and EF. Although ToM may be important for EF to develop, executive control later on becomes important for the flexible application of mental state knowledge in social and nonsocial contexts.

To test whether children with impaired action control have greater difficulty than normal controls in online representation of mental states when faced with conflicting behavioral outcomes, we administered a task based on Pillow's work (2001, 2002; Pillow, Hill, Boyce, & Stein, 2000) that requires subjects to rate the certainty of a speaker under various conditions of informational access. In particular, it requires children to set aside the speaker's correct statement of facts in cases of guessing and to distinguish between guessing and valid inference based on the speaker's access to premise information. Understanding inference as a source of knowledge is part of higher order ToM development and is normally mastered around the age of 6 years (Sodian & Wimmer, 1987). When certainty ratings were required, instead of absolute judgments, Pillow (2001, 2002; Pillow et al., 2000) found that normally developing children in the early elementary school grades were far from ceiling. Thus, the certainty rating task appears to be suitable for investigating specific difficulties in the application of advanced mental state knowledge.

To replicate previous findings on higher order ToM in ADHD children, we included a second-order belief task and Happé's (1994) strange stories in our study. We did not aim to investigate children's executive problems in detail but included one EF task (Luria's hand game) to test for possible correlations with ToM tasks. We also included two delay of gratification tasks (Kochanska, Murray, Jaques, Koenig, & Vandegeest., 1996) to test for a pervasive deficit in action control in the clinical group.

Method

Subjects. Thirty-two ADHD–diagnosed children and 101 normally developing children participated in the study. The ADHD children had been diagnosed by child psychiatrists and were recruited through a school for children with learning and behavioral problems and through the child psychiatry ward of the University of Würzburg, Germany. There were 25 boys and 7 girls in the ADHD group. The age range was 6 years and 9 months to 11 years and 5 months ($M = 8.9$). At the time of the study, 78% of the children were taking medication.

The normally developing group consisted of 56 girls and 45 boys with a mean age of 8.0 years, 29 kindergarteners (16 girls, 13 boys, mean age 6.6, range 5.9 to 6.11), 22 first graders (13 girls and 9 boys, mean age 7.5, range 6.11 to 7.11), 21 second graders (10 girls, 11 boys, mean age 8.4, range 7.10 to 9.1), and 29 third graders (17 girls and 12 boys, mean age 9.8, range 8.10 to 10.11).

Procedure and Design.   All children received three ToM tasks and three action–control tasks in the following order:

1. *The second-order false belief task.* This task was modeled after Perner and Wimmer (1985). Children were presented with a story about two children, Max and Anna, that was enacted with puppets. Max and Anna were playing in their room with crayons until Max decided to get a drink. He packed his crayons into a box and left. Max knows that his sister, Anna, often tricks him and therefore peeps through the keyhole before leaving. When Anna sees that Max has left, she decides to trick him, takes his crayons from the box, and puts them into the wastebasket. Max watches Anna do this, but Anna cannot see him. The child was then asked the following questions.

Control question 1: Can Max see Anna?

Control question 2: Where does Max think his crayons are?

Control question 3: Does Anna think that Max can see her?

Test question 1: Where does Anna think Max will look for his crayons when he returns?

Test question 2: Why does she think so?

Children received a score from 0 to 2 on the test questions: a score of 2 reflected correct answers and justifications, and a score of 1, a correct answer to test question 1, without an adequate justification.

2. *Training.* To introduce the certainty rating scale, children were instructed in which face to indicate when they were certain that their answer was correct (full smile), when they were completely uncertain (sad face), and when they were not quite certain (neutral face). They were then asked to tell their age and, subsequently, to rate the certainty of their answer. Then they were asked to judge the experimenter's age and to rate the certainty of their answer. If their certainty ratings following the two answers did not differ, they were corrected, and the scale was explained once more. The procedure was repeated, using two drawings, one that unambiguously depicted flowers and one that showed an uninterpretable child drawing. After children had given their answers to the questions about the drawings and rated the certainty of their answers, they were

told that the uninterpretable picture was meant to show a butterfly. Then a green hippopotamus toy figure was introduced to those who thought the object on the drawing might be a butterfly. Children were then asked to rate the hippo's certainty. If they attributed high certainty to the hippo, they were reminded that they themselves had been uncertain about what the picture showed. They were then given another trial (rating the hippo's certainty).

3. *Happé's strange stories.* Children were presented with six of Happé's (1994) strange stories in a close translation, accompanied by drawings. The protagonist's utterances in the stories represented a lie, a white lie, metaphors, a double bluff, and irony. Children were asked whether the protagonist's statement was true and why he had said this. Children's answers were coded as correct if they adequately justified the protagonist's statement. Justifications were coded independently by two coders following Happé's (1994) criteria.

4. *Epistemic State Attribution Task.* Children were again presented with the green hippo and were told that their task was to judge how certain the hippo was that his answers were correct. The hippo's job was to judge the contents of an opaque cup under each of the following conditions:

- *Inferential knowledge.* The hippo was shown three cups and three brown cats and was told that the experimenter was going to hide a cat under each of the cups. The hippo then had to leave and was hiding under the table while the experimenter and the child moved the cats under the cups. Then the experimenter returned the hippo, who was put in front of one of the cups and judged that the cup contained a brown cat. Then the child was asked to rate the hippo's certainty. If children rated the hippo as uncertain, they were given an explanation and were asked to correct their judgment. Then they were told that the game was now going to be more difficult for the hippo.
- *Guess wrong condition.* A white and a brown cat were hidden in the hippo's absence. Then the hippo was asked to find the white cat. The hippo chose the wrong cup. Again, the child was asked to rate the hippo's certainty and was corrected if necessary.

After these two training trials, each child received three test trials: a guess right trial followed by a valid inference trial and an invalid inference trial. In the guess right trial, the hippo correctly guessed the location of the brown cat. In the inference trial, the hippo looked under one of the cups, detected the white cat, and then correctly inferred the color of the cat under the other cup. In the invalid inference trial, the hippo detected one of the brown cats and then drew the invalid inference that a white cat was under one of the two other cups. The whole procedure was repeated with another set of materials, this time without corrective feedback on the first two trials.

Children could obtain a maximum score of 8 (4 on each of the material sets) on the certainty rating task if they correctly judged guess wrong as less certain than valid inference, judged guess right as equally uncertain as guess wrong, judged valid inference as more certain than guess right, and judged invalid inference as less certain than valid inference.

5. *Snack delay task.* The experimenter put a piece of candy under a glass and a bell next to the glass. She then explained to the child that the child was allowed to take the candy as soon as the bell rang. The experimenter waited 10 s before touching the bell. After another 10 s she rang it.

6. *Luria's hand game.*[1] A slightly modified version of a task by Hughes (1998a, 1998b) was employed. There were four cards, a red and a green square, and a red and a green circle. Children were first instructed to imitate the experimenter's gesture (thumb up, thumb down, fist, flat hand) when a green card was shown. After a practice trial, they were instructed to perform the opposite gesture when a red card was shown. In the second experimental trial, the rule was altered: Now children had to imitate the gesture when a circle was shown, and to do the opposite when a square was shown. In the last experimental trial, the rule was changed back to color, but children now had to imitate when red was shown and to show the opposite gesture when green was shown.

7. *Gift delay task.* Children were told that they were going to get a surprise present. They were asked to turn their back toward the experimenter. The experimenter then started to unwrap the present with noticeable noise. In a 1-minute interval the number of times the children turned around was recorded.

Results

Second-Order Belief. A one-way ANOVA with group (ADHD vs. normal) as the between subjects factor and age and gender as control variables yielded no effect of group, $F (1, 130) = .14$, $p > .05$. As expected, there was a significant effect of age, $F = (1, 130) = 15.37$, $p < .01$). In the normal group, 76% of the children gave the correct answer to the test question, and 45% correctly justified their answer. In the ADHD group, 78% of the children gave the correct answer, and 56% gave an adequate justification.

Happé's Strange Stories. Normal children obtained a mean score of $M = 2.73$ (maximum = 6; $SD = 1.38$), ADHD children a mean of $M = 3.44$ ($SD = 1.48$). The difference between groups was not significant, $F (1, 130) = 2.53$, $p > .05$. There was, however, a significant effect of age, $F = (1, 130) = 13.36$, $p < .01$.

Epistemic State Attribution Task. ADHD children attained a mean score of $M = 2.72$, $SD = 2.1$ (maximum = 8) in their certainty ratings, whereas normally developing children had a mean score of $M = 4.2$, $SD = 2.12$ (see Fig. 8.1). The one-way ANOVA yielded a significant dif-

---

[1]Due to testing time limitations, this task could only be administered to 18 ADHD children and 30 normally developing children (15 first graders and 15 second graders).

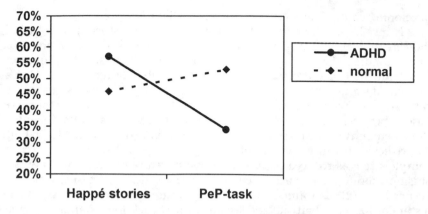

FIG. 8.1.   Mean percent correct in Happé's strange stories and epistemic state attribution (PeP) tasks by group.

ference between groups, $F = (1, 130) = 25.83$, $p < .01$, with a significant effect of age as covariate, $F = (1, 130) = 30.88$; $p < .01$). A comparison of the subgroup of ADHD children who were on medication at the time of testing with the subgroup who were not yielded no significant effect of medication on performance. ADHD children's poor performance on the epistemic states task cannot be attributed to a poor understanding of the rating scale because there was no difference between ADHD and normally developing children on the tasks that were used to introduce the scale.

Delay of Gratification.   ADHD children committed a transgression significantly more often than normally developing children did in both the snack delay and the gift delay tasks. However, even in the ADHD group only a minority did so (19% touched the glass in the snack delay, and 25% turned around in the gift delay task).

Luria's Hand Game.   In the control group, children made an average of 4.2 ($SD = 3.5$) mistakes (out of 24 trials), whereas the 18 ADHD children made a mean number of 6.5 mistakes ($SD = 6.5$). Forty-eight percent of the children made fewer than five mistakes. A stepwise logistic regression with age as covariate, group as independent variable, and action control (below vs. at or above five mistakes) as dependent variable showed significant effects of age, $\chi^2(1) = 9.96$, $p < .01$, and of group $\chi^2(1) = 10.42$, $p < .01$). Action control was correlated significantly with the score for the epistemic states task, $r = .346$, $p < .01$, when age was partialled out. No other correlations between action control and ToM tasks were significant.

Discussion and Conclusions

Consistent with previous findings on advanced ToM reasoning in ADHD children we found no difference between ADHD children and normally developing controls in second-order false belief understanding or on a test of advanced social understanding (Happé's strange stories). Our results indicate, however, that ADHD children were delayed on a test of advanced understanding of epistemic states, requiring online representation of a person's informational access, independently of behavioral outcome. EF was correlated significantly with the epistemic state attribution task (certainty ratings), even when age was partialled out. This was not the case for correlations between our EF measure and the other ToM tasks. Thus, the inhibitory demands of the epistemic state attribution task appeared to be high, as predicted. Because we did not assess EF comprehensively, and because sample size was reduced on our executive measure, we cannot draw conclusions about the executive demands of the other ToM tasks. Note that Perner et al. (2002) found significant correlations between EF (assessed by a standardized test battery) and second-order belief understanding, as well as other advanced ToM tasks in normally developing children.

The present findings indicate that the development of action control may in fact be important for higher order ToM development but that the effects may be fairly specific and more important for online mind reading than for ToM reasoning in general. As predicted, we found that children with ADHD were impaired on a task requiring online mental state representation when a protagonist's mental states conflicted with his verbal utterances. This difficulty cannot be attributed to a misunderstanding of the task format because ADHD children did not perform worse than controls on the tasks introducing the rating scale. Moreover, it cannot be easily attributed to verbal demands of the task, mental state language, or other demands common to ToM tasks because there were no performance differences between the ADHD children and normal controls on the other ToM tasks, especially Happé's strange stories, which were more demanding in terms of language and mental vocabulary than the certainty rating task. The correlation of the epistemic state task with the EF task points to the inhibitory demands of the certainty rating task. This finding is consistent with our analysis that the epistemic state task requires inhibition because a mental state has to be inferred independently of a protagonist's statement of fact. Whereas the other ToM tasks invited fairly complex mental state inferences, the epistemic attribution task implied the danger of mental state neglect. Thus, the present finding, although preliminary, is consistent with the view that ADHD children tend to neglect mental states when faced with high inhibitory demands.

Because the present finding is, to our knowledge, the first demonstration of a mind-reading impairment in children with deficient action control, interpretations can only be tentative. Further research is necessary to distinguish between a lean and rich interpretation of the present results. A lean interpretation is based on the assumption that ADHD children possess intact mental state concepts but are unable to express them in some situations with high inhibitory demands. Such an interpretation is consistent with deficits in social information processing as well as in metacognitive monitoring that have been reported in the literature (Barkley,

1997). If this is the case, then variations of task demands should lead to significant performance differences in ADHD children. In contrast, a richer interpretation of mind-reading deficits in children with executive problems is based on the idea that inhibitory demands of ToM tasks interact with conceptual content, in the sense that some mental concepts are more difficult to grasp than others because, independently of superficial features of tasks, to gain information about some mental states, we have to inhibit prepotent behavioral tendencies. An example of such mental concepts might be complex emotion concepts such as moral emotion concepts. Young children tend to base their emotion attributions solely on a person's intentions: An action outcome that matches the person's intention leads to happiness, whereas an outcome that mismatches the person's intention leads to sadness. They thereby neglect moral norms and social standards and attribute happiness to a wrongdoer who violated moral norms. Moral emotions such as shame and guilt are conceptualized in normal development in the early elementary school years (Nunner-Winkler & Sodian, 1988). Based on the present analysis of possible interactions between conceptual content and inhibitory demands of the tasks, we would predict that a conceptual understanding of moral emotions is delayed in ADHD children because such an understanding requires an inhibition of the prepotent tendency to focus on the relation between a character's intention and an action outcome.

How do the present findings bear on theories of the developmental relation between ToM and EF? As was outlined in the introduction, mind-reading impairments in ADHD children are to be expected under the assumption that action control is an important prerequisite for gaining insight into one's own and others' mental states (e.g., Russell, 1997). That no such impairments were previously found in children with ADHD is the strongest piece of evidence against executive accounts of ToM development. If the present findings can be replicated and generalized across a range of advanced mental state tasks in future research, executive accounts could gain some support. It should be noted, however, that several studies, including the present one, have found no impairments in ADHD children in some core concepts of advanced mental state understanding, including second-order false belief reasoning. Therefore, the present findings appear to be best compatible with the view that there is a bidirectional relation between the development of EF and ToM—with the acquisition of a ToM around the age of 4 years being important for gaining self-control and enhanced self-control in turn allowing the flexible application of mental state knowledge to situations with high inhibitory demands.

ACKNOWLEDGMENT

This research was supported by a grant from the German Research Council (DFG FOR 261/2-1). It was conducted while the authors were at the University of Würzburg.

REFERENCES

Barkley, R. A. (1997). Behavioral inhibition, sustained attention, and executive functions: Constructing a unifying theory of ADHD. *Psychological Bulletin, 121,* 65–94.

Buitelaar, J. K., van der Wees, M., Swaab-Barneveld, H., & van der Gaag, R. (1999). Theory of mind and emotion-recognition functioning in autistic spectrum disorders and in psychiatric control and normal children. *Development and Psychopathology, 11,* 39–58.

Carlson, S. M., & Moses, L. J. (2001). Individual differences in executive control and children's theory of mind. *Child Development, 72,* 1032–1053.

Carlson, S. M., Moses, L. J., & Breton, C. (2002). How specific is the relation between executive function and theory of mind? Contributions of inhibitory control and working memory. *Infant and Child Development, 11,* 73–92.

Carlson, S. M., Moses, L. J., & Hix, H. R. (1998). The role of inhibitory processes in young children's difficulties with deception and false belief. *Developmental Psychology, 69,* 672–691.

Charman, T., Carroll, F., & Sturge, C. (2001). Theory of mind, executive function and social competence in boys with ADHD. *Emotional and Behavioral Difficulties, 6,* 31–49.

deVilliers, J. (2001, April). *Complex language but not executive functioning predicts false belief reasoning in orally taught deaf children.* Paper presented at the Society for Research in Child Development, Minneapolis, MN.

Diamond, A., Prevor, M. B., Callender, G., & Druin, D. P. (1997). Prefrontal cortex cognitive deficits in children treated early and continuously for PKU. *Monographs of the Society for Research in Child Development, 62*(4, Serial No. 252).

Douglas, V. I., & Benezra, E. (1990). Supraspan verbal memory in attention deficit disorder with hyperactivity, normal and reading-disabled boys. *Journal of Abnormal Child Psychology, 18,* 613–638.

Frye, D., Zelazo, P. D., & Palfai, T. (1995). Theory of mind and rule-based reasoning. *Cognitive Development, 10,* 483–527.

Hala, S., Hug, S., & Henderson, A. (2003). Executive function and false-belief understanding in preschool children: Two tasks are harder than one. *Journal of Cognition and Development, 4,* 275–298.

Happé, F. (1994). An advanced test of theory of mind: Understanding of story characters' thoughts and feelings by able autistic, mentally handicapped, and normal children and adults. *Journal of Autism and Developmental Disorders, 24,* 129–154.

Happé, F., & Frith, U. (1996). Theory of mind and social impairment in children with conduct disorder. *British Journal of Developmental Psychology, 14,* 385–398.

Hughes, C. (1998a). Executive function in preschoolers: Links with theory of mind and verbal ability. *British Journal of Developmental Psychology, 16,* 233–253.

Hughes, C. (1998b). Finding your marbles: Does preschoolers' strategic behavior predict later understanding of mind? *Developmental Psychology, 34,* 1326–1339.

Hughes, C. (2002). Executive functions and development: Emerging themes. *Infant and Child Development, 11,* 201–209.

Kochanska, G., Murray, K., Jaques, T. Y., Koenig, A. L., & Vandegeest, A. (1996). Inhibitory control in young children and its role in emerging internalization. *Child Development, 67,* 490–507.

Kochanska, G., Murray, K., & Koy, K. C. (1997). Inhibitory control as a contributor to conscience in childhood: From toddler to early school age. *Child Development, 68,* 263–277.

Lang, B., & Perner, J. (2002). Understanding intention and false belief and the development of self control. *British Journal of Developmental Psychology, 20,* 67–76.

Milch-Reich, S., Campbell, S. B., Pelham, W. E., Connelly, L. M., & Geva, D. (1999). Developmental and individual differences in children's on-line representations of dynamic social events. *Child Development, 70,* 413–431.

Nunner-Winkler, G., & Sodian, B. (1988). Children's understanding of moral emotions. *Child Development, 59,* 1323–1338.

Ozonoff, S., Pennington, B. F., & Rogers, S. J. (1991). Executive function deficits in high-functioning autistic children: Relationship to theory of mind. *Journal of Child Psychology and Psychiatry, 32,* 1081–1105.

Pacherie, E. (1997). On being the product of one's failed actions. In J. Russell (Ed.), *Autism as an executive disorder* (pp. 215–255). Oxford, UK: Oxford University Press.

Pennington, B., Rogers, S., Bennetto, L., Grifith, E. M., Reed, D. T., & Shyu, V. (1997). Validity tests of the executive dysfunction hypothesis of autism. In J. Russell (Ed.), *Autism as an executive disorder* (pp. 143–179). Oxford, UK: Oxford University Press.

Perner, J. (1998). The meta-intentional nature of executive functions and theory of mind. In P. Carruthers & J. Boucher (Eds.), *Language and thought: Interdisciplinary themes* (pp. 270–283). Cambridge, UK: Cambridge University Press.

Perner, J., Kain, W., & Barchfeld, P. (2002). Executive control and higher-order theory of mind in children at risk of ADHD. *Infant and Child Development, 11,* 141–158.

Perner, J., & Lang, B. (1999). Development of theory of mind and executive control. *Trends in Cognitive Sciences, 3,* 337–344.

Perner, J., & Lang, B. (2000). Theory of mind and executive function: Is there a developmental relationship? In S. Baron-Cohen, H. Tager-Flusberg, & Cohen, D. (Eds.), *Understanding other minds: Perspectives from autism and developmental cognitive neuroscience* (2nd ed., pp. 150–181). Oxford, UK: Oxford University Press.

Perner, J., Lang, B., & Kloo, D. (2002). Theory of mind and self control: More than a common problem of inhibition. *Child Development, 73,* 752–767.

Perner, J., & Wimmer, H. (1985). "John thinks that Mary thinks that . . ." Attribution of second order beliefs by 5–10 year old children. *Journal of Experimental Child Psychology, 39,* 437–471.

Pillow, B. H. (2001, April). *Children's differentiation of deductive inference and guessing: Certainty evaluation for self vs. others.* Poster presented at the Society for Research in Child Development, Minneapolis, MN.

Pillow, B. H. (2002). Children's and adults' evaluation of the certainty of deductive inferences, inductive inferences, and guesses. *Child Development, 73,* 779–792.

Pillow, B. H., Hill, V., Boyce, A., & Stein, C. (2000). Understanding inference as a source of knowledge: Children's ability to evaluate the certainty of deduction, perception, and guessing. *Developmental Psychology, 36,* 169–179.

Russell, J. (1996). *Agency. Its role in mental development.* Hove, UK: Psychology Press.

Russell, J. (1997). How executive disorders can bring about an inadequate theory of mind. In J. Russell (Ed.), *Autism as an executive disorder* (pp. 256–304). Oxford, UK: Oxford University Press.

Seidel, W. T., & Joschko, M. (1990). Evidence of difficulties in sustained attention in children with ADDH. *Journal of Abnormal Child Psychology, 18,* 217–229.

Sodian, B., & Wimmer, H. (1987). Children's understanding of inference as source of knowledge. *Child Development, 58,* 424–433.

Welsh, M. C., Pennington, B. F., & Groissier, D. B. (1991). A normative-developmental study of executive function: A window on prefrontal function in children. *Developmental Neuropsychology, 7,* 131–149.

Wimmer, H. (1989). Common-sense mentalismus und emotion: Entwicklungspsychologische Implikationen [Common sense mentalism and emotion: Developmental implications. In E. Roth (Ed.), *Denken und Fühlen* (pp. 56–66). Berlin, Germany: Springer.

Zelazo, P. D., Carter, A., Reznick, J. S., & Frye, D. (1997). Early development of executive function: A problem-solving framework. *Review of General Psychology, 1,* 1–29.

Chapter 9

What fMRI Can Tell Us About the ToM–EF Connection: False Beliefs, Working Memory, and Inhibition

Winfried Kain
Josef Perner
University of Salzburg

There is now well-established evidence that the acquisition of theory of mind (ToM) around 3 to 5 years is developmentally related to executive functions (EF). Several theories have been proposed explaining this ToM–EF connection (Perner & Lang, 1999). Among them is the suggestion that ToM and EF are mediated by the same region in the prefrontal cortex. In the last 10 years, a boom in cognitive neuroscience has set in, and functional magnetic resonance imaging (fMRI) has become increasingly popular as a non-invasive tool for exploring brain activations during ToM and EF tasks. Therefore, it is timely to scrutinize this suggestion more closely.

After a brief review of the ToM–EF connection in developmental psychology, we look at the current evidence for the neural basis of ToM and of two dimensions of EF: working memory and inhibition. Whenever possible, emphasis is placed on developmental fMRI studies to explore the important question about brain activation being different for children than for adults. We conclude with a short summary of what fMRI can currently tell us about the ToM–EF connection and with proposals for future studies in this important research area.

THE ToM-EF CONNECTION
IN DEVELOPMENTAL PSYCHOLOGY

According to the meta-analysis by Perner and Lang (1999), the mean effect size of the observed correlations between ToM and different EF tasks in the age range of 3 to 6 years is 1.08 and can be considered as strong. Three dimensions of executive functioning have been considered central to the developmental link with ToM development: working memory, inhibition, and set shifting/attentional flexibility. Because we discussed the neurobiological interrelationship between shifting/attentional flexibility and ToM in another publication (Kain & Perner, 2003), we concentrate in this chapter on working memory and inhibition.

All existing studies found significant although often moderate correlations between working memory and ToM tasks (Carlson, Moses, & Breton, 2002; Davis & Pratt, 1996; Gordon & Olson, 1998; Hala, Hug, & Henderson, 2003; Hughes, 1998; Jenkins & Astington, 1996; Keenan, 1998; Perner, Kain, & Barchfeld, 2002). However, several of these studies found that the significant relationship disappeared once age and verbal or nonverbal ability were partialled out (Carlson et al., 2002; Hughes, 1998; Jenkins & Astington, 1996; Perner, Kain, et al., 2002).

Most studies also confirm significant associations between ToM tasks and inhibition (Carlson & Moses, 2001; Carlson et al., 2002; Hala et al., 2003; Hughes, 1998; Perner, Kain, et al., 2002; Perner, Lang, & Kloo, 2002) even when age and verbal or nonverbal ability were controlled for. This relationship appears, therefore, to be more robust than the relationship between ToM and working memory.

It is important to note that not all inhibition tasks appear equally associated with ToM. For example, Hughes (1998) found that her inhibition tasks (Luria's hand game, detour-reaching box) correlated significantly only with a deception task and not with false belief tasks (explanation and prediction) once age and verbal/nonverbal ability were controlled for. In the Perner, Lang, et al. (2002) study, inhibition (go/no-go task) was associated only with false belief explanation and not prediction. This association disappeared once age, verbal ability, and control questions were partialled out. In another study by Perner, Kain, et al. (2002), the same go/no-go task was not related to second-order false belief but a variant of Luria's hand game was related to both of them (knock and tap from the NEPSY).

Carlson and Moses (2001) made an important differentiation between two categories of inhibition tasks. Delay tasks, such as the classical gift delay task used by Kochanska, Murray, Jacques, Koenig, and Vandegeest (1996), measure the ability to delay a prepotent response. Conflict tasks are a kind of inhibition task that require the ability not only to withhold an impulsive response but also to give a novel response that is incompatible with the prepotent response, for example, the day/night Stroop task developed by Gerstadt, Hong, and Diamond (1994). In addition to differences in their cognitive processing demands (conflict tasks are more demanding), these tasks, especially the classical gift delay task, also involve different emotional-motivational processing because delay tasks depend more on reward incentive than do conflict tasks. Nevertheless, both kinds of tasks were significantly associated with ToM, but the relationship seems stronger for conflict tasks than for delay tasks (Carlson & Moses, 2001).

Hala et al. (2003) also used these two kinds of inhibition tasks (gift and snack delay tasks vs. day/night and Luria's tapping tasks). For these authors, the important difference between these tasks lies in working memory load. Whereas the gift and snack delay tasks impose minimal memory but strong inhibitory demands, day/night and Luria's tapping tasks combine a high working memory load with inhibitory demands. Contrary to the study by Carlson and Moses (2001) but similar to the study by Carlson et al. (2002), Hala et al. found no relationship between the gift delay task (the snack task was excluded because of ceiling effects) and ToM, in contrast to a strong association between the combined score of the day/night and Luria's tapping tasks with ToM. Carlson and Moses, as well as Hala et al., therefore, suggest that inhibitory control alone is not a powerful predictor for ToM performance, but inhibitory control in combination with more demanding cognitive processes (more load on working memory) becomes powerful.

These authors, however, give no further reason for their claim that the gift delay task poses markedly lower memory demands than the conflict tasks pose. At face value, this claim is not particularly convincing because children have to keep reminding themselves for some time that they were instructed to not peek under the gift wrap. Thus, we suggest that emotional and reward factors could provide another reason why gift delay bears a lower and less robust correlation with ToM tasks than does the conflict task. The gift delay task classically activates emotional and reward processing, which we know from other tasks (e.g., gambling task by Bechara, Damasio, Tranel, & Anderson, 1998) is related to the orbito-frontal cortex, whereas conflict tasks activate the dorsolateral prefrontal cortex (DL-PFC) and the anterior cingulate cortex (ACC; Barch et al., 2001). The ACC is also involved in ToM (Frith & Frith, 2003). This commonality might explain why ToM is developmentally more closely related to conflict tasks than to delay tasks.

Overall, these studies show that working memory and, even more so, inhibitory control are associated with ToM performance in an important way. The specific causal relations among these factors, though, are far from clear. More elaborate theoretical conceptualizations of the relationship between ToM and EF are needed. The different types of processing requirements in different ToM, inhibition, and working memory tasks need to be identified. One useful way of stimulating our theoretical understanding of the ToM–EF connection is to look at the neurological basis of these processes. Neuroimaging studies can reveal whether tasks tapping ToM, working memory, and inhibition activate identical or different brain regions. Similarity and differences in brain activations found in these tasks can lead to important research hypotheses, which may deepen our understanding of the ToM–EF connection in development.

THE CYTOARCHITECTURE
OF THE PREFRONTAL CORTEX

Before proceeding to fMRI studies of ToM, inhibition, and working memory, it is helpful to give an overview of the cytoarchitecture (structure of nerve cells) of the prefrontal cortex. The prefrontal cortex lies in the front of the posterior part of the frontal cortex, which comprises the premotor cortex and the supplementary motor area SMA (BA 6) and the primary motor cortex (BA 4). One can roughly distinguish the following regions in the prefrontal cortex: dorsolateral prefrontal cortex (DL-PFC), ventrolateral prefrontal cortex (VL-PFC), medial prefrontal cortex (MPFC), frontal pole, and orbitofrontal cortex (OFC). We now briefly describe these regions in terms of Brodmann's (1909) areas (BA, see Fig. 9.1A and Fig. 9.1B). When relevant, we also refer to the amendments to Brodmann's classification by Petrides and Pandya (Petrides, 1994; Petrides & Pandya, 1999, 2001) in their comparative cytoarchitectonic analyses of human and monkey brains.

Dorsolateral Prefrontal Cortex

The dorsolateral prefrontal cortex lies superior to the inferior frontal gyrus and consists of the cytoarchitectonic areas BA 9, BA 46, and—according to Pandya and Yeterian (1998)—also BA 8. Area 9 occupies the superior frontal gyrus extending medially to the paracingulate cortex (for location of the gyri see Fig. 9.2). Area 46 occupies the middle sector of the middle frontal gyrus. Contrary to Brodmann's classical map, Petrides and Pandya (1999) labeled one part of area 9 as 9/46 because of its cytoarchitectonic similiarities with area 46.

Ventrolateral Frontal Cortex

The ventrolateral prefrontal cortex corresponds to Brodmann areas 44, 45, and 47 (Fletcher & Henson, 2001). Area 44 is the most posterior part. Area 45 lies in front of area 44 and occupies the pars triangularis of the inferior frontal gyrus (see Fig. 9.2). Area 47 lies on the most rostral part of the inferior frontal gyrus and extends onto the caudal half of the orbitofrontal cortex. Petrides and Pandya (2001) label this region also 47/12.

Medial Prefrontal Cortex

The medial prefrontal cortex comprises mainly the cytoarchitectonic areas 24, 25, 32, and 10 (Öngür & Price, 2000) and also parts of areas 8 and 9. Area 24 overlies the corpus callosum. On its ventral border beneath the corpus callosum lies area 25. In front of area 24 lies area 32, which extends to area 10 (frontal poles).

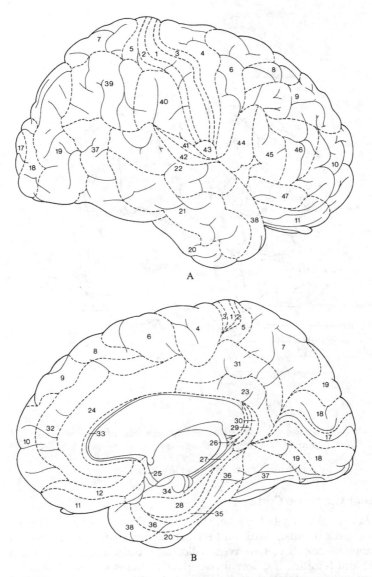

FIG. 9.1.   Cytoarchitectonic map of the human cerebral cortex by Brodmann. (A) Lateral surface; (B) Medial surface. Nieuwenhuys, R., Voogd,
J., & van Huijzen, Chr. (1991). *Das Zentralnervensystem des Menschen*. 2.
vollständig überarbeitete p. 10, Abb. 5 A,B. Auflage, Berlin. © 1991 by
Springer-Verlag. Reprinted with permission.

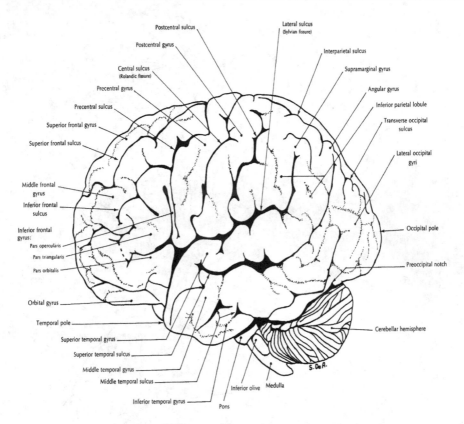

FIG. 9.2. Gyri and sulci of the cerebral hemispheres. From *Structure of the Human Brain: A Photographic Atlas*, 3/E by S. J. DeArmond, M. M. Fusco, & M. M. Dewey, © 1974, 1976, 1989 by Oxford University Press, Inc. Used by permission of Oxford University Press, Inc.

Anterior Cingulate Cortex

The ACC is also located medially and overlies the corpus callosum above and beneath it. Bush, Luu, and Posner (2000) distinguish two major subdivisions of the ACC. One region lies above the corpus callosum (BA 24 & 32) and is called the dorsal cognitive division (ACcd). The other region lies anterior and beneath the corpus callosum (rostral part BA 24 and 32; ventral part 25 & 33) and is called the rostral–ventral affective division (ACad). These subdivisions are shown in Fig. 9.3.

Orbitofrontal Cortex

The orbitofrontal cortex consists of areas 10, 11, 12, 25, and 47. According to Elliott, Dolan, and Frith (2000), it is important to differentiate between the medial and lateral orbitofrontal cortex. The medial orbitofrontal cortex extends forward to area 10 and ventrally to area 11, whereas areas 25 and 12 form the caudal part. The lateral orbitofrontal cortex also includes parts of areas 10 and 11 and extends caudally to area 47. Often the term *ventromedial cortex* is used interchangeably with OFC, although Bechara, Damasio, and Damasio (2000) also include areas 32 and 13 (this area is not shown in Fig. 9.11A; it lies in the caudal part of the OFC behind area 11; see Pandya & Yeterian, 1998, Fig. 5.2a).

Connectivity of the Prefrontal Cortex With Other Brain Regions

An important feature of the prefrontal cortex is its high connectivity with other brain regions. Although we are far from understanding its connectivity in detail, there is evidence that the different prefrontal regions have distinct patterns of connections. Thus, the dorsolateral and ventrolateral

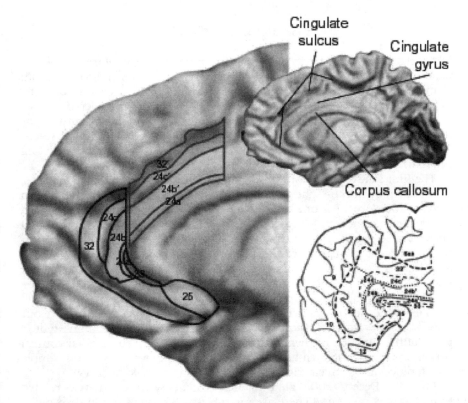

FIG. 9.3. Cytoarchitectonic map of the anterior cingulate cortex. Light gray: cognitive division areas; dark gray: affective division areas. From "Cognitive and Emotional Influences in Anterior Cingulate Cortex," by G. Bush, P. Luu, and M. I. Posner, 2000, *Trends in Cognitive Sciences, 4,* p. 216. Adapted with permission.

prefrontal cortex are more strongly connected to the sensory and motor cortex and to the posterior temporal, parietal, and occipital association areas than to the orbitofrontal cortex (Cummings, 1995; Miller & Cohen, 2001). In contrast, orbitofrontal and parts of medial prefrontal cortex have direct connections to limbic structures, such as the amygdala and hippocampus, whereas there are only indirect connections between these areas and the dorsolateral and ventrolateral cortex (Miller & Cohen, 2001). Moreover, there is evidence that the medial and lateral orbitofrontal cortex have different patterns of connections. For example, the most caudal part of the lateral orbitofrontal cortex has strong connections with the amygdala (Elliott et al., 2000). As Bush et al. (2000) state, the cognitive division of the anterior cingulate has strong connections to lateral prefrontal cortex, parietal cortex and motor areas, whereas the ACad of the anterior cingulate has connections to the orbitofrontal cortex, amygdala, hippocampus, and so on.

THE NEURAL BASIS OF ToM

We currently know of 15 brain imaging studies that explore the neural basis of ToM tasks (for a more detailed review, see Gallagher & Frith, 2003; Kain & Perner, 2003). Due to space limitations, we concentrate on activations found in the prefrontal cortex only, which is considered specific to mentalizing (imputing mental states to agents), and ignore activations often reported during ToM tasks in the posterior superior temporal sulcus (STS) and the temporal poles bilaterally, which relate to processes assisting mentalizing (Gallagher & Frith, 2003).

The first study (SPECT study using a region-of-interest approach) was undertaken by Baron-Cohen et al. (1994), who presented participants with two lists of words. For one list, participants had to raise their finger when they heard a mind-related word and, for the other list, when they heard a body-related word (control condition). Compared with the control condition, there was increased activity in the right orbitofrontal cortex (BA 11) and decreased activity in the left frontal-polar region (BA 10) during the mental state term recognition task.

Goel, Grafman, Sadato, and Hallett (1995) presented a set of 150 stimuli of man-made old and modern artifacts, and participants had to figure out how someone with a basic knowledge of Christopher Columbus would guess at the function of these artifacts. Compared with three other control conditions involving visual perception, memory retrieval, and simple interference, a selective activation occurred in the left MPC (BA9).

Ruby and Decety (2003) gave medical students written sentences related to health sciences (e.g., "There are more births when the moon is round"). Subjects then had to press a two-button mouse to indicate if these sentences were true or false from their own perspective (heading: according to you) or from the perspective of a layperson (heading: according to the other). Comparing third-person with first-person perspective, bilateral activations were found in the medial part of the superior frontal gyrus, in the left inferior frontal gyrus, and in the frontopolar gyrus.

There are four studies using written ToM stories (Fletcher et al., 1995; Gallagher et al., 2000; Happé et al., 1996; Vogeley et al., 2001), comparing brain activation while reading a ToM story with activation in a control condition (reading a passage of unrelated sentences or physical events). All of these studies found unique activations (more on the left side) in the MPC (BA 8, extending into area 9 and the anterior cingulate cortex, BA 32) while reading ToM stories.

The study by Gallagher et al. (2000) also used ToM cartoons requiring the attribution of false belief or ignorance to one character. As control conditions, non-ToM cartoons (requiring no mental state attribution) and jumbled pictures were used. Compared with the ToM stories, activations were also found in the MPC, but to a lesser extent and restricted to BA 8. In a similar vein, Brunet, Sarfati, Hardy-Baylé and Decety (2000) used ToM cartoons requiring mental state attribution and contrasted them with physical control stories (involving characters or objects). Activations were found in the right middle and medial prefrontal cortex (BA 8 & 9), bilaterally in the anterior cingulate gyrus (BA 24) and in the right inferior prefrontal cortex (BA 47).

Castelli, Happé, Frith, and Frith (2000) used abstract computer animations of geometric shapes. In one condition, the shapes depicted random movements and in another, simple interaction. In the ToM animation, the complex interactions of the shapes evoked mental state attributions in the participants' descriptions of what was happening in the animations. Similar to other studies, activation occurred in MPC (BA 9). Using the same paradigm, Castelli et al. found reduced activations in the MPC (BA 9) in able adults with autism or Asperger's Syndrome compared with a normal control group.

Another paradigm exploring online mentalizing was used in two other studies (Gallagher et al., 2003; McCabe, Houser, Ryan, Smith, & Trouard, 2001). In the study by McCabe et al., volunteers played three types of games (trust, punish, and mutual advantage), each with a human or computer as opponent. The rationale behind this design was that playing with a human opponent would elicit mentalizing (what the other will do) in contrast to playing against the computer. Contrasting human and computer conditions, activations were found in the MPC and the frontal pole (BA 10).

Using a computerized version of the competitive game "stone, paper, scissors," Gallagher et al. (2003) found activations in the anterior paracingulate cortex bilaterally (BA 32, 9/32) when comparing the mentalizing (playing against the experimenter) and rule-solving conditions (playing against the computer with a predetermined rule-based strategy).

In a recent study by Sanfey, Rilling, Aronson, Nystrom, and Cohen (2003), subjects participated in the role of the responder in the ultimatum game. Although this game is usually used for studying decision-making processes, mentalizing is also required as players judge the fairness of the other player. In this game, two players have the opportunity to split a sum of money. The so-called proposer makes an offer for splitting the money and the responder can accept or reject the offer. In the case of acceptance, the money is split as proposed; but in the case of rejection, neither player receives any money. Subjects played a total of 30 rounds, 10 with a human partner, 10 with a computer partner, and 10 control rounds, where they got money for pressing a button. The fairness of the offer was manipulated so that half of the offers were fair ($5:$5) and the other half were unfair ($9:$1; $8:$2; $7:$3). Unfair offers made by a human partner were rejected significantly more than offers made by a computer partner. Three brain regions were significantly more activated in unfair than in fair offers when playing with a human partner: bilateral anterior insula, DL-PFC, and ACC. Additionally, regions of the bilateral anterior insula were sensitive to the degree of unfairness and were more activated in the human than in the computer task condition.

Three other studies used the eyes task developed by Baron-Cohen et al. (1994) as an advanced ToM test and compared brain activations in a normal control group versus persons with autism (Baron-Cohen et al., 1999) and persons with schizophrenia (Russell et al., 2000). This task involves more emotional processing than the other tasks, because subjects are instructed to decide from photographs of eyes what that person is feeling or thinking. In the control task, subjects had to decide if the depicted eyes were those of a man or a woman. In the study by Baron-Cohen et al. (1999), activations in the normal control group were seen in the left DL-PFC and VL-PFC (BA 44, 45, 46), and left MPFC (BA 9). Additional limbic structures were activated: left amygdala, left hippocampal gyrus, and left striatum. In the study by Russell et al. (2000), the left inferior frontal gyrus reaching into the insula (BA 44, 45, 47) and medial frontal lobe (BA 45/9) were activated. In contrast to the control groups, less activations of the prefrontal regions were found in the autism and schizophrenia group. Moreover, the autism group showed no activation of the amygdala at all.

In a study by Wicker, Perret, Baron-Cohen, and Decety (2003), subjects were presented with short video clips showing eye regions of male and female actors with averted and direct gaze. Subjects were to judge whether the expressions were friendly or hostile. Contrasting emotional versus nonemotional stimuli with judgments, increased activity was found in the medial dorsofrontal gyrus (BA 9 and 9/10), medial frontal gyrus (BA 8), medial orbitofrontal cortex (BA 11) and anterior cingulate cortex (BA 24/32). Additionally, when contrasting emotion attribution in the direct versus averted gaze condition, the only prefrontal region that was activated was the orbitofrontal cortex (BA 10/11).

Overall, existing neuroimaging studies show that the most consistent brain activations in the prefrontal cortex during ToM processing occur in the medial prefrontal cortex (BA 8, especially BA 9). According to Gallagher and Frith (2003), these regions can be more precisely described as lying at the most anterior part of the paracingulate cortex (anterior to the genu of the corpus callosum and the ACC). Interestingly, the eyes task employed by Baron-Cohen et al. (1999) additionally activated prefrontal areas lying beneath these regions, including limbic structures in the Baron-Cohen study. It seems, therefore, that the more emotional a mentalizing task gets, the more ventral areas become involved.

This impression fits with social judgment studies involving emotional components. Winston, Strange, O'Doherty, and Dolan (2002) showed faces to subjects and asked them to judge (by pressing a button) whether the face was trustworthy or not (experimental task) or whether the face depicted a high school or university student (control task). Strong activations occurred in the amygdala, STS, insula, and OFC. Moll, de Oliveira-Souza, Bramati, and Grafman (2002) found that the processing of moral or nonmoral statements associated with unpleasant emotions activated different subregions of the OFC: Moral statements activated the left medial OFC (BA 10/11), and nonmoral social judgments, the lateral OFC (BA 11/47) and amygdala.

Nevertheless, the exact role that the MPFC and OFC play in the processing of emotional contents is far from clear. Phan, Wager, Taylor, and Liberzon (2002) pointed to the dominant role of the MPFC for cognitive aspects of emotional processing, such as attention to emotions and their appraisal. Recently, Schaefer et al. (2003) argued that, in contrast to more cognitive components in emotional tasks, processes leading to the generation of emotional responses are more strongly activated in orbitofrontal regions (BA 10, 10/32).

THE NEURAL BASIS OF WORKING MEMORY

There is clear evidence that the prefrontal cortex plays a central role in working memory (Fletcher & Henson, 2001; Smith & Jonides, 1997). A central issue in the current research concerning the neural basis of working memory is the question of whether there are discrete regions in the prefrontal cortex that are specialized for different types of tasks or stimuli.

Concerning lateralization, one of the first studies on this topic by Smith, Jonides, and Koeppe (1996) found activations for verbal working memory (retaining and remembering letters) primarily in the left hemisphere, whereas, for spatial working memory (retaining and remembering the location of spots), more activation occurred in the right hemisphere. Therefore, they concluded that verbal and object working memory are typically activated in the left hemisphere, whereas spatial working memory is right lateralized (Smith & Jonides, 1997).

Newer accounts (Fletcher & Henson, 2001) report that this left-right lateralization seems to apply to storing processes in posterior brain regions, whereas the evidence for lateralization of rehearsal processes of verbal and spatial stimuli in the prefrontal cortex is mixed. Gruber and von Cramon (2003) argue that the inconsistency in the findings regarding the dissociation between verbal and visuospatial working memory is due to the tasks employed. In studies using n-back tasks, no clear evidence for such a dissociation is found. This is attributable to the more heterogeneous character of these tasks requiring additional cognitive processes, such as memory for serial order, sequencing, and updating. In contrast, pure item-recognition tasks reveal different activations dependent on stimulus type. In their own study, Gruber and von Cramon found activations for verbal working memory in a left-lateralized premotor-parietal network underlying verbal rehearsal and a bilateral anterior-prefrontal/inferior-parietal network subserving nonarticulatory maintenance of phonological information. For visuospatial working memory, however, no such differentiation between active rehearsal and passive storage mechanisms could be found; both activated the same bilateral prefrontal-parietal regions.

Another influential theory was proposed by Goldman-Rakic (1987), derived from her research on single cell recordings in monkeys. Her domain-specificity model posits a functional segregation of the prefrontal cortex for the temporary maintenance of different types of stimuli. Specifically, she argued that the VL-PFC is responsible for the temporary storage of object information, and the DL-PFC, for spatial information.

An alternative model to Goldman-Rakic's (1987) was formulated by Petrides (1994). His process-specificity model, derived from animal lesion studies, draws a distinction between maintenance and manipulation processes in working memory. He argued that the VL-PFC supports processes for transferring or maintaining information in working memory independent of stimuli type. In contrast, the DL-PFC is recruited only if additional monitoring or manipulation of information held in working memory is required.

In their reviews of the current research in this controversy, using fMRI studies, D'Esposito and colleagues (D'Esposito et al., 1998; D'Esposito & Postle, 2002) conclude (contra Goldman-Rakic, 1987) that there is no evidence for a clear dorsal/ventral dissociation in the prefrontal cortex according to stimulus type. It seems that maintenance-related processes of different stimulus types are distributed broadly across both hemispheres. For the maintenance of verbal material, a strong lateralization can be found in the left prefrontal cortex, whereas the maintenance of spatial versus nonspatial material seems to be weakly lateralized in the right versus left prefrontal cortex, respectively. Evidence for Petrides's (1994) process-specificity model is somewhat better, although recruitment of the DL-PFC is influenced by various factors, such as how efficiently the retained information is actively scanned.

Developmental fMRI Studies on Working Memory

Compared with fMRI studies with adults, studies using fMRI with children and adolescents are scarce. According to Gaillard, Grandin, and Xu (2001), problems with data acquisition and interpretation of developmental fMRI studies abound, especially among children younger than 5 years of age. First, the difficulty of getting young children to remain still during scanning and their short stature increase motion artifacts. Second, children's higher anxiety levels caused by the scanner lead to physiological reactions (hyperventilations, elevated heart rates) affecting the hemody-namic response. Third, differences in head circumference and thickness of skull (thinner in younger children) can lead to signal distortions. Fourth, the brain of children is still developing, and, therefore, the sizes of differ-ent brain regions, gray/white matter relations, neuronal connectivity, and synaptic density are different than for adult brains. This makes the nor-malization process of mapping individual brains onto the standard tem-plate even more error prone than it is for adults. This is especially true for the frontal lobes, which are the last to mature. The consequences of these structural and functional immaturities on data acquisition and compara-bility to adult studies are still unknown.

Existing neuroimaging studies on working memory clearly focus on the neural basis of spatial working memory because there are only two published neuroimaging studies (Casey et al., 1995; Sowell, Delis, Stiles, & Jernigan, 2001) exploring developmental aspects of verbal working memory. Casey et al. (1995) explored activations in the prefrontal cortex in six children ages 9 to 11 years during a nonspatial working memory task (n-back task). In the experimental task, children had to press a button whenever a letter in a random sequence of letters was similar to the one presented two items previously. In the control task, they had to press a button whenever they saw the letter X. Using a region-of-interest approach, the most consistent prefrontal activations were found in infe-rior and middle frontal gyri (BA 46, 10). These activations were compara-ble to those in a study with adults by Cohen et al. (1994) using the same task. Furthermore, half of the children showed activation in the anterior cingulate (BA 32, mostly right) and superior frontal lobe (BA 11).

A different approach using MRI (without "f") was undertaken by Sowell et al. (2001). They analyzed frontal lobe gray ratio in 35 children ages 7 to 16 years and compared these ratios with the children's delayed recall scores on the California Verbal Learning Test for Children, deemed to be an index for verbal working memory. There was a significant relationship between thinning of frontal lobe gray matter and better performance on the delayed recall score, underpinning the central role of frontal lobe mat-uration for the development of verbal working memory.

Thomas et al. (1999) compared six children (age range 8–10 years) with six adults (age range 19–26 years) on a spatial n-back task. Subjects were instructed to fixate on a central crossbar and to monitor a linear array of four boxes for the location of a dot. In the two control conditions, subjects either made no response (visual condition) or indicated the current loca-tion of the dot by pressing the corresponding button (motor condition). For the memory condition, subjects were first pretested outside the scanner to assess level of performance (75–95 % accuracy required) and then, depend-ing on their performance level (to eliminate performance as a confound-ing factor), they were asked to indicate the location of the dot one or two trials back. In both groups, the right superior frontal gyrus (BA 8), middle frontal gyrus (BA 10/46), superior parietal lobule (BA 7) and bilateral inferior parietal lobule were activated (comparison of memory and motor conditions). In contrast, only adults showed activation of the right cingulate gyrus (BA 24/32), bilateral supplementary motor area (BA 6), postcentral gyrus (BA 2), middle temporal gyrus (BA 21) and left cerebellum, whereas only children showed activation of the left precuneus cortex (BA 7) and right cerebellum. According to the authors, the lack of activation of the cingulate gyrus in children shows that the ability to modulate competition (as a function of the cingulate cortex) is not fully developed in this age range. In contrast to other studies on nonspatial working memory, deactivations were seen in the left inferior frontal gyrus (BA 47) for adults and right inferior frontal gyrus (BA 45) for the children. The authors argue that stronger activation of the dorsolateral cortex leads to less activation of the ventrolateral cortex.

Nelson et al. (2000) used the same task design (visual, motor, and memory condition) as had Thomas et al. (1999), in nine children (age range 8–11 years). In the memory condition, only a spatial 1-back task was explored. Contrasting memory to motor condition, they found prefrontal activations in the right middle frontal gyrus (BA 46 & BA 10), in the right superior frontal gyrus (BA 9 & BA 6), and in the left ACC (BA 24 & BA 32).

Two other studies used a voxel-based approach looking at direct voxel-by-voxel comparisons of regional changes in brain activity with age. In the first study, Kwon, Reiss, and Menon (2002) examined age-related increases in brain activations during a 2-back spatial working memory task in three age groups: eight children (age range 7–12), eight adolescents (age range 13–17) and young adults (age range 18–22). Participants saw the letter O once every 2 s at one of nine distinct locations on the screen. In the memory condition, they were to respond if the current location was the same as presented two stimuli previously. In the control condition, subjects were to respond when the stimuli appeared at the center. Brain regions showing significant age-related increases during the working memory task were the bilateral dorsolateral prefrontal cortex (BA 9/46), ventrolateral prefrontal cortex (BA 44), PMC (BA 6), SFG (BA 8), SMA, bilateral IPC (BA 39/40) and SPL (BA 7).

In the second study, Klingberg, Forssberg, and Westerberg (2002) examined 13 children between 9 and 18 years of age. In the control condition, subjects saw green circles presented sequentially in a 4 × 4 grid in one of the four corner boxes and had to press a button when an unfilled green circle appeared in the middle of the grid after a 1,500-ms delay. In the memory condition, subjects saw red circles (in one version there were three to remember, in the other version, five) presented sequentially in the grid. After a 1,500-ms delay, participants had to press a button when the new circle was in the same location as any of the circles presented previously. Significant age-related increases were found bilaterally in the superior frontal sulcus, in the intraparietal and superior parietal cortex, and in the left occipital cortex. Interestingly, a negative interaction between age and activity was found in the right inferior frontal sulcus.

Further evidence for the role of the prefrontal cortex in spatial working memory in children comes from studies of clinical populations with known executive deficits such as Turner syndrome and fragile X syndrome (Haberecht et al., 2001; Kwon et al., 2001). In both studies, the same task design was used as in the study by Kwon et al. (2002) with the only difference being that both spatial 1-back and 2-back working memory tasks were used. Haberecht et al. (2001) compared 14 control subjects ages 7–18 years (mean age 14.5 years) with 11 subjects with Turner syndrome ages 7–18 years (mean age 12.6 years) and didn't find any difference in brain activity in the 1-back task. But in the 2-back task, greater prefrontal activations in the bilateral inferior frontal gyrus (BA 44) and middle frontal gyrus (BA 9 and BA 8/9) were found in the control group. When using IQ as a covariate, subjects with Turner syndrome also showed decreased prefrontal activation in the bilateral middle frontal gyrus (BA 9) and the right middle frontal gyrus (BA 9/46).

Kwon et al. (2001) compared 10 female subjects with fragile X syndrome ages 10–23 years (mean age 17.2 years) with 15 female control subjects ages 8–22 years (mean age 15.1 years) on the spatial *n*-back task. Using a region-of-interest analysis, no difference in activation between these two groups could be detected on the 1-back and 2-back tasks. However, the control group showed a significant prefrontal increase between the 1-back and 2-back tasks in the inferior frontal gyrus and in the middle frontal gyrus, which could not be found in the subjects with fragile X syndrome. Further, a significant relationship between performance accuracy on the *n*-back tasks and brain activation could be found only in the control group. Both studies show that children within clinical populations with known executive deficits do not demonstrate increased activations in central prefrontal regions when working memory load increases, whereas normal children do.

What is the overall picture that emerges from these existing developmental fMRI studies? Clearly this field is at its very beginning, and more studies are urgently needed, especially studies on verbal working memory, for which we could find but a single study (Casey et al., 1995). Two fMRI studies looking at age-related increases in brain activations during nonspatial working memory tasks (Klingberg et al., 2002; Kwon et al., 2002) found that the DL-PFC and VL-PFC are more activated in adults than in children. This confirms the assumption that functional specialization in the prefrontal cortex for working memory takes place throughout childhood. This observation also applies to the cingulate gyrus, which showed increased activation with age in the study by Thomas et al. (1999). However, what is missing are fMRI studies of different working memory tasks within the same group of children in analogy to studies with adults contrasting spatial versus nonspatial and maintenance versus manipulation tasks. Nevertheless, the finding of more right-lateralized activations for spatial working memory tasks in the studies by Kwon et al. (2002), Nelson et al. (2000), and Thomas et al. (1999) provides some evidence for functional segregation in children. Finally, the studies by Haberecht et al.

(2001) and Kwon et al. (2001) show that working memory deficits in clinical disorders are also associated with reduced activations in the DL-PFC and VL-PFC. These findings underpin the central role of these prefrontal regions for working memory in children.

THE NEURAL BASIS OF INHIBITION

Inhibition is a very broad construct used widely in developmental, cognitive, and clinical psychology, as well as in neuroscience. In developmental psychology, the term *inhibition* is generally used in two facets. One facet is as a general heritable temperamental trait appearing in late infancy (Kagan, Reznick, Clarke, Snidman, & Garcia-Coll, 1984; Rothbart, 1989). In this sense, inhibition is defined as wariness of unfamiliar people, objects, or events and can be regarded as a personality construct involving strongly emotional processes. The other facet of inhibition refers to distinct cognitive tasks requiring response suppression and, therefore, can be regarded as a cognitive processing mechanism. This different conceptualization shows that inhibition can be analyzed within a behavioral-emotional and a cognitive framework. The important difference between these two forms of inhibition lies in the type of processing information.

fMRI Studies on Inhibition

Several tasks have been used to delineate the neural correlates of executive inhibition. Prominent among them are variants of the Stroop task and go/no-go tasks, the Eriksen flanker task and antisaccade tasks. All of them have in common that a response conflict is induced and a response has to be made on the basis of stimulus evaluation and selection. Various fMRI studies indicate several brain regions in the prefrontal cortex (more on the right side) that are important for executive inhibition. These are, in particular, the dorsolateral prefrontal cortex, ventral lateral cortex, and anterior cingulate cortex (Barch et al., 2001; Bunge, Dudukovic, Thomason, Vaidya, & Gabrieli, 2002, Bunge, Hazeltine, Scanlon, Rosen, & Gabrieli, 2001; de Zubicaray, Zelaya, Andrew, Williams, & Bullmore, 2000; Garavan, Ross, Murphy, Poche, & Stein, 2002; Konishi et al., 1999).

There is now converging evidence that the ACC is central for processing response conflict tasks, although its exact role is still controversial. One influential theory concerning the role of the ACC in conflict response tasks is proposed by Carter et al. (1998) and Botvinick, Braver, Barch, Carter, and Cohen (2001). In their account, the rostral cingulate zone (rCZ) of the ACC is specifically involved in conflict monitoring. The ACC then signals demands of increased cognitive control to other brain regions (especially to the lateral prefrontal cortex).

Furthermore, the extensive review by Barch, Braver, Akbudak, Conturo, Ollinger, and Snyder (2001) indicates that the same regions in the ACC are activated by different response conflict tasks that vary in response modalities (vocal vs. manual vs. oculomotor) and stimulus types (verbal vs. spatial). So, then, there is no evidence for functional segregation within the ACC for different types of response conflicts. Two recent studies using the Flanker paradigm also support the view that the ACC is involved only in evaluating response conflict and not in detecting stimulus conflict (Bunge et al., 2001, 2002; van Veen, Cohen, Botvinick, Stenger, & Carter, 2001).

The position outlined previously implies that the ACC evaluates response conflicts but does not implement strategic processes to resolve conflicts or inhibit responses. So what additional prefrontal regions are central for response inhibition? Important candidates are the ventral prefrontal cortex and dorsolateral cortex because they are also involved in response inhibition as shown in go/no-go and stop signal tasks (Casey et al., 1997; Garavan et al., 2002; Konishi et al., 1999; Rubia et al., 2001).

To reveal common networks activated by different inhibition tasks, Rubia et al. (2001) compared two go/no-go task and three stop task versions. Common areas of activation in all five inhibition tasks were the bilateral inferior gyrus (BA 47/44), right middle frontal gyrus (BA 9/6), right anterior cingulate (BA 8/32), right pre-SMA (BA 6), right inferior parietal lobe (BA 40), and predominantly left middle temporal cortex (BA 21). It seems important to note that Rubia et al. attribute the activation in the parietal lobe not to motor inhibition per se but to movement-related visuospatial attentional demands.

Garavan et al. (2002), using a go/no-go task (with individually tailored stimulus timing), tried to separate the processes of response inhibition, error detection, and behavioral correction. Response inhibition was associated with right dorsolateral prefrontal and right inferior parietal areas. Comparing easy and difficult inhibition conditions (based on the speed of target responses that immediately preceded the successful inhibition), they found greater activations in the right dorsolateral prefrontal cortex (BA 9, 46, 6) for easy inhibitions but in the anterior cingulate cortex (BA 24) for difficult inhibitions. The authors therefore postulate two inhibitory systems. One is in the right prefrontal system, which becomes active when more deliberative or controlled inhibition is required. The other involves the anterior cingulate and may be especially important for urgent inhibitions of fast or very automatic behaviors. In addition, Garavan et al. suggest laterality effects, in which the right prefrontal cortex is associated with response inhibition, whereas the left prefrontal cortex is involved in behavioral correction following an error.

Whereas anterior cingulate cortex and ventrolateral and dorsolateral cortex are heavily involved in different response conflict tasks requiring cognitive inhibition, there is good evidence from lesion studies (Bechara et al., 1998, 2000) as well as from fMRI studies (Elliott et al., 2000) that the orbitofrontal cortex is essential for inhibition in emotion- or reward-related contexts.

Bechara et al. (1998) compared patients with lesions in the dorsolateral prefrontal cortex and patients with lesions in the ventromedial prefrontal cortex on the gambling task. In this task, subjects have to select cards from four decks, whereby they experience different monetary gains and losses. Two of the decks are the good decks in terms of long-term gain. The other two decks are the bad decks. Although subjects occasionally get a very high monetary gain (reward) by choosing the bad decks, they encounter money loss (punishment) in the long run. There was no difference in performance between normal subjects and patients with lesions in the dorsolateral prefrontal cortex. After initial attraction to the bad decks with their seductive high rewards, with experience participants switched to drawing from the safe decks. In contrast, patients with ventromedial lesions were insensitive to long-term consequences and did not alter their behavior in response to reinforcement contingencies. Their behavior is similar to the cognitive impulsiveness of young children with problems in delaying gratification (Bechara et al., 2000).

Elliott et al. (2000) conclude from their review of fMRI studies that the orbitofrontal cortex is especially activated in tasks where the reward values of past and future stimuli have to be monitored and kept in mind. They suggest further that the lateral orbitofrontal cortex is especially activated when previously rewarded responses have to be inhibited.

In a similar vein, Rolls (2000) postulates that the orbitofrontal cortex is particularly involved when the control of behavior depends on the evaluation of reinforcement associations of environmental stimuli. In this sense, reward and punishment aspects of stimuli and information are represented in the OFC (Rolls, 2002). This is well demonstrated in a study by O'Doherty, Kringelbach, Rolls, Hornak, and Andrews (2001), in which subjects were confronted with rewards and punishments in dealing with symbolic monetary gains and losses. Rewarded events were significantly associated with prefrontal activations in the medial OFC compared with punishment events. Moreover, this activation was related to the magnitude of the obtained reward. In contrast, punishment events activated more lateral areas of the anterior OFC (BA 10/11) and a region of the nearby ventral prefrontal cortex.

Developmental fMRI Studies on Inhibition

Although several developmental fMRI studies explore the neural basis of motor and cognitive inhibition, we could not find any studies using emotion- and reward-oriented inhibition tasks.

Studies Involving Go/No-Go Paradigms. In one of the first studies, Casey et al. (1997) employed a go/no-go paradigm, comparing nine children ages 7 to 12 years to nine adults ages 21 to 24 years. In their task, subjects had to simply press a button when shown all presented letters except the letter X. Two comparison conditions were used to control for stimulus and response parameters. They found no difference between children and adults in the general activation. In both populations, anterior cingulate, inferior and middle frontal gyri, and orbitofrontal gyri were activated, although these regions were activated to a greater degree in children (especially dorsolateral regions). Moreover, for both populations, activation in the orbitofrontal cortex was associated with better behavioral performance, whereas the inverse was true for the ACC. Dorsolateral activity was also related to better performance but only in children and not in adults. Casey et al. (1997), therefore, suggest that children use different strategies in performing this task, recruiting more and different prefrontal regions. In a second study, Casey, Giedd, and Thomas (2000) manipulated the probability of the nontarget X and found that dorsolateral activity in adults was related to higher nontarget probability only, whereas in children it was related to low and high nontarget probability. This again supports the claim that functional segregation of EF increases with age.

Tamm, Menon, and Reiss (2002) used the same task paradigms as did Casey et al. (1997) and explored brain activations in 19 children and young adults (age range 8–20, mean age 14.4). Contrasting the experimental condition (no-go vs. go trials) with the control condition (only go trials), participants showed significant prefrontal activations in the right frontal operculum/inferior frontal gyrus, in the left middle frontal gyrus (BA 8/9), and in the right superior frontal gyrus (BA 6). Age-related increases in prefrontal activations were found in the left inferior frontal gyrus/insula extending to the orbitofrontal gyrus, whereas age-related decreases were found in the left superior frontal gyrus (BA 8), extending to the middle frontal gyrus and cingulate.

Durston, Thomas, Yang, et al. (2002) also used a go/no-go paradigm, comparing brain activations in 10 adults (mean age 28.0 years) and 10 children (mean age 8.7 years). They also manipulated the effects of interference on neural processes by parametrically varying the number of go trials (1, 3, or 5 go trials) before responding to a no-go trial. To increase the children's interest, Pokemon characters were used as stimuli. Comparing effects of condition (go vs. no-go trials), bilateral activations were found in both children and adults in the ventral prefrontal cortex (BA 44/47), the right dorsolateral prefrontal cortex (BA 9/46), and the right parietal lobe (BA 40). In all three regions, activations were larger in children. Additional activations were found for adults only in the bilateral inferior frontal gyrus (BA 44), left anterior cingulate gyrus (BA 24/32), and left caudate nucleus. Using event-related fMRI, Bunge et al. (2002) explored brain activations of cognitive control in 16 children ages 8–12 years (mean age 10 years) and in 16 adults (mean age 24). They combined the Eriksen flanker task with a go/no-go paradigm to assess two forms of cognitive control: interference suppression and response inhibition, respectively. Subjects viewed an array of five stimuli on the screen and were instructed to react to the central arrow and ignore the flankers by pressing a left or right button when the central arrow pointed to the left or right. To reveal neural processes of interference suppression, two contrasts—incongruent versus neutral—were compared: In the incongruent condition, the flankers also consisted of arrows but pointing in a different direction than the central arrow. In the neutral condition, the flankers were diamond shapes not associated with a response. Comparing these conditions, differences in lateralization of prefrontal activation were found in children and adults. Significantly more activations in adults than in children were seen in the right ventrolateral prefrontal cortex (BA 44, 45, and 47), insula bilaterally (BA 13), and putamen. In children, more activations were found in the left ventrolateral prefrontal cortex (BA 45), left insula (BA 13), right inferior parietal lobe (BA 40), and left superior temporal lobe (BA 38). Furthermore, Bunge et al. (2002) looked for regions that were associated with efficiency of interference suppression (measured by the amount of slowing of reaction times for incongruent vs. neutral trials). Again, they found a lateralization effect, whereby in adults the right inferior frontal gyrus/anterior insula (BA 47/13) and right middle frontal gyrus (BA 10/46) were associated with efficiency, whereas in children these regions included the left anterior insula (BA 13, extending into the left caudate nucleus) and the left pulvinar nucleus of the thalamus.

Looking at the neural processes during response inhibition, no-go and neutral conditions were compared. In the no-go condition, subjects were instructed to refrain from pressing a button when the flankers were Xs. Significantly more activations in adults than in children were found in the bilateral ventrolateral prefrontal cortex (right BA 44, left BA 44), bilateral dorsolateral prefrontal cortex (BA 9/46), right anterior and posterior cingulate cortices (BA 32, 30/23), left inferior parietal lobe (BA 39), and right temporal lobe (BA 39, 21). There were no regions that were significantly more activated in children than in adults. Further analyses revealed that no specific regions were associated with efficiency of response inhibition in adults, whereas in children this was the case for several regions: the right premotor cortex (BA 6), bilateral parietal cortex (right BA z, left BA 39), right globus pallidus, bilateral middle temporal gyrus (right BA 39, left BA 21, 37), and bilateral occipital cortex (BA 17, 18, 19). Dividing each of the two groups into above- and below-average performers revealed a difference only for children. Low performers showed activation in the left ventrolateral and bilateral dorsolateral prefrontal cortex in contrast to high performers, whose activations were in the bilateral inferior parietal lobule. From these results, Bunge and colleagues (2002) conclude that, unlike in adults, cognitive control in children is associated with immature prefrontal activation but that this immaturity differs according to type of control demanded. For instance, in interference suppression, adults were activated more on the right side, children more on the left side, which the authors attribute to different task strategies (children rely more on verbal strategies than adults do). In contrast, for response inhibition, instead of a laterality effect, a posterior-prefrontal effect was found. In adults, it was prefrontal regions, but in children it was posterior areas, that were associated with successful response inhibition.

Another response inhibition task was employed by Luna et al. (2001). Using a region-of-interest approach, they compared eleven 8- to 13-year-old children, fifteen 14- to 17-year-old adolescents, and ten 18- to 30-year-old adults performing an antisaccade task (suppressing a reflexive eye movement to a prepotent novel visual stimulus). A prosaccade task was used as a comparison condition. Compared with adults, children showed increased activation in the supramarginal gyrus (SMG), which the authors attribute to more reliance on visuospatial processing in this task. Different from the results by Casey et al. (1997, 2000), increased dorsolateral activity (on the right side) was seen only in adolescents. Luna and colleagues (2001) offer the following explanation for these discrepant findings. They cite evidence that performance on the antisaccade task matures later than on the go/no-go task. This is mirrored in the error proneness of the younger children in this study, which opens the possibility that only adolescents begin to recruit the dorsolateral cortex efficiently to accomplish this task. This result is in line with the results by Bunge et al. (2002) that younger children fail to recruit prefrontal regions in response inhibition.

The fMRI activations in go/no-go tasks have also been explored in ADHD children, who are known for their core deficit in response inhibition (Barkley, 1997). Vaidya et al. (1998) compared 10 ADHD boys ages 8–13 years with 6 age- and IQ-matched controls on two versions of a go/no-go task. In the response-controlled task version (go & no-go blocks were equated in the number of key presses but differed in the number of trials and rate of stimulus presentation), greater bilateral activation of the frontal cortex (especially in the cingulate) was found in the ADHD group. This astonishing result of hypermetabolism in the prefrontal cortex is attributed to greater inhibitory efforts, which ADHD children must undertake to resolve this task. In the stimulus–controlled version of the task, go and no-go blocks were equated in the rate of presentation and number of trials but differed in the number of key presses. ADHD children showed reduced striatal activation but no differences in prefrontal activation. Langleben et al. (2001) used the same task and compared 20 ADHD boys and 4 normal controls (age range for the whole group was 8–12 years, mean age, 10.2 years). Contrary to the results of the study by Vaidya et al. (1998), they found decreased activations in the right prefrontal cortex (BA 9, 44, 46) relative to the left in ADHD children with severe or moderate hyperactivity, whereas this was not the case in ADHD children with low hyperactivity.

In another study, Rubia et al. (1999) explored a stop and delay task in seven male adolescents (ages 12–18 years, mean age, 15.7 years) and nine male controls (ages 12–17 years, mean age, 15.0). In the stop task, subjects saw an airplane appearing on a screen. In the control task, a zeppelin followed in 50% of the trials, and the subjects had to press a button whenever the airplane appeared, whether or not a zeppelin followed. In the experimental task, a bomb followed in 50% of the trials instead of the zeppelin, and subjects were instructed not to press the button when the bomb appeared next. In the delay task, a visual stimulus appeared on a screen in a short-event-rate condition (interstimulus interval 600 ms) and in a long-event-rate condition (interstimulus interval 5 s). Subjects had to synchronize their motor response to the visual stimulus. In the stop task, normal controls showed significantly greater prefrontal activations in the right medial frontal cortex (BA 8/32) at the border with the ACC and in the right inferior and medioinferior frontal lobe (BA 45 & 9/45) than did the ADHD adolescents. In the delay task, greater activations were found in the anterior and posterior cingulate gyrus (BA 32 & 31, respectively).

Studies Involving Stroop Paradigms.   One of the most frequently employed task paradigms for studying brain activation during inhibition in adults is the classical Stroop task. Adleman et al. (2002) investigated 8 children (ages 7–11 years, mean age, 10.1 years), 11 adolescents (ages 12–16 years, mean age, 14.7 years) and 11 young adults (ages 17–22 years, mean age, 20.0 years). To rule out motion artifacts from vocalizing, subjects were instructed to identify and say quietly to themselves the color of the Xs (control condition) and the incongruent color in which the color word was printed (experimental condition). The Stroop task was also performed outside the scanner to assess age-related changes in performance. Several prefrontal brain regions showed higher activation with increasing age: the left ACC (BA 24/32), the left superior frontal gyrus (BA 6), and the bilateral middle frontal gyrus (BA 9).

Tamm, Menon, Johnston, Hessl, and Reiss (2002) compared 14 females with fragile X syndrome and 14 age-matched control females (age range for both groups was 10–22, mean age, 15.4) on a counting Stroop task. In the control task, the word *fish* was presented 1, 2, 3, and 4 times on the screen, and subjects had to press the corresponding button. In the interference, the number words *one*, *two*, *three*, and *four* were depicted. In the interference condition, prefrontal activations in the control group were found in the left inferior and middle frontal gyrus (BA 9, 46, 47). In the fragile X group, similar activations could be found, although more bilateral (left BA 45, 46, and right BA 9/47). Between-group comparisons controlling for IQ as a covariate showed differences in prefrontal brain activations in the right orbitofrontal gyrus, left insular cortex, and orbitofrontal gyrus bordering on the frontal operculum.

Summary

Looking at the different results in fMRI studies on inhibition, one can conclude that, in adults, three specific brain regions are heavily involved in cognitively oriented response inhibition tasks such as the Stroop or go/no-go paradigm: the DL-PFC, VL-PFC and ACC. There is evidence that the ACC is responsible for detecting and monitoring conflict (Botvinick et al., 2001), whereas the DL-PFC and VL-PFC, along with posterior brain regions, are more involved in resolving conflict. The DL-PFC and VL-PFC are probably differentially activated depending on process and memory load requirements in the task used. In contrast, inhibition in emotional and reward/punishment contexts is related to activations in the OFC (Elliott et al., 2000; Rolls, 2002). This is also confirmed by human lesion studies (Bechara et al., 1998). Therefore, current studies support the suggestion that the capacity to inhibit responses is differently modulated depending on whether cognitive or emotional reward aspects are tapped. Unfortunately, we could not find any studies that explored these different inhibition requirements within the same group of subjects.

All available fMRI studies with children and adolescents focus almost exclusively on the more cognitive inhibition tasks, especially go/no-go tasks. The studies by Durston, Thomas, Young, et al. (2002) indicate that more and larger prefrontal regions are generally activated in children than in adults. This is compatible with the reliable evidence that functional segregation of inhibition with respect to the DL-PFC, VL-PFC and ACC increases with age (Adleman et al., 2002; Bunge et al., 2002; Casey et al., 1998; Durston, Thomas, Worden, et al., 2002, 2002b; Tamm et al., 2002). Similarly, fMRI studies of working memory in clinical populations, such as ADHD children (Langleben et al., 2001; Rubia et al., 1999), demonstrate that inhibition deficits are associated with hypometabolism of the prefrontal cortex, although Vaidya et al. (1998) report hypermetabolism in their ADHD group.

WHAT fMRI TELLS US ABOUT THE ToM–EF CONNECTION

There are several suggestions that can be made on the basis of current evidence of fMRI studies of ToM, working memory, and inhibition that are of relevance for exploring the developmental link between ToM and EF. One explanation for this relationship is the assumption that ToM and EF recruit the same brain regions. However, there is little evidence that this is the case in terms of a precise overlap, at least in adults. Working memory is especially associated with the DL-PFC (dorsolateral part of BA 9 & 46) and VL-PFC (BA 44, 45, 47); in contrast, classical ToM tasks are strongly related to activations in the medial prefrontal cortex—for example, in the medial part of BA 8 and 9 and especially in the anterior paracingulate cortex. The closest executive brain region to this ToM area is the ACC, which plays a dominant role in detecting and monitoring response conflict as required in Stroop and go/no-go tasks.

Although we cannot find a region that is functionally responsible for EF tasks as well as for ToM tasks, at least the close spatial proximity between the ToM area (in the anterior rostral part of the ACC and paracingulate cortex) and the area responsible for cognitive inhibition processes (posterior part of the rostral cingulated zone) is compatible with the finding that ToM and conflict inhibition tasks are particularly strongly related (Carlson & Moses, 2001; Carlson et al., 2002). Moreover, if one takes into consideration that, in children, prefrontal regions are more broadly recruited during executive tasks, it could well be that the areas of activation in conflict tasks and ToM tasks are not just neighbors but actually overlapping in childhood.

The common brain regions explanation of developmental synchronies can be sensibly generalized to the common maturation of brain regions hypothesis. That is, the developmental correlation between mental abilities is a function of the correlation between the maturation levels of the supporting brain regions. Currently, there are data only on the maturation of the prefrontal lobes as a whole (Casey et al., 2000; Kanemura, Aihara, Aoki, Araki, & Nakazawa, 2003), although some studies are starting to look at the differential maturation rates of subregions (e.g., Reiss, Abrams, Singer, Ross, & Denckla, 1996). However, there are no detailed maturational trajectories for subregions of the PFC and their correlations. In absence of evidence on precise maturational correlations for different regions within the PFC, we make the gross simplification that the closer two regions are to each other, the more likely they are to share their maturational schedule. For the subregions that we have emphasized, the following exemplary predictions can be made:

1. For investigating relations of specific brain areas with working memory, the distinction between manipulation (based on the DL-PFC) and maintenance processes (based on the VL-PFC) needs to be made. Then the prediction follows that manipulation processes should be more strongly related to ToM than are maintenance processes because the DL-PFC is closer to the ToM region of ACC than is the VL-PFC. Unfortunately, existing investigations of the link between ToM and working memory development do not systematically compare manipulation and maintenance aspects of working memory. Therefore, it is left to future studies to test our prediction.

2. Conflict tasks (based on a subregion of ACC) and ToM tasks (based on a neighboring subregion of ACC) should correlate more strongly with each other than either of them with emotional delay tasks (based on OFC). This prediction has already received support in recent developmental studies (Carlson & Moses, 2001; Carlson et al., 2002; Hala et al., 2003). A closer inspection of the intercorrelations of these three groups of tasks shows that, in all three studies, ToM tasks correlate quite strongly with conflict tasks, much more strongly than with delay tasks. Particularly surprising, and not especially emphasized in these publications, is that conflict tasks have a much higher correlation with ToM tasks than with delay tasks, even though these two tasks are both considered EF tasks. Future studies should, therefore, pay closer attention to the distinction between the more cognitive inhibition tasks (conflict) and inhibition in the context of emotion-laden rewards (delay tasks, gambling tasks).

In sum, imaging studies emphasize that the relationship between ToM and EF depends very much on the particular kind of EF one is investigating. The developmental relationship tends to be stronger with those EF that are subserved by neighboring brain regions than with those based on more distant regions. This lesson also applies to ToM, where one needs to minimally distinguish the more cognitive tasks (understanding false belief and other forms of perspective taking) from tasks with a strong emotional and moral component (e.g., judgment of facial expressions, eye gaze, and processing of moral statements).

ACKNOWLEDGMENT

This chapter was written while the first author received financial support from the Austrian Science Fund (FWF-Project P11397-SOZ).

REFERENCES

Adleman, N. E., Menon, V., Blasey, C. M., White, C. D., Warsofsky, I. S., Glover, G. H., & Reiss, A. L. (2002). A developmental fMRI study of the stroop color-word task. *Neuroimage, 16,* 61–75.

Barch, D. M., Braver, T. S., Akbudak, E., Conturo, T., Ollinger, J. & Snyder, A. (2001). Anterior cingulate cortex and response conflict: Effects of response modality and processing domain. *Cerebral Cortex, 11,* 837–848.

Barkley, R. A. (1997). *ADHD and the nature of self-control.* New York: Guilford Press.

Baron-Cohen, S., Ring, H., Moriarty, J., Schmitz, B., Costa, D., & Ell, P. (1994). Recognition of mental state terms. *British Journal of Psychiatry, 165,* 640–649.

Baron-Cohen, S., Ring, H. A., Wheelwright, S., Bullmore, E. T., Brammer, M. J., Simmons, A., & Williams, S. C. R. (1999). Social intelligence in the normal and autistic brain: An fMRI study. *European Journal of Neuroscience, 11,* 1891–1898.

Bechara, A., Damasio, H., & Damasio, A. R. (2000). Emotion, decision making and the orbitofrontal cortex. *Cerebral Cortex, 10,* 295–307.

Bechara, A., Damasio, H., Tranel, D., & Anderson, S. W. (1998). Dissociation of working memory from decision making within the human prefrontal cortex. *Journal of Neuroscience, 18,* 428–437.

Botvinick, M. M., Braver, T. S., Barch, D. M., Carter, C. S., & Cohen, J. D. (2001). Conflict monitoring and cognitive control. *Psychological Review, 108,* 624–652.

Brodmann, K. (1909). *Vergleichende Lokalisationslehre der Grosshirnrinde in ihren Prinzipien dargestellt auf Grund des Zellenbaues.* Leipzig, Germany: Barth.

Brunet, E., Sarfati, Y., Hardy-Baylé, M.-C., & Decety, J. (2000). A PET investigation of the attribution of intentions with a nonverbal task. *Neuroimage, 11,* 157–166.

Bunge, S., Dudukovic, N. M., Thomason, M. E., Vaidya, C. J., & Gabrieli, J. D. E. (2002). Immature frontal lobe contributions to cognitive control in children: Evidence from fMRI. *Neuron, 33,* 1–20.

Bunge, S. A., Hazeltine, E., Scanlon, M. D., Rosen, A. C., & Gabrieli, J. D. E. (2001). Dissociable contributions of prefrontal and parietal cortices to response selection. *Neuroimage, 17,* 1562–1571.

Bush, G., Luu, P., & Posner, M. I. (2000). Cognitive and emotional influences in anterior cingulate cortex. *Trends in Cognitive Sciences, 4,* 215–222.

Carlson, S. M., & Moses, L. J. (2001). Individual differences in inhibitory control and children's theory of mind. *Child Development, 72,* 1032–1053.

Carlson, S. M., Moses, L. J., & Breton, C. (2002). How specific is the relation between executive function and theory of mind? Contributions of inhibitory control and working memory. *Infant and Child Development, 11,* 73–92.

Carter, C. S., Braver, T. S., Barch, D. M., Botvinick, M. M., Noll, D., & Cohen, J. D. (1998). Anterior cingulate cortex, error detection, and the online monitoring of performance. *Science, 280,* 747–749.

Casey, B. J., Cohen, J. D., Jezzard, P., Turner, R., Noll, D. C., Trainor, R. J., Giedd, J., Kaysen, D., Hertz-Pannier, L., & Rapoport, J. L. (1995). Activation of prefrontal cortex in children during a nonspatial working memory task with functional MRI. *Neuroimage, 2,* 221–229.

Casey, B. J., Giedd, J. N., & Thomas, K. M. (2000). Structural and functional brain development and its relation to cognitive development. *Biological Psychology, 54,* 241–257.

Casey, B. J., Trainor, R. J., Orendi, J. L., Schubert, A. B., Nystrom, L. E., Giedd, J. N., Castellanos, F. X., Haxby, J. V., Noll, D. C., Cohen, J. D., Forman, S. D., Dahl, R. E., & Rapaport, J. L. (1997). A developmental functional MRI study of prefrontal activation during performance of a go-no-go task. *Journal of Cognitive Neuroscience, 9,* 835–847.

Castelli, F., Happé, F., Frith, U., & Frith, C. (2000). Movement and mind: A functional imaging study of perception and interpretation of complex intentional movement patterns. *Neuroimage, 12,* 314–325.

Cohen, J. D., Forman, S. D., Braver, T. S., Casey, B. J., Servan-Schreiber, D., & Noll, D. C. (1994). Activation of the prefrontal cortex in a nonspatial working memory task with functional MRI. *Human Brain Mapping, 1,* 293–304.

Cummings, J. L. (1995). Anatomic and behavioral aspects of frontal-subcortical circuits. In J. Grafman, K. J. Holyoak, & F. Boller (Eds.), *Structure and functions of the human prefrontal cortex* (pp. 1–13). New York: Academy of Sciences.

Davis, H. L., & Pratt, C. (1996). The development of children's theory of mind: The working memory of explanation. *Australian Journal of Psychology, 47,* 25–31.

DeArmond, S. J., Fusco, M. M., & Dewey, M. M. (1989). *Structure of the human brain: A photographic atlas.* Third edition. New York: Oxford University Press.

D'Esposito, M., Aguirre, G. K., Zarahn, E., Ballard, D., Shin, R. K., & Lease, J. (1998). Functional MRI studies of spatial and nonspatial working memory. *Cognitive Brain Research, 7,* 1–13.

D'Esposito, M., & Postle, B. R. (2002). The organization of working memory function in lateral prefrontal cortex: Evidence from event-related functional MRI. In D. T. Stuss & R. T. Knight (Eds.), *Principles of frontal lobe function* (pp. 168–187). New York: Oxford University Press.

de Zubicaray, G. I., Zelaya, F. O., Andrew, C., Williams, S. C., & Bullmore, E. T. (2000). Cerebral regions associated with verbal response initiation, suppression and strategy use. *Neuropsychologia, 38,* 1292–1304.

Durston, S., Thomas, K. M., Worden, M. S., Yang, Y., & Casey, B. J. (2002). The effect of preceding context on inhibition: an event-related fMRI study. *Neuroimage, 16,* 449–453.

Durston, S., Thomas, K. M., Yang, Y., Ulug, A. M., Zimmerman, R. D., & Casey, B. J. (2002). A neural basis for the development of inhibitory control. *Developmental Science, 5,* 9–16.

Elliott, R., Dolan, R. J., & Frith, C. D. (2000). Dissociable functions in the medial and lateral orbitofrontal cortex: Evidence from human neuroimaging studies. *Cerebral Cortex, 10,* 308–317.

Fletcher, P. C., Happé, F., Frith, U., Baker, S. C., Dolan, R. J., Frackowiak, R. S. J., & Frith, C. D. (1995). Other minds in the brain: A functional imaging study of "theory of mind" in story comprehension. *Cognition, 57,* 109–128.

Fletcher, P. C., & Henson, R. N. (2001). Frontal lobes and human memory: Insights from functional neuroimaging. *Brain, 124,* 849–881.

Frith, U. & Frith, C. D. (2003). Development and neurophysiology of mentalising. *Philosophical Transactions of the Royal Society of London series B, 358,* 459–473.

Gaillard, W. D., Grandin, C. B., & Xu, B. (2001). Developmental aspects of pediatric fMRI: Considerations for image acquisition, analysis, and interpretation. *Neuroimage, 13,* 239–249.

Gallagher, H. L., & Frith, C. D. (2003). Functional imaging of "theory of mind." *Trends in Cognitive Sciences, 7,* 77–83.

Gallagher, H. L., Happé, F., Brunswick, N., Fletcher, P. C., Frith, U., & Frith, C. D. (2000). Reading the mind in cartoons and stories: An fMRI study of "theory of mind" in verbal and nonverbal tasks. *Neuropsychologia, 38,* 11–21.

Garavan, H., Ross, T. J., Murphy, K., Poche, R. A. P., & Stein, E. A. (2002). Dissociable executive functions in the dynamic control of behavior: Inhibition, error detection, and correction. *Neuroimage, 17,* 1820–1829.

Gerstadt, C. L., Hong, Y. J., & Diamond, A. (1994). The relationship between cognition and action: Performance of children 3.5–7 years old on a Stroop-like day-night test. *Cognition, 53,* 129–153.

Goel, V., Grafman, J., Sadato, N., & Hallett, M. (1995). Modeling other minds. *NeuroReport, 6,* 1741–1746.

Goldman-Rakic, P. S. (1987). Circuitry of the prefrontal cortex and the regulation of behavior by representational memory. In F. Plum & V. Mountcastle (Eds.), *Handbook of physi-*

ology, section 1. The nervous system (Vol. 5, pp. 373–417). Bethesda, MD: American Physiological Society.

Gordon, A. C. L., & Olson, D. R. (1998). The relation between acquisition of a theory of mind and the capacity to hold in mind. *Journal of Experimental Child Psychology, 68,* 70–83.

Gruber, O., & von Cramon, D. Y. (2003). The functional neuroanatomy of human working memory revisited: Evidence from 3-T fMRI studies using classical domain-specific interference tasks. *Neuroimage, 19,* 797–809.

Haberecht, M. F., Menon, V., Warsofsky, I. S., White, C. D., Dyer-Friedman, J., Glover, G. H., Neely, E. K., & Reiss, A. L. (2001). Functional neuroanatomy of visuo-spatial working memory in Turner syndrome. *Human Brain Mapping, 14,* 96–107.

Hala, S., Hug, S., & Henderson, A. (2003). Executive functioning and false-belief understanding in preschool children: Two tasks are harder than one. *Journal of Cognition and Development, 4,* 275–298.

Happé, F., Ehlers, S., Fletcher, P., Frith, U., Johansson, M., Gillberg, C., Dolan, R., Frackowiak, R., & Frith, C. (1996). "Theory of mind" in the brain. Evidence from a PET scan study of Asperger syndrome. *NeuroReport, 8,* 197–201.

Hughes, C. (1998). Executive function in preschoolers: Links with theory of mind and verbal ability. *British Journal of Developmental Psychology, 16,* 233–253.

Jenkins, J. M., & Astington, J. W. (1996). Cognitive factors and family structure associated with theory of mind development in young children. *Developmental Psychology, 32,* 70–81.

Kagan, J., Reznick, J. S., Clarke, C., Snidman, N., & Garcia-Coll, C. (1984). Behavioral inhibition to the unfamiliar. *Child Development, 55,* 2212–2225.

Kain, W., & Perner, J. (2003). Do children with ADHD not need their frontal lobes for theory of mind? A review of brain imaging and neuropsychological studies. In M. Brüne, H. Ribbert, & W. Schiefenhövel (Eds.), *The social brain: Evolution and pathology* (pp. 197–230). Chichester, UK: Wiley.

Kanemura, H., Aihara, M., Aoki, S., Araki, T., & Nakazawa, S. (2003). Development of the prefrontal lobe in infants and children: A three-dimensional magnetic resonance volumetric study. *Brain and Development, 25,* 195–199.

Keenan, T. (1998). Memory span as a predictor of false belief understanding. *New Zealand Journal of Psychology, 27,* 36–43.

Klingberg, T., Forssberg, H., & Westerberg, H. (2002). Increased brain activity in frontal and parietal cortex underlies the development of visuospatial working memory capacity during childhood. *Journal of Cognitive Neuroscience, 14,* 1–10.

Kochanska, G., Murray, K., Jacques, T. Y., Koenig, A. L., & Vandegeest, K. A. (1996). Inhibitory control in young children and its role in emerging internalization. *Child Development, 67,* 490–507.

Konishi, S., Nakajima, K., Uchida, I., Kikyo, H., Kameyama, M., & Miyashita, Y. (1999). Common inhibitory mechanism in human inferior prefrontal cortex revealed by event-related functional MRI. *Brain, 122,* 981–991.

Kwon, H., Menon, V., Eliez, S., Warsofsky, I. S., White, C. D., Dyer-Friedman, J., Taylor, A. K., Glover G. H., & Reiss, A. L. (2001). Functional neuroanatomy of visuospatial working memory in fragile X syndrome: Relation to behavioral and molecular measures. *American Journal of Psychiatry, 158,* 1040–1051.

Kwon, H., Reiss, A. L., & Menon, V. (2002). Neural basis of protracted developmental changes in visuo-spatial working memory. *Proceedings of the National Academy of Science, 99,* 13336–13341.

Langleben, D. D., Austin, G., Krikorian, G., Ridlehuber, H. W., Goris, M. L., & Strauss, H. W. (2001). Interhemispheric asymmetry of regional cerebral blood flow in prepubescent boys with attention deficit hyperactivity disorder. *Nuclear Medicine Communications, 22,* 1333–1340.

Luna, B., Thulborn, K. R., Munoz, D. P., Merriam, E. P., Garver, K. E., Minshew, N. J., Keshavan, M. S., Genovese, C. R., Eddy, W. F., & Sweeney, J. A. (2001). Maturation of widely distributed brain function subserves cognitive development. *Neuroimage, 13,* 786–793.

McCabe, K., Houser, D., Ryan, L., Smith, V., & Trouard, T. (2001). A functional imaging study of cooperation in two-person reciprocal exchange. *Proceedings of the National Academy of Science, 98,* 11832–11835.

Miller, E. K., & Cohen, J. D. (2001). An integrative theory of prefrontal cortex function. *Annual Review of Neuroscience, 24,* 167–202.

Moll, J., de Oliveira-Souza, R., Bramati, I. E., & Grafman, J. (2002). Functional networks in emotional moral and nonmoral social judgments. *Neuroimage, 16,* 696–703.

Nelson, C. A., Monk, C. S., Lin, J., Carver, L. J., Thomas, K. M., & Truwit, C. L. (2000). Functional neuroanatomy of spatial working memory in children. *Developmental Psychology, 36,* 109–116.

Nieuwenhuys, R., Voogd, J., & van Huijzen, Chr. (1991). *Das Zentralnervensystem des Menschen.* 2. vollständig überarbeitete. Auflage, Berlin.

O'Doherty, J., Kringelbach, M. I., Rolls, E. T., Hornak, J. & Andrews, C. (2001). Abstract reward and punishment representations in the human orbitofrontal cortex. *Nature Neuroscience, 4,* 95–102.

Öngür, D., & Price, J. L. (2000). The organization of networks within the orbital and medial prefrontal cortex of rats, monkeys and humans. *Cerebral Cortex, 10,* 206–219.

Pandya, D. N., & Yeterian, E. H. (1998). Comparison of prefrontal architecture and connections. In A. C. Roberts, T. W. Robbins, & L. Weisskrantz (Eds.), *The prefrontal cortex: Executive and cognitive functions* (pp. 51–66). Oxford, UK: Oxford University Press.

Perner, J., & Lang, B. (1999). Development of theory of mind and executive control. *Trends in Cognitive Science, 3,* 337–344.

Perner, J., Kain, W., & Barchfeld, P. (2002). Executive control and higher-order theory of mind in children at risk of ADHD. *Infant and Child Development, 11,* 141–158.

Perner, J., Lang, B., & Kloo, B. (2002). Theory of mind and self-control: More than a common problem of inhibition. *Child Development, 73,* 752–767.

Petrides, M. (1994). Frontal lobes and working memory: Evidence from investigations of the effects of cortical excisions in nonhuman primates. In F. Boller & J. Grafman (Eds.), *Handbook of neuropsychology* (pp. 59–84). Amsterdam: Elsevier Science.

Petrides, M., & Pandya, D. N. (1999). Dorsolateral prefrontal cortex: Comparative cytoarchitectonic analysis in the human and the macaque brain and corticocortical connection patterns. *European Journal of Neuroscience, 11,* 1011–1036.

Petrides, M., & Pandya, D. N. (2001). Comparative cytoarchitectonic analysis of the human and macaque ventrolateral prefrontal cortex and corticocortical connection patterns in the monkey. *European Journal of Neuroscience, 16,* 291–310.

Phan, K. L., Wager, T., Taylor, S. F., & Liberzon, I. (2002). Functional neuroanatomy of emotion: A meta-analysis of emotion activation studies in PET and fMRI. *Neuroimage, 16,* 331–348.

Reiss, A. L., Abrams, M. T., Singer, H. S., Ross, J. L., & Denckla, M. B. (1996). Brain development, gender and IQ in children: A volumetric imaging study. *Brain, 119,* 1763–1774.

Rolls, E. T. (2000). The orbitofrontal cortex and reward. *Cerebral Cortex, 10,* 284–294.

Rolls, E. T. (2002). The functions of the orbitofrontal cortex. In D. T. Stuss & R. T. Knight (Eds.), *Principles of frontal lobe function* (pp. 354–375). New York: Oxford University Press.

Rothbart, M. K. (1989). Temperament and development. In G. A. Kohnstamm, J. E. Bates, & M. K. Rothbart (Eds.), *Temperament in childhood* (pp. 187–247). Chichester, UK: Wiley.

Rubia, K., Overmeyer, S., Taylor, E., Brammer, M., Williams, S. C. R., Simmons, A., & Bullmore, E. T. (1999). Hypofrontality in attention deficit hyperactivity disorder during higher-order motor control: A study with functional MRI. *American Journal of Psychiatry, 156,* 891–896.

Rubia, K., Russell, T., Overmeyer, S., Brammer, M. J., Bullmore, E. T., Sharma, T., Simmons, A., Williams, S. C. R., Giampietro, V., Andrew, C. M., & Taylor, E. (2001). Mapping motor inhibition: Conjunctive brain activations across different versions of go/no-go and stop tasks. *Neuroimage, 13,* 250–261.

Ruby, P., & Decety, J. (2003). What do you believe vs. what do you think they believe: A neuroimaging study of conceptual perspective-taking. *European Journal of Neuroscience, 17,* 1–6.

Russell, T. A., Rubin, K., Bullmore, E. T., Soni, W., Suckling, J., Brammer, M. J., Simmons, A., Williams, S. C. R., & Sharma, T. (2000). Exploring the social brain in schizophrenia: Left prefrontal underactivation during mental state attribution. *American Journal of Psychiatry, 157*, 2040–2042.

Sanfey, A. G., Rilling, J. K., Aronson, J. A., Nystrom, L. E., & Cohen, J. D. (2003). The neural basis of economic decision-making in the ultimatum game. *Science, 300*, 1755–1758.

Schaefer, A., Collette, F., Philippot, P., Van der Linden, M., Laureys, S., Delfiore, G., Degueldre, C., Maquet, P., Luxen, A., & Salmon, E. (2003). Neural correlates of «hot» and «cold» emotional processing: A multilevel approach to the functional anatomy of emotion. *Neuroimage, 18*, 938–949.

Smith, E. E., & Jonides, J. (1997). Working memory: A view from neuroimaging. *Cognitive Psychology, 33*, 5–42.

Smith, E. E., Jonides, J., Koeppe, R. A. (1996). Dissociating verbal and spatial working memory using PET. *Cerebral Cortex, 6*, 11–20.

Sowell, E. R., Delis, D., Stiles, J., & Jernigan, T. L. (2001). Improved memory functioning and frontal lobe maturation between childhood and adolescence: A structural MRI study. *Journal of the International Neuropsychological Society, 7*, 312–322.

Tamm, L., Menon, V., Johnston, C. K., Hessl, D. R., & Reiss, A. L. (2002). fMRI study of cognitive interference processing in females with fragile X syndrome. *Journal of Cognitive Neuroscience, 14*, 160–171.

Tamm, L., Menon, V., & Reiss, A. L. (2002). Maturation of brain function associated with response inhibition. *Journal of the American Academy of Child and Adolescent Psychiatry, 41*, 1231–1238.

Thomas, K. M., King, S. W., Franzen, P. L., Welsh, T., Berkowitz, A. L., Noll, D. C., Birmaher, V., & Casey, B. J. (1999). A developmental functional MRI study of spatial working memory. *Neuroimage, 10*, 327–338.

Vaidya, C. J., Austin, G., Kirkorian, G., Ridlehuber, H. W., Desmond, J. E., Glover, G. H., & Gabrieli, J. D. E. (1998). Selective effects of methylphenidate in attention deficit hyperactivity disorder: A functional magnetic resonance study. *Proceedings of the Nationall Academy of Sciences of the United States of America, 95*, 14494–14499.

van Veen, V., Cohen, J. D., Botvinick, M. M., Stenger, V. A., & Carter, C.S. (2001). Anterior cingulate cortex, conflict monitoring, and levels of processing. *Neuroimage, 14*, 1302–1308.

Vogeley, K., Bussfeld, P., Newen, A., Herrmann, S., Happé, F., Falkai, P., Maier, W., Shah, N. J., Fink, G. R., & Zilles, K. (2001). Mind reading: Neural mechanisms of theory of mind and self-perspective. *Neuroimage, 14*, 170–181.

Wicker, B., Perrett, D. I., Baron-Cohen, S., & Decety, J. (2003). Being the target of another's emotion: A PET study. *Neuropsychologia, 41*, 139–146.

Winston, J. S., Strange, B. A., O'Doherty, J., & Dolan, R. J. (2002). Automatic and intentional brain responses during evaluation of trustworthiness of faces. *Nature Neuroscience, 5*, 277–283.

Chapter 10

Theory of Mind, Working Memory, and Verbal Ability in Preschool Children: The Proposal of a Relay Race Model of the Developmental Dependencies

Marcus Hasselhorn
Claudia Mähler
Dietmar Grube
Georg-August-Universität Göttingen, Germany

Research on theory of mind (ToM) has expanded vastly during the last 20 years. Since the discovery of young preschoolers' problems with the understanding of false belief by Wimmer and Perner (1983), more than 750 studies have been reported. The issues within this research field have somewhat changed during all these years. Whereas in the beginning the description of the phenomena dominated research, later the theoretical explanation of the typical behavior of preschoolers, and especially of the characteristic developmental changes at this age, became most important. The analysis of the typical deficits found in autistic children (e.g., Baron-Cohen, Leslie, & Frith, 1985) contributed a great deal to the latter focus of research. Only recently has research begun to identify aspects of cognitive development that develop concurrently with the emergence of children's ToM and, thus, could be cognitive correlates or even precursors of ToM development. Among the cognitive areas that are being explored, as to what extent they contribute to or even determine ToM development, executive functioning plays an important role (cf. Moses, Carlson, & Sabbagh, this volume). Executive functioning comprises several cognitive functions, such as inhibition, working memory, cognitive flexibility, and planning processes—taken together, different aspects of monitoring and control of thought. It has been argued that especially working memory and inhibition are necessary to solve standard false belief tasks, which are a central measure of ToM (Moses et al., this volume; Perner & Lang, 1999). Substantial correlations were reported between ToM and central executive tasks, such as backward memory span, whereas possible influences, such as age, receptive vocabulary, or memory span (phonological working memory), were held constant (Davis & Pratt, 1996). Measures of inhibition control also proved to be related to several ToM tasks (Carlson & Moses, 2001). Although all of these relationships are both conceptually and statistically very convincing, other possible candidates that may influence ToM development must be taken into account. The studies presented in the present chapter were dedicated to this latter aim. They were undertaken to explore the developmental dependencies of ToM, phonological working memory, and verbal ability in preschool children.

ToM is defined as the capacity to impute mental states to oneself and to others (Premack & Woodruff, 1978). It has been investigated across a variety of tasks assessing concepts such as false belief understanding, appearance-reality distinction, level of perspective taking, or deception. The synchronous development usually is amazing; nevertheless, the studies presented here concentrate only on the understanding of false belief. An important reason for this decision is that there is evidence for a developmental change during the preschool years. Not only the emergence of the capacity at the age of about 3.5 years but also the improvement of ToM by the end of the preschool years or the beginning of the school years are of interest to the present studies.

A strong consensus has been established among ToM researchers that children first become capable of understanding mental states such as false belief between 3 and 4 years of age. The understanding of second-order embedded mental states, however, requires the capacity to represent not only a person's perception of a social situation but also different individuals' concern about the other's mental states. There is much less agreement about the age at which this capacity is within the competence of young children. In the original studies by Perner and Wimmer (1985), using the well-known story of the ice cream van, children succeeded in attributing second-order false belief at about 6 or 7 years. Data in later studies reveal that, under certain conditions, children younger than the age of 7 years are able to understand second-order false belief. Reducing the information-processing demands in the tasks, Sullivan, Zaitchik, and Tager-Flusberg (1994) made even younger preschoolers successful at solving the second-order false belief problem. Yet the question remains open as to what exactly causes the 1- or 2-year lag between the understanding of first- and second-order false belief. Exploring the developmental dependencies between ToM and other cognitive capacities, such as working memory and verbal abilities, may help to explain the age differences in the understanding of first- and second-order false belief.

During the last couple of years, the relationship between young children's false belief performance and various basic cognitive competencies has been explored by several researchers. In a number of studies, close relationships could be demonstrated between the performance in typical ToM tasks and measures of verbal intelligence (Schneider, Perner, Bullock, Stefanek, & Ziegler, 1999), vocabulary (Hughes, 1998), and syntactic abilities (Astington & Jenkins, 1999). Although these results are compatible with the view that the development of ToM depends on language, there are at least two alternative interpretations for the reported correlational relationships. The first alternative is that the causality is in the opposite direction. That is, it might be that it is not ToM development that depends on language but rather language development that depends on ToM. The other alternative is that both ToM development and language development do depend on a third factor.

To rule out the validity of the first alternative, Astington and Jenkins (1999) started a longitudinal study with children 3.5 years old. ToM was assessed with first-order false belief tasks and with appearance-reality tasks. Language ability was assessed with a standardized measure of reception and production of syntax and semantics. Earlier language abilities—especially syntax competence—predicted later ToM test performance, although the authors statistically controlled for earlier ToM test scores, but earlier ToM did not predict later language test performance (controlling for earlier language). The authors provided these findings as an empirical argument for their position that language is fundamental to ToM development. However, although this interpretation seems rational, the dependency of both language and ToM on a third factor was explicitly mentioned by Astington and Jenkins as a further possibility that was not ruled out by the results of their own study.

One such third factor that may determine both ToM and language development is phonological working memory. It is obvious that solving false belief tasks, especially at the second-order level, puts high demands on information processing. Keeping in mind the most important details of the false belief story is a necessary precondition of understanding such complex problems. Reducing the information-processing demands of the false belief tasks—as Sullivan et al. (1994) did in their study—made it possible for younger children to come up with correct solutions. Thus, a dependency between phonological working memory and ToM development is very reasonable.

Other researchers reported close relationships between phonological working memory and language acquisition in the early childhood years. Baddeley, Gathercole, and Papagno (1998) reviewed a series of longitudinal studies with children at preschool age (4 to 6 years), where up to 19% of the variance in vocabulary could be explained by memory span performance. The repetition of spoken nonwords, which is one of the most preferred measures of phonological working memory, explained 10% (at 3 years of age) to 28% (at 6 years of age) of the variance in vocabulary—even after controlling statistically for general nonverbal intelligence. Although such correlational connections do not inevitably implicate a causal influence of phonological working memory on vocabulary acquisition, it is indicative of a close relationship between the two areas.

The following chapter consists of three sections. First, two studies are reported,[1] both aimed at the investigation of age differences and covariations in ToM (false belief understanding), working memory, and verbal abilites. Age differences in the crucial variables are reported within the description of the studies, whereas correlational analyses are documented in the second part. The second section deals with the question of what ToM development is the development of. In this section, we especially analyze the impact of phonological working memory and verbal abilities on the developmental increase in children's first- and second-order false belief performance between about 4 and 6 years of age. Finally, in the third section, a hypothetical model is provided to offer a preliminary description of the developmental dependencies between ToM, phonological working memory, and verbal abilities.

TWO STUDIES ON THE DEVELOPMENT OF ToM, PHONOLOGICAL WORKING MEMORY, AND VERBAL ABILITIES

Study 1

Subjects.   Participants were 30 younger children with a mean age of 3 years, 9 months (range 38–53 months), and 30 older preschoolers at the mean age of 5 years, 2 months (range 55–71 months). Children were tested individually in their kindergarten in one or two sessions. They had to complete a battery of tasks described in the next section.

Measures.   To investigate the developmental changes concerning false belief understanding in the preschool years, we administered both a first- and a second-order false belief task (typical unexpected change of location tasks).

The story told to the children in testing first-order false belief was about two mice; one of them, Max, has cheese. He eats some and puts the rest in a box in front of his hole before he goes to sleep. While he is sleeping, his friend Frieda comes and transfers the cheese into a box in front of her own hole. Max wakes up and comes out of his hole. Children are then asked the critical test questions:

First-order ignorance: "Does Max know where the cheese is right now?"

---

[1] Many thanks to Sassa Kittelmann, Lothar Steinke, Ulrike Oberschelp, and Vivien Kurtz for their help in collecting the data.

First-order false belief: "Where does Max think the cheese is?"
Justification: "Why does he think that?"

While the story is told, the experimenter plays the little scene out and makes sure the child has got the story right using the following questions: Where is the cheese now (beginning)? Do you remember where Max put the cheese? Where is the cheese now (end)? Did Max see that the cheese was put into the other box?

For every correct answer to the test questions, the child was credited a point, so the maximum for a correct answer to the ignorance, the false belief question, and the justification was 3 points.

The second-order false belief task was administered to the children in a similar way. Because we had only preschool children in the sample, we decided to use one of the stories published by Sullivan et al. (1994), which was supposedly not too difficult for that crucial age. In the story of the birthday puppy, a young boy hopes that he will get a puppy for his birthday, but his mother, who wants to surprise him with a puppy, misinforms him by telling him that he will get a nice toy. Then the boy goes out to play, and on the way he passes through the basement to get his roller skates and finds the puppy. He is very excited, but his mother does not know what has happened. Then the grandmother calls on the telephone to find out what time the birthday party is. She asks the mother if the boy knows what his mother really got him for his birthday. (Now the children are asked second-order ignorance question: "What does Mom say to Grandma?" (p. 402). Then she asks the mother what the boy believes he will get for his birthday. (The second-order false belief question follows: "What does Mom say to Grandma?" and finally the justification question is asked: "Why does Mom say that?" [p. 402]).

Of course this story is also played out for the children and accompanied by several probe questions and memory aids.

All the tasks described later (with the exception of the nonword repetition task) that were administered to assess phonological working memory and verbal ability were taken from the Wiener Entwicklungstest (Kastner-Koller & Deimann, 1998). This is a German and Austrian test of general development for children at preschool age (3 to 6 years) and consists of 13 subtests assessing different aspects of development (motor development, visual perception, memory, cognitive development, language development). For the present study, measures of memory and language development were chosen.

In the digit span task, children heard acoustically presented series of digits, beginning with two digits and continuing up to six digits. When a child failed at an item of any given length, he or she was given a second chance with another version of the same length. Only when both items of the same length were not repeated correctly was the task finished. The maximum number of digits (i.e., the longest sequence) repeated correctly was taken as a score of memory span.

In the nonword repetition task—a German version constructed by Hasselhorn and Körner (1997)—children heard 18 wordlike nonwords consisting of two, three, and four syllables, which they had to repeat immediately. The number of correctly repeated nonwords constituted the nonword repetition score.

Three subtests of the Wiener Entwicklungstest (Kastner-Koller & Deimann, 1998) were given to the children to assess verbal abilities, two of them measuring vocabulary and the third testing the understanding of syntactic information. The first task was called Explain Words, in which the child was asked to explain 10 different words in his or her own words. Following the test criteria, the children were credited 0, 1, or 2 points for every explanation, depending on the quality of the answer. The second indicator of vocabulary was the Contrasts task; here, the children heard 15 sentences that were begun by the experimenter and had to be finished by the child (e.g., "Sugar is sweet, lemon is . . ."; "The sun shines at daytime; the moon shines at . . ."). The number of correct answers was used as the relevant test score. The understanding of syntactic information was assessed by a subtest called Puppet Play. With given puppets (a family, a dog, and a wooden block), the child was to play out a little scene that showed the meaning of a sentence given by the experimenter (e.g., "The dog is given food by the girl"; "The dog bites the father, who is holding the boy"). A total of 13 sentences were read to the child, with every correct play being credited with a point.

Results

Because children's performance with regard to ToM was of special interest, we analyzed their answers to the different questions in the first-order as well as in the second-order false belief task in more detail. Figure 10.1 presents the percentages of children with correct answers on both of these tasks, separated by question and age. As can easily be seen, older children outperformed the younger ones in all respects. Moreover, the age differences were very similar in both the first-order and the second-order false belief task.

Given these results, we decided to compute a sum score for both first- and second-order false belief understanding (see Sullivan et al., 1994, for similar scoring). The maximum of this score is 3 points if all three test questions are answered correctly. In a next step of analysis, we used the sum scores of all the scales described in the method section and examined whether there were age differences in all the measures used to assess ToM, phonological working memory, and verbal abilities. In Table 10.1, means and standard deviations are presented for all measures by age, and also t-values are provided, which were estimated to test whether there were substantial age differences in all areas under scrutiny.

As expected, age differences were found for all variables representing abilities with regard to ToM, phonological working memory, and verbal ability. Thus, the data collected in Study 1 seem to be useful to further

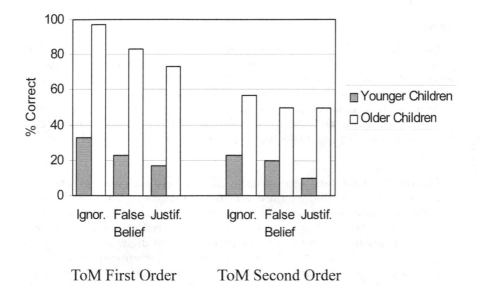

FIG. 10.1. Study 1: Younger and older children's percentage of correct answers to ignorance, false belief, and justification questions for ToM—first and second order.

explore the relationships between all three cognitive areas to get more insight into the causal influences and developmental dependencies of ToM, phonological working memory, and verbal abilities during the preschool years. However, the language subtests taken from the Wiener Entwicklungstest (Kastner-Koller & Deimann, 1998) in Study 1 do not seem to be typical with regard to the assessment of children's syntactical language abilities. We therefore decided to conduct another study to replicate Study 1 with an amplification of the language measures.

TABLE 10.1
Study 1: Means (SD) of Measures of Phonological Working Memory
(WM), Syntax (S), Vocabulary (V), and Theory of Mind (ToM)

	Younger Children	Older Children	t(58)
WM: Digit Span	2.80 (0.71)	3.87 (0.68)	5.92**
WM: Nonword Repetition	10.57 (4.30)	13.40 (3.42)	2.82**
S: Understanding	7.80 (2.68)	10.03 (1.88)	3.73**
V: Explaining	7.43 (3.05)	10.33 (2.87)	3.80**
V: Contrasts	7.77 (3.54)	11.70 (2.59)	4.91**
ToM: First order	0.73 (1.01)	2.53 (0.86)	7.41**
ToM: Second order	0.53 (0.90)	1.57 (1.28)	3.62**

Note. **p < .01.

Study 2

Subjects. Again, participants were two groups of preschoolers: 30 younger children with a mean age of 4 years, 1 month, with a range between 40 and 55 months, and 33 older preschoolers at the mean age of 6 years, 1 month, with a range between 65 and 79 months.

As in Study 1, children were tested individually in their kindergarten in one or two sessions and had to complete the test battery, this time consisting of more adequate tasks for assessing the different aspects of verbal abilities.

Measures. First- and second-order false belief tasks were exactly the same as in Study 1. Phonological working memory again was assessed by digit span and by the German nonword repetition test (Hasselhorn & Körner, 1997). The digit span task was administered in a slightly different way in this study. Children reproduced series of digits presented with a rate of one digit per second. The set size was incremented after four trials of a given set size. Subjects were assigned a span score according to the longest set size they were able to repeat. The nonword repetition task also was very similar to that used in Study 1. However, to avoid ceiling effects, a more difficult version of the Hasselhorn and Körner task was administered.

To assess language, or verbal ability, four different subscales were used from German tests of language development. Two subtests were chosen from the Heidelberger Sprachentwicklungstest (Grimm & Schöler, 1991); both claimed to be tests of children's morphosyntactical abilities. In the first one, named Imitation of Grammatical Structures, children had to repeat grammatically complex sentences (e.g., "This is the man, whose son is ill"). The answers were rated 0, 1, or 2 points depending on the exactness of the repetition. The maximum score was 24.

In the second task, children had to understand the grammatical structure of sentences including an action and had to demonstrate the content of the action with the help of wooden puppets and animals (e.g., "Before the dog runs, the horse jumps"); this task was similar to the Puppet Play task in Study 1. A total of 17 sentences were given as long as the child followed the directions; after a series of four mistakes, the task was stopped. Every correct demonstration was credited with 1 point (maximum 17).

A third subtest for assessing syntactical ability was taken from a standardized German test of language abilities in preschool years (Kindersprachtest für das Vorschulalter, KISTE; Häuser, Kasielke, & Scheidereiter, 1994). In the chosen subscale, the child's task was to identify grammatical inconsistencies within a sentence and to repeat the sentence in the grammatically correct form. Twenty sentences were presented, 14 being grammatically inconsistent and 6 being distractor items. A maximum score of 14 correct answers could be received.

Finally, expressive vocabulary was also assessed by a standardized German vocabulary test (Aktiver Wortschatztest, AWST; Kiese & Kozielsky,

1996) for children from 3 to 6 years of age. Children had to name objects presented by means of line drawings. The original test consisted of 82 items, but a short form of 40 items was given to the children. For every correctly named item, children received a point, the maximum score being 40.

Results

The same steps of data analysis that were done in Study 1 were also done in Study 2. Thus, we first looked for age differences in the children's first-order as well as second-order ignorance, false belief, and justification. Figure 10.2 contains the percentage of children in both age groups who correctly answered the different test questions.

As we expected, the results of Study 1 were replicated. The older children performed better on all test questions. Furthermore, as reported in the literature, attributing ignorance is easier than attributing false belief, and justification is most difficult. This is true for first- and second-order problems for both younger and older children. However, despite the obvious similarities of the children's answers to the false belief questions in both studies, there are also apparent dissimilarities, especially with regard to the younger children's first-order false belief performance. The percentage of younger children's correct answers was much lower in Study 1, compared with Study 2. Because the same false belief tasks were administered to the children in both studies, the difference between the results might best be

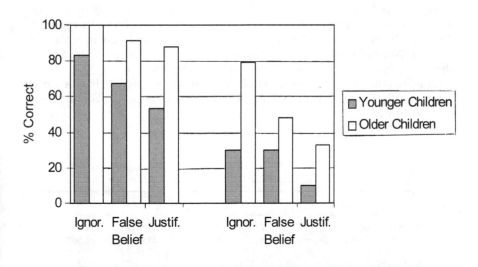

FIG. 10.2. Study 2: Younger and older children's percentage of correct answers to ignorance, false belief, and justification questions for ToM—first and second order.

explained by the fact that the younger children in Study 1 were on average about 4 months younger than the younger children in Study 2. Given the tremendous empirical evidence that an appropriate first-order false belief behavior emerges in the second half of the 4th year of life, these rather small age differences between Study 1 and Study 2 may have produced such great differences in the percentage of children with correct answers.

If we compare our results to other results reported in the literature, we must admit that our children did not succeed as well as expected. Not all of the children in the 4-year-old group passed the first-order false belief question (only 66 %), and also the sum score reveals no complete understanding. The older children did not have general problems with first-order false belief but still did not justify their answers at a perfect level. Much variation resulted for the second-order false belief problems. Only a few 4-year-olds, but nevertheless one third of the 6-year-olds, were able to answer second-order questions correctly. For second-order mental states, the older children are the interesting group. Their sum score makes evident that they also cannot completely solve this kind of problem. Only half of them made no mistake when answering the second-order false belief question.

Performance on second-order false belief tasks of the sample in the study by Sullivan et al. (1994) was actually better than in our study. But, taken together, our results represent a typical finding: They show the lag of almost 2 years between the understanding of first- and second-order false belief.

Table 10.2 presents the means and standard deviations of the ToM sum scores as well as the phonological working memory and verbal ability measures, separated by age. Again, the pattern of results with regard to these analyses is a complete replication of the findings documented for Study 1. Not only ToM but also phonological working memory and verbal ability significantly increase between ages 4 and 6 years.

This increase of cognitive capabilities is not unexpected. It is a rather trivial result that there is developmental increase of performance in almost every cognitive domain. However, the question remains as to what devel-

TABLE 10.2

Study 2: Means (SD) of Measures of Phonological Working Memory
(WM), Syntax (S), Vocabulary (V), and Theory of Mind (ToM)

	Younger Children	Older Children	t(61)
WM: Digit span	3.07 (0.87)	3.94 (0.79)	4.18**
WM: Nonword repetition	8.07 (4.35)	13.03 (4.05)	4.69**
S: Imitation	7.93 (6.02)	16.88 (6.22)	5.79**
S: Understanding	8.73 (3.33)	13.27 (2.32)	6.32**
S: Inconsistencies	10.93 (4.71)	16.03 (4.01)	4.64**
V: Object naming	21.70 (6.10)	31.97 (5.58)	6.98**
ToM: First order	2.03 (1.16)	2.79 (0.60)	3.29**
ToM: Second order	0.70 (0.95)	1.61 (1.12)	3.45**

Note. **p < .01.

opmental relationships do exist between the age increases in these different areas of cognitive functioning. Exploring the developmental dependencies between these areas might help us to better understand what ToM development is the development of. Thus, we further analyzed the data of both studies to explore whether ToM development at least partly is the outcome of phonological working memory development, verbal abilities development, or both.

THE CONTRIBUTION OF VERBAL ABILITY AND PHONOLOGICAL WORKING MEMORY TO ToM DEVELOPMENT

As we referred to in the introduction, several researchers reported substantial correlations between children's performance in ToM tasks and their performance in other cognitive areas, such as language and working memory. If there are true developmental dependencies between different cognitive domains, substantial correlations should be observed among related variables.

To examine whether this prerequisite of developmental dependencies also existed in our data, in a next step of analyses we explored the relationships among phonological working memory, verbal ability, and ToM by calculating the Pearson correlations of all the measures separately for both age groups in Study 1 and Study 2. These product-moment correlations are shown in Tables 10.3 and 10.4.

As might have been anticipated because of the low variability of first-order false belief performance in both studies and both age groups, most of the measures did not correlate significantly with first-order ToM. There were only two exceptions; both were found in Study 1 for the younger children. In this subsample, significant correlations with first-order false belief performance were observed for digit span as well as for explaining. That is, although ToM performance within the age range focused on in our studies scarcely is related to phonological working memory and verbal ability, such relationships could be found for the group of younger children in Study 1. No such relationships were found in either of the studies for the children of the older age group, nor were they found for the younger children in Study 2. Although alternative interpretations are possible, we think that relationships between first-order ToM, phonological working memory, and verbal ability are restricted to children younger than 4 years of age. Compatible with this interpretation is that the younger children in Study 1 were about 4 months younger on average than the younger children in Study 2. Given that our interpretation is correct, it might be that developmental dependencies between first-order false belief performance and working memory or verbal ability are restricted to the age range where the ToM core competence emerges.

However, second-order false belief performance was significantly correlated with vocabulary in the younger sample in Study 1 and the

TABLE 10.3
Study 1: Partial Correlations (With Age Partialed Out) Between Measures
of Phonological Working Memory (WM), Syntax (S), Vocabulary (V),
and Theory of Mind (ToM), Separated for Younger and Older Children

	1	2	3	4	5	6	7
Younger Children (n = 30)							
1. WM: Digit Span	—	.61**	.15	.49**	.71**	.41*	.28
2. WM: Nonword Repetition		—	.29	.52**	.68**	.28	.30
3. S: Understanding			—	.09	.16	−.01	−.12
4. V: Explaining				—	.66**	.42*	.37*
5. V: Contrasts					—	.33	.44*
6. ToM: First order						—	.52**
7. ToM: Second Order							—
Older Children (n = 30)							
1. WM: Digit span	—	.41*	.12	.31	.42*	−.01	.37*
2. WM: Nonword repetition		—	.10	.29	.33	.13	.21
3. S: Understanding			—	.11	.04	.17	.30
4. V: Explaining				—	.46**	.15	.39*
5. V: Contrasts					—	.09	.49**
6. ToM: First order						—	.09
7. ToM: Second order							—

Note. *p < .05. **p < .01.

correlation barely missed significance in Study 2 (r = .35; p < .06). In addition, second-order false belief performance was significantly related to phonological working memory and nearly all language abilities in the samples of the 5- to 6-year-olds. The clear consistency of these results between both studies encourages us to provide an interpretation of this pattern of results, too. Obviously, at the age of about 6 years, strong relationships do exist between second-order false belief performance and both measures of working memory as well as measures of verbal ability. Applying the same kind of reasoning we used for the interpretation of the first-order false belief data, one might argue that 6 years is quite a sensible age period for the emergence of second-order false belief abilities. Thus, those children who are developmentally more advanced with regard to phonological working memory and language abilities are also more advanced in the related ToM emergence.

Although we have interpreted the correlational patterns reported so far in terms of a functional contribution of verbal abilities and phonological working memory in the emergence of ToM, there is still room for alternative interpretations as well as for alternative empirical analyses of the data. To explore whether the reported developmental increase in second-order false belief performance can be explained in terms of the development of working memory or verbal abilities, we ran a series of analyses of covariance on the second-order false belief data, with age as a between-

TABLE 10.4
Study 2: Partial Correlations (With Age Partialed Out) Between Measures
of Phonological Working Memory (WM), Syntax (S), Vocabulary (V),
and Theory of Mind (ToM), Separated for Younger and Older Children

	1	2	3	4	5	6	7	8
Younger Children (n = 30)								
1. WM: Digit span	—	.58**	.49**	.44*	.59**	.51**	.22	−.13
2. WM: Nonword repetition		—	.40*	.53**	.36*	.25	.01	.01
3. S: Imitation			—	.40*	.61**	.65**	.00	.18
4. S: Understanding				—	.44*	.55**	.30	.34
5. S: Inconsistencies					—	.53**	.28	−.02
6. V: Object naming						—	.27	.35
7. ToM: First order							—	.27
8. ToM: Second order								—
Older Children (n = 33)								
1. WM: Digit span	—	.55**	.56**	.21	.57**	.33	.03	.58**
2. WM: Nonword repetition		—	.30	.22	.54**	.36*	.12	.44**
3. S: Imitation			—	.38*	.72**	.52**	−.07	.50**
4. S: Understanding				—	.43*	.63**	.15	.28
5. S: Inconsistencies					—	.64**	−.06	.62**
6. V: Object naming						—	.08	.37*
7. ToM: First order							—	.08
8. ToM: Second order								—

Note. *$p < .05$. **$p < .01$.

subject factor and each of the other measures used in our study as covariates. These series of analyses provided us with two pieces of information for all covariates. The first piece of information is about the relevance of the relationship between the ability, assessed by the covariate, and second-order false belief performance across age groups. The second piece of information concerns whether the developmental increase in second-order false belief performance depends on the addressed covariate or not. Tables 10.5 and 10.6 present the results of these analyses for the data from Study 1 and Study 2, respectively.

As can easily be determined from Table 10.5, with the exception of the measure for the understanding of syntactic information, all covariates significantly contributed to second-order false belief performance across age groups. However, for only two of the measures, namely digit span (working memory) and contrasts (vocabulary), an elimination of the second-order false belief age difference was revealed by controlling it statistically as a covariate. This pattern of results confirms the view of high developmental dependencies of ToM, phonological working memory, and verbal ability within the age range under scrutiny. Moreover, this view was also supported by the results of Study 2, presented in Table 10.6. In this study, all used measures of phonological working memory and

TABLE 10.5
Study 1: Results of Analyses of Covariance Regarding Theory of Mind—
Second Order: Contribution of the Covariate to ToM
and Elimination of the Age Difference of ToM

Covariate	Covariate Contributes Significantly to ToM		Control of Covariate Eliminates ToM Age Difference	
Working memory				
Digit span	Yes	$F(1,57) = 10.25*$	Yes	$F(1,57) = 1.24$
Nonword repetition	Yes	$F(1,57) = 7.94*$	No	$F(1,57) = 6.83*$
Verbal ability				
S: Understanding	No	$F(1,57) = 2.04$	No	$F(1,57) = 7.04*$
V: Explaining	Yes	$F(1,57) = 9.10*$	No	$F(1,57) = 4.47*$
V: Contrasts	Yes	$F(1,57) = 18.23*$	Yes	$F(1,57) = 1.33$

Note. F value of the age difference in ToM—second order (ANOVA): $F(1,58) = 13.12$.
$*p < .05$.

TABLE 10.6
Study 2: Results of Analyses of Covariance Regarding Theory of Mind—
Second Order: Contribution of the Covariate to ToM
and Elimination of the Age Difference of ToM

Covariate	Covariate Contributes Significantly to ToM		Control of Covariate Eliminates ToM Age Difference	
Working Memory				
Digit span	Yes	$F(1,60) = 7.79*$	Yes	$F(1,60) = 3.56$
Nonword repetition	Yes	$F(1,60) = 4.18*$	Yes	$F(1,60) = 3.91$
Verbal ability				
S: Imitation	Yes	$F(1,60) = 10.26*$	Yes	$F(1,60) = 1.14$
S: Understanding	Yes	$F(1,60) = 6.40*$	Yes	$F(1,60) = 1.45$
S: Inconsistencies	Yes	$F(1,60) = 7.54*$	Yes	$F(1,60) = 2.94$
V: Object Naming	Yes	$F(1,60) = 10.30*$	Yes	$F(1,60) = 0.39$

Note. F value of the age difference in ToM—second order (ANOVA): $F(1,61) = 11.89$.
$*p < .05$.

verbal ability contributed significantly to second-order false belief across age groups and revealed an elimination of second-order ToM age differences after their statistical control in an analysis of covariance.

In sum, there is a high degree of consistency across the two studies with regard to the impact of phonological working memory and verbal abilities on the developmental increase in children's second-order false belief performance. At the very least, digit span and vocabulary not only contributed significantly to second-order false belief performance, but they also demonstrated good explanatory power to interpret the age differences regarding second-order ToM as a consequence of age-related improvements in phonological working memory and verbal abilities.

This pattern of results is compatible with different interpretations of the developmental dependencies of ToM, phonological working memory, and verbal abilities in the age range under scrutiny. For example, if the emergence of second-order false belief between 4 and 6 years of age was an epiphenomenon of working memory and vocabulary development, then the observed pattern of results would have been expected. However, the results reported might also fit with alternative developmental models of the emergence of ToM. For instance, if developmental increases in phonological working memory cause both vocabulary development as well as second-order ToM development, or if the rise of children's receptive vocabulary between 4 and 6 years of age is followed functionally by related increases in working memory capacity and second-order ToM performance, then the same close relationships between the measures reported in the two studies would have been obtained. To explore which of these alternative developmental scenarios fit best with the data from Study 1 and Study 2, we calculated partial correlations between digit span and second-order ToM performance, with age and vocabulary partialled out on the one hand, and between vocabulary and second-order ToM performance, with age and digit span partialled out on the other hand. Again, a high consistency could be found across the two studies. In Study 1, digit span was not reliably correlated with second-order ToM when vocabulary and age were partialled out, $r(56) = .13$, ns, but vocabulary was significantly related to second-order ToM when digit span and age were partialled out, $r(56) = .35$, $p < .01$. Similarly in Study 2, digit span was no longer related to second-order ToM when vocabulary and age were partialled out, $r(59) = .19$, ns, but vocabulary remained significantly related to second-order ToM when digit span and age were partialled out, $r(59) = .27$, $p < .05$. Although in each study, the two partial correlation coefficients do not differ significantly, the reliability of the correlation between the different vocabulary scores and second-order ToM might be taken as an argument for the position that vocabulary knowledge is the major pacemaker in the developmental relationship between phonological working memory and verbal abilities on the one hand and second-order ToM on the other hand.

Even though we have argued that vocabulary knowledge seems to be the most important pacemaker in the developmental throng of the cognitive capabilities under scrutiny within the age range between 4 and 6 years, we do not believe that phonological working memory development is merely a by-product of vocabulary development. In another recent study from our laboratory (Götze, Hasselhorn, & Kiese-Himmel, 2000), vocabulary knowledge and digit span were tested in a sample of more than 100 children, ranging in age from 3 years, 6 months, to 5 years, 11 months. Although age differences in receptive vocabulary remained significant even when digit span was partialled out, age differences in digit span also proved to be significant even when vocabulary was partialled out. Thus, we prefer thinking about phonological working memory and vocabulary knowledge as two independent sources and resources of ToM development as well as of cognitive development in general during the preschool years.

A RELAY RACE MODEL OF THE DEVELOPMENTAL DEPENDENCIES OF ToM, PHONOLOGICAL WORKING MEMORY, AND VERBAL ABILITY

To encourage a critical discussion about the developmental relationships between ToM, phonological working memory, and verbal ability, we decided to summarize the interpretations of our findings within a hypothetical model of the developmental dependencies between these cognitive areas. Figure 10.3 presents a rough sketch of our model.

The model presented in Fig. 10.3 is a kind of relay race model. One assumption of this model is that very early in the developmental trajectory addressed in this chapter phonological working memory capacity constrains the development of different verbal abilities and thus becomes a major pacemaker of cognitive development in the 2nd and—perhaps—the 3rd year of life. Another assumption inherent to our model is that the area of verbal abilities, especially vocabulary knowledge, takes the baton from phonological working memory at least in the 5th and 6th year of a child's life and plays the part of the major relay runner in the cognitive field during these years.

Although the studies presented in this chapter provide only some empirical evidence for the second assumption of the relay race model, the assumption of the early relay runner function of phonological working memory is supported by a number of studies conducted by Susan Gathercole and her coworkers (Gathercole, Hitch, Service, & Martin, 1997; Gathercole, Willis, Emslie, & Baddeley, 1992) during the last decade. In these studies, the connection between central achievements of language acquisition and phonological working memory were explored in some detail. Especially the acquisition of new words, which is one of the most remarkable phenomena in the acquisition of language, seems to be strongly and bidirectionally related to phonological working memory. In their longi-

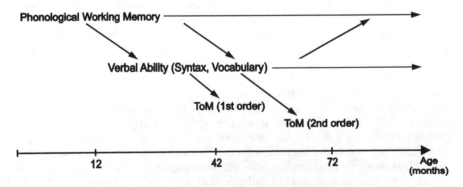

FIG. 10.3. Hypothetical model of developmental dependencies between phonological working memory, verbal abilities, and ToM.

tudinal studies with children of preschool age, Gathercole and coworkers found that 4% to 19% of the variance in vocabulary test scores between the ages of 4 and 6 years can be explained by memory span performance. Moreover, nonword repetition performance was able to explain even higher proportions of vocabulary variance, namely between 10% at the age of 3 years and 28% among the 6-year-olds, even after the statistical control of general nonverbal intelligence. Although those results are of correlational nature and do not necessarily implicate a causal influence of phonological working memory on vocabulary acquisition, Gathercole and colleagues provided further evidence for the assumption that vocabulary acquisition depends on phonological working memory.

For instance, Gathercole et al. (1992) made use of cross-lagged correlational techniques to resolve this issue. Eighty children participated in their longitudinal study, completing a vocabulary test and a nonword repetition test at the ages of 4, 5, 6, and 8 years. Between 4 and 5 years, the connection between the earlier nonword repetition performance and the gain in vocabulary was significantly greater than the corresponding connection between the earlier vocabulary and the gain in the performance of nonword repetition. However, between 5 and 6 and between 6 and 8 years of age the reverse cross-lagged correlational pattern was obtained. These findings indicate a bidirectional developmental dependency between phonological working memory and vocabulary. During early preschool age, the capacity of phonological working memory seems to determine the developmental increase of vocabulary; from the age of 5 years, it appears rather that the available vocabulary seems to influence the further development of working memory efficiency.

In a more recent study with 5-year-old children, Gathercole et al. (1997) reported a strong association between memory span as well as between nonword repetition and the capability to learn word–nonword pairs (e.g. table–bleximus), but not word–word pairs (e.g. table–rabbit).

Further evidence for a strong developmental relationship between phonological working memory and language production is presented by Adams and Gathercole (1995, 1996). Nineteen children with high and 19 children with low phonological memory scores (digit span and nonword repetition) were selected from a cohort of 108 children between the ages of 34 and 37 months. The groups did not differ significantly on the measure of articulation rate. Seven months later, Adams and Gathercole (1995) assessed children`s receptive vocabulary (British Picture Vocabulary Scale) and their natural language, which they produced in another session and in play times with the experimenter and a parent. The differences in phonological store capacity remained stable over the 7 months ($r = .62$). Surprisingly, the differences between the children with low versus high phonological working memory performance in receptive vocabulary proved not to be significant. But in qualitative and quantitative analyses of speech output, reliable differences in performance were found. Children with high phonological working memory performance produced more different words, which refers to their richer productive vocabulary.

FINAL REMARKS

Researchers in cognitive development are used to looking for causal influences within the interplay among different areas of cognitive capabilities. In this regard, the present chapter focused on the developmental dependencies among ToM, phonological working memory, and verbal ability. On the basis of two studies, the interindividual covariability of these areas within certain age groups during the preschool years, as well as the mutual influences on the variability between about 4 and 6 years of age, were explored. Some arguments were proposed to disentangle the threads of the three closely related cognitive areas, from a developmental point of view. As a consequence of the age groups incorporated in our studies, the results were more informative for the emergence of second-order ToM than for first-order ToM.

Overgeneralizing the results from the two studies presented, we provided a hypothetical model of the developmental dependencies between phonological working memory, verbal abilities, and ToM. This model was called a relay race model because its main idea is that the relay runner function within the areas under scrutiny changes as a function of age. According to this model, the baton was carried by phonological working memory during the early preschool years and then delivered to the area of verbal abilities, predominately to vocabulary knowledge. We know that most details of this model are more speculative than evidence based. However, we hope that critical discussions of the proposed model, as well as further studies to test some of the assumptions, will enhance our knowledge of the developmental dependencies of phonological working memory, verbal ability, and ToM in the near future.

REFERENCES

Adams, A.-M., & Gathercole, S. E. (1995). Phonological working memory and speech production in preschool children. *Journal of Speech and Hearing Research, 38*, 403–414.
Adams, A.-M., & Gathercole, S. E. (1996). Phonological working memory and spoken language development in young children. *Quarterly Journal of Experimental Psychology, 49A*, 216–233.
Astington, J. W., & Jenkins, J. M. (1999). A longitudinal study of the relation between language and theory-of-mind development. *Developmental Psychology, 35*, 1311–1320.
Baddeley, A. D., Gathercole, S. E., & Papagno, C. (1998). The phonological loop as a language learning device. *Psychological Review, 105*, 158–173.
Baron-Cohen, S., Leslie, A. M., & Frith, U. (1985). Does the autistic child have a "theory of mind"? *Cognition, 21*, 37–46.
Carlson, S. M., & Moses, L. J. (2001). Individual differences in inhibitory control and children's theory of mind. *Child Development, 72*, 1032–1053.
Davis, H. L., & Pratt, C. (1996). The development of children's theory of mind: The working memory explanation. *Australian Journal of Psychology, 47*, 25–31.
Gathercole, S. E., Hitch, G. J., Service, E., & Martin, A. J. (1997). Phonological short-term memory and new word learning in children. *Developmental Psychology, 33*, 966–979.

Gathercole, S. E., Willis, C., Emslie, H., & Baddeley, A. D. (1992). Phonological working memory and vocabulary development during the early school years: A longitudinal study. *Developmental Psychology, 28,* 887–898.

Götze, B., Hasselhorn, M., & Kiese-Himmel, C. (2000). Phonologisches Arbeitsgedächtnis, Wortschatz und morpho-syntaktische Sprachleistungen im Vorschulalter [Phonological working memory, productive vocabulary knowledge, and morphosyntactical language skills in preschool-age children]. *Sprache und Kognition, 19,* 15–21.

Grimm, H., & Schöler, H. (1991). *Heidelberger Sprachentwicklungstest (H-S-E-T)* [Heidelberg Language Development Test] (2. Aufl.). Göttingen, Germany: Hogrefe.

Hasselhorn, M., & Körner, K. (1997). Nachsprechen von Kunstwörtern: Zum Zusammenhang zwischen Arbeitsgedächtnis und syntaktischen Sprachleistungen bei Sechs- und Achtjährigen [Nonword repetition: The role of working memory in the development of syntactical language abilities]. *Zeitschrift für Entwicklungspsychologie und Pädagogische Psychologie, 29,* 212–224.

Häuser, D., Kasielke, E., & Scheidereiter, U. (1994). *KISTE—Kindersprachtest für das Vorschulalter* [Verbal abilities test for preschool children]. Weinheim, Germany: Beltz.

Hughes, C. (1998). Executive function in preschoolers: Links with theory of mind and verbal ability. *British Journal of Developmental Psychology, 16,* 233–253.

Kastner-Koller, U., & Deimann, P. (1998). *Wiener Entwicklungstest (WET): Ein allgemeines Entwicklungstestverfahren für Kinder von 3 bis 6 Jahren* [Vienna Developmental Test]. Göttingen, Germany: Hogrefe.

Kiese, C., & Kozielski, P. M. (1996). *Aktiver Wortschatztest für 3–6jährige Kinder (AWST 3–6)* [Active vocabulary test for 3- to 6-year-old children] (2. Aufl.). Weinheim, Germany: Beltz.

Perner, J., & Lang, B. (1999). Development of theory of mind and executive control. *Trends in Cognitive Sciences, 3,* 337–344.

Perner, J., & Wimmer, H. (1985). "John *thinks* that Mary *thinks* that . . .": Attributions of second-order beliefs by 5- to 10-year-old children. *Journal of Experimental Child Psychology, 39,* 437–471.

Premack, D., & Woodruff, G. (1978). Does the Chimpanzee have a theory of mind? *Behavioral and Brain Sciences, 4,* 515–526.

Schneider, W., Perner, J., Bullock, M., Stefanek, J., & Ziegler, A. (1999). Development of intelligence and thinking. In F. E. Weinert & W. Schneider (Eds.), *Individual development from 3 to 12: Findings from the Munich Longitudinal Study* (pp. 9–28). Cambridge, UK: Cambridge University Press.

Sullivan, K., Zaitchik, D., & Tager-Flusberg, H. (1994). Preschoolers can attribute second-order beliefs. *Developmental Psychology, 30,* 395–402.

Wimmer, H., & Perner, J. (1983). Beliefs about beliefs: Representation and constraining function of wrong beliefs in young children's understanding of deception. *Cognition, 13,* 103–128.

Chapter 11

Theory of Mind, Language, and Executive Functions in Autism: A Longitudinal Perspective

Helen Tager-Flusberg
Robert M. Joseph
Boston University School of Medicine

The syndrome of autism is diagnosed on the basis of behavioral characteristics that emerge during infancy or the early preschool years. The core diagnostic features include qualitative impairments in social functioning; qualitative impairments in communication, which usually include delays and deficits in spoken language; and restricted repetitive and stereotyped patterns of behavior, activities, and interests (American Psychiatric Association, 1994). Although all children with autism share these main symptoms, their expression can be extremely variable. In addition, children with autism often experience secondary symptoms including mood or anxiety disorders, severe behavioral problems, such as sleep disturbance, aggression or self-injury, sensory sensitivities, or isolated skills—for example, in music, mathematics, or memory. In recent years, there has been considerable interest among cognitive scientists and neuropsychologists in searching for core cognitive deficits that may explain the range of symptoms found in this complex and heterogeneous disorder (e.g., Frith, Morton, & Leslie, 1991). In this context, there has been a strong emphasis on investigating two key cognitive domains in autism: theory of mind (ToM) and executive functions (EF).

Research on autism has focused on several interrelated issues regarding core deficits in ToM and EF. In this chapter, we discuss two key questions:

(1) Do children with autism have fundamental impairments in these aspects of cognition? (2) What is the relationship between EF and ToM impairments in autism? In the first part of the chapter, we provide a brief review of the literature on ToM and EF in autism. In the second part, we present the initial findings from a longitudinal investigation that was designed specifically to address the relationship between ToM and EF in autism from a developmental perspective.

ToM AND EF DEFICITS IN AUTISM

ToM in Autism

The ToM hypothesis proposes that autism involves a primary impairment in the ability to understand and use mental states concepts to predict and explain human behavior (Baron-Cohen, Tager-Flusberg, & Cohen, 1993). Baron-Cohen and his colleagues were the first to demonstrate that the majority of children with autism failed false belief tasks, in contrast to normally developing preschoolers and children with Down syndrome (Baron-Cohen, Leslie, & Frith, 1985). Follow-up experimental studies provided further support for their hypothesis that autistic children are impaired in their acquisition of a representational ToM: They fail to understand stories that involve deception or false belief (Baron-Cohen, Leslie, & Frith, 1986), they do not understand the connection between perception and knowledge (Baron-Cohen 1989), they lack imagination (Scott & Baron-Cohen, 1996), and they do not engage in spontaneous pretend play (Baron-Cohen, 1987; Lewis & Boucher, 1988).

Over the past two decades, Baron-Cohen's studies have been replicated by many other research groups (for a recent review, see Baron-Cohen, 2000). Across a wide range of tasks, children with autism fail ToM tasks at rates that are significantly higher than those found among comparison groups. Nevertheless, across all studies, there are always some children with autism who pass ToM tasks, including false belief. The single best predictor of passing ToM tasks among children with autism is language ability (Dahlgren & Trillingsgaard, 1996; Eisenmajer & Prior,1991; Happé, 1995; Sparrevohn & Howie, 1995; Tager-Flusberg & Sullivan, 1994). Children with better language skills, as measured on standardized tests of vocabulary or syntax, are more likely to pass ToM tasks.

ToM is also integrally linked to language use (cf. Bartsch & Wellman, 1995). Studies of language acquisition in children with autism suggest that they are selectively impaired in acquiring terms that refer to mental states, especially terms referring to epistemic states, such as knowledge or belief (e.g., Hobson & Lee, 1989; Tager-Flusberg, 1992; Ziatas, Durkin, & Pratt, 2003). Pragmatic deficits in autism have been related to ToM impairments. For example, children with autism express only a limited range of speech acts—they rarely use language to seek or share attention or provide new information (Loveland, Landry, Hughes, Hall, & McEvoy, 1988; Tager-

Flusberg, 1993, 1997; Wetherby, 1986). They have difficulty understanding the different perspectives of speaker and listener, as illustrated, for example, in pronoun reversal errors (Lee, Hobson, & Chiat, 1994; Tager-Flusberg, 1994). They fail to distinguish between given and new information and do not conform to conversational rules (Baltaxe, 1977; Fine, Bartolucci, Szatmari, & Ginsberg, 1994). They cannot appropriately maintain an ongoing topic of discourse (Tager-Flusberg & Anderson, 1991); instead, they introduce irrelevant comments or fail to extend a topic by adding new relevant information. Capps and her colleagues (Capps, Kehres, & Sigman, 1998) found a significant correlation in children with autism between performance on ToM tasks and the ability to respond to a conversational partner with contingent relevant new information. Experimental studies also suggest that children with autism who fail ToM tasks do not adhere to Gricean maxims, which are concerned with conversational relevance (Surian, Baron-Cohen, & Van der Lely, 1996). The conversational deficits in autism reflect fundamental problems in understanding that communication is about the expression and interpretation of intended rather than literal meaning (Happé, 1993; Sperber & Wilson, 1986).

In sum, there is strong evidence that autism involves fundamental impairments in ToM. This hypothesis has theoretical significance in that it provides a cognitive explanation for a range of symptoms that characterize the syndrome, especially the deficits in social reciprocity and communication (Baron-Cohen, 1988; Frith, 1989; Happé, 1994).

EF in Autism

A second important perspective on primary neuropsychological impairments in autism has been the EF hypothesis (Pennington & Ozonoff, 1996; Russell, 1997), which focuses on deficits in executive control over information processing and the regulation of behavior. EF are typically required in nonroutinized, problem-solving tasks and include mental operations such as planning, working memory, maintenance and shifting of attention and mental set, and inhibition of automatic or prepotent responses.

Initial findings indicative of executive dysfunction in autism (see Joseph, 1999, for a recent review) were based largely on omnibus clinical measures, such as the Wisconsin Card Sorting Test. Such measures, however, do not allow identification of the specific executive control functions that may be impaired in autism, and they confound executive and nonexecutive cognitive skills. More recent research has adopted information-processing paradigms to explore whether a specific pattern of executive deficit might be linked to autism and its core symptoms (see Ozonoff, 1997). For example, Ozonoff and colleagues (Ozonoff & Strayer, 1997; Ozonoff, Strayer, McMahon, & Filloux, 1994) found that children with autism were able to inhibit a simple response (e.g., pressing a button for circles but not for squares) but had difficulty when required to shift from one response set to another (e.g., pressing a button for squares instead of circles). Deficits in set shifting were confirmed in a recent large-scale study comparing matched groups of children and adults with autism on the Intradimensional/Extradimensional shift task from the CANTAB (Ozonoff et al., in press).

There is also substantial evidence that tasks that simultaneously tax working memory and inhibitory control are particularly challenging for individuals with autism (Hughes, 1996; Hughes & Russell, 1993; Russell, 1997). This evidence includes poor performance by participants with autism on such tasks as the Tower of Hanoi (Hughes, Russell, & Robbins, 1994; Ozonoff, Pennington, & Rogers, 1991) and the related CANTAB Stockings of Cambridge (Ozonoff et al., in press); the Luria hand game (Hughes, 1996); the no-opponent Windows task; and the detour-reaching task (Hughes & Russell, 1993). One possibility is that children with autism are impaired in the ability to use inner speech to maintain a rule in mind and to guide behavior in standard conflict tasks that simultaneously tax working memory and inhibitory control (Russell, 1997). Research with younger children has also found deficits on a range of EF tasks, especially those tasks tapping working memory, inhibitory control, and set-shifting capacities, including a spatial reversal task (McEvoy, Rogers, & Pennington,1993) and a delayed response task (Dawson, Meltzoff, Osterling, & Rinaldi, 1998). It should be noted, however, that Griffith, Pennington, Wehner, and Rogers (1999) found that although preschoolers with autism were impaired a series of EF tasks, their performance was not different from a group of nonautistic preschoolers with mental retardation.

Thus, evidence from many studies provides support for the view that EF deficits are found across a broad range of individuals with autism, suggesting the possibility of frontal lobe pathology (Ozonoff et al., in press). Deficits in EF have been proposed as the key neuropsychological explanation for a range of autism symptoms, especially the rigid and repetitive behavior problems (Damasio & Maurer, 1978; Turner, 1997).

The Relationship between ToM and lack of EF in Autism

The executive dysfunction account of autism has been proposed as an alternative to the ToM hypothesis. Its proponents have argued that executive deficits are potentially more primary and may possibly account for the ToM impairment in autism (Pennington et al., 1997; Russell, 1997), based on evidence that EF tasks are better at discriminating individuals with autism than are ToM tasks (Ozonoff et al., 1991) and that performance on measures of EF and false belief understanding are correlated in autism (Ozonoff et al., 1991; Russell, Mauthner, Sharpe, & Tidswell, 1991). Numerous studies have documented the relationship between ToM and EF in normally developing children (e.g., Carlson & Moses, 2001; Carlson, Moses, & Breton, 2002; Hughes, 1998a; see also Hasselhorn, Mahler, & Grube, this volume), and one longitudinal study of normally developing preschoolers demonstrated that growth in executive processes predicted developmental changes in ToM, but not the reverse (Hughes, 1998b). These findings suggest that there are significant developmental links between EF and ToM. Yet there have been no longitudinal investigations in autism comparable to Hughes's (1998b) important study. In the remainder of this chapter, we present findings from our longitudinal study that was designed to address the developmental links between these cognitive domains in autism.

A LONGITUDINAL STUDY OF ToM AND EF IN AUTISM

Specific Aims

In this study, we explored concurrent and longitudinal relations between language, EF, and ToM in a relatively large group of well-characterized children with autism. We included a range of developmentally appropriate tasks tapping different EF and several tasks to provide a reliable measure of representational ToM abilities (Hughes et al., 2000) to address the key question of which EF components are related to ToM performance in autism. We collected ToM data from our sample at two time points, spaced about 1 year apart, so that we could address a second key question: Are EFs related to the acquisition of ToM? Finally, because, as noted earlier, ToM abilities in individuals with autism are strongly correlated with language ability (Happé, 1995; Tager-Flusberg & Sullivan, 1994; Yirmiya, Erel, Shaked, & Solomonica-Levi, 1998), and it has been proposed that language deficits contribute to executive problems in autism (Hughes, 1996; Liss et al., 2001; Russell, 1997; Russell, Jarrold, & Hood, 1999), we specifically included measures of language in our investigation to address the question of whether the relationship between component EF and ToM might be mediated by language in autism.

Participants

The study included 43 children (38 boys) with DSM-IV diagnoses of autism spectrum disorder (either autism or pervasive developmental disorder not otherwise specified) who ranged in age from 5 years 7 months to 14 years 2 months at the beginning of the study. All children were diagnosed by expert clinicians and met diagnostic criteria on the Autism Diagnostic Interview–Revised (ADI-R; Lord, Rutter, & LeCouteur, 1994) and the Autism Diagnostic Observation Schedule (ADOS; Lord et al., 2000). Children with Rett syndrome, childhood disintegrative disorder, or autism-related medical conditions (e.g., neurofibromatosis, tuberous sclerosis, fragile X syndrome) were excluded from this study.

The children's IQ scores were obtained using the Differential Ability Scales (DAS; Elliot, 1990), which provide full-scale, verbal, and nonverbal standard scores. We also administered two standardized language tests: the Peabody Picture Vocabulary Test (PPVT-III; Dunn & Dunn, 1997) and the Expressive Vocabulary Test (EVT; Williams, 1997), which measure

TABLE 11.1
Descriptive Characteristics of the Children With Autism

	M	SD	Range
Age	8.5	2.5	5.7–14.2
DAS full scale IQ	83	19.3	51–141
DAS verbal IQ	82	19.2	51–118
DAS nonverbal IQ	88	21.0	49–153
EVT standard score	79	18.9	40–114
PPVT-III standard score	84	19.8	40–134

single word receptive and expressive vocabulary, respectively. Table 11.1 presents the descriptive characteristics of the 43 children at the first time point (Time 1). At the second time point, 1 year later (Time 2), there were 31 children who returned and had not reached ceiling on our experimental measures. At Time 2, children were retested on the ToM battery.

Experimental Measures

Language.   Language measures included age-equivalent scores from the EVT and the PPVT-III. Because the PPVT-III and EVT were developed with the same normative sample, and the two scores were strongly correlated in our sample, $r(41) = .75, p < .001$, we averaged the age-equivalent scores from these tests to generate a composite language score for each child. We used age-equivalent scores rather than age-adjusted standard scores in our analyses because they were more suitable for comparison to the ToM and EF measures, which were also not adjusted for age.

Nonverbal Mental Age.   Nonverbal mental age served as our measure of general cognitive ability and was calculated by averaging the age-equivalent scores for all the DAS nonverbal subtests for each participant. As with language level, an age-equivalent rather than a standardized score was used because the other measures were not adjusted for age.

ToM.   Three standard tasks designed to assess knowledge and false belief attribution were administered in randomized order to each child:

1. *Perception/Knowledge:* Based on Pillow (1989) and Pratt and Bryant (1990), this task tested the ability to infer knowledge from perceptual access. On each of two test trials, children observed one doll that looked in a box and another doll that simply touched the box, and children were then asked a knowledge question ("Does X know what's in the box?"). Scores on this task ranged from 0 to 2.
2. *Location-Change False Belief:* Based on Wimmer and Perner (1983) and Baron-Cohen et al. (1985), this task included two stories in which an object was moved while the main character was absent. The stories were told using props, and participants were asked a knowledge ("Does X know

where Y is?"), prediction ("Where will X look first for Y?"), and justification question ("Why?"). Scores on this task ranged from 0 to 6.

3. *Unexpected-Contents False Belief:* Based on Perner, Leekam, and Wimmer (1987), participants were shown two different familiar containers that had unexpected objects inside. Test questions included representational change ("When you first saw this container, what did you think was inside?"), knowledge ("If I show this container to X, will X know what is inside?"), and false belief ("What will X think is inside?"). Scores on this task ranged from 0 to 6.

Two trials of each test question yielded a possible score of 0–2, for a total possible ToM score across the seven test questions of 0–14. Chronbach's alpha for the seven test questions comprising the ToM measure was .89, indicating high internal consistency. Different versions of the ToM tasks were developed, and children were randomly assigned to one of the versions in the 1st year of testing. At Time 2, they were given a different version to avoid repeated testing effects.

Executive Functions. We administered five different EF tasks in randomized order. These tasks provided measures of working memory (word span, block span), working memory and inhibitory control (day-night, NEPSY knock-tap), and planning (NEPSY tower). Each task was preceded by a brief training procedure, consisting of a maximum of four practice trials, to ensure that the children understood the task instructions. We gave no corrective feedback during test trials.

1. *Word Span:* The word span task was similar to the nonverbal recall span task used by Russell, Jarrold, and Henry (1996), except that we included a backward as well as a forward condition. In the forward task, children heard the examiner speak a sequence of words at the rate of one word per second. For each trial, a fixed sequence was randomly preselected from a set of nine words, all of which were single-syllable, high-frequency concrete nouns (*arm, boat, brush, chair, dress, knife, mouse, ring, tree*). After each sequence was spoken, children were immediately presented with a 3 × 3 grid containing nine line drawings corresponding to the set of nine words and were told to touch the pictures in the same order as the words were spoken. For each trial, the arrangement of the pictures in the grid changed to prevent children from using a fixed visual representation of the array to help encode the word sequence and to introduce a visual search component to the task (thus requiring participants to maintain the word sequence in working memory while searching for and pointing to each successive item). Following the word span forward task, all children were administered a word span backward task, which was exactly the same as the forward task except that the children were instructed to touch the pictures in the reverse order from the spoken sequence. For both the forward and backward tasks, children were given two different trials of each sequence length, which ranged from two to seven words. One point

was given for each correct trial. Testing was discontinued when a child failed both trials of any one sequence length.

2. *Block Span:* In the block span test (Isaacs & Vargha-Khadem, 1989), children were asked to watch as the examiner pointed to an unstructured array of nine identical, black blocks affixed to a white board and to point to the blocks in the same sequence as the examiner in the blocks forward test and in the reverse order from the examiner in the blocks backward test. Children were administered two different trials of each sequence length, which ranged from two to eight blocks, and they earned 1 point for each trial correct. Testing was discontinued when a child failed both trials of any one sequence length. The word and block span tasks were similar in that they required participants to update, rehearse, and maintain information in working memory and to use that information to carry out a response. Although the word and block span tasks differed in the modality of input (auditory vs. visual), and the backward tasks were more demanding of working memory capacities than the forward tasks in that they required mental manipulation of the response sequence, scores on all four tasks were highly intercorrelated. Therefore, a composite score was generated for each participant for a total working memory score of 0–52. Chronbach's alpha for the four component tests was .78, indicating high internal consistency for the working memory measure.

3. *Day-Night:* Following the same procedure as Gerstadt, Hong, and Diamond (1994), children were instructed to say "day" to a picture of the moon and stars and "night" to a picture of the sun. Participants were presented with 8 moon and 8 sun stimuli in pseudorandom order for a total of 16 test trials.

4. *Knock-Tap:* This task was taken from the NEPSY (Korkman, Kirk, & Kemp, 1998) and was administered according to the standard procedure. Children were instructed to knock with their knuckles on the table when the examiner tapped with flat palm and vice versa. A total of 15 trials were given in pseudorandom order.

Both the day-night and knock-tap tasks required participants to hold an arbitrary response rule in working memory and to inhibit a prepotent response (to name the picture shown, to copy the hand movement of the examiner). Scores on these tasks were correlated ($r = .33, p < .05$) and were therefore combined to create a composite working memory and inhibitory control score with a possible range of 0–31.

5. *Tower:* NEPSY Tower (Korkman et al., 1998), modeled after Shallice's (1982) tower of London, was used as a measure of planning ability and administered according to the standard NEPSY procedure. Children were asked to rearrange three different colored balls situated on three vertical pegs to reach a goal state, shown on a picture board, in a prescribed number of moves without violating the rules (moving only one ball at a time directly from one peg to another). There was a total of 20 possible trials, which increased in difficulty from one to seven moves for the correct solution. Following NEPSY procedures, only trials solved in the optimum (i.e., fewest possible) number of moves were scored as correct

and awarded 1 point, for a total possible score of 0–20. Testing was discontinued after four consecutive incorrect responses.

Results

Table 11.2 presents the children's scores on all measures at Time 1. Prior to statistical analyses, we conducted a screen to check for skewness and kurtosis in the distribution of the data for each test variable. At an alpha level of .01, the screening revealed negative skew in the distribution of scores for the working memory and inhibitory control composite measure. Because of the negative skewness, the variable was reflected and a logarithmic transformation was applied, resulting in a normal distribution. The transformed variable was rereflected to shift values in the correct direction.

We first investigated the effects of age, nonverbal mental age (NVMA), and language on EF and ToM scores. Both NVMA and language were significantly correlated with chronological age, $r(41) = 0.48$, $p < .001$ and $r(41) = 0.50$, $p < .001$, respectively, and with each other, $r(41) = 0.63$, $p < .001$. When either NVMA or language was covaried, age was not significantly correlated with any of the EF or ToM measures. Therefore, age was not considered in subsequent analyses.

Table 11.3 presents the full and partial correlations among the main EF measures. Before the effects of NVMA or language level were removed, all EF scores were significantly correlated with each other. The partial correlations indicated that planning was related to working memory independently of language level and that planning was related to working memory and inhibitory control independently of both NVMA and language level. Table 11.4 presents the full and partial correlations for ToM collected at the first and second time points. As can be seen, language was significantly correlated with ToM scores, after NVMA was covaried. Furthermore, the two ToM scores were highly correlated, independently of either NVMA or language.

Table 11.5 presents the full and partial correlations between the EF and ToM scores collected at the beginning of the study and those collected 1 year

TABLE 11.2
Experimental Measures Obtained at Time 1

	M	SD	Range
Nonverbal mental age	7.0	2.7	3.6–16.3
Language age equivalent	6.2	2.3	2.9–12.11
Executive functions			
Working memory	15.1	6.4	4–26
Working memory + inhibitory control	23.2	6.6	2–31
Planning	7.0	4.1	2–16
Theory of mind	6.9	4.8	0–14

TABLE 11.3
Full and Partial Correlations Among EF Measures

	Working Memory + Inhibitory Control	Planning
Working memory	.52**	.49***
NMVA removed	.35	.19
Language removed	.35	.38*
Working memory + inhibitory control		.51***
NMVA removed		.49**
Language removed		.45*

*p < .05. **p < .01. ***p < .001.

TABLE 11.4
Full and Partial Correlations Among ToM Measures

	ToM—Time 1	ToM—Time 2
Age	.42**	.03
NMVA removed	−.14	−.30
Language removed	.06	−.22
Nonverbal mental age	.57***	.39*
Language removed	.20	.01
Language age	.77***	.58***
NVMA removed	.60***	.46**
ToM at Time 1		.82***
NVMA removed		.79***
Language removed		.71***

*p < .05. **p < .01. ***p < .001.

TABLE 11.5
Full and Partial Correlations Between EF and ToM Measures

	ToM—Time 1	ToM—Time 2
Working memory	.48***	.25
NMVA removed	.08	.00
Language removed	.14	−.02
Working memory + inhibitory control	.55***	.39*
NMVA removed	.40*	.32
Language removed	.37*	.27
Planning	.57***	.66***
NVMA removed	.47**	.59***
Language removed	.46**	.48***

*p < .05. **p < .01. ***p < .001.

later. The correlations show that both the composite of working memory and inhibitory control and planning were significantly correlated with the concurrent measure of theory of mind ability at the first time point, even when NVMA and language level were partialled. However, at Time 2, only planning maintained significant NVMA- and language-independent correlations with ToM.

In addition to the correlational analyses, multiple regression analyses were conducted to examine the combined contribution of EF to ToM ability at Time 1 and Time 2. For Time 1 ToM, NVMA and language level were entered into the equation as control variables because of their significant correlations with both the EF and ToM measures. Next, the EF variables were entered in the order of highest statistical significance using a forward stepwise procedure. Table 11.6 shows the regression coefficients and the increments in variance at each step in the model.

Language level was a much stronger predictor of Time 1 ToM ability, $\beta = .69$, $t = 5.3$, $p < .001$, than was NVMA, $\beta = .13$, $t = 1.0$, ns. Together, NVMA and language level accounted for 60% of the variance in Time 1 ToM score, $F(2, 40) = 29.3$, $p < .001$. After the control variables were

TABLE 11.6
Hierarchical Regression Analyses Predicting ToM at Time 1 and Time 2

Variable	β	R^2	ΔR^2
DV: Time 1 Theory of Mind			
Step 1			
Nonverbal mental age	.13		
Language	.69***	.60	.60***
Step 2			
Nonverbal mental age	.08		
Language	.61***		
Working memory + inhibitory control	.26*	.65	.05*
DV: Time 2 Theory of Mind			
Step 1			
Nonverbal mental age	−.15		
Language	−.02		
Time 1 ToM	.92***	.68	.68***
Step 2			
Nonverbal mental age	−.34*		
Language	.01		
Time 1 ToM	.75***		
Planning	.37*	.73	.05*

Note. For each dependent variable, control variables were forced into the model on the first step and EF variables were then entered stepwise in the order of highest statistical significance until the threshold criterion of $p = .05$ was reached.
*$p < .05$. **$p < .01$. ***$p < .001$.

entered into the model, the composite of working memory and inhibitory control variable accounted for an additional 5% of variance, F_{inc} (1, 39) = 5.7, p < .05. The other two EF measures did not contribute to any increment in the variance explained.

For Time 2 ToM ability, the Time 1 ToM score was the only significant predictor from among the control variables, β = .92, t = 5.3, p < .001, which together explained 68% of the variance in Time 2 ToM, F(3, 27) = 18.3, p < .001. Planning score from the NEPSY tower task accounted for an additional 5% of variance, F_{inc} (1, 26) = 5.0, p < .05, in Time 2 ToM ability.

Summary of Findings

In our sample of children with autism, we found a wide range of performance on both our ToM tasks and the EF measures. Language ability was strongly linked to both ToM and EF. The two important components of EF that contributed to ToM performance in our sample of children with autism were both the composite of working memory and inhibitory control and planning; in contrast, measures of working memory were not found to be significantly related to ToM independent of either general cognitive ability or language. Finally, we found that working memory and inhibitory control was a significant concurrent predictor of ToM, whereas planning ability was a significant factor predicting developmental change in ToM over the course of 1 year.

EF AND ToM IN AUTISM

It has been argued that executive control deficits contribute to and are possibly the primary cause of the well-documented deficits in mental state understanding in individuals with autism (Hughes, 2001; Russell, 1997). However, evidence supporting these claims has been limited (Ozonoff et al., 1991; Russell et al., 1991). In the current study, we examined representational ToM abilities in a group of rigorously diagnosed, school-age children with autism for whom understanding of knowledge and false belief was developmentally within the range of their cognitive and linguistic abilities. As such, this group of children could be expected to provide a revealing picture of the factors affecting the understanding of representational mental states in autism. Furthermore, we included a battery of EF measures that tapped a range of executive control processes and that were selected to be developmentally appropriate for the children in this study. We found that children's ToM performance was consistently related to the components of executive control we measured and that some of these associations held up when the shared effects of nonverbal ability and language level on these two variables were controlled.

First, we found a concurrent relationship between ToM and our combined measure, working memory and inhibitory control, that was independent of both nonverbal mental age and language ability. The knock-tap task required children to combine inhibition and working memory to withhold a prepotent motor response (to copy the examiner's hand movement) by maintaining an arbitrary response rule (to knock when the examiner tapped and vice versa) in active memory. Similarly, the day-night Stroop task required to the child to withhold a prepotent verbal response (saying "night" to a picture of the moon and stars) and to maintain an arbitrary response rule (saying "day" to the night picture) in active memory. The requirements of these tasks are formally similar to other executive tasks on which autism-specific deficits have been found (Hughes, 1996; Hughes & Russell, 1993) and to at least one other executive task that has been associated with false belief performance in autism (Russell et al., 1991).

Second, we found a robust relationship between tower performance and ToM. This measure of planning was related to both concurrent and longitudinal changes in ToM ability in our sample of children with autism. Performance on tower taps a broad range of executive skills, including attention and planning and attention, working memory (keeping planned moves in active memory) and inhibitory control (to formulate a set of moves prior to making an initial response and to inhibit direct placement of a disk to its final destination). More generally, it taps the ability to flexibly rerepresent perceptual reality into a sequence of moves that will result in the attainment of the final goal state. At its heart, tower is an important measure of central executive control, which is critical for coordinating other EFs in solving novel problems.

Our finding of an association between knock-tap and ToM performance suggests that domain-general executive processes, specifically the capacity for combined working memory and inhibitory control, may mediate or at least provide the necessary conditions for success on ToM tasks in children with autism, which has also been suggested for typically developing children (Carlson & Moses, 2001; Hughes, 1998a, 1998b). This makes sense given that successful attribution of false beliefs requires an individual to maintain a false representation of a given state of affairs in working memory and to resist the normal tendency to ascribe mental states on the basis of a prepotent reality. These findings support the idea of a mediating role of EF in ToM in autism, although it remains a question whether these components of EF are mainly important for performance on ToM tasks or whether they are also involved in the conceptual developments that are necessary for a representational understanding of mind (Moses, 2001). Given that we found significant concurrent links between working memory and inhibitory control, but no longitudinal relationship, this suggests that these aspects of EF are more closely related to performance.

In contrast, the significant concurrent and longitudinal relationships between tower and ToM suggest that that planning skills are more deeply related to the ability to pass ToM tasks in children with autism. One possibility is that children with autism are more dependent on general problem-solving skills in reasoning through a false belief or related representational ToM tasks. This is consistent with evidence from Happé and her colleagues (1996), based on their functional imaging studies of ToM with adults with autism or Asperger's syndrome. Nonautistic adults generally activate critical regions in the medial prefrontal cortex in the paracingulate region (BA 8/9) when they process tasks that depend on ToM abilities (Fletcher et al., 1995). This region is specifically associated with ToM or mentalizing ability (Frith & Frith, 2003). In contrast, adults with Asperger's syndrome activated a different area, BA 9/10, which is associated with problem solving and general cognitive abilities (Happé et al., 1996). These areas of prefrontal cortex, particularly in the left hemisphere, have been associated with performance on tower tasks in recent functional imaging studies (van den Heuvel et al., 2003).

A second possibility is that language is an important mediator in performance on both planning tasks and ToM. Although in this study we found that performance on tower was a significant longitudinal predictor of ToM after controlling for language age, our language measure was somewhat limited in that it only assessed vocabulary knowledge, not more complex grammatical knowledge. Other studies suggest that grammatical abilities are more strongly related to ToM than single-word vocabulary both in children with autism (Tager-Flusberg & Sullivan, 1994) and in normally developing children (Astington & Jenkins, 1999). If we had included a measure of higher order syntax or, more specifically, embedded sentential complements in our analyses (cf. de Villiers & Pyers, 2002; Tager-Flusberg, 2000), we may have been able to test for the role of language in mediating the relationship between planning and ToM. This remains an important issue for future studies on EF and ToM in children with autism.

We make one final note: The present data provide support for a role of EF in one specific aspect of ToM development, which normally occurs around age 4 years and involves the ability to represent epistemic mental states, such as knowledge and belief. Numerous authors have proposed a broader perspective on ToM that would include the ability to read mental states from more immediately available perceptual information, such as body movements, eye gaze, and facial expressions (Hobson, 1989, 1991; Klin, Jones, Schultz, Volkmar, & Cohen, 2002; Ruffman, 2000; Tager-Flusberg, 2001; Tager-Flusberg & Sullivan, 2000). It is likely that these domain-specific, more direct aspects of mentalizing are less dependent on higher order, domain-general cognitive capacities than is the ability to reason about people's beliefs, but there has been no research investigating the relationship between EF and these other aspects of ToM.

ACKNOWLEDGMENTS

This research was supported by a grant from the National Institute on Deafness and Other Communication Disorders (U19/PO1 DC03610) and was conducted as part of the NICHD/NIDCD funded Collaborative Programs of Excellence in Autism. We thank the following individuals for their assistance in collecting and preparing the data reported in this paper:

Susan Bacalman, Laura Becker, Karen Condouris, June Chu, Susan Folstein, Anne Gavin, Courtney Hale, Margaret Kjelgaard, Lauren McGrath, Echo Meyer, and Shelly Steele. We are especially grateful to the children and families who generously participated in this study.

REFERENCES

American Psychiatric Association. (1994). *Diagnostic and statistical manual of mental disorders* (4th ed.). Washington, DC: Author.

Astington, J., & Jenkins, J. (1999). A longitudinal study of the relation between language and theory of mind development. *Developmental Psychology, 35,* 1311–1320.

Baltaxe, C. A. M. (1977). Pragmatic deficits in the language of autistic adolescents. *Journal of Pediatric Psychology, 2,* 176–180.

Baron-Cohen, S. (1987). Autism and symbolic play. *British Journal of Developmental Psychology, 5,* 139–148.

Baron-Cohen, S. (1988). Social and pragmatic deficits in autism: Cognitive or affective? *Journal of Autism and Developmental Disorders, 18,* 379–402.

Baron-Cohen, S. (1989). Perceptual role-taking and protodeclarative pointing in autism. *British Journal of Developmental Psychology, 7,* 113–127.

Baron-Cohen, S. (2000). Theory of mind and autism: A fifteen year review. In S. Baron-Cohen, H. Tager-Flusberg, & D. J. Cohen (Eds.), *Understanding other minds: Perspectives from developmental cognitive neuroscience* (pp. 3–20). Oxford, UK: Oxford University Press.

Baron-Cohen, S., Leslie, A. M., & Frith, U. (1985). Does the autistic child have a "theory of mind"? *Cognition, 21,* 37–46.

Baron-Cohen, S., Leslie, A. M., & Frith, U. (1986). Mechanical, behavioral, and intentional understanding of picture stories in autistic children. *British Journal of Developmental Psychology, 4,* 113–125.

Baron-Cohen, S., Tager-Flusberg, H., & Cohen, D. J. (Eds.). (1993). *Understanding other minds: Perspectives from autism.* Oxford, UK: Oxford University Press.

Bartsch, K., & Wellman, H. (1995). *Children talk about the mind.* New York: Oxford University Press.

Capps, L., Kehres, J., & Sigman, M. (1998). Conversational abilities among children with autism and children with developmental delays. *Autism, 2,* 325–344.

Carlson, S., & Moses, L. J. (2001). Individual differences in inhibitory control and children's theory of mind. *Child Development, 72,* 1032–1053.

Carlson, S., Moses, L., & Breton, C. (2002). How specific is the relation between executive function and theory of mind? Contributions of inhibitory control and working memory. *Infant and Child Development, 11,* 73–92

Dahlgren, S., & Trillingsgaard, A. (1996). Theory of mind in non-retarded children with autism and Asperger's syndrome: A research note. *Journal of Child Psychology and Psychiatry, 37,* 759–763.

Damasio, A. R., & Maurer, R.G. (1978). A neurological model for childhood autism. *Archives of Neurology, 35,* 777–786.

Dawson, G., Meltzoff, A. N., Osterling, J., & Rinaldi, J. (1998). Neuropsychological correlates of early symptoms of autism. *Child Development, 69,* 1276–1285.

de Villiers, J., & Pyers, J. (2002). Complements to cognition: A longitudinal study of the relationship between complex syntax and false-belief understanding. *Cognitive Development, 17,* 1037–1060.

Dunn, L. M., & Dunn, L. M. (1997). *Peabody picture vocabulary test* (3rd ed.). Circle Pines, MN: American Guidance Service.

Eisenmajer, R., & Prior, M. (1991). Cognitive linguistic correlates of "theory of mind" ability in autistic children. *British Journal of Developmental Psychology, 9,* 351–364.

Elliott, C. D. (1990). *Differential ability scales: Introductory and technical handbook.* New York: Psychological Corporation.

Fine, J., Bartolucci, G., Szatmari, P., & Ginsberg, G. (1994). Cohesive discourse in pervasive developmental disorders. *Journal of Autism and Developmental Disorders, 24,* 315–329.

Fletcher, P., Happé, F., Frith, U., Baker, S., Dolan, D., Frackowiak, R., & Frith, C. (1995). Other minds in the brain: A functional imaging study of "theory of mind" in story comprehension. *Cognition, 57,* 109–128.

Frith, U. (1989). *Autism: Explaining the enigma.* Oxford, UK: Blackwell.

Frith, U., & Frith, C. (2003). Development and neurophysiology of mentalizing. *Philosophical Transactions of the Royal Society, 258,* 459–473.

Frith, U., Morton, J., & Leslie, A. M. (1991). The cognitive basis of a biological disorder: Autism. *Trends in Neuroscience, 14,* 433–438.

Gerstadt, C., Hong, Y., & Diamond, A. (1994). The relationship between cognition and action: Performance of 3–7-year-old children on a Stroop-like day-night test. *Cognition, 53,* 129–153.

Griffith, E. M., Pennington, B. F., Wehner, E. A., & Rogers, S. (1999). Executive functions in young children with autism. *Child Development, 70,* 817–832.

Happé, F. (1993). Communicative competence and theory of mind in autism: A test of relevance theory. *Cognition, 48,* 101–119.

Happé, F. (1994). *Autism: An introduction to psychological theory.* London: University College London Press.

Happé, F. (1995). The role of age and verbal ability in the theory of mind task performance of subjects with autism. *Child Development, 66,* 843–855.

Happé, F., Ehlers, S., Fletcher, P., Frith, U., Johansson, M., Gillberg, C., Dolan, R., Frackowiak, R., & Frith, C. (1996). "Theory of mind" in the brain: Evidence from a PET scan study of Asperger syndrome. *NeuroReport, 8,* 197–201.

Hobson, R. P. (1989). Beyond cognition: A theory of autism. In G. Dawson (Ed.), *Autism* (pp. 22–48). New York: Guilford Press.

Hobson, R. P. (1991). Against the theory of "theory of mind." *British Journal of Developmental Psychology, 9,* 33–51.

Hobson, R. P., & Lee, A. (1989). Emotion-related and abstract concepts in autistic people: Evidence from the British Picture Vocabulary Scale. *Journal of Autism and Developmental Disorders, 19,* 601–623.

Hughes, C. (1996). Control of action and thought: Normal development and dysfunction in autism: A research note. *Journal of Child Psychology and Psychiatry, 37,* 229–236.

Hughes, C. (1998a). Executive function in preschoolers: Links with theory of mind and verbal ability. *British Journal of Developmental Psychology, 16,* 233–253.

Hughes, C. (1998b). Finding your marbles: Does preschoolers' strategic behavior predict later understanding of the mind? *Developmental Psychology, 34,* 1326–1339.

Hughes, C. (2001). Executive dysfunction in autism: Its nature and implications for the everyday problems experienced by individuals with autism. In J. Burack, T. Charman, N. Yirmiya, & P. Zelazo (Eds.), *The development of autism: Perspectives from theory and research* (pp. 255–275). Mahwah, NJ: Lawrence Erlbaum Associates.

Hughes, C., Adlam, A., Happe, F., Jackson, J., Taylor, A., & Caspi, A. (2000). Good test-retest reliability for standard and advance false-belief tasks across a wide range of abilities. *Journal of Child Psychology and Psychiatry, 41,* 483–490.

Hughes, C., & Russell, J. (1993). Autistic children's difficulty with mental disengagement from an object: Its implications for theories of autism. *Developmental Psychology, 29,* 498–510.

Hughes, C., Russell, J., & Robbins, T. W. (1994). Evidence for executive dysfunction in autism. *Neuropsychologia, 32,* 477–492.

Isaacs, E. B., & Vargha-Khadem, F. (1989). Differential course of development of spatial and verbal memory span: A normative study. *British Journal of Developmental Psychology, 7,* 377–380.

Joseph, R. M. (1999). Neuropsychological frameworks for understanding autism. *International Review of Psychiatry, 11,* 309–325.

Klin, A., Jones, W., Schultz, R., Volkmar, F., & Cohen, D. (2002). Visual fixation patterns during viewing of naturalistic social situations as predictors of social competence in individuals with autism. *Archives of General Psychiatry, 59*(9), 809–816.

Korkman, M., Kirk, U., & Kemp, S. (1998). *NEPSY: A developmental neuropsychological assessment*. San Antonio, TX: Psychological Corporation.

Lee, A., Hobson, R. P., & Chiat, S. (1994). I, you, me and autism: An experimental study. *Journal of Autism and Developmental Disorders, 24*, 155–176.

Lewis, V. & Boucher, J. (1988). Spontaneous, instructed and elicited play in relatively able autistic children. *British Journal of Developmental Psychology, 6*, 325–339.

Liss, M., Fein, D., Allen, D., Dunn, M., Feinstein, C., Morris, R., Waterhouse, L., & Rapin, I. (2001). Executive functioning in high-functioning children with autism. *Journal of Child Psychology and Psychiatry, 42*, 261–270.

Lord, C., Risi, S., Lambrecht, L., Cook, E. H., Lenventhal, B. L., DiLavore, P. S., Pickles, A., & Rutter, M. (2000). The Autism Diagnostic Observation Schedule–Generic: A standard measure of social and communication deficits associated with the spectrum of autism. *Journal of Autism and Developmental Disorders, 30*, 205–223.

Lord, C., Rutter, M., & LeCouteur, A. (1994). Autism Diagnostic Interview–Revised: A revised version of a diagnostic interview for caregivers of individuals with possible pervasive developmental disorders. *Journal of Autism and Developmental Disorders, 24*, 659–668.

Loveland, K., Landry, S., Hughes, S., Hall, S., & McEvoy, R. (1988). Speech acts and the pragmatic deficits of autism. *Journal of Speech and Hearing Research, 31*, 593–604.

McEvoy, R. E., Rogers, S. J., & Pennington, B. F. (1993). Executive function and social communication deficits in young autistic children. *Journal of Child Psychology and Psychiatry, 34*, 563–578.

Moses, L. (2001). Executive accounts of theory-of-mind development. *Child Development, 72*, 688–690.

Ozonoff, S. (1997). Components of executive function in autism and other disorders. In J. Russell (Ed.), *Autism as an executive disorder* (pp. 179–211). Oxford, UK: Oxford University Press.

Ozonoff, S., Cook, I., Coon, H., Dawson, G., Joseph, R. M., Klin, A., McMahon, W., Minshew, N., Munson, J., Pennington, B., Rogers, S., Spence, A., Tager-Flusberg, H., Volkmar, F., & Wrathall, D. (2004). Performance on CANTAB subtests sensitive to frontal love function in people with autistic disorder: Evidence from the CPEA Network. *Journal of Autism and Developmental Disorders, 34*, 139–150.

Ozonoff, S., Pennington, B. F., & Rogers, S. J. (1991). Executive function deficits in high-functioning autistic individuals: Relationship to theory of mind. *Journal of Child Psychology and Psychiatry, 32*, 1081–1105.

Ozonoff, S., & Strayer, D. L. (1997). Inhibitory function in nonretarded children with autism. *Journal of Autism and Developmental Disorders, 27*, 59–77.

Ozonoff, S., Strayer, D. L., McMahon, W. M., & Filloux, F. (1994). Executive function abilities in autism and Tourette syndrome: An information processing approach. *Journal of Child Psychology and Psychiatry, 35*, 1015–1032.

Pennington, B. F., & Ozonoff, S. (1996). Executive functions and developmental psychopathology. *Journal of Child Psychology and Psychiatry, 37*, 51–87.

Pennington, B. F., Rogers, S. J., Bennetto, L., Griffith, E. M., Reed, D. T., & Shyu, V. (1997). Validity tests of the executive dysfunction hypothesis of autism. In J. Russell (Ed.), *Autism as an executive disorder* (pp. 143–178). Oxford, UK: Oxford University Press.

Perner, J., Leekam, S., & Wimmer, H. (1987). Three-year-olds' difficulty with false belief: The case for a conceptual deficit. *British Journal of Developmental Psychology, 5*, 125–137.

Pillow, B. (1989). Early understanding of perception as a source of knowledge. *Journal of Experimental Child Psychology, 47*, 116–129.

Pratt, C., & Bryant, P. (1990). Young children understand that looking leads to knowing (so long as they are looking into a single barrel). *Child Development, 61*, 973–982.

Ruffman, T. (2000). Nonverbal theory of mind: Is it important, is it implicit, is it simulations, is it relevant to autism? In J. W. Astington (Ed.), *Minds in the making: Essays in honor of David R. Olson* (pp. 250–266). Malden, MA: Blackwell.

Russell, J. (1997). How executive disorders can bring about an inadequate "theory of mind." In J. Russell (Ed.), *Autism as an executive disorder* (pp. 256–304). Oxford, UK: Oxford University Press.

Russell, J., Jarrold, C., & Henry, L. (1996). Working memory in children with autism and with moderate learning difficulties. *Journal of Child Psychology and Psychiatry, 37,* 673–686.

Russell, J., Jarrold, C., & Hood, B. (1999). Two intact executive capacities in children with autism: Implications for the core executive dysfunctions in the disorder. *Journal of Autism and Developmental Disorders, 29,* 103–112.

Russell, J., Mauthner, N., Sharpe, S., & Tidswell, T. (1991). The "windows task" as a measure of strategic deception in preschoolers and autistic subjects. *British Journal of Developmental Psychology, 9,* 331–349.

Scott, F., & Baron-Cohen, S. (1996). Imagining real and unreal objects: An investigation of imagination in autism. *Journal of Cognitive Neuroscience, 8,* 400–411.

Shallice, T. (1982). Specific impairments of planning. *Philosophical Transactions of the Royal Society of London, 298,* 199–209.

Sparrevohn, R., & Howie, P. (1995). Theory of mind children with autistic disorder: Evidence of developmental progression and the role of verbal ability. *Journal of Child Psychology and Psychiatry, 36,* 249–263.

Sperber, D., & Wilson, D. (1986). *Relevance: Communication and cognition.* Cambridge, MA: Harvard University Press.

Surian, L., Baron-Cohen, S., & Van der Lely, H. (1996). Are children with autism deaf to Gricean maxims? *Cognitive Neuropsychiatry, 1,* 55–72.

Tager-Flusberg, H. (1992). Autistic children talk about psychological states: Deficits in the early acquisition of a theory of mind. *Child Development, 63,* 161–172.

Tager-Flusberg, H. (1993). What language reveals about the understanding of minds in children with autism. In S. Baron-Cohen, H. Tager-Flusberg, & D. J. Cohen (Eds.), *Understanding other minds: Perspectives from autism* (pp. 138–157). Oxford, UK: Oxford University Press.

Tager-Flusberg, H. (1994). Dissociations in form and function in the acquisition of language by autistic children. In H. Tager-Flusberg (Ed.), *Constraints on language acquisition: Studies of atypical children* (pp. 175–194). Hillsdale, NJ: Lawrence Erlbaum Associates.

Tager-Flusberg, H. (1997). The role of theory of mind in language acquisition: Contributions from the study of autism. In L. Adamson & M. A. Romski (Eds.), *Communication and language acquisition: Discoveries from atypical development* (pp. 133–158). Baltimore, MD: Paul Brookes.

Tager-Flusberg, H. (2000). Language and understanding minds: Connections in autism. In S. Baron-Cohen, H. Tager-Flusberg, & D. J. Cohen (Eds.), *Understanding other minds: Perspectives from developmental cognitive neuroscience* (2nd ed., pp. 124–149). Oxford, UK: Oxford University Press.

Tager-Flusberg, H. (2001). A re-examination of the theory of mind hypothesis of autism. In J. Burack, T. Charman, N. Yirmiya, & P. Zelazo (Eds.), *The development of autism: Perspectives from theory and research* (pp. 173–193). Mahwah, NJ: Lawrence Erlbaum Associates.

Tager-Flusberg, H., & Anderson, M. (1991). The development of contingent discourse ability in autistic children. *Journal of Child Psychology and Psychiatry, 32,* 1123–1134.

Tager-Flusberg, H., & Sullivan, K. (2000). A componential view of theory of mind: Evidence from Williams syndrome. *Cognition, 76,* 59–89.

Tager-Flusberg, H., & Sullivan, K. (1994). Predicting and explaining behavior: A comparison of autistic, mentally retarded and normal children. *Journal of Child Psychology and Psychiatry, 35,* 1059–1075.

Turner, M. (1997). Towards an executive dysfunction account of repetitive behavior in autism. In J. Russell (Ed.), *Autism as an executive disorder* (pp. 57–100). Oxford, UK: Oxford University Press.

Van den Heuvel, O., Groenewegen, H., Barkhoff, F., Lazeron, R., van Dyck, R., & Veltman, D. (2003). Frontostriatal system in planning complexity: A parametric functional magnetic resonance version of Tower of London task. *Neuroimage, 18,* 367–374.

Wetherby, A. (1986). Ontogeny of communication functions in autism. *Journal of Autism and Developmental Disorders, 16,* 295–316.

Williams, K. T. (1997). *Expressive vocabulary test.* Circle Pines, MN: American Guidance Service.

Wimmer, H., & Perner, J. (1983). Beliefs about beliefs: Representation and constraining function of wrong beliefs in young children's understanding of deception. *Cognition, 13,* 103–128.

Yirmiya, N., Erel, O., Shaked, M., & Solomonica-Levi, D. (1998). Meta-analyses comparing theory of mind abilities of individuals with autism, individuals with mental retardation, and normally developing individuals. *Psychological Bulletin, 124,* 283–307.

Ziatas, K., Durkin, K., & Pratt, C. (2003). Differences in assertive speech acts produced by children with autism, Asperger syndrome, specific language impairment and normal development. *Development and Psychopathology, 15,* 73–94.

Chapter 12

Interrelationships Among Theory of Mind, Executive Control, Language Development, and Working Memory in Young Children: A Longitudinal Analysis

Wolfgang Schneider
Kathrin Lockl
Olivia Fernandez
University of Würzburg, Germany

This chapter describes a longitudinal study that was carried out to examine relationships among different aspects of young children's cognitive development, which seem theoretically connected but typically have been studied in isolation. In particular, the study assessed interrelationships among children's working memory, language proficiency, social cognition (theory of mind), and their ability to control and regulate their actions. Although developmental research on this issue has accumulated over the last few years (e.g., Carlson & Moses, 2001; Hughes, 1998a, 1998b; Jenkins & Astington, 1996; Perner & Lang, 2000; Perner, Lang, & Kloo, 2002), findings do not seem to be consistent. This is why we designed a new longitudinal study that included all of the relevant cognitive domains and aimed at exploring the interdependencies among these related concepts and their changes over time. Before we get to the description of the study, the relevant constructs and their theoretical relationships are briefly discussed.

THEORY OF MIND AND METACOGNITION

In the early 1980s, a number of studies focused on young children's knowledge about the mental world, better known as theory of mind (ToM) research. This wave is still very much in motion and may have produced more than 800 publications within the last two decades. ToM deals with very young children's understanding of mental life and age-related changes in this understanding, for instance, their knowledge that mental representations of events need not correspond to reality. In retrospect, it appears that this paradigm emerged from two initially independent lines of inquiry. One line was directly linked to research on metacognitive development, assessing children's understanding of mental verbs such as *knowing* or *forgetting* (Johnson & Wellman, 1980; Wellman, 1985). Wellman and coworkers conceptualized young children's developing metacognitive knowledge and their understanding of mental verbs as the development of a ToM. The other line of developmental research was mainly stimulated by a philosophical discussion (see Premack & Woodruff, 1978) on the issue of whether chimpanzees have a ToM, that is, possess the concept of belief. In a now classic study, Wimmer and Perner (1983) transferred this issue to the human species. They tested young children's understanding of false belief, confirming the assumption that children younger than about four years of age find it impossible to believe that another person could hold a belief that the child knows to be false. A little later, beginning at about age 4 years, children come to recognize assertions as the expression of someone's belief, which is not necessarily true. Subsequent ToM research has addressed young children's understanding of mental states, such as desires, intentions, emotions, attention, consciousness, and so on.

Differences Between the Metacognitive and ToM Approaches

Although researchers in both traditions share the same general objective—that is, to explore children's knowledge about and understanding of mental phenomena—the research literature has been distinct and unconnected because researchers focused on different developments (for a more detailed discussion, see Flavell, 2000; Kuhn, 1999, 2000). For instance, whereas ToM researchers have investigated children's initial knowledge about the existence of various mental states, such as desires and intentions, metacognitive researchers have focused more on task-related mental processes, such as strategies for improving performance on various tasks or attempts to monitor improvements. Flavell (2000) conceives of this latter approach as problem centered and suggests that it may be labeled applied theory of mind.

A second distinction between the two research paradigms concerns the age groups under study. Because ToM researchers are mainly interested in the origins of knowledge about mental states, they predominantly study infants and young children. On the other hand, metacognitive researchers investigate knowledge components and skills that require some previous understanding of mental states, and, thus, they mainly test older children and adolescents. A further distinction concerns the fact that developmental research on metacognition deals with what a child knows about his or her own mind rather than somebody else's. As noted by Flavell, how and how often other people use their minds in similar situations is not of primary interest. In contrast, it is the participant's understanding of some other person's mind that is usually of central concern in ToM studies.

Kuhn (1999, 2000) recently developed a conceptual framework to connect the ToM paradigm to related theoretical constructs, such as metacognition. She chose the heading of *metaknowing* as an umbrella term to encompass any cognition that has cognition—either one's own or others'—as its object. The dichotomy between procedural knowing (knowing how) and declarative knowing (knowing that) was used to distinguish between types of metaknowing. Knowing about declarative knowledge (as a product) was labeled metacognitive knowing, whereas knowing about procedural knowledge (knowing how) was addressed as metastrategic knowing. In Kuhn's framework, the metacognitive knowing component addresses young children's understanding of mental states and thus refers to ToM research, whereas metastrategic knowing refers to what children know about their cognitive processes and what impact this has on performance, an issue typically addressed in research on metacognitive development, such as metamemory. Although the labels chosen by Kuhn seem debatable (e.g., metamemory comprises more than knowledge about strategies; cf. Schneider & Pressley, 1997), the idea of linking the two research lines in a common framework is important and deserves further attention.

Based on these theoretical analyses, we assumed that early ToM competencies should be related to subsequent metacognitive knowledge, in particular, metastrategic knowledge. To our knowledge, this relationship has not yet been tested empirically within a longitudinal framework. Thus, both ToM measures and indicators of metacognitive knowledge were included in our study to explore the empirical link.

ToM AND EXECUTIVE CONTROL

Numerous studies have shown that striking changes take place in children's performance on ToM tasks during the preschool years (for reviews, see Flavell & Miller, 1998; Taylor, 1996). Whereas 3-year-olds typically perform very poorly on measures of false belief and deception and various kinds of perspective taking, most 4- to 5-year-olds master such tasks without any problem. One interpretation of this finding is that young children suffer from a conceptual deficit, lacking a concept of belief or a concept of mental representation (cf. Perner, 1991). An alternative interpretation is that many of the developmental differences observed for ToM performance reflect changes in children's executive functioning skills (e.g., Frye, Zelazo, & Palfai, 1995; Russell, 1996). According to this view, younger children's difficulties with ToM tasks may not be due to purely conceptual limitations but may rather stem from problems in translating conceptual knowledge into action.

One problem with the study of executive function (EF) is that it has to be conceived of as a rather complex cognitive construct. The term is used to describe processes such as planning, inhibitory control, and attentional flexibility. Although there is now a rapidly growing interest in EF within the field of developmental psychopathology, comparably little is known about its normal development (see Hughes, 1998a). There is broad agreement that the frontal lobes of the brain are heavily implicated in EF development, both in inhibitory processes and executive functioning more generally. Although the frontal lobes develop rapidly during infancy, they undergo another growth spurt between about 4 and 7 years of age, with subsequent growth being slow and gradual into young adulthood (Luria, 1973; Thatcher, 1992). There is reason to assume that developmental changes in the prefrontal cortex observed during the preschool and kindergarten years correspond with improvements in EF documented for the same time period.

In a recent theoretical account, Zelazo and colleagues (Frye et al., 1995; Zelazo, Carter, Resnick, & Frye, 1997; Zelazo & Frye, 1997) focused on young children's ability to use one or more rules (if-then statements) to control behavior. Their cognitive complexity and control (CCC) theory of deliberate reasoning and intentional action was developed to explain why task complexity predicts task difficulty. According to the CCC theory, there are age-related changes in the complexity of the situations that elicit perseveration—that is, inability to switch rules according to task requirements. Thus, Zelazo and colleagues assume that there are age-related changes in the complexity of the rule systems that children can represent: During the 3rd year of life, children can represent a single rule ("If red, then here") but not more. By 36 months, children can reflect on two different rules but are unable to represent a higher order relation between two incompatible pairs of rules, which is required to select between rule pairs (e.g., "If color, then if red, then here"). It is not until the age of 4 or 5 years that children can represent such a higher order rule. A modified version of the Wisconsin Card Sorting game seems well suited to illustrate this change. Here, children are told to first sort a series of test cards according to one dimension (e.g., for color) and then asked to switch to a new sorting criterion (e.g., shape). Regardless of which dimension is presented first, 3-year-olds typically continue to sort cards by that dimension despite being told the new rule on every trial. On the other hand, 4-year-olds no longer show signs of perseveration.

Is there any link between the development of EF and ToM? The literature suggests that EF (inhibition) tasks and ToM tasks are mastered at about the same developmental level. So far, several theoretical explanations for a systematic relationship have been offered. Frye et al. (1995) suggested that advances in children's ToM task performance reflect improvement in their embedded rule reasoning that enables children to switch judgments across different settings. Another theoretical claim is that the experience of agency (based on desires and volitions and leading to goal-directed behavior) is necessary for acquiring the concept of intentionality, which is central to understanding mental states (Russell, 1996). An opposite theoretical position has been taken by Perner (1998) and Carruthers (1996), who claim that the metarepresentational skills involved in understanding mental states are a necessary prerequisite for executive control. Researchers arguing from an evolutionary perspective believe that one critical ability in the evolution of social intelligence and in the subsequent development of other forms of cognition is the ability to inhibit thoughts and behaviors in certain contexts (cf. Bjorklund, Cormier, & Rosenberg, this volume; Bjorklund & Kipp, 2002).

Although the theoretical accounts vary considerably, there is plenty of empirical evidence for a close relationship between EF and ToM. Support for an association between the two constructs can be inferred from two different research areas. First, research on childhood autism has shown that individuals with autism are severely impaired on tests of both understanding mental states and on EF tasks (Baron-Cohen, Leslie, & Frith, 1985; Hughes, 1998a). Second, research with young, normal children has yielded substantial correlations between indicators of inhibitory control and ToM (cf. Carlson & Moses, 2001; Carlson, Moses, & Hix, 1998; Hughes, 1998a, 1998b; Perner et al., 2002). On average, correlations were in the 0.6 to 0.7 range, indicating a rather close association between the two constructs. Although this interdependence is not debated, the causal direction of the relationship is not clear. Whereas several researchers assume that individual differences in EF (in particular, inhibitory control) influence the development of ToM (e.g., Carlson & Moses, 2001; Carlson, Moses, & Breton, 2002; Hughes, 1998a, 1998b), others argue that the relationship between EF and ToM is not due to common executive demands (Perner et al., 2002). One general problem is that longitudinal studies exploring the chicken-egg issue are still rare. In one of these studies, Hughes (1998b) presented 4-year-olds with a battery of ToM and EF tasks and retested them about a year later. She found that the relation between EF and ToM was not symmetric: Whereas early EF performance predicted subsequent ToM performance, early individual differences in ToM did not account for any of the variance in later EF. Given the scarce longitudinal evidence on this issue, we decided to carry out another longitudinal study that included measures of both EF and ToM.

The Impact of Language Ability and Working Memory on ToM and EF Development

From an evolutionary theoretical perspective, most important aspects of cognition are domain specific in nature, that is, modular and not influenced by other cognitive abilities. ToM, for example, is proposed to be such a modular ability (Baron-Cohen, 1995). On the other hand, the ability to inhibit thoughts or behaviors is assumed to be domain general, cutting across domains or types of cognitive tasks. Similarly, working memory and language ability are conceived of as domain-general competencies. The question of how changes in a domain-general ability can play a role in the development of domain-specific aspects of cognition such as ToM remains an interesting one. Some authors (e.g., Bjorklund & Kipp, 2002) argue that the two types of cognition coexist in contemporary people but that enhanced domain-general skills (inhibitory control, language ability, working memory) are required before more domain-specific abilities can be developed. According to this assumption, EF, language ability, and working memory should serve as predictors of ToM development, whereas the opposite should not be the case.

Longitudinal evidence supporting this assumption was provided by Astington and Jenkins (1999). In this study, 3-year-olds were tested three times over a period of 7 months to assess the contribution of ToM to language development (syntax and semantics) and of language development to ToM development. As a main result, this study showed that language competence predicted ToM development but that the reverse was not true. Astington and Jenkins concluded that linguistic ability is required for successful performance on ToM tasks, with syntactical skills turning out to be more relevant than aspects of semantics (pragmatic aspects were not assessed). Although these findings seem to suggest that ToM performance depends on language ability, the authors acknowledged that their data could be interpreted differently. That is, it could also be that ToM and language both depend on some other internal factor not assessed in their study, such as working memory or EF. Given that Hughes (1998b) and Carlson et al. (2002) presented evidence for a strong impact of EF on ToM, this possibility cannot be ruled out. On the other hand, Carlson et al. also showed that EF tasks predicted ToM measures over and above working memory and intelligence, indicating that not all measures of domain-general competencies predict young children's ToM development.

Overall, the empirical findings are complex and not always easy to reconcile. One of the main problems with causal interpretations in this field is that most studies were cross-sectional in nature. Moreover, most studies focused on only two or three of the relevant constructs, which makes it difficult to judge the relative impact of variables. Thus, one main goal of our longitudinal study was to assess all theoretically relevant variables simultaneously and to analyze the interrelationships of constructs over time.

THE WÜRZBURG LONGITUDINAL STUDY

When planning our longitudinal study, we considered two aspects to be particularly important for the study's subsequent success: the initial age of the children and the time intervals between adjacent measurement points.

Regarding the first issue, previous research has clearly shown that major changes in young children's ToM and executive functioning occur between the ages of 3 and 4 years. Thus, precautions were taken to recruit children for our longitudinal study who on average were about 3 years old. As to the optimal timing of measurement points, we were confronted with a dilemma. Theoretically, it would have been preferable to assess intraindividual changes in the critical variables within rather short time intervals, for instance, within 2 to 3 months. However, due to organizational constraints, the time interval between adjacent measurement points that could be practically handled in our study was about 6 months (similar time intervals were also chosen in the longitudinal studies by Astington & Jenkins, 1999, and Hughes, 1998b). From a methodological point of view, choosing such a long time interval also reduces the probability of substantial testing effects. The longitudinal study is designed to explore developmental changes within the age range from 3 to 6 years. So far, three measurement points have been completed. Thus, only changes occurring during the course of 1 year, that is, between the age of (a little more than) 3 years to (a little more than) 4 years are considered in this chapter.

In total, 183 children (92 boys, 91 girls) from 18 kindergartens in the city and surroundings of Würzburg, Germany, were recruited for our ongoing project. The kindergartens are located in areas with mixed social backgrounds ranging from lower working class families to upper middle class families. Children's mean age at the first time of testing was 3 years 4 months (range: 3 years 0 months to 3 years 10 months). Overall, the attrition rate has been rather low. At the second measurement point, four children did not participate in the testing (one child had died and three children had moved to another area). Three more children left the study before the third time of testing. Accordingly, 176 children participated in all three assessments described in this chapter.

Design of the Longitudinal Study

At each time of testing, children participated in three sessions within an interval of 2 weeks. Testing took part in a quiet room at the children's kindergarten and lasted between 20 and 30 min per session. Session 1 consisted of the ToM tasks as well as a hiding task (only at the third time of testing). In Session 2, a German battery of language development (SET-K 3-5; Grimm, 2001) was administered. Finally, in Session 3, children were given various tasks designed to measure executive control and working memory.

The order of the sessions was counterbalanced in such a way that half of the children started with the ToM tasks, and the other half of the children began with the test of language development. Moreover, the tasks within each session were presented in two different orders (with the exception of the test of language development, which was always presented in the same standardized order).

Materials and Procedure

Theory of Mind. At each test time, children were given three ToM tasks:

1. A standard change-in-location false belief task (Wimmer & Perner, 1983) was given. The children listened to a tape recording of the following story, which was also acted out with dolls:

> Mother returns from her shopping trip. She bought chocolate for a cake. Maxi helps her to put away the things. He puts the chocolate into the blue cupboard. Maxi remembers exactly where he put the chocolate so that he could come back and get some later. Then he leaves for the playground. While Maxi is gone, mother starts to prepare the cake and takes the chocolate out of the blue cupboard. She grates a bit into the dough and then she does not put it back into the blue but into the green cupboard. Then she leaves to get some eggs. Now Maxi comes back from the playground and wants to get some chocolate.

Children were asked, "Does Maxi know where the chocolate is?" and "Where will Maxi look for the chocolate?" Furthermore, the story was interrupted for a control question to ensure that the children remembered where Maxi had left the chocolate. A credit was given when children answered both the control question and the test question concerning Maxi's false belief correctly.

2. A standard appearance-reality task (Flavell, Flavell, & Green, 1983) was given. Children were shown a candle that looked like an apple. They were asked what the object looked like and what it really was. Both of these questions had to be answered correctly for a credit to be given.

3. A standard unexpected-contents false belief task (Gopnik & Astington, 1988; Wimmer & Hartl, 1991) was also administered. Children were asked what was inside a familiar box. In most cases they answered with the usual content (e.g., "Smarties"). Then the box was opened and was found to have unexpected contents (e.g., a pen). After these unusual contents were put back in the box, the children were again asked what was inside the box. Then they were asked what they had thought was inside before it was opened and what another child, who had not seen inside the box, would think was inside it before it was opened. At each time of testing, a different box and contents were used (a Smarties box containing a pen, a crayon box containing a handkerchief, a soap-bubble box containing candies). Children received 2 points for the correct answers on this task, 1 for their own false belief, and 1 for the other child's false belief. Control questions had to be answered correctly for credit to be given.

Language. A German battery of language development (Sprachentwicklungstest für Kinder, SETK 3-5; Grimm, 2001) was administered. This battery measures general language ability by assessing receptive and expressive language skills as well as phonological memory skills. The battery has good validity and reliability, with internal consistency of the subtests ranging between .62 and .89. It contains two different test versions depending on the age of the children (a version for 3-year-olds and a version for 4- and 5-year-olds). At the first and second time of testing, children were given the following three subtests (test version for 3-year-olds):

1. *Sentence comprehension:* This subtest measures the ability to understand sentences of various complexity. It includes two different parts: In the first part, children were presented nine cards depicting different pictures. For each card, a sentence was stated, and the child had to point to the appropriate picture (e.g., "the man cooks"). In the second part, children received instructions of various grammatical complexity, which they had to translate into actions (e.g., "Put the blue pencil under the pillow").

2. *Encoding of semantic relations:* This subtest examines the ability to describe pictures verbally. The test material consists of 11 picture cards. Children were asked to describe what they could see in these pictures (e.g., a horse standing on a table).

3. *Morphological rules:* This subtest assesses the ability to use the plural form of different words. Children were shown 10 picture cards, which depicted a single object on the left side and several of these objects on the right side. Children were given the name of the single object (e.g., car), and then were asked to name the object set (e.g., cars).

At the third time of testing, the subtests were partly changed or replaced (test version for 4- and 5-year-olds). Again, three subtests were administered:

1. *Sentence comprehension:* As in the second part of the version for 3-year-olds, children were given instructions that they had to translate into actions. However, the subtest for 4- and 5-year-olds includes more complex instructions than the subtest for 3-year-olds (e.g., "Show me: The white ball is under the book because the teddy has hidden it there.")

2. *Sentence memory:* Children had to repeat sentences that differed in their length and meaningfulness. The first six sentences were meaningful sentences (e.g., "The duck is sitting beside the car"); the following nine sentences were nonmeaningful sentences (e.g., "A hat that feeds mountains sleeps").

3. *Morphological rules:* The first part of this subtest was the same as in the version for 3-year-olds. That is, children had to produce the plural form of common objects. However, in the second part, children were shown picture cards that depicted fantasy objects, such as Tulo, and children were asked to name the object sets.

In addition to the battery of language development, at the second and third time of testing children were given a vocabulary test, which was taken from a German intelligence test (HAWIVA; Schuck & Eggert, 1976). Children were asked to explain 20 different words, such as *dog*, *knife*, and *polite*. Depending on the accuracy of the statements, 2, 1, or 0 points were given for each answer. The test was discontinued after five consecutive 0-point answers.

Executive Control. At the first time of testing, children were given three tasks, and at the second and third time of testing children were given four tasks to measure executive control:

1. *Luria's hand game:* This task, which was originally designed by Luria (Luria, Pribram, & Homskaya, 1964), was used in a recently developed version by Hughes (1998b). The hand game includes two conditions: the imitative (control) condition and the conflict (test) condition. In the imitative condition, children were instructed to produce the same hand shape as the experimenter (point a finger or show a fist). In the conflict condition, children were asked to produce the opposite hand action, that is, point a finger if the experimenter shows a fist and show a fist if the experimenter points a finger. The instructions were repeated until the child made six consecutive correct responses (or up to a maximum of 15 trials), and feedback was provided for every trial. Fist and finger trials were intermingled in a pseudorandom sequence, and the two conditions were presented in a counterbalanced order across children. Performance was rated by the number of trials to criterion (6–15).

2. *Go/no-go task* (e.g., Perner et al., 2002). Our version of the go/no-go task consisted of a practice trial (10 items) and two test trials (25 items each). A laptop was used on which one of two stimuli, a red square or a yellow square (6.5 cm × 6.5 cm), was presented (one at a time) in the center of the display. Stimulus duration was 2 s for the practice trial and 0.75 s for the test trials. Time from stimulus offset to next stimulus onset (ISI) was 2 s for the practice trial and 0.5 s for the test trials. The proportion of go–items was 75% in the practice trial and the first test trial, and 50% in the second test trial. Children responded by pressing a 10 cm × 10 cm plastic panel.

Before the practice trial started, the experimenter explained the rules of the task: "If a yellow square appears, you press this panel, and if a red square appears, you do not press the panel." During the practice trial, children received feedback about their performance. Before starting the first test trial, the rules were repeated. Before starting the second trial, the experimenter explained, "Now we are going to play a different game. Now you press the panel if a red square appears and you do not press the panel if a yellow square appears." During the test trials, no more feedback was given. To determine each child's performance, the percentages of hits, false alarms, omission errors, and correct rejections were registered by the computer.

3. *Card sorting:* At the first and second time of testing, a standard Dimensional Change Card Sorting (DCCS) task was administered (see Perner & Lang, 2002). A set of cards (8 cm × 8 cm) was used, which consisted of 2 target cards (a red teddy bear and a yellow ball) and 12 test cards (six yellow teddy bears and six red balls). The target cards were affixed to a box into which the test cards had to be posted through a slit. In the preswitch phase, the experimenter explained the two dimensions (color and shape) of the target cards. The experimenter said, "Now we are going to play the color game. In this game, all the yellow cards go here, but the red cards go in there." The children and the experimenter sorted two cards together (one yellow and one red), and then the children were asked to sort five cards on their own. Feedback was given on each of the preswitch trials. After five preswitch trials, the experimenter explained, "Now we are going to play a different game, the shape game. This time, all teddy bears go here, but all balls go in there." Again, the children had to sort five cards. In the postswitch phase, no more feedback was given. The order of the rules (color and shape) was counterbalanced. Each child's performance was rated by the number of correctly sorted cards during the postswitch phase (0–5).

Because the standard DCCS task showed ceiling effects at the second time of testing, this task was replaced by a different card-sorting task at the third time of testing (set-shifting task; Hughes, 1998b). In contrast to the standard DCCS task, the rule change was not announced in this task, and a new set of cards was used for each rule. Again, children were required to learn two rules, a color rule and a shape rule. The sets of cards consisted of yellow and green books or yellow and green pencils and grey and black hats or grey and black rabbits (eight cards of each type). As props, two toy characters well-known to children (Samson and Elmo from *Sesame Street*) were included. Children were introduced to the first toy character and were told that some of the cards that would be shown were Samson's (or Elmo's) favorites, and some he did not like at all. The experimenter instructed the child to put Samson's (or Elmo's) favorites into a box. The cards teddy didn't like were placed face down on the table. The cards were shown one by one to the child in a pseudorandom sequence. On each trial, the experimenter asked whether Samson (or Elmo) liked the card or not, noted the child's response, and provided feedback (e.g., "Yes, Samson likes that one, so you put it in the box"). The rule order and card set used were counterbalanced across children. For each rule, a maximum of 20 trials was presented, and performance was rated by the mean number of trials needed to achieve the criterion run of six correct trials across rules (6–20).

4. *Stroop task:* At the second and third time of testing, a Stroop task was added. This task was designed by Gerstadt, Hong, and Diamond (1994) and requires inhibitory control of action plus learning and remembering two rules. Children were shown 2 training cards and 16 testing cards (8 cm × 8 cm). Half of the cards were black depicting a yellow moon and stars; the other half of the cards were white depicting a bright sun.

Children were instructed to say "day" whenever a black card with a moon and stars appeared and to say "night" when shown a white card with a bright sun. During the two practice trials, children received feedback and were reminded of the rules if necessary. No feedback was given during the 16 test trials. Sun and moon cards were presented in a pseudorandom sequence. Children's performance was indexed by the number of correct answers (0–16).

Working Memory.   At each time of testing, three tasks were administered to measure working memory:

1. *Phonological memory for pseudowords:* This task, which is taken from the German battery of language development (SETK 3-5; Grimm, 2001), is designed to measure the ability to represent new and unfamiliar phonological patterns in phonological memory. Children were instructed to repeat pseudowords such as *billop* or *kalifeng*. The pseudowords differed in their length, with the number of syllables ranging from two to five. The task was made more engaging for young children by using funny-looking figures, which they had to call by certain names. Performance was rated by the number of correctly recalled pseudowords (0–13 for 3-year-olds; 0–18 for 4-year-olds).

2. *Word span task:* Children were asked to reproduce sequences of words. All words used in this task consisted of one syllable (e.g., *shoe, bed*). During the practice phase, children had to repeat a sequence of one and a sequence of two words. The test phase consisted of two trials at each level: two-, three-, four-, and five-item lists. Testing was discontinued after two failures at a given level. Scores on this task were determined by the children's span, that is, the longest list length for which a child succeeded on at least one out of two trials.

3. *Pointing task:* This task was adopted from the noisy book working memory task developed by Hughes (1998b). In this task, children were asked to point at picture cards in order to recreate a sequence of items given as a verbal list. First, children were shown an array of nine 5 cm × 8 cm cards depicting objects and animals. To ensure that all children were familiar with the items, children were asked to name the pictures. Next, the experimenter covered up the pictures and said the names of two items. After that, the children were instructed to point at the corresponding pictures in the correct order. The training phase consisted of two sequences of two items. During the test phase, children had to recreate sequences of two, three, and four pictures (and five pictures at the third time of testing). Again, performance on this task was indexed by the child's span (i.e., the longest list length for which a child succeeded on at least one out of two trials).

Results

In general, the relevant literature has shown that, in early childhood, intercorrelations within a domain and also between different domains are

TABLE 12.1
Percentage of Children Passing the ToM Tasks

	Time 1	Time 2	Time 3
Change-in-location false belief	27.1	41.9	64.7
Unexpected content			
Representational change	35.2	60.3	65.7
False belief	14.4	45.3	53.8
Appearance-reality	34.6	40.6	46.6

highly dependent on age. Therefore, correlations are often considerably lower when age is partialled out. Preliminary analyses showed that, in our study, correlation coefficients remained approximately the same when individual differences in chronological age were taken into account. This is due to the fact that our sample is very homogeneous, as far as age is concerned. Hence, in the following, only uncorrected Pearson correlations are reported.

Theory of Mind. Table 12.1 shows the percentages of children passing the ToM tasks at each time of testing. Cochran's Q-tests indicated that there was a significant increase over time in the number of children succeeding on each of the ToM tasks (all $Qs > 6.22$; all $ps < .05$). As can be seen from Table 12.1, however, even at the third time of testing, ToM performance was far from being perfect.

At the first time of testing, intercorrelations among individual scores on ToM tasks ranged between $rs = .07$ and $.33$. The strongest correlations were found between both parts of the unexpected-content task ($r = .33$, $p < .01$) and between the change-in-location task and the unexpected-content task ($r = .31$, $p < .01$; $r = .28$; $p < .01$ for the false belief and the representational change question, respectively). There were no significant correlations between the appearance-reality task and any other of the ToM tasks. At the second time of testing, five out of six correlations reached significance, indicating a developmental increase in coherence within children's ToM performance (range: $r = .01$ to $.46$). Again, the strongest correlations were observed between the change-in-location task and the unexpected-content task ($r = .46$, $p < .01$; $r = .25$, $p < .01$ for the false belief and the representational change question, respectively) and between both parts of the unexpected-content task ($r = .38$, $p < .01$). The correlations between the appearance-reality task and other ToM tasks were generally lower. However, two out of three correlations were significant ($r = .19$, $p < .05$; $r = .18$, $p < .05$ for the representational change question of the unexpected-content task and the change-in-location task, respectively). At the third time of testing, a similar pattern of intercorrelations emerged, with the strongest correlations occurring between both parts of the unexpected-content task ($r = .42$, $p < .01$) and between the change-in-location task and the unexpected-content task ($r = .37$, $p < .01$; $r = .33$, $p < .01$ for the false belief and the representational change question, respectively).

Again, correlations of the appearance-reality task with other ToM tasks were comparably lower and nonsignificant (range: r = .01 to .14).

To create a more robust measure of ToM performance, sum scores were calculated for each time of testing. These scores are the sum total of all items passed, and they have a possible range of 0 to 4 points. A one-way analysis of variance with these sum scores as a within-subject factor confirmed that ToM performance increased over time, $F(2,342)$ = 70.54; $p <$ .01 (M = 1.11, SD = 1.09; M = 1.88, SD = 1.30; M = 2.29, SD = 1.26 for Times 1, 2, and 3, respectively). The correlation between sum scores at Times 1 and 2 was r = .39, $p <$ .01. The corresponding correlation between the sum scores at Times 2 and 3 was somewhat higher, r = .47, $p <$ .01. Overall, these coefficients indicate a moderate stability of ToM performance.

Language.   Because children had to complete a different version of the Language Development Battery (SETK 3-5; Grimm, 2001) at the third time of testing, developmental changes can be reported only for Time 1 and Time 2 (see Table 12.2). A t test revealed that children's ability to understand complex sentences significantly improved over time, $t(175)$ = 11.15, $p <$ .01. Similarly, there was a significant increase in the ability to encode semantic relations, $t(174)$ = 9,60, $p <$ .01. In addition, a developmental increase was found for the ability to use morphological rules, $t(173)$ = 6.34, $p <$ .01.

To examine whether our data correspond to the data of the normative sample of the Language Development Battery (SETK 3-5; Grimm, 2001) we converted the raw scores obtained in our study into T scores according to the test manual. At Time 1, the mean T scores were 51.2 (SD = 10.2), 50.7 (SD = 10.3), and 53.2 (SD = 11.0) for sentence comprehension, encoding of semantic relations, and morphological rules respectively. Because our T scores were very similar to those of the normative sample (Ms = 50, SDs = 10), it can be concluded that our sample is representative in the domain of language development.

In addition to the Battery of Language Development, a vocabulary test was administered at the second and third time of testing. A t test indicated that there was a significant increase in children's vocabulary, $t(163)$ = 8.1, $p <$ .01.

TABLE 12.2
Mean Raw Scores on the Subtests of the Battery of Language
Development and the Vocabulary Test at Time 1 and Time 2 (SD)

	Time 1	Time 2
Sentence comprehension	12.25 (3.98)	14.81 (3.21)
Encoding of semantic relations	3.29 (1.31)	4.14 (1.28)
Morphological rules	13.65 (5.09)	15.59 (4.10)
Vocabulary test	—	13.73 (4.24)

At each time of testing, substantial intercorrelations were found among the subtests of the Battery of Language Development (all rs ranging between $r = .45$ and $r = .67$; all $ps < .01$). These intercorrelations correspond well to those obtained in the normative sample. The relations of the vocabulary test with the subtests of the Battery of Language Development were somewhat lower, ranging from $r = .34, p < .01$ to $r = .53, p < .01$.

Each of the subtests of the Battery of Language Development proved to show substantial stability from Time 1 to Time 2 ($rs = .65, .59, .61$ for Sentence Comprehension, Encoding of Semantic Relations, Morphological Rules, respectively; all $ps < .01$). Moreover, individual differences on the subtests Sentence Comprehension and Morphological Rules remained stable from Time 2 to Time 3, even though the corresponding subtests were partly changed and expanded at Time 3 ($r = .57, .50$ for Sentence Comprehension and Morphological Rules, respectively; all $ps < .01$). For the vocabulary test, a moderate stability was found from Time 2 to Time 3, $r = .47, p < .01$.

Because performances on individual language scores were reasonably well correlated with each other, aggregate scores were computed for each time of testing. Therefore, all raw scores were converted into standard z scores, and then mean z scores were computed for the domain language. At Time 1, the mean z score contained the subtests Sentence Comprehension, Encoding of Semantic Relations, and Morphological Rules. At Time 2, additionally, the vocabulary test was included. At Time 3, the mean z score consisted of the subtests Sentence Comprehension, Sentence Memory, and Morphological Rules and the vocabulary test. The correlations of these z scores were $r = .76, p < .01$ for Time 1 and Time 2, and $r = .74, p < .01$ for Time 2 and Time 3. Hence, these coefficients demonstrate strong associations among language scores across the time period under study.

Executive Control. Table 12.3 shows the mean scores on EF tasks at each time of testing. A t test indicated that there was a significant increase in the number of correctly sorted cards during the postswitch phase from Time 1 to Time 2, $t(164) = 4.09, p < .01$. At Time 2, performance on this task was almost at ceiling, with 80% of the children attaining perfect scores of 5 points.

To examine developmental changes on Luria's hand game, a two-way repeated measures analysis of variance with condition and time as within-subject factors was carried out. Results revealed a main effect of time, $F(2,302) = 29.5, p < .01$, a main effect of condition, $F(1,151) = 69.4, p < .01$, and a significant time × condition interaction, $F(2, 302) = 14.6, p < .01$. As can be seen from Table 12.3, children's performance in the control condition was superior to that in the conflict condition, and developmental improvement was greater for the conflict condition than for the imitation condition.

For the go/no-go task, a discrimination index A', which is a nonparametric equivalent to d' known from signal detection theory (Grier, 1971),

TABLE 12.3
Mean Scores on EF and Working Memory Tasks (SD)

Tasks	Measure	Time 1	Time 2	Time 3
Card sorting				
DCCS	Correct sorted cards (0–5)	3.6 (2.0)	4.2 (1.7)	—
Set Shifting	Trials to criterion (6–20)	—	—	11.0 (2.8)
Hand game				
Imitation	Trials to criterion (6–15)	6.8 (2.0)	6.7 (2.0)	6.3 (1.4)
Conflict	Trials to criterion (6–15)	9.7 (4.1)	8.2 (3.6)	7.0 (2.6)
Go/no-go task				
Trial 1	Discrimination Index A´ (0–1)	.66 (.22)	.80 (.17)	.88 (.14)
Trial 2	Discrimination Index A´ (0–1)	.60 (.24)	.75 (.22)	.82 (.18)
Day and night Stroop	Number of correct answers (0–16)	—	11.3 (5.0)	13.0 (4.4)
Pseudowords	Correct repeated words	6.4 (2.9)	8.0 (3.0)	11.9 (3.6)
Word span	Max. sequence length	3.2 (0.8)	3.5 (0.8)	3.8 (0.8)
Pointing task	Max. sequence length	2.5 (0.9)	2.5 (1.0)	2.7 (1.1)

was calculated. In a pilot study, this score has proven to be the most reliable of different available measures (e.g., hits, false alarms). A two-way repeated measures analysis of variance with trial and time as within-participants factors revealed a main effect of time, $F(2,236) = 78.1$, $p < .01$, and a main effect of trial, $F(1,118) = 18.4$; $p < .01$, but no significant interaction trial × time. Overall, there was a significant improvement over time in children's ability to discriminate targets from distractors (i.e., the ability to respond to red rectangles but not to yellow ones or vice versa). The discrimination index was consistently lower in Trial 2, in which a new rule had to be applied.

At the second and third time of testing, a Stroop task was added to the test battery. As indicated by a t test, there was a significant increase in the number of correct answers to sun and moon cards, $t(170) = 3.5$, $p < .01$.

Trials to criterion on the hand game and the set-shifting task were reversed to obtain consistent positive scoring on individual tasks. At Time 1, four out of six correlations between the EF tasks were significant, with coefficients ranging between $r = .07$ (ns) and $r = .32$, $p < .01$. Scores on the conflict condition of the hand game were significantly correlated with scores on the DCCS task and scores on Trial 1 and Trial 2 of the go/no-go task, $r = .21, .32, .16$, respectively, $ps < .05$, and scores on the DCCS task were also correlated with scores on Trial 2 of the go/no-go task, $r = .22$, $p < .01$.

At Time 2, all 10 coefficients were significant, suggesting a developmental increase in coherence within children's EF skills (range: $rs = .16$ to .41; $p < .01$). The strongest correlations were found between Trial 1 and Trial 2 of the go/no-go task and between the conflict condition of the hand game and Trial 2 of the go/no-go task, $rs = .41$ and .29, respectively, $ps < .01$.

Unexpectedly, however, only 1 out of 10 correlations reached significance at the third measurement point (range: rs = .03 to .32). The only significant correlation was found between Trial 1 and Trial 2 of the go/no-go task, r = .32 p < .01. All other relations remained nonsignificant, which was probably due to ceiling effects in both the Luria's hand game and the go/no-go task.

Aggregate scores were calculated to obtain a robust measure of EF skills. As for the domain of language, raw scores were converted into standardized z scores, and mean z scores were computed. Mean z scores at Time 1 were significantly correlated with those at Time 2, r = .44, p < .01, as well as mean z scores at Time 2 with mean z scores at Time 3, r = .34, p < .01. Accordingly, a moderate stability was found for the domain executive control.

Working Memory.   Results on working memory tasks are displayed in the lower part of Table 12.3. To examine developmental changes in separate repeated measures, analyses of variance on individual working memory tasks were carried out. Results revealed that there was a significant increase in the number of repeated pseudowords, $F(2,304)$ = 239.7, p < .01, as well as in the word span, $F(2, 316)$ = 42.5, p < .01. However, the repeated measures analysis of variance on the pointing task did not reach significance, $F(2,324)$ = 1.9; ns. Performance on this task remained low over time.

At Time 1, correlations among the various working memory tasks were rather low, with coefficients ranging between r = .19 and r = .20; all ps < .01. At Time 2, relations between working memory tasks were somewhat higher (range: r = .22 and r = .38; all ps < .01). Finally, at Time 3, moderate correlations between individual tasks were found (range: r = .24 and r = .47; all ps < .01). Taken together, results demonstrate that coherence within children's working memory skills increased over time.

Mean z scores were calculated as a measure of overall working memory skills. Mean z scores at Time 1 were correlated (with r = .36, r = .50; ps < .01) with mean z scores at Time 2 and Time 3, respectively. The correlation between mean z scores at Time 2 with those at Time 3 was r = .61, p < .01, indicating an augmenting stability of working memory skills.

Relations Between ToM, EF, Working Memory, and Language.   Table 12.4 presents the intercorrelations between aggregate scores for ToM, EF, working memory, and language at each time of testing. Overall, the strongest correlations were found between language and all other domains. That is, at each time of testing, children with better language skills also showed better performances on tests of ToM, executive control, and working memory. Surprisingly, there were only relatively weak associations between executive control and working memory, even though correlations tended to be stronger at Times 2 and 3. Hence, in this study, there was no evidence that performances on working memory and EF tasks reflect the same underlying concept. The main question for this study,

TABLE 12.4
Intercorrelations Between Theory of Mind, Executive Control,
Working Memory, and Language at Time 1, Time 2, and Time 3

	ToM	Executive Control	Working Memory
Executive control	.19*[a]	—	
	.34**[b]	—	
	.33**[c]	—	
Working memory	.19*[a]	.20**[a]	—
	.31**[b]	.26**[b]	—
	.29**[c]	.28**[c]	—
Language	.31**[a]	.44**[a]	.48**[a]
	.48**[b]	.49**[b]	.32**[b]
	.48**[c]	.37**[c]	.46**[c]

Note. *$p < .05$. **$p < .01$. [a]Time 1; [b]Time 2; [c]Time 3.

however, concerned the relation between ToM and executive control. As can be seen from Table 12.4, only a weak association between both domains emerged at the first measurement point. However, moderate correlations were found at Times 2 and 3, indicating a developmental increase in the relation between performances on tests of ToM and executive control.

Because language proficiency was considerably correlated with all other domains, further analyses were conducted to investigate which specific language skills contribute to these correlations. Accordingly, correlations among scores on individual subtests of language development and aggregate scores for ToM, executive control, and working memory were computed. At each time of testing, all of these correlations were significant (except for the correlation between the vocabulary test and executive control at Time 3, $r = .12$, ns), with coefficients ranging between $r = .23$ and $r = .53$; all $ps < .01$. Altogether, the strongest correlations were found between the subtest Sentence Comprehension and the aggregate scores for ToM, executive control, and working memory. Particularly, at Time 2, the subtest Sentence Comprehension was highly correlated with ToM, $r = .51$, $p < .01$, and with executive control, $r = .51$, $p < .01$. Furthermore, there was also a strong correlation between sentence memory and the aggregate score for working memory at Time 3, $r = .53$, $p < .01$.

Given that the main question in our study addressed the relation of ToM and executive control, it seemed important to examine whether a third variable accounts for this association. In the relevant literature, partial correlations controlling for age and verbal ability are usually reported. Most often, verbal ability is rated by scores on a vocabulary test (e.g. the PPVT-R; Dunn & Dunn, 1981). When the correlations between ToM and executive control obtained in our study were controlled for age, they remained significant at each time of testing, $r = .15, .28, .28$, all $ps < .05$, for Time 1, Time 2, and Time 3, respectively. When age and scores on the vocabulary test were taken into account, similar results were found, $r = .24, .32, p < .01$, for Time 2 and Time 3, respectively (at Time 1, the vocabulary test was not administered). However, when age and the subtest Sentence Comprehension were partialled out, a significant correlation between ToM and executive control emerged only at the third measurement point, $r = .25$, $p < .01$. The corresponding correlations at Time 1 and Time 2 were nonsignificant, $rs = .05$ and $.09$, $p > .05$. These results indicate that, until the age of about 4 years, the association between ToM and executive control is explained to a large extent by individual differences in sentence comprehension skills.

Predicting ToM From Executive Control, Working Memory, and Language. To assess the contribution of individual differences in executive control, working memory, and language to variability in ToM scores at a later time point, hierarchical regression analyses were computed. In each regression analysis, age and ToM performance at an earlier time point were entered as Step 1. Scores on executive control, working memory, and language at the earlier time point were entered as Step 2. Table 12.5 shows the results of the analyses from Time 1 to Time 2, from Time 2 to Time 3, and from Time 1 to Time 3. Only significant predictors are presented, and the regression coefficients shown are those obtained at the final step. First, when ToM at Time 2 served as the dependent variable, ToM performance at Time 1 accounted for 14% of the variance in ToM scores obtained 6 months later. When executive control, working memory, and language scores were added as predictors, only language performance at Time 1 reliably improved the amount of variance explained in the criterion variable, $\Delta R^2 = .14$. Together, earlier ToM and language performances now predicted 28% of the variance in later ToM scores. Similarly, when ToM at Time 3 was the criterion variable, ToM and language performance at Time 2 accounted for 35% of the variance in ToM scores obtained 6 months later. However, the addition of executive control performance at Time 2 also reliably improved the amount of variance explained in the dependent variable, $\Delta R^2 = .02$. Finally, when ToM assessed at Time 3 was predicted from Time 1 scores, ToM and language performance at Time 1 accounted for 25% of the variance in ToM scores 1 year later. No significant predictive relation between early executive control performance and later ToM scores was found. Overall, language proved to be the strongest predictor of later ToM performance, as indicated by the beta weights depicted in Table 12.5. In none of the various regression analyses did age or working memory make a contribution to the prediction of ToM performance.

Predicting Executive Control From ToM, Working Memory, and Language. A similar set of analyses was performed to assess the contribution of scores on ToM, working memory, and language to variability in executive control scores at a later time point. In each regression analysis, age and executive control performance assessed at an earlier time point were entered as Step 1. Next, ToM, working memory, and language variables assessed at the earlier time point were entered as Step 2. Table 12.6

TABLE 12.5
Summary of Hierarchical Regression Analyses Predicting ToM
From Executive Control, Working Memory, and Language

Variable	Corrected R^2	ΔR^2	β
	Time 1 to Time 2[a]		
Step 1			
ToM, Time 1	.14**	.14	.26
Step 2			
Language, Time 1	.28**	.14	.40
	Time 2 to Time 3[b]		
Step 1			
ToM, Time 2	.22**	.22	.25
Step 2			
Language, Time 2	.35**	.13	.35
Executive Control, Time 2	.37*	.02	.17
	Time 1 to Time 3[b]		
Step 1			
ToM, Time 1	.07 ($p < .07$)	.07	.13
Step 2			
Language, Time 1	.25**	.18	.45

Note. *$p < .05$. **$p < .01$. [a]Dependent variable = ToM,
Time 2. [b]Dependent variable = ToM, Time 3.

shows the results of the analyses predicting Time 2 performance from
Time 1 data, Time 3 performance from Time 2 data, and Time 3 performance from Time 1 data. Again, only significant predictors are presented,
and the regression coefficients shown are those obtained at the final step.
First, when executive control at Time 2 was chosen as the dependent variable, performance on executive control tasks at Time 1 predicted 20% of the
variance in executive control scores assessed 6 months later. The addition
of language performance at Time 1 reliably improved the amount of variance explained in the dependent variable, $\Delta R^2 = .12$. Likewise, when executive control at Time 3 was the criterion variable, performance on executive
control and language tasks at Time 2 accounted for 13% of the variance in
executive control scores obtained 6 months later. Interestingly, however,
language performance assessed at Time 1 did not predict executive control
measured at Time 3. Obviously, the contribution of early language skills
for predicting later scores on executive control tasks declined over time.
In contrast, scores on working memory tasks assessed at Time 1 reliably
improved the amount of variance explained in executive control assessed
at Time 3, $\Delta R^2 = .04$. Age differences and early ToM performance did not
make significant contributions to the prediction of executive control performance at any time point.

General Discussion

The data analyzed for the first three measurement points of the Würz-burg Longitudinal Study revealed several interesting findings. First, it turned out that developmental changes obtained for the various domains and tasks differed considerably. For instance, a closer look at Table 12.1 reveals that ToM tasks remained rather difficult across the three measure-ment points, even though intraindividual improvements were significant over time. On the other hand, the various tasks chosen to represent exec-utive control turned out to be rather easy from the very beginning on. Not surprisingly, then, ceiling effects were observed for these measures at Time 3. Similar problems were observed for some of the language vari-ables in that new test items had to be worked on at the third measurement point. Apparently, changes in the relevant features of executive function-ing and language take place at a more rapid pace than those observed for the ToM tasks. Consequently, different tasks tapping the same construct have to be considered during rather short time intervals within the same longitudinal study, which makes it difficult and sometimes even impos-sible to describe the course of individual changes in the relevant concept over time. This certainly constitutes a serious methodological problem for

TABLE 12.6
Summary of Hierarchical Regression Analyses Predicting
Executive Control From ToM, Working Memory, and Language

Variable	Corrected R^2	ΔR^2	β
Time 1 to Time 2[a]			
Step 1			
Executive Control, Time 1	.20**	.20	.28
Step 2			
Language, Time 1	.32**	.12	.40
Time 2 to Time 3[b]			
Step 1			
Executive Control, Time 2	.11**	.22	.25
Step 2			
Language, Time 2	.13*	.02	.18
Time 1 to Time 3[b]			
Step 1			
Executive Control, Time 1	.07**	.07	.22
Step 2			
Working Memory, Time 1	.11**	.04	.23

Note. *$p < .05$. **$p < .01$. [a]Dependent variable = Executive Control, Time 2. [b]Dependent variable = Executive Control, Time 3.

longitudinal studies dealing with young children, a problem that has been neglected in both past and current discussions (see Schneider, 1989, for a more comprehensive treatment of such problems). In contrast, longitudinal research on working memory is not plagued with this problem, given that the same tasks can be used (and also measure similar functions) from early childhood to late adulthood.

Related to this methodological problem, assessments of intertask coherence and test-retest stability within a given domain varied as a function of the domain under consideration. With the exception of the language domain, intertask correlations obtained for the 3-year-olds were low to moderate, indicating that children's performance varied considerably across similar tasks. This points to the problem that experimental studies with 3-year-olds are generally difficult to conduct. That these young children are not familiar with the test situation and that they often feel uncomfortable when interacting with an adult stranger may add to the measurement problem, despite extended warming up phases, which were included in our study to reduce this problem. The general difficulty already observed in similar studies carried out decades ago is that it is not sufficient to make young children understand what you want them to do, but it is at least as important to get them to want to do it (Brown & DeLoache, 1978). Given that both intertask coherence and test-retest stability increased as a function of measurement point, it is obvious that this problem disappears with time and increasing age of the children. After the age of 3.6 years, studies of this type seem generally feasible and can be conducted rather objectively and reliably. Nonetheless, the general dilemma we are faced with when conducting a longitudinal study with 3- to 4-year-olds is that measurement issues particularly salient at the very beginning complicate the assessment of intraindividual changes within and across cognitive domains. So a caveat is certainly in order when we interpret the main outcomes of this study.

One of the most important findings concerns the close relationship between language proficiencies on the one hand and all other domains on the other hand, particularly at the beginning of the study. Overall, the strongest correlations were found for the subtest Sentence Comprehension and the aggregate scores for ToM, executive control, and working memory. The relevance of language skills for ToM development was already emphasized in the longitudinal study by Astington and Jenkins (1999). In that study, however, tests of executive control and working memory were not included. Consequently, as noted by the authors, the possibility that the relationship between language skills and ToM was caused by a common third factor, such as executive control or working memory, could not be excluded. Given that the present study included measures of all of these constructs, the issue seems clearer now. We did not find any evidence for the assumption that the relationship between language proficiency and ToM is mediated by executive control or working memory. Rather, there is clear-cut evidence that early performance on ToM tasks and measures of executive performance (as well as on working memory tasks) strongly depends on specific language skills—particularly, the ability to decode, memorize, and understand sentences. Much of the variability of findings obtained at the first measurement point seems due to the young children's problems with understanding what they were supposed to do, that is, with understanding the instructions. If this assumption is correct, we would expect more intertask coherence in the ToM, executive functioning, and working memory domains for those children with initially higher levels of sentence comprehension.

Interestingly, the impact of language skills on performance in the other cognitive domains decreased over time, indicating that most 4-year-olds understood task requirements. This development was accompanied by increasing within-domain coherence and also increasing across-domain intercorrelations. This finding is in accord with the outcomes of other relevant studies (e.g., Carlson & Moses, 2001; Hughes, 1998b).

Unexpectedly, we did not find the strong associations between measures of ToM and executive control reported in the literature (Carlson & Moses, 2001; Carlson et al., 1998; Frye et al., 1995; Hughes, 1998a, 1998b; Perner & Lang, 2000; Perner et al., 2002). For instance, Carlson and Moses (2001) reported a correlation of $r = .66$ between inhibitory (executive) control and ToM. As can be seen from Table 12.4, correlations between these two concepts obtained in our study varied from .19 to .34. Although all of these correlations were statistically significant, they clearly differed from those found by Carlson and Moses and other researchers. However, a closer look at the previous studies reveals that findings may not be as discrepant as one might assume. For some reason, age-heterogeneous samples were recruited in most previous studies, which made it necessary to partial out age differences to assess the true relationship between the relevant concepts. As noted previously, we strived to obtain a sample that was rather homogeneous regarding chronological age. When uncorrected and partial correlations were calculated in our study, results did not differ. However, quite substantial differences between uncorrected and partial correlations were found in most other studies. Whereas 46 out of the 48 uncorrected correlations among 12 inhibitory control and 4 ToM measures reported in the Carlson and Moses (2001; cf. their Table 7) study were significant and also substantial, ranging between .25 and .55, only 20 of these correlations remained significant after controlling for age, gender, and verbal ability. The correlation of .66 mentioned earlier, which was calculated for the aggregate scores of the inhibitory control and ToM batteries, dropped to .41 when age differences were taken into account. Differences between uncorrected and partial correlations were even more pronounced in the Perner et al. (2002) study (cf. their Table 6). These findings no longer differ much from our results. In our view, this indicates that the relationship between ToM and executive control may have been overestimated due to sampling procedures used in previous research, that is, the recruiting of age-heterogeneous samples.

Although we had hoped to contribute substantially to the discussion regarding the causal direction of the relationship between executive control and ToM, our findings so far have not been conclusive. Our regression analyses showed that language skills accounted for much of the variance in the criterion variables, regardless of whether ToM or executive control served as dependent variables. Although there were indications that early executive control additionally contributed to the prediction of subsequent ToM (and not vice versa), the evidence was not strong enough to support the statement that executive functioning should be conceived of as a precursor of ToM. As noted earlier, previous longitudinal research (Hughes, 1998b) supported such an assumption, and other recent work seems to indicate that both inhibitory control and working memory predict ToM (false belief) performance (Carlson & Moses, 2001; Carlson et al., 2002; but see Perner & Lang, 2002; Perner et al., 2002). Unfortunately, however, the available results from our longitudinal study are not clearcut in this respect and, thus, do not contribute significantly to this controversial discussion.

Finally, one of the positive outcomes of our study was that both coherence and stability of our ToM measures increased over time. So the concept can be reliably assessed, and individual differences in ToM performance seem rather stable from an early point. This is a necessary prerequisite to testing our assumption outlined previously, that children's knowledge about the mental world (i.e., ToM) will predict subsequent metacognitive knowledge, in particular, metastrategic knowledge sensu Kuhn. Given that measures of metacognitive knowledge are just now being assessed in the ongoing study, however, it is still too early to speculate about the empirical relation.

ACKNOWLEDGMENTS

This research was supported by a grant from the German Research Foundation (SO 213 12-2, TP 3).

REFERENCES

Astington, J. W., & Jenkins, J. M. (1999). A longitudinal study of the relation between language and theory-of-mind development. *Developmental Psychology, 35*, 1311–1320.

Baron-Cohen, S. (1995). *Mindblindness: An essay on autism and theory of mind.* Cambridge, MA: MIT Press

Baron-Cohen, S., Leslie, A. M., & Frith, U. (1985). Does the autistic child have a "theory of mind"? *Cognition, 21*, 37–46.

Bjorklund, D. F., & Kipp, K. (2002). Social cognition, inhibition, and theory of mind: The evolution of human intelligence. In R. J. Sternberg & J. C. Kaufman (Eds.), *The evolution of intelligence* (pp. 27–54). Mahwah, NJ: Lawrence Erlbaum Associates.

Brown, A. L., & DeLoache, J. S. (1978). Skills, plans, and self-regulation. In R. S. Siegler (Ed.), *Children's thinking: What develops?* (pp. 3–35). Hillsdale, NJ: Lawrence Erlbaum Associates.

Carlson, S. M., & Moses, L. J. (2001). Individual differences in inhibitory control and children's theory of mind. *Child Development, 72*, 1032–1053.

Carlson, S. M., Moses, L. J., & Breton, C. (2002). How specific is the relation between executive function and theory of mind? Contributions of inhibitory control and working memory. *Infant and Child Development, 11*, 73–92.

Carlson, S. M., Moses, L. J., & Hix, H. R. (1998). The role of inhibitory processes in young children's difficulties with deception and false belief. *Child Development, 69*, 672–691.

Carruthers, P. (1996). Autism as mindblindness: An elaboration and partial defence. In P. Carruthers & P. K. Smith (Eds.), *Theories of theories of mind* (pp. 257–273). Cambridge, UK: Cambridge University Press.

Dunn, B. M., & Dunn, L. M. (1981). *Peabody picture vocabulary test* (rev. ed.). Circle Pines, MN: American Guidance Service.

Flavell, J. H. (2000). Development of children's knowledge about the mental world. *International Journal of Behavioral Development, 24*, 15–23.

Flavell, J. H., Flavell, E. R., & Green, F. L. (1983). Development of the appearance-reality distinction. *Cognitive Psychology, 15*, 95–120.

Flavell, J. H., & Miller, P. H. (1998). Social cognition. In D. Kuhn & R. S. Siegler (Eds.), W. Damon (Series Ed.) *Handbook of child psychology: Vol. 2. Cognition, perception, and language* (5th ed., pp. 851–898). New York: Wiley.

Frye, D., Zelazo, P. D., & Palfai, T. (1995). Theory of mind and rule-based reasoning. *Cognitive Development, 10*, 483–527.

Gerstadt, C. L., Hong, Y. J., & Diamond, A. (1994). The relationship between cognition and action: Performance of children 3½–7 years old on a Stroop-like day-night test. *Cognition, 53*, 129–153.

Gopnik, A., & Astington, J. W. (1988). Children's understanding of representational change and its relation to the understanding of false belief and the appearance-reality distinction. *Child Development, 59*, 26–37.

Grier, J. B. (1971). Nonparametric indexes for sensitivity and bias: Computing formulas. *Psychological Bulletin, 75*, 424–429.

Grimm, H. (2001). *Sprachentwicklungstest für Kinder (SETK 3–5)* [Language development test for 3- to 5-year-old children]. Göttingen, Germany: Hogrefe.

Hughes, C. (1998a). Executive function in preschoolers: Links with theory of mind and verbal ability. *British Journal of Developmental Psychology, 16*, 233–253.

Hughes, C. (1998b). Finding your marbles: Does preschoolers' strategic behavior predict later understanding of mind? *Developmental Psychology, 34*, 1326–1339.

Jenkins, J., & Astington, J. W. (1996). Cognitive factors and family structure associated with theory of mind development in young children. *Developmental Psychology, 32*, 70–78.

Johnson, C. N., & Wellman, H. M. (1980). Children's developing understanding of mental verbs: Remember, know, and guess. *Child Development, 51*, 1095–1102.

Kuhn, D. (1999). Metacognitive development. In L. Balter & C. S. Tamis-LeMonda (Eds.), *Child psychology: A handbook of contemporary issues* (pp. 259–286). Philadelphia: Psychology Press.

Kuhn, D. (2000). Theory of mind, metacognition, and reasoning: A life-span perspective. In P. Mitchell & K. J. Riggs (Eds.), *Children's reasoning and the mind* (pp. 301–326). Hove, UK: Psychology Press.

Luria, A. R. (1973). *The working brain: An introduction to neuropsychology.* New York: Basic Books.

Luria, A. R., Pribram, K. H., & Homskaya, E. D. (1964). An experimental analyses of the behavioral disturbance produced by a left frontal arachnoidal endothelioma (meningioma). *Neuropsychologia, 2*, 257–280.

Perner, J. (1991). *Understanding the representational mind.* Cambridge, MA: MIT Press.

Perner, J. (1998). The meta-intentional nature of executive functions and theory of mind. In P. Carruthers & J. Boucher (Eds.), *Language and thought* (pp. 270–283). Cambridge, UK: Cambridge University Press.

Perner, J., & Lang, B. (2000). Theory of mind and executive function: Is there a developmental relationship? In S. Baron-Cohen, H. Tager-Flusberg, & D. Cohen (Eds.), *Understanding other minds: Perspectives from autism and developmental cognitive neuroscience* (2nd ed., pp. 150–181). Oxford, UK: Oxford University Press.

Perner, J., & Lang, B. (2002). What causes 3-year-olds' difficulty on the dimensional change card sorting task? *Infant and Child Development, 11*, 93–105.

Perner, J., Lang, B., & Kloo, D. (2002). Theory of mind and self-control: More than a common problem of inhibition. *Child Development, 73*, 752–767.

Premack, D., & Woodruff, G. (1978). Does the chimpanzee have a theory of mind? *Behavioral and Brain Sciences, 1*, 515–526.

Russell, J. (1996). *Agency: Its role in mental development.* Hove, UK: Erlbaum (UK) Taylor and Francis.

Schneider, W. (1989). Problems of longitudinal studies with children: Practical, conceptual, and methodological issues. In M. Brambring & F. Lösel (Eds.), *Children at risk: Assessment and longitudinal research and intervention* (pp. 313–335). New York: De Gruijter.

Schneider, W., & Pressley, M. (1997). *Memory development between 2 and 20.* Mahway, NJ: Lawrence Erlbaum Associates.

Schuck, K.-D., & Eggert, D. (1976). *Hannover-Wechsler-Intelligenztest für das Vorschulalter* [Hannover-Wechsler Intelligence Test for Pre-school Children]. Bern, Switzerland: Huber.

Taylor, M. (1996). A theory of mind perspective on social cognitive development. In R. Gelman & T. Kit-Fong (Eds.), *Handbook of perception and cognition: Perceptual and cognitive development* (2nd ed., pp. 283–329). San Diego, CA: Academic Press.

Thatcher, R. W. (1992). Cyclic cortical reorganization during early childhood. *Brain and Cognition, 20*, 24–50.

Wellman, H. M. (1985). A child's theory of mind: The development of conceptions of cognition. In S. R. Yussen (Ed.), *The growth of reflection in children* (pp. 169–206). New York: Academic Press.

Wimmer, H., & Hartl, M. (1991). Against the Cartesian view on mind: Young children's difficulty with own false beliefs. *British Journal of Developmental Psychology, 9*, 125–138.

Wimmer, H., & Perner, J. (1983). Belief about beliefs: Representation and constraining function of wrong beliefs in young children's understanding of deception. *Cognition, 13*, 103–128.

Zelazo, P. D., Carter, A., Reznick, J. S., & Frye, D. (1997). Early development of executive function: A problem-solving framework. *Review of General Psychology, 1*, 1–29.

Zelazo, P. D., & Frye, D. (1997). Cognitive complexity and control: A theory of the development of deliberate reasoning and intentional action. In M. Stamenov (Ed.), *Language stucture, discourse and access to consciousness* (pp. 113–153). Amsterdam: John Benjamins.

Chapter 13

Executive Functions, Working Memory, Verbal Ability, and Theory of Mind— Does It All Come Together?

Klaus Oberauer
University of Potsdam

Research on the development of a theory of mind (ToM) in children has been one of the success stories of cognitive psychology, as the collection of chapters in this volume clearly shows. The heterogeneity of the backgrounds of the contributors documents that, at least in one sense, much comes together: our growing understanding of the child's understanding of the mind is based in large part on the integration of conceptual work in developmental psychology (most obviously, the concepts of a ToM and of metarepresentation; e.g., Perner, 1991) and in experimental psychology with adult participants (i.e., the concept of working memory and executive functions [EF], e.g., Baddeley, 1986). The progress that has been made over the last 20 years certainly owes much to the joint perspectives gained from experimental, correlational, clinical, evolutionary, and neuroscience approaches. My task in this final chapter is to reflect on where we stand and whether the conceptual building blocks and—a more difficult issue—whether the data begin to fit together into a coherent picture. I think they do.

Figure 13.1 is my personal summary of what I have learned from the chapters in this book about the relationship between working memory (WM), EF, verbal abilities, and ToM. In a moment of boldness, I composed

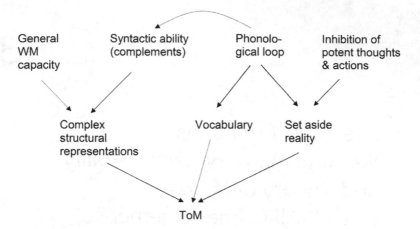

FIG. 13.1.   Hypothetical sources of developmental and individual differences in ToM.

this summary in the form of a causal diagram. Several of the causal paths are highly speculative, but for some we already have considerable empirical evidence. The individual paths are mostly borrowed from the theoretical accounts proposed in the chapters of this book. In what follows, I discuss them one by one.

EXECUTIVE FUNCTIONS

One thing that might be immediately apparent is that I failed to include EF in the picture. This has to do with my wariness about this concept. The term *executive functions* has different histories in the various traditions of psychology and the neurosciences that come together working on the development of ToM, and this bears the potential for considerable confusion. In the experimental tradition, EFs have been treated as part of the WM system (Baddeley, 1986) or as being mainly identical to WM (Engle, Kane, & Tuholski, 1999), whereas it plays a much more marginal role as a separate entity in the model of Cowan (1995, see Towse & Cowan, chap. 2). In neuropsychology, WM tends to be subsumed under EF, together with other functions such as selective attention, flexibility of attention, and various inhibition functions.

I am skeptical about the viability of a broad, encompassing construct of EF. Several correlational studies with young adults showed that tasks assumed to indicate inhibition or attentional flexibility (i.e., task set switching) correlate little, if at all, with measures of WM capacity (Miyake et al., 2000; Oberauer, Süß, Wilhelm, & Wittmann, 2003). This dissociation seems to generalize to preschool children because Schneider, Lockl, and Fernandez (chap. 12) also found little correlation between WM and

EF measures (but see Carlson, Moses, & Breton, 2002, for a correlation between WM and one class of inhibition tasks). Thus, it seems premature at the moment to subsume WM under a broad umbrella called *executive functions*. I propose to treat WM and EF as separate constructs, neither of which conceptually implies the other, thereby leaving their interdependency open to empirical investigation.

A narrow definition of EF would focus on supervisory and control processes employed to ascertain that thought and behavior comply with the person's current goal. This involves maintaining an operative representation of this goal—that is, a representation that guides ongoing action, as opposed to one that is merely held in long-term memory or WM so that it can be recalled when asked for. An operative goal representation can be called a task set—a set of procedures or parameters that specifies which action to perform under what condition (Logan & Gordon, 2001). Complementary to maintenance of a task set, sometimes switching to a new task set is required by a higher order goal, and achieving the flexibility to switch between task sets certainly belongs to EF in a narrow sense. Finally, this concept of EF also involves prevention of distraction through inhibition of irrelevant information and of potent, but inadequate thoughts and actions.

Even the narrow concept of EF as outlined here is not yet a well-established construct. Several attempts to obtain construct validity for EF through factor-analytic studies with adults yielded mixed results at best: Tasks supposedly measuring EF tend to correlate weakly, if at all, with each other (Miyake et al., 2000; Shilling, Chetwynd, & Rabbitt, 2002; Ward, Roberts, & Phillips, 2001). In a recent study, Friedman and Miyake (2004) were able to confirm two factors of inhibition tasks, one representing the common variance of tasks that require inhibition of prepotent responses or of visual distractors, the other representing resistance to proactive interference in verbal recall. The first factor, which corresponds to the inhibition factor in the previous study of Miyake et al. (2000), was highly correlated to task-set switching costs. Thus, there is at least preliminary evidence for the construct validity of a narrow EF concept.

Studies investigating the correlations of various EF measures in children yield a converging picture. For example, Espy, Kaufmann, McDiarmid, and Glisky (1999) found positive correlations between a version of Piaget's A-not-B task, a delayed alternation task, and a self-control task. These tasks have in common that the child must suppress a response that is potent either because it was successful in the immediately preceding trial or because it is motivationally tempting (as in the self-control task, which consists merely of refraining from touching an attractive object). They were uncorrelated, however, with two so-called *reversal* tasks that required mainly WM (i.e., remembering the last response and repeating it). Hughes (1998) reported little coherence between measures of EF at the first time of testing in her longitudinal study after controlling for age and verbal ability, but there were several significant associations between her EF tasks at the second time of testing. Again, two of these were tasks that required inhibition of a strongly suggested response (Luria's hand game: not imitating the experimenter; detour-reaching box: not reaching directly for the object). Carlson and Moses (2001) reported substantial coherence among 10 tasks measuring inhibitory control, even after partialling out age and verbal abilities.

Several chapters in this book add important evidence to the issue of construct validity of EF. Schneider et al. (chap. 12) observed moderate coherence among three EF tasks, which arguably all require inhibition of a prepotent response. Again, coherence increased from the first to the second time of measurement. Zoelch, Seitz, and Schumann-Hengsteler (chap. 3) investigated the relationship between seven tasks reflecting EF in the comprehensive sense, including WM. The pattern of their correlations is not easily interpreted, but it seems that, after partialling out age, the strongest remaining commonalities involve tasks that, among other things, require suppression of a strong response tendency (Stroop: don't say the color you see; decision making: ignore salient features; trail making B: switch away from the previously relevant feature; backward color span: don't recall in forward order).

To summarize, what little evidence we have for construct validity of EF tends to converge on the inhibition of prepotent responses as the common denominator of tasks that share some variance after statistical control of age. This, I think, is not an unfortunate outcome. Downsizing EF to the ability to inhibit strong thought or action tendencies makes the construct conceptually precise and specific enough to make interesting predictions about its relationship with other variables. We would not expect EF to correlate with every cognitive performance variable—for instance, it should not necessarily be associated to WM—but only with those that require suppression of some strongly suggested cognitive or physical action. This is the case in many tasks used to measure ToM: False-belief tasks require giving an answer based on the (invisible) representation of another person, instead of on the much more salient real state of affairs. Appearance-reality tasks require switching between answers based on appearance, suppressing the real nature of the object, or vice versa. Therefore, a relationship between EF and ToM is to be expected precisely for the narrow definition of EF suggested here, at least for ToM tasks that require suppression of a salient aspect of reality. The evidence—most notably the chapters of Sodian and Hülsken (chap. 8) and of Tager-Flusberg and Joseph (chap. 11)—seems to support this very specific link.

An interpretation of the ToM–EF link based on inhibition as the source of common variance has been questioned by Perner and Lang (1999; see also Perner, Lang, & Kloo, 2002) because strong correlations with EF measures were also obtained for ToM tasks that did not require suppression of a prepotent response. In these tasks, children were not required to predict what a protagonist would say or do based on a false belief but rather, to explain the protagonist's action. As Moses, Carlson, and Sabbagh (chap. 6) pointed out, these findings help to narrow down the role of inhibition in the development of ToM. It is probably not the inhibition of a strong but wrong answer in the false belief test situation that is limited by EF. Instead, the ability to suppress the prepotent representation of reality might be crucial for establishing a representation of a false belief—including its referent, a nonexisting state of the world—alongside the correct belief. This would be a prerequisite to understanding false beliefs and, thereby, also for giving an explanation for a person's behavior on the basis of his or her false belief. In other words, inhibition of prepotent thoughts (more than actions) would be needed for the emergence of an understanding of ToM, not for its expression.

One open issue is whether even the narrow EF concept proposed here should be subdivided further. Moses and his colleagues (chap. 6) draw a distinction between conflict inhibition tasks and delay inhibition tasks. Whereas the latter require only the suppression of a potent action, doing nothing for a while, the former require, in addition, the execution of an alternative, less potent action. Moses et al. point out that several studies consistently found a stronger link of ToM with conflict inhibition tasks than with delay inhibition tasks. They argue that the conflict, but not the delay inhibition tasks, includes a load on WM, because the alternative response must be held in mind for successful performance. This is a highly plausible interpretation: Because both inhibition and WM seem to contribute to ToM, a task that taps both sources of variance would be expected to be a very good predictor. One alternative explanation for the differential predictive power of conflict and delay inhibition tasks, however, is that the former are measured with higher reliability. Only one of the studies comparing the two groups of inhibition tasks as predictors of ToM (Carlson & Moses, 2001) reports estimates of reliabilities for them, and in this study the reliability of the conflict scale was considerably higher than that of the delay scale.

Zelazo and Qu (chap. 4) propose another subdivision of EF. They distinguish between cool and hot EF and claim that ToM is related particularly to hot EF, based on an overlap in brain regions that are activated in hot EF tasks and in ToM tasks (i.e., ventromedial prefrontal cortex and anterior cingulate). In their review of brain imaging studies on ToM and EF, Kain and Perner (chap. 9) also make the distinction between cognitive and emotional inhibition, but they see little overlap in the brain regions associated with emotional inhibition tasks (the orbitofrontal cortex) and the regions activated by ToM tasks (medial prefrontal cortex and anterior cingulate). Moreover, Kain and Perner point out that one task that clearly falls in the hot category—inhibiting the impulse to look at or touch a gift for an extended period of time—was less correlated to ToM than the cool conflict inhibition tasks. Kain and Perner propose that delay inhibition tasks don't predict ToM as well as conflict inhibition tasks do precisely because they involve emotion and reward—contrary to the hypothesis of Zelazo and Qu. Thus, the fractionation of inhibitory functions into hot and cool promises to develop into still another fruitful refinement of our concept of EF. Which of the two is more closely related to ToM, however, is still an open question for future research.

To conclude, developmental research on EF and ToM not only furthers our understanding of how children acquire mental concepts, but it also contributes to the sharpening and validation of EF as a concept in theories of cognition. Moreover, the specific relationship between EF—narrowly defined as the ability to inhibit salient cognition or action tendencies—and ToM is, to the best of my knowledge, the first robust evidence for criterion validity of the EF construct.

WORKING MEMORY

Most researchers define WM as a system responsible for holding a limited amount of information in a state of immediate accessibility for intentional (i.e., goal-directed) manipulation. Towse and Cowan (chap. 2) give an overview of two representative approaches. In Fig. 13.1, I distinguished between general WM capacity and the capacity of the phonological loop. This distinction is justified by a dissociation between measures of WM capacity (mostly complex span tasks that combine maintenance with manipulation of information) and measures of the phonological loop (i.e., serial recall of verbal material, such as digit span, word span, and nonword repetition). This dissociation has been observed with adult participants in factor-analytic studies (Cantor, Engle, & Hamilton, 1991; Conway, Cowan, Bunting, Therriault, & Minkoff, 2002; Engle, Tuholski, Laughlin, & Conway, 1999; Oberauer et al., 2003) and through neuroimaging (Postle, Berger, & D'Esposito, 1999; Smith et al., 2001). Moreover, Kail and Hall (2001) reported a factorial dissociation of simple and complex spans with children. In Baddeley's model, the phonological loop is a specialized subsystem dedicated to the short-term maintenance of phoneme sequences. Its contribution to cognitive development is seen mainly as an aid in vocabulary acquisition (Baddeley, Gathercole, & Papagno, 1998). I come back to the contribution of the phonological loop to the development of ToM in the section on language. Here I am concerned with the role of general WM capacity.

General WM is not easy to characterize. Traditionally, its capacity has been measured by so-called complex span tasks combining serial recall with some additional processing demand, such as the reading span task (Daneman & Carpenter, 1980) and counting span task (Case, Kurland, & Goldberg, 1982). Meanwhile, we know that a much broader variety of task paradigms load on a common WM factor (Oberauer, Süß, Schulze, Wilhelm, & Wittmann, 2000; Oberauer et al., 2003). These studies also show that the variance associated with WM capacity is largely domain general.

The common denominator of tasks with high loadings on a WM capacity factor seems to be that they require the construction of relatively complex structural representations. Therefore, I think of general WM as a cognitive space that brings together several representational elements in a common coordinate system, thereby enabling the construction of new relations between them (Oberauer, Süß, Wilhelm, & Sander, in press; cf. Halford, Wilson, & Phillips, 1998). This cognitive space corresponds closely to the focus of attention in Cowan's model (cf. Towse & Cowan, chap. 2). Such a system seems to be what is needed to build complex, embedded representations such as envisioned in the cognitive complexity and control (CCC) theory developed by Zelazo and his colleagues (Frye, Zelazo, & Burack, 1998; Zelazo & Frye, 1998).

As Zelazo and Qu (chap. 4) argued convincingly, solving typical ToM tasks, such as false belief and appearance-reality tasks, requires the construction of relatively complex structures. These structures can either be thought of as embedded rules (e.g., "If asked about appearance, then if the object looks like X, say 'X,' but if asked about what it really is, then if it is Y, say 'Y'") or as coordinated mental models of representational relations (as illustrated in Fig. 13.2). I prefer the latter variant because I think that understanding of mental states involves more than acquiring the rules that enable one to execute a specific condition–action link. Mental models can be used more flexibly in thinking about one's own and other people's mental states, including inferences about the causes of these mental states (e.g., the change of belief was caused by looking into the Smarties box) and their consequences (e.g., that another person who believes that an object is in place X will say that it is in place X, will look for it at place X, will be surprised when it turns out not to be at place X, and many others), as well

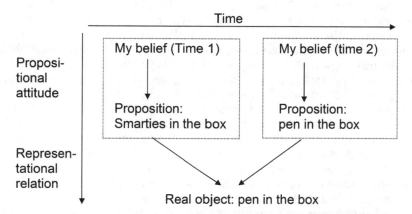

FIG. 13.2. Mental models of representational states in a belief-change task: At Time 1, the child believed that there were Smarties in the Smarties box. At Time 2, the child knows that there is a pen in the box. Understanding of the situation requires a mental model integrating relations in two dimensions of a cognitive coordinate system, one reflecting time, the other reflecting the relationship between the person and his or her belief (the propositional attitude) and the representational relation between the believed proposition and the corresponding objects in the world. The corresponding model for understanding false belief in others would replace "my belief (Time 1)" with "your belief," and the time dimension would be replaced by a social dimension.

as the ability to explain the actions of another person who acts on a false belief (e.g., "Why has the protagonist looked for the chocolate at place X?"). All these abilities emerge at around the same age (Sodian, chap. 5). The rule systems envisioned by Zelazo and his colleagues don't allow such flexibility of application. Their own work shows that the representations they assume have "omnidirectional access" (Frye et al., 1998, p. 119): Each component can be inferred from the remaining components. This is more suggestive of a mental model on which the child can operate with various if-then rules than of a rule structure in which the roles of condition and action are fixed. A recent study by Andrews, Halford, Bunch, Bowden, and Jones (2003) supports this interpretation by showing that several tasks requiring representations of a comparable complexity to false-belief tasks are good predictors of false-belief understanding, regardless of whether or not these representations have the hierarchical rule structure assumed by Zelazo and Frye.

It seems reasonable, then, to expect that WM capacity, defined as the ability to integrate relations into complex mental models, is a prerequisite for the development of understanding mental states. Unfortunately, the evidence supporting a relationship between WM capacity and ToM is relatively sparse. For instance, although they obtained reliable measures of WM capacity, Tager-Flusberg and Joseph (chap. 11) could not find an association of their WM scale with ToM in autistic children once language proficiency or nonverbal mental age were statistically controlled. Schneider and his colleagues (chap. 12) also found that WM did not account for unique variance in ToM after language ability was entered as predictor into the equation (see also Carlson et al., 2002; Hala, Hug, & Henderson, 2003).

Some previous studies are ambiguous as well. Gordon and Olson (1998), for instance, reported a strong correlation between two dual-task paradigms and ToM tasks. To pass the dual tasks, children had to maintain two goals simultaneously. This accomplishment could be limited by their ability to construct the representations of a combined task set, including temporal relations between individual acts, which might be complex enough to tax their WM capacity. Alternatively, however, the goal of the task executed first could become so strong that children fail to switch away from it to the second goal. Thus, these tasks could also reflect the ability to inhibit strong response tendencies. More convincing evidence for a link between ToM and WM comes from a study by Keenan (1998), who found a strong correlation between false belief task performance and the counting span task (Case et al., 1982), even after controlling for verbal ability. The results of Andrews et al. (2003) can also be interpreted as support for a role of WM in ToM development because their complexity measures were reasoning tasks with contents unrelated to understanding of mental concepts, which were designed to measure the construction and integration of relations.

Unfortunately, there is relatively little work to establish WM as an individual-differences construct in young children and to investigate which tasks constitute reliable and valid indicators of this construct. As pointed out earlier, work on EF (and in particular inhibitory control) is more advanced in that regard, and this could be one reason why EF tasks and language tests fare better than WM tasks as predictors of ToM. The study of Schneider and colleagues (chap. 12) provides a good starting point for the development of a WM test battery for preschool children. The modest coherence and stability of their set of tests show that there is substantial room for improvement in the construct validity of WM indicators among young children.

One other reason why measures of WM tend to account for little unique variance in ToM could be that WM is so closely related to general cognitive abilities as measured in intelligence tests (Engle, Tuholski, et al., 1999; Süß, Oberauer, Wittmann, Wilhelm, & Schulze, 2002). This close link seems to be present also in preschool children (see Carlson et al., 2002, for the relationship of WM with general intelligence and Schneider et al., chap. 12, for the association of WM with language ability). Thus, after entering intelligence or verbal abilities into the regression equation, most of the variance that WM could explain in ToM performance is already accounted for.

To conclude, there are good theoretical reasons to expect that WM capacity contributes to the emergence of ToM understanding, and there is preliminary support for this hypothesis. More work is needed, however, to firmly establish a link between WM and ToM.

LANGUAGE ABILITY I: SYNTAX

Several chapters in this volume highlight the particularly strong relationship between language abilities and ToM (Hasselhorn, Mähler, & Grube; Schneider et al.; Tager-Flusberg & Joseph). These new results converge with numerous previous studies (e.g., Astington & Jenkins, 1999; Ruffman, Slade, Rowlandson, Rumsey, & Garnham, 2003). The evidence for this relationship is remarkably strong because several of these studies involve longitudinal designs and show that earlier language competence predicts later ToM, but not the other way around. Currently, it is not clear whether this relationship exists on the general level of overall language competence or on a more specific level, such as syntactic abilities or vocabulary. Correspondingly, there is little agreement about why language relates to the development of ToM.

One highly specific hypothesis, introduced by de Villiers and de Villiers (2000), is that acquisition of the syntax of complementation is crucial for an understanding of mental concepts. Complement structures have the form "N thinks/says/hopes . . . that X." This is precisely the syntactic structure needed to express beliefs about mental states. A recent training study (Lohmann & Tomasello, 2003) showed that a training based on discourse, in which the experimenter used complementation structures, improved children's performance on false belief and appearance-reality tasks. On the other hand, several studies showing a strong association between language and ToM did not even measure the degree to which children mastered this specific syntactic structure. There must be a more general connection as well.

I find it plausible that the use of syntactic structures with hierarchical embedding of constituents—not only complement structures—advances the ability to construct embedded mental models as needed for the understanding of mental states. This hypothesis, however, seems to clash with the assumption that syntax is processed by a special module, separate from general WM. For instance, Caplan and Waters (1999) argued for a syntactic WM system separate from general WM. If their theory is correct, not only for adults but also for preschool children, this would imply that syntactic structures are not processed by the same cognitive mechanisms as are representations of mental states. Now, one could of course question the modularity of syntax processing and argue that, at least early in life, general WM is also responsible for the construction of complex syntactic structures—in particular, as long as these structures are not yet well mastered. However, this would still leave the question of why syntactic structures should have a privileged role in advancing the child's ability to build complex representational structures in general.

There is a more elegant way to conceptualize the role of syntactic abilities, and it happens to be compatible with syntactic modularity. The attainment of complex syntax enables one to formulate complex sentences expressing complex thoughts. These sentence structures can be used not only to guide other people's attention but also to guide one's own. Zelazo and Qu (chap. 4) pointed out the role of verbal self-instruction for the management of rule systems. More generally, self-instruction might guide the child's mind in constructing complex representations—including rule systems and mental models. Thus, the degree of complexity achieved in a hypothetical syntactic WM might lead to corresponding complexity of structures built in general WM. Thus, even if general WM capacity is not yet sufficient to maintain all the elements of a structure such as that in Fig. 13.2 simultaneously, as long as a sentence expressing this structure can be held in syntactic WM, the model described by that sentence can easily be recovered. It is conceivable that the complexity attained by syntactic WM supersedes that of general WM, at least during some developmental period. Self-instruction could be a means to exploit this head start of the syntactic system for nonlinguistic cognitive processes.

Evidence for the use of language for the construction of nonlinguistic relational representations comes from a series of experiments by Hermer-Vasquez, Spelke, and Katsnelson (1999). They showed that constant verbal shadowing prevented adults from using a conjunction of geometric features (long vs. short walls) and nongeometric features (the color of a wall) in their search for an object hidden in space. The authors hypothesized that language is used to encode and maintain links between information from different modules (e.g., spatial and color features), for instance by phrases such as "on the left of the blue wall." Additional evidence reported in that article suggests that children spontaneously begin to use language for this purpose at the age of 4 years. This study not only demonstrates the reliance on language for relating representations from different domains but also points to the exciting possibility of investigating the role of language in ToM tasks by using dual-task methods to interfere selectively with aspects of language processing (e.g., shadowing or articulatory suppression).

LANGUAGE ABILITY II: VOCABULARY AND THE PHONOLOGICAL LOOP

The work of Gathercole, Baddeley, and their colleagues (Baddeley et al., 1998) has revealed an important role of the phonological loop in children's vocabulary learning. Vocabulary also seems to be associated strongly with ToM (e.g., Tager-Flusberg & Joseph, chap. 11). In their chapter, Hassel-horn, Mähler, and Grube have built a causal model around this relationship: The development of the phonological loop drives vocabulary acquisition, which in turn drives the child's understanding of ToM later in development. I agree with the first part of this causal chain, but I find it difficult to understand how a rich vocabulary can help one to understand mental concepts. Even when we focus on mentalistic vocabulary, I find it implausible that learning the phonological form of words such as *believe* and *appear* helps in understanding their meaning unless one is able to construct the appropriate mental models of what these terms refer to.

But maybe there is another role for the phonological loop in the emergence of ToM. Recent research with adult populations on one EF, switching between task sets, has revealed that switching is slowed considerably under conditions of articulatory suppression (Baddeley, Chincotta, & Adlam, 2001; Emerson & Miyake, 2003). This has been interpreted as evidence for a contribution of the phonological loop to the control of task sets. Presumably, even adults use verbal self-instruction to guide their actions when the selection of the right task set becomes difficult. It seems plausible that the phonological loop plays a similar, if not more important role for EF in children. Thus, the contribution of the phonological loop to ToM could be to assist in the suppression of strong but misleading thoughts and actions.

Baddeley et al. (1998) speculated that the phonological loop might be a device not only for the acquisition of individual words but also of grammatical structures. The evidence for this hypothesis is sparse at present, but we should consider the possibility that the link between the phonological loop and ToM might be mediated through the development of syntactic skills.

GENERAL AND SPECIFIC SOURCES OF DEVELOPMENTAL VARIANCE

Research on the development of ToM, EF, WM, and verbal abilities is informative for cognitive psychology in general because it reveals associations and dissociations of cognitive functions. Developmental psychologists working with preschool children seem to be blessed with phenomena that are neither completely specific nor completely general. On the one hand, the consistent covariation of ToM task performance with other cognitive variables is clear evidence that ToM is not a module in a strict sense, developing autonomously along its predetermined path. Bjorklund, Cormier, and Rosenberg (chap. 7) argued for a variant of the modularity hypothesis that leaves room for interdependencies between the ToM module and other cognitive competencies. On the other hand, ToM development arguably cannot be reduced to the development of general cognitive abilities—at least in one study, accounting for the variance of IQ did not eliminate the relationship between ToM and EF (Carlson et al., 2002).

Still, it is not yet clear to what degree the sources of individual and age differences in ToM identified so far—in particular EF and language abilities—can themselves be reduced to very general factors, such as mental speed (Fry & Hale, 1996). I think this issue deserves more attention in future research. On the other end of the life cycle, in research on cognitive aging, the single-factor theory of cognitive decline has been very popular and strikingly robust against empirical falsification for some time (Cerella, 1990; Salthouse, 1996). Meanwhile, it is becoming increasingly clear that, although a general factor of mental speed explains a large part of the age-related variance in cognition, there are specific age-related deficits, as well as invariances, in addition to these general factors (Mayr & Kliegl, 1993; Mayr, Kliegl, & Krampe, 1996). WM capacity (Oberauer, Wendland, & Kliegl, 2003) and EF (Mayr, Spieler, & Kliegl, 2001) have been identified as cognitive functions suffering a specifically pronounced decline in old age, whereas other abilities seem to be largely preserved. Thus, in old age, not all of our mental abilities go together when they go (Rabbitt, 1993). It seems likely, then, that early in life not everything comes together when it comes; WM capacity and EF might again constitute clusters of cognitive functions that follow a specific developmental trajectory. In this regard, this volume can also be read as a toolbox for methods (such as longitudinal designs, Schneider et al., Tager-Flusberg et al.; and developmental dissociations, Zoelch et al.) that make use of interindividual and temporal variance simultaneously to investigate the specific associations and dissociations between various cognitive functions. This illustrates the unique contribution of developmental cognitive psychology to our understanding of what belongs together in the human mind.

REFERENCES

Andrews, G., Halford, G., Bunch, K. M., Bowden, D., & Jones, T. (2003). Theory of mind and relational complexity. *Child Development, 74*, 1476–1499.

Astington, J. W., & Jenkins, J. M. (1999). A longitudinal study of the relation between language and theory-of-mind development. *Developmental Psychology, 35*, 1311–1320.

Baddeley, A. D. (1986). *Working memory.* Oxford, UK: Clarendon Press.

Baddeley, A. D., Chincotta, D., & Adlam, A. (2001). Working memory and the control of action: Evidence from task switching. *Journal of Experimental Psychology: General, 130,* 641–657.

Baddeley, A. D., Gathercole, S., & Papagno, C. (1998). The phonological loop as a language learning device. *Psychological Review, 105,* 158–173.

Cantor, J., Engle, R. W., & Hamilton, G. (1991). Short-term memory, working memory, and verbal abilities: How do they relate? *Intelligence, 15,* 229–246.

Caplan, D., & Waters, G. S. (1999). Verbal working memory and sentence comprehension. *Behavioral and Brain Sciences, 22,* 77–126.

Carlson, S. M., & Moses, L. J. (2001). Individual differences in inhibitory control and children's theory of mind. *Child Development, 72,* 1032–1053.

Carlson, S. M., Moses, L. J., & Breton, C. (2002). How specific is the relation between executive function and theory of mind? Contributions of inhibitory control and working memory. *Infant and Child Development, 11,* 73–92.

Case, R., Kurland, M., & Goldberg, J. (1982). Operational efficiency and the growth of short-term memory span. *Journal of Experimental Child Psychology, 33,* 386–404.

Cerella, J. (1990). Aging and information processing rate. In J. E. Birren & K. W. Schaie (Eds.), *Handbook of the psychology of aging* (3rd ed., pp. 201–221). San Diego, CA: Academic Press.

Conway, A. R. A., Cowan, N., Bunting, M. F., Therriault, D. J., & Minkoff, S. R. B. (2002). A latent variable analysis of working memory capacity, short-term memory capacity, processing speed, and general fluid intelligence. *Intelligence, 30,* 163–183.

Cowan, N. (1995). *Attention and memory: An integrated framework.* New York: Oxford University Press.

Daneman, M., & Carpenter, P. A. (1980). Individual differences in working memory and reading. *Journal of Verbal Learning and Verbal Behavior, 19,* 450–466.

de Villiers, J., & de Villiers, P. (2000). Linguistic determinism and the understanding of false beliefs. In K. J. Riggs (Ed.), *Children's reasoning and the mind* (pp. 191–228). Hove, UK: Psychology Press.

Emerson, M. J., & Miyake, A. (2003). The role of inner speech in task switching: A dual-task investigation. *Journal of Memory and Language, 48,* 148–168.

Engle, R. W., Kane, M. J., & Tuholski, S. W. (1999). Individual differences in working memory capacity and what they tell us about controlled attention, general fluid intelligence, and functions of the prefrontal cortex. In A. Miyake & P. Shah (Eds.), *Models of working memory. Mechanisms of active maintenance and executive control* (pp. 102–134). Cambridge, UK: Cambridge University Press.

Engle, R. W., Tuholski, S. W., Laughlin, J. E., & Conway, A. R. A. (1999). Working memory, short-term memory and general fluid intelligence: A latent variable approach. *Journal of Experimental Psychology: General, 128,* 309–331.

Espy, K. A., Kaufmann, P. M., McDiarmid, M. D., & Glisky, M. L. (1999). Executive functioning in preschool children: Performance on A-not-B and other delayed response format tasks. *Brain and Cognition, 41,* 178–199.

Friedman, N. P., & Miyake, A. (2004). The relations among inhibition and interference control functions: a latent variable analysis. *Journal of Experimental Psychology: General, 133,* 101–135.

Fry, A., & Hale, S. (1996). Processing speed, working memory, and fluid intelligence. *Psychological Science, 7,* 237–241.

Frye, D., Zelazo, P. D., & Burack, J. A. (1998). Cognitive complexity and control: I. Theory of mind in typical and atypical development. *Current Directions in Psychological Science, 7,* 116–121.

Gordon, A. C. L., & Olson, D. R. (1998). The relation between acquisition of a theory of mind and the capacity to hold in mind. *Journal of Experimental Child Psychology, 68,* 70–83.

Hala, S., Hug, S., & Henderson, A. (2003). Executive function and false-belief understanding in preschool children: Two tasks are harder than one. *Journal of Cognition and Development, 4,* 275–298.

Halford, G. S., Wilson, W. H., & Phillips, S. (1998). Processing capacity defined by relational complexity: Implications for comparative, developmental, and cognitive psychology. *Behavioral and Brain Sciences, 21,* 803–864.

Hermer-Vasquez, L., Spelke, E. S., & Katsnelson, A. S. (1999). Sources of flexibility in human cognition: Dual-task studies of space and language. *Cognitive Psychology, 39,* 3–36.

Hughes, C. (1998). Finding your marbles: Does preschoolers' strategic behavior predict later understanding of the mind? *Developmental Psychology, 34,* 1326–1339.

Kail, R., & Hall, L. K. (2001). Distinguishing short-term memory from working memory. *Memory and Cognition, 29,* 1–9.

Keenan, T. (1998). Memory span as a predictor of false belief understanding. *New Zealand Journal of Psychology, 27,* 36–43.

Logan, G. D., & Gordon, R. D. (2001). Executive control of visual attention in dual-task situations. *Psychological Review, 108,* 393–434.

Lohmann, H., & Tomasello, M. (2003). The role of language in the development of false belief understanding: A training study. *Child Development, 74,* 1130–1144.

Mayr, U., & Kliegl, R. (1993). Sequential and coordinative complexity: Age-based processing limitations in figural transformations. *Journal of Experimental Psychology: Learning, Memory and Cognition, 19,* 1297–1320.

Mayr, U., Kliegl, R., & Krampe, R. T. (1996). Sequential and coordinative processing dynamics in figural transformation across the life span. *Cognition, 59,* 61–90.

Mayr, U., Spieler, D. H., & Kliegl, R. (Eds.). (2001). *Aging and executive control.* Hove, UK: Psychology Press.

Miyake, A., Friedman, N. P., Emerson, M. J., Witzki, A. H., Howerter, A., & Wager, T. D. (2000). The unity and diversity of executive functions and their contributions to complex "frontal lobe" tasks: A latent variable analysis. *Cognitive Psychology, 41,* 49–100.

Oberauer, K., Süß, H. M., Schulze, R., Wilhelm, O., & Wittmann, W. W. (2000). Working memory capacity—Facets of a cognitive ability construct. *Personality and Individual Differences, 29,* 1017–1045.

Oberauer, K., Süß, H.-M., Wilhelm, O., & Sander, N. (in press). Individual differences in working memory capacity and reasoning ability. In A. R. A. Conway, C. Jarrold, M. J. Kane, A. Miyake, & J. N. Towse (Eds.), *Variation in working memory.* New York: Oxford University Press.

Oberauer, K., Süß, H. M., Wilhelm, O., & Wittmann, W. W. (2003). The multiple faces of working memory—Storage, processing, supervision, and coordination. *Intelligence, 31,* 167–193.

Oberauer, K., Wendland, M., & Kliegl, R. (2003). Age differences in working memory: The roles of storage and selective access. *Memory and Cognition, 31,* 563–569.

Perner, J. (1991). *Understanding the representational mind.* Cambridge: MIT Press.

Perner, J., & Lang, B. (1999). Development of theory of mind and executive control. *Trends in Cognitive Science, 3,* 337–344.

Perner, J., Lang, B., & Kloo, D. (2002). Theory of mind and self-control: More than a common problem of inhibition. *Child Development, 73,* 752–767.

Postle, B. R., Berger, J. S., & D'Esposito, M. (1999). Functional neuroanatomical double dissociation of mnemonic and executive control processes contributing to working memory performance. *Proceedings of the National Academy of Science, 96,* 12959–12964.

Rabbitt, P. (1993). Does it all go together when it goes? The nineteenth Bartlett memorial lecture. *Quarterly Journal of Experimental Psychology, 46,* 385–434.

Ruffman, T., Slade, L., Rowlandson, K., Rumsey, C., & Garnham, A. (2003). How language relates to belief, desire, and emotion understanding. *Cognitive Development, 18,* 139–158.

Salthouse, T. A. (1996). The processing speed theory of adult age differences in cognition. *Psychological Review, 103,* 403–428.

Shilling, V. M., Chetwynd, A., & Rabbitt, P. M. A. (2002). Individual inconsistency across measures of inhibition: an investigation of the construct validity of inhibition in older adults. *Neuropsychologia, 40,* 605–619.

Smith, E. E., Geva, A., Jonides, J., Miller, A., Reuter-Lorenz, P., & Koeppe, R. A. (2001). The neural basis of task-switching in working memory: Effects of performance and aging. *Proceedings of the National Academy of Science, 98,* 2095–2100.

Süß, H. M., Oberauer, K., Wittmann, W. W., Wilhelm, O., & Schulze, R. (2002). Working memory capacity explains reasoning ability—And a little bit more. *Intelligence, 30,* 261–288.

Ward, G., Roberts, M. J., & Phillips, L. H. (2001). Task-switching costs, Stroop-costs, and executive control: A correlational study. *Quarterly Journal of Experimental Psychology, 54A,* 491–511.

Zelazo, P. D., & Frye, D. (1998). Cognitive complexity and control: II. The development of executive function in childhood. *Current Directions in Psychological Science, 7,* 121–125.

Author Index

Subject Index

Theory theory, 114–117
Tower, 250–252
  of Hanoi, 83, 242
  of London, 74, 246

V

Verbal ability, 2, 5, 110, 132–136, 140,
  190, 220–226, 228–234, 236, 276,
  281, 285, 287, 288, 292, 293, 295
Vocabulary, 2, 13, 110, 114, 184, 220–
  222, 224, 226, 231–236, 240, 243,
  244, 252, 268, 272, 273, 276, 290,
  293, 295

W

Wisconsin Card Sorting Test, 73, 74, 77,
  79, 83, 241, 262
Working memory, 2–6, 9–34, 39–45, 50,
  59, 62–64, 72, 81, 82, 84, 133–142,
  159, 176, 190–192, 199–204, 211,
  212, 220–222, 229–231, 233, 241,
  242, 245–247, 249–251, 259, 263–
  265, 270, 275–277, 279–282, 285–
  290, 292–294
  capacity, 6, 22, 23, 30–33, 41, 43, 64,
    133, 233–235, 246, 251, 286, 290,
    292, 296
  development of, 3, 12–15, 18, 23, 32,
    39, 40, 43, 44, 61, 190, 191, 212,
    230, 235
  maintenance, 82, 200, 203, 212, 290
  manipulation, 40, 45, 200, 203, 212,
    290
  models of, 2, 10 –13, 15–19, 30, 40–42,
    64
  phonological working memory, 5, 11,
    12, 31, 41, 43, 200, 220–226, 228–
    236, 270
Würzburg Longitudinal Study, 6, 264, 279